WEST ACADEMIC PUBLISHING'S LAW SCHOOL ADVISORY BOARD

INTERNATIONAL HUMAN RIGHTS

IN A NUTSHELL®

SIXTH EDITION

DAVID P. STEWART
Professor from Practice
Co-Director, Center on Transnational Business and the Law
Georgetown University Law Center
Former Member, Inter-American Juridical Committee

DINAH SHELTON
Manatt/Ahn Professor Emeritus of International Law
The George Washington University Law School
Former Member, Inter-American Commission on Human Rights

EVELYN ASWAD
Herman G. Kaiser Chair in International Law
University of Oklahoma College of Law

MICHAEL K. ADDO
Professor of Law, Notre Dame Law School
Former Member, UN Working Group on
Business and Human Rights

WEST ACADEMIC

860 Blue Gentian Road, Suite 350
Eagan, MN 55121
1-877-888-1330

Published in the United States of America

ISBN: 978-1-68561-523-9

PREFACE

The sixth edition of this book follows the basic format of the previous editions. The purpose of the book remains the same: both to serve as a self-contained introduction to the international law of human rights and to complement other course materials by providing the reader with a concise overview of human rights norms and the institutional context within which they evolve. The book continues to grow in size, however, to take account of many new developments in the field.

The fifth edition was published in 2017. While the geo-political changes that have occurred since then have been less dramatic than those that took place during the interval between the first and second editions (which saw the collapse of the Soviet empire, the end of the Cold War, and the abolition of apartheid in South Africa), they are nonetheless important in the evolution of international human rights law. As was the case for the interval between the third and fourth editions, continuing internal and international armed conflicts have brought increased attention to the interaction of humanitarian law and international human rights law. In particular, the disastrous civil war in Syria, the broader conflict in the Mid-East, the ongoing war in Ukraine, and other crises in Africa and Central Asia have created humanitarian crises unparalleled since the end of World War II. Human rights and fundamental freedoms remain under threat in every corner of the globe, and the international community continues to struggle to hold individuals accountable for wartime and peacetime atrocities.

At the same time, the international community continues its efforts to strengthen the normative and institutional framework for dealing with human rights problems. Institutionally, the United Nations human right treaty bodies have continued to strengthen their monitoring functions while the Office of the UN High Commissioner for Human Rights has further promoted the world-wide enjoyment of human rights through the creation of numerous field offices. The most extensive institutional change over a decade ago came with the replacement of the UN Commission on Human Rights and abolition of its Sub-Commission on the Promotion and Protection of Human Rights. The UN Human Rights Council, which reports directly to the General Assembly, was elected and began functioning in 2006. At the regional level, the African Court on Human Rights was elected, drafted its rules of procedure, and began hearing cases. It decided numerous matters of its jurisdiction and issued its first merits determination in 2014.

Overall, the revisions to this edition take into account many of the developments that are new or have gained greater importance since the last edition.

DAVID P. STEWART
DINAH SHELTON
EVELYN ASWAD
MICHAEL ADDO

December 2024

ACKNOWLEDGMENTS

A book of this scope is generally the product of efforts beyond those of the authors; this volume is no exception.

Dinah Shelton would like to thank persons at the Council of Europe and the European Court of Human Rights who provided information on recent developments in the European system. Particular thanks are owed to Andrew Drzemczewski, Michael O'Boyle, Caroline Ravaud and Hans Christian Kruger. Similar gratitude must be expressed to Carlos Villan Duran of the Office of the United Nations High Commissioner for Human Rights and to Martin Oelz and Lee Swepston of the International Labour Organization.

David P. Stewart gratefully acknowledges the very able assistance of Saherish Surani and Rahul Satija for their contributions to this edition.

Evelyn Aswad would like to thank her research assistants, Skylar Hill, Madison Estes, Madison Taylor, and Jason Kersey for their excellent research contributions to this edition.

Michael Addo would like to thank Rachel Murray for her valuable advice and Lehlohonolo January for research assistance.

Finally, we would like to express our mutual gratitude to each other for an exceptionally pleasant collaboration and the opportunity to work together.

FOREWORD

The relevance and importance of international human rights as a field of study continues to grow. Indeed, when the first edition of this book was published in 1988, only a handful of American law schools offered courses or seminars on International Human Rights Law. Today the majority do.

This development is due to the recognition of the ever more pervasive impact International Human Rights Law has on contemporary international relations and the behavior of state and non-state entities as well as on the rights of individuals, on international treaties as well as customary international law, on the law of international and regional organizations, on the growth and legal status of non-governmental international organizations, on the domestic implementation of international law, and on related subjects.

Put otherwise, while International Human Rights Law once played a relatively minor role on the international scene, it has over the years become a major branch of public international law and transformed it and international relations to an extent not previously imagined. Human rights law and principles have become an integral part of the international system. Knowledge of the field, and an appreciation of its relevance and importance, is now an essential part of the "toolkit" of every lawyer practicing in the international space, including with respect to international business affairs.

Beginning with the first edition, the aim of this volume has always been to provide a useful introduction for those without prior knowledge of (or experience in) the field. The continuing challenge has been to keep it to a manageable size while at the same time providing the necessary and practical information. Nonetheless, the book has more than doubled in size when compared to its first edition, which reflects the incredible growth of this field.

This 6th edition of the book is the first to be published without the direct contributions of its original author, Thomas Buergenthal, who passed away just as we were beginning the task. We have endeavored to keep to his original concept and approach. As he wrote in the introduction to the 5th edition, the Nutshell was "the love of my academic publications because of my lifelong commitment to the promotion of international human rights through education and scholarship." We deeply miss working with him but share that commitment and are privileged to try to maintain the quality of scholarship and sound educational standards that he demanded.

THE AUTHORS

December 2024

OUTLINE

PREFACE III

ACKNOWLEDGMENTS VII

FOREWORD IX

TABLE OF CASES XXI

TABLE OF AUTHORS XXVII

Chapter 1. The Origins and Evolution of International Human Rights Law 1

I. Introduction 1

II. Pre-World War II Law 2

§ 1–1. Introduction 2

§ 1–2. Human Rights and Traditional International Law 2

§ 1–3. Humanitarian Intervention 4

§ 1–4. Early Human Rights Treaties 7

§ 1–5. The League of Nations 8

1. The Mandates System 8

2. International Labor Standards 10

3. The Minorities System 10

§ 1–6. State Responsibility for Injury to Aliens 14

§ 1–7. Responsibility of Non-Governmental Individuals and Entities 18

§ 1–8. International Humanitarian Law 20

§ 1–9. Contemporary International Human Rights Law 22

§ 1–10. A Note About Categorizations and Terminology 28
§ 1–11. A Note About References and Citations 30

Chapter 2. The United Nations Human Rights System 35

I. Introduction 35
II. The UN Charter 35
§ 2–1. Introduction 35
§ 2–2. The San Francisco Conference and Human Rights 36
§ 2–3. Human Rights in the UN Charter 37
III. The International Bill of Human Rights 42
§ 2–4. Introduction 42
§ 2–5. The Universal Declaration of Human Rights 43
1. The Rights and Freedoms 44
2. Legal Effect and Political Importance 47
§ 2–6. The International Covenants on Human Rights 51
§ 2–7. International Covenant on Civil and Political Rights (ICCPR) 52
§ 2–8. The Human Rights Committee 56
1. The Reporting Procedure 57
2. General Comments 62
3. Inter-State Disputes 63
§ 2–9. The (First) Optional Protocol to the Covenant on Civil and Political Rights 65

§ 2–10. Second Optional Protocol to the International Covenant on Civil and Political Rights ... 67
§ 2–11. The International Covenant on Economic, Social and Cultural Rights ... 68
1. Nature of the Obligations ... 70
2. Overseeing Implementation ... 74
IV. Other Core UN Human Rights Treaties ... 77
§ 2–12. Introduction ... 77
§ 2–13. The Convention on the Prevention and Punishment of the Crime of Genocide ... 80
§ 2–14. International Convention on the Elimination of All Forms of Racial Discrimination ... 83
§ 2–15. Convention on the Elimination of All Forms of Discrimination Against Women ... 85
§ 2–16. Convention Against Torture and Other Cruel, Inhuman or Degrading Treatment ... 89
§ 2–17. Convention on the Rights of the Child and Its Protocols ... 91
§ 2–18. International Convention on the Protection of the Rights of All Migrant Workers and Members of Their Families ... 94
§ 2–19. Convention on the Rights of Persons with Disabilities ... 96
§ 2–20. International Convention for the Protection of All Persons from Enforced Disappearance ... 97

V. UN Charter-Based Institutions 99
§ 2–21. Introduction 99
§ 2–22. Principal UN Organs 99
1. The General Assembly 99
2. The Security Council 100
3. The High Commissioner for Human Rights 101
4. The International Court of Justice 102
§ 2–23. The UN Human Rights Council 104
§ 2–24. Commission on the Status of Women 106
§ 2–25. Procedures for Dealing with Gross Violations of Human Rights 108
§ 2–26. UN Human Rights Conferences 110
VI. Specialized Agencies 112
§ 2–27. Introduction 112
§ 2–28. The International Labor Organization 112
§ 2–29. UNESCO, WHO and FAO 114

Chapter 3. The European System for the Protection of Human Rights 121
I. Introduction 121
II. Council of Europe 121
III. The European Convention on Human Rights: An Overview 125
§ 3–1. Introduction 125
§ 3–2. Rights Guaranteed 126
§ 3–3. Convention Institutions 128

IV. The Enforcement Mechanism of the Convention 135
§ 3–4. Introduction 135
§ 3–5. Jurisdiction of the European Court of Human Rights 136
§ 3–6. Inter-State Complaints 136
§ 3–7. Advisory Opinions 138
§ 3–8. Individual Petitions 140
§ 3–9. Admissibility: Incompatible, Ill-Founded, or Abuse of the Right of Petition 143
§ 3–10. Exhaustion of Domestic Remedies and the Four-Months Rule 145
§ 3–11. "Significant Disadvantage" 149
§ 3–12. Preliminary Matters 151
§ 3–13. Proceedings on the Merits 153
§ 3–14. Judgments of the Court 154
§ 3–15. Enforcement of Judgments 155
§ 3–16. Assessment 157
V. The European Social Charter 159
§ 3–17. Introduction 159
§ 3–18. The Catalog of Rights 160
§ 3–19. Legal Obligations of Contracting Parties 162
§ 3–20. International Measures for Enforcement of Charter Rights 163
§ 3–21. The European Convention Against Torture 165
§ 3–22. Protection of National Minorities 166
§ 3–23. Human Rights and Biomedicine 169
§ 3–24. Convention on Action Against Trafficking in Human Beings 171

§ 3–25. Convention on Preventing and Combating Violence Against Women and Domestic Violence 172
VI. The European Union 174
§ 3–26. Absorbing the European Convention on Human Rights 174
§ 3–27. The Charter of Fundamental Rights of the European Union 177
§ 3–28. Non-Judicial EU Human Rights Bodies 179
VII. Organization for Security and Cooperation in Europe 182
§ 3–29. Introduction 182
§ 3–30. The Helsinki Final Act 183
§ 3–31. The OSCE Process 186
§ 3–32. The Non-Binding Character of OSCE Commitments 187
§ 3–33. The OSCE Catalog of Rights 188
§ 3–34. The OSCE's Human Dimension Mechanism 189
§ 3–35. The High Commissioner on National Minorities 191
§ 3–36. Representative on Freedom of the Media 193

Chapter 4. The Inter-American Human Rights System 197
I. Introduction 197
II. The OAS Charter-Based System 199
§ 4–1. Introduction 199
§ 4–2. The OAS Charter 200
§ 4–3. The American Declaration of the Rights and Duties of Man 201

§ 4–4. Commission as Charter Organ: Its Institutional Evolution 203
§ 4–5. The Commission as Charter Organ: Its Practice 208
1. Country Studies and On-Site Investigations 208
2. Individual Petitions 212
3. Precautionary Measures 214
III. The Convention-Based System 216
§ 4–6. Introduction 216
§ 4–7. The Convention and Its Guarantees 218
§ 4–8. The Convention Organs 222
IV. The Inter-American Commission on Human Rights 223
§ 4–9. The Commission as Convention Organ 223
1. Examination of Petitions 224
2. Role Before the Court 231
V. The Inter-American Court of Human Rights 232
§ 4–10. Jurisdiction of the Court 232
§ 4–11. Contentious Jurisdiction 233
§ 4–12. The Court's Powers in Contentious Cases 236
§ 4–13. Provisional Measures 242
§ 4–14. Advisory Jurisdiction 243
§ 4–15. Legal Effect of Advisory Opinions 246
§ 4–16. Case Law 248
§ 4–17. Other Inter-American Human Rights Instruments 259

§ 4–18. Democracy and Human Rights in the Inter-American System 260

Chapter 5. The African and Other Regional Systems 269

I. Overview of the African System 269

II. The Rights and Duties 272

§ 5–1. Introduction 272

§ 5–2. Individual Rights............................. 273

§ 5–3. Peoples' Rights................................. 277

§ 5–4. Duties 279

III. State Obligations and Measures of Implementation 281

§ 5–5. Introduction 281

§ 5–6. State Obligations 281

§ 5–7. The African Commission on Human and Peoples' Rights 283

§ 5–8. Interstate Complaints 289

§ 5–9. Individual Complaints................... 292

§ 5–10. The African Court of Human and Peoples' Rights 306

§ 5–11. ECOWAS Court of Justice 315

IV. Arab and ASEAN Developments.................. 318

§ 5–12. The Arab Charter on Human Rights 318

§ 5–13. Association of South East Asian Nations (ASEAN)........................... 325

Chapter 6. International Human Rights Law in the United States 335

I. Introduction 335

II. The United States and Human Rights Treaties 342
§ 6–1. Introduction 342
§ 6–2. Treaties and the U.S. Constitution 344
§ 6–3. The U.S. Senate and Human Rights Treaties 345
§ 6–4. Legal and Policy Considerations Affecting Ratification 351
§ 6–5. The Conditional Approach: Ratification with Reservations, Understandings and Declarations 357
III. Human Rights Legislation 368
§ 6–6. Introduction 368
§ 6–7. Terminating Military and Economic Aid: Laws of General Applicability 369
§ 6–8. Country-Specific Legislation 375
§ 6–9. International Financial Institutions 376
§ 6–10. The Bureau of Democracy, Human Rights and Labor 377
IV. International Human Rights Law in U.S. Courts 380
§ 6–11. Introduction 380
§ 6–12. Human Rights Treaties 382
§ 6–13. Customary International Law 389

Chapter 7. Non-State Actors and International Human Rights Law 407
I. Introduction 407

II. Non-Governmental Organizations 410
§ 7–1. Types and Roles 410
§ 7–2. NGO Engagement with International Bodies 419
§ 7–3. Universal Periodic Review 423
§ 7–4. Engagement in Judicial and Quasi-Judicial Processes 424
§ 7–5. NGOs and National Policies and Legislation 427
III. Business and Human Rights 429
§ 7–6. The Role and Responsibility of Corporations 429
§ 7–7. U.S. Human Rights Litigation Against Corporations 433
§ 7–8. International Standards and Codes of Conduct for Business 436
1. UN Measures 437
2. Regional Initiatives 440
3. Other Actions 443
§ 7–9. The Draft UN Treaty on Business and Human Rights 445
IV. Financial Institutions 451
§ 7–10. Future Developments 454

INDEX 459

TABLE OF CASES

References are to Pages

Acevedo Buendía v. Perú, 220
Advisory Opinion on Access to German Minority Schools in Upper Silesia, 12
Advisory Opinion on Greco-Bulgarian Communities, 12
Advisory Opinion on Hearings of Petitioners, 9
Advisory Opinion on Minority Schools in Albania, 12
Advisory Opinion on Nationality Decrees Issued in Tunis and Morocco, 7
Advisory Opinion on the Consistency of Certain Danzig Legislative Decrees with the Constitution of the Free City, 12
Advisory Opinion on the International Status of South-West Africa, 9
Advisory Opinion on the Legal Consequences for States of the Continued Presence of South Africa in Namibia, 9
Advisory Opinion on Voting Procedure, 9
African Commission on Human and Peoples' Rights v. Republic of Kenya, 278
Agim Behrami & Bekir Behrami v. France, 141
Airey Case, 144
Akdivar and others v. Turkey, 146
Aksoy v. Turkey, 148
Alex Thomas v. Tanzania, 311
Alhassan Abubakar v. Ghana, 299
Amnesty International (on behalf of Banda and Chinula) v. Zambia, 299
Angés Uwimana-Nkusi & Saidati Mukakibibi v. Rwanda, 304
Article 19 v. Eritrea, 277, 298
Assanidze v. Georgia, 155
Bamaca Velásquez v. Guatemala, 249
Behrami and Behrami v. France, 127
Belilos v. Switzerland, 358
Belozorov v. Russia and Ukraine, 127
Blake Case, 256
Bond v. United States, 345, 354

Bosnia and Herzegovina v. Yugoslavia, 82
Boyce et al. v. Barbados, 219
Brumarescu v. Romania, 155
Bueno-Alves v. Argentina, 203, 237
Burden v. the United Kingdom, 140
Caballero Delgado Case, 227
Case of Almonacid-Arellano et al., 254
Case of Gutierrez-Soler, 254
Case of Klass and Others, 140
Case of La Cantuta, 203, 248
Case of The Last Temptation of Christ (Olmedo-Bustos et al.), 253
Case of Yvon Neptune v. Haiti, 257
Case of Zambrano Vélez et al. v. Ecuador, 250
Case Relating to Certain Aspects of the Laws on the Use of Languages in Education in Belgium, 131
Castells v. Spain, 146
Castillo Petruzzi Case, 237, 256
Cayara Case, 227
Cesti Hurtado Case, 256
Chaparro Alvarez and Lap Iníguez v. Ecuador, 255
Civil Liberties Organisation, Legal Defence Centre, Legal Defence and Assistance Project v. Nigeria, 299
Commission Nationale des Droits de l'Homme et des Libertes v. Chad, 276
Commission v. France, 176
Constitutional Court Case, 256
Constitutional Rights Project (in respect of Wahab Akamu, G. Adeaga and others) v. Nigeria, 297
Constitutional Rights Project and Civil Liberties Organization v. Nigeria, 299, 305
Cook v. United States, 344, 381
Costa v. ENEL, 174
Dame Hadijatou Mani Koraou v. La République du Niger, 316
De Becker Case, 130
De Geofroy v. Riggs, 348, 353
De Wilde, Ooms and Versyp Cases, 147
Defrene v. Sabena, 176
Democratic Republic of the Congo v. Uganda, 64
Demopoulos and Others v. Turkey, 144
Doe I v. Cisco Systems, Inc., 401

Droits de l'Homme v. Côte d'Ivoire, 309
EEOC v. Arabian American Oil Co., 397
Erie R. Co. v. Tompkins, 390, 393
Ethiopia and Liberia v. South Africa, 9
Ethiopia v. South Africa, 103
Fairen Garbi and Solis Corrales Case, 255
Fairen Garbi Case, 226, 237
Ferrazzini v. Italy, 144
Filártiga v. Peña-Irala, 352, 392
Forum of Conscience v. Sierra Leone, 297
Foster v. Neilson, 383
Free Legal Assistance Group et al. v. Zaire, 298
García Asto and Ramirez Rojas Case, 237
Geofroy v. Riggs, 344
Georgia v. Russian Federation, 17
Giusti v. Italy, 151
Godínez Cruz Case, 236
Godínez-Cruz Case, 255
González et al. (Cotton Field) v. Mexico, 258
Government of South Africa v. Grootboom, 72
Gratzinger and Gratzingerova v. the Czech Republic, 144
Guillaume Kigbafori Soro v. the Republic of Coté D'Ivoire, 314
Handelsgesellschaft v. Einfuhr-und Vorratsstelle fur Getreide und Futtermittel, 175
Houngue Eric Noudehouenou v. Republic of Benin, 312
Igartua-De La Rosa v. United States, 387
Indigenous Communities of the Lhaka Honhat (Our Land) Association v. Argentina, 258
Indigenous Community Sawhoyamaxa v. Paraguay, 258
Indigenous Community Yakye Axa v. Paraguay, 258
Institute for Human Rights Development in Africa v. Republic of Angola, 299
Interights et al. (on behalf of Mariette Sonjaleen Bosch) v. Botswana, 299
International Pen, Constitutional Rights Project, Interights on behalf of Ken Saro-Wiwa Jr. and Civil Liberties Organization v. Nigeria, 297
Ireland v. United Kingdom, 137, 154
Issiaka KEÏTA and Others v. Republic of Mali, 312
Italy, United States v., 17
Ituango Massacres v. Colombia, 236, 237

Jesner v. Arab Bank, PLC, 399, 434
John Lazaro v. United Republic of Tanzania, 314
Kadić v. Karadszić, 352
Katangese Peoples' Congress v. Zaire, 301
Kennedy Gihana and Others v. the Republic of Rwanda, 314
Kennedy Owino Onyachi & Another v. United Republic of Tanzania, 312
Kevin Mgwanga Gunme v. Cameroon, 277
Kimel v. Argentina, 253
Kiobel v. Royal Dutch Petroleum Co. (Kiobel I), 434
Kiobel v. Royal Dutch Petroleum Co. (Kiobel II), 396, 434
Konate v. Burkina Faso, 309
Korolev v. Russia, 150
Kouadio Kobena Fory v. Republic of Coté d'Ivoire, 312
Kuna Indigenous Peoples of Madungandí and the Emberá Indigenous Peoples of Bayano and their members v. Panama, 241
Law Office of Ghazi Suleiman v. Sudan, 297
Lawyers for Human Rights v. Swaziland, 303
Legal and Human Rights Centre and Human Rights and Tanzania Human Rights Defenders Coalition v. United Republic of Tanzania, 312
Legal Consequences of the Construction of a Wall in the Occupied Palestinian Territory, 103
Legal Resources Foundation v. Zambia, 303
Lemoth Morris et. al. v. Honduras, 259
Liesbeth Zegveld and Mussic Ephremr v. Eritrea, 298
Loayza Tamayo Case, 238
Lopez, United States v., 354
Malawi African Association v. Mauritania, 297
Mangold v. Helm, 175
Maria da Penha Maia Fernandes v. Brazil, 259
Mavrommatis Palestine Concessions (Jurisdiction), 14
Mayagna (Sumo) Awas Tingni Community v. Nicaragua, 250, 258
Medellín v. Texas, 344, 354, 363, 385
Media Rights Agenda, Constitutional Rights Project, et al. v. Nigeria, 301
Mexico v. United States, 385
Microsoft Corp. v. AT&T Corp., 397
Missouri v. Holland, 345, 348, 353

Morrison v. National Australia Bank Ltd., 397
Morrison, United States v., 354
Mouvement Burkinabé des Droits de L'Homme v. Burkina Faso, 303
Moya Chacon et. al v. Costa Rica, 253
Mtikila v. Tanzania, 312
Murray v. The Schooner Charming Betsy, 382
Neira Alegría Case, 227, 237
Nestlé USA, Inc. v. Doe, 400, 435
New York v. United States, 353
Nicaragua v. Costa Rica, 17
Olga Tellis v. Bombay Municipal Corp., 72
Open Society Justice Initiative v. Côte d'Ivoire, 304
Oyama v. California, 346
Pink, United States v., 345
Prais v. Council, 176
Printz v. United States, 353
Raxcaco Reyes v. Guatemala, 219
Registered Trustees of The Socio-Economic Rights And Accountability Project (SERAP), The v. The Federal Republic Of Nigeria And Universal Basic Education Commission, 317
Reid v. Covert, 344, 348, 353, 356
Republic of Guinea v. DRC, 17, 64
Reservations to the Convention on the Prevention and Punishment of the Crime of Genocide, 103
Reverend Christopher R. Mtikila v. Tanzania, 277
Ribitsch v. Austria, 154
Ricardo Canese Case, 237
Romward William v. United Republic of Tanzania, 312
Ruzhdi Saramati v. France, Germany & Norway, 141
Saramaka People v. Suriname, 227
Saramati v. France, Germany and Norway, 127
Sarei v. Rio Tinto, PLC, 395
Sawhoyamaxa Indigenous Community v. Paraguay, 18
Scozzari and Giunta v. Italy, 155
Sébastien Germain Ajavon v. Republic of Benin, 282
Sébastien Germain Marie Aikoué Ajavon v. Republic of Benin, 313
Sei Fujii v. California, 346, 382
Sosa v. Alvarez-Machain, 393, 436
Stauder v. Ulm, 175

Stögmüller Case, 146
Stran Greek Refineries and Stratis Andreadis v. Greece, 140
Suárez Rosero Case, 256
Sunday Times Case, The, 140
Tănase v. Moldova, 140
Tanganyika Law Society and the Legal and Human Rights Centre v. Tanzania, In the Consolidated Matter of, 277
The Paquete Habana, 389
Union Syndicale-Amalgamated European Pub. Serv. Union v. Council, 176
Van Oosterwijck Case, 146
VBBB & VBVB v. Commission, 176
Velásquez Rodríguez Case, 221, 227, 255
Velásquez Rodríguez v. Honduras, 19, 236
Veliz Franco et al. v. Guatemala, 259
Villagran Morales (Street Children) Case, 255
Viviana Gallardo, Matter of, 231
Whitney v. Robertson, 344, 381, 384
Zimbabwe Human Rights NGO Forum v. Zimbabwe, 303
Zimbabwe Lawyers for Human Rights and the Institute for Human Rights and Development v. Republic of Zimbabwe, 296
Zongo et al v. Burkina Faso, 312
Zschernig v. Miller, 383

TABLE OF AUTHORS

References are to Pages

Abe, O., 332
Abramovic, 265
Abrusci, E., 118
Adeola, A., 332
Ahmad, H., 401
Ahmed, M., 334
Akande, D., 32
Alfadhel, K.A., 33
Al-Midani, 333
Ambos, K., 34
Amis, L., 456
Anaya, S.J., 31
Angeleri, 194
Antkowiak, 265
Ayers, P., 401, 404
Bachman, J.S., 33
Backer, 456
Baderin, 333
Baluarte, 265
Bantekas, I., 31
Barsky, B.A., 402
Bassiouni, C.M., 334
Bellamy, A., 33
Bonfanti, Angelica, 456
Borchard, E., 33
Born, G., 405
Boulding, 428
Bradley, 381, 390, 403
Breau, S., 33
Brett, R, 195
Buergenthal, T., 32, 265, 402, 403, 405
Burbano-Herrera, 266
Butler, 450
Butler, M., 32
Carozza, 268
Castan, M., 119

Celario, R., 31
Charnovitz, 429
Christopher, Ewell, 404
Clapham, A., 33
Clara, Petch, 404
Clark, 428
Clarke, K.M., 333
Clément, 332
Cone, 267
Corre, G.M., 456
Correa, 450
Cotton-Betteridge, 428
Crawford, E., 32
Crawford, J., 33
Crowle, 428
Crowley, 428
Curling, R., 309
Czech, 194
Danyi, 428
Dau, 332
Dinstein, Y., 32
Dittrich, 34
Dugar, J., 118
Dulitzky, 266
Dummet, 450, 456
Dunne, T., 33
Edwards, 429
El Demery, A.M., 334
Ellis, T., 401
Evans, G., 33
Forsythe, 371
Foster, S., 333
Garcia-Sayan, 266
Garve, 404
Gerards, 195
Ghandhi, P.R., 118
Glennon, 402
Goldsmith, 381, 390
Grossman, 266, 426
Guida, S.D., 332
Hannum, H., 31
Harris, 195

Harris, D., 31
Harvey, C., 31
Hathaway, O., 404
Heinze, A., 34
Henderson, C., 32
Henkin, L., 32, 119, 402
Hervey, 195
Heschle, 194
Hillebrecht, 267
Hollis, 403
Horn, A., 33
Horowitz, B., 267
Howard, D.M., 390, 405
Hugo, Grotius, 4
Huneeus, 267
Illingworth, R., 33
Inboden, R.S., 334
Ishay, M., 31
Israeli, R., 334
Jabri, A., 34
Jacobs, 195
Jain, 34
Jalloh, C.C., 333
Jessberger, F., 34
John, L., 4
John, R., 19
Joseph, S., 119
Kaufman, 404
King, 450
Kinley, D., 119
Kishanthi, P., 456
Knox, 33
Kollontai, P., 31
Ku, 403
Laine, 456
Lauren, P.G., 32
Lee, J., 404
Levin, 457
Lohmann, F., 31
Long, D., 31, 306
Louw, 306
Luban, 34

Lukas, 194, 195
Marchak, M.P., 32
Mbaye, K., 279
Mbazira, 305
McCorquodal, R., 450, 456
McGaughey, F., 118
McKanders, K., 334
McNeilly, K., 31
Mendez, 267
Moeckli, D., 31
Moinet, A., 402
Moon, 405
Moore, 390
Moyn, S., 32
Murray, 306
Murray, R., 31
Mutelo, I., 332
Mutua, M.W., 332
Neier, A., 32, 118
Neuman, 267
Nohle, E., 404
Nollkaemper, A., 402
Norris, 265
Nowak, 194
Ntirushwamaboko, A., 333
Nussberger, 195
O'Boyle, 195
O'Sullivan, 34
Odinkalu, 305
Oette, L., 31
Overleitner, 194
Ovey, 195
Pasqualucci, 268
Peak, T., 32
Peers, 195
Pert, A., 32
Peterson, 450
Pinto, 267
Popa, 267
Porter, B., 118
Press, D., 332
Quataert, J., 32

Ramcharan, B.G., 333
Ramirez, 268
Ramsey, 403
Reid, 195
Reventlow, J., 309
Richards, 403
Rivera, H.C., 118
Roberson, L., 404
Roberts, C., 333
Rudner, N., 332
Saul, B., 32, 119
Schabas, W., 34, 195
Shah, S., 31
Shany, Y., 402
Shelton, 268, 278, 428
Shelton, D., 31, 119, 268, 429
Siri, 268
Sisay, A., 305
Sivakumaran, S., 31
Sloane, 402
Sloss, D., 402
Sohn, 50
Solis, G., 32
Ssenyonjo, 305
Stapel, S., 332
Stearns, P., 31
Stephens, 404
Stewart, 34, 403
Storey, 457
Subedi, S., 118
Tananbau, D., 404
Taylor, P., 118
Teshome, R.G., 34
Teson, F., 32
Tripkovic, 195
Tzanakopoulos, A., 402
Udombana, 305
Ulferts, 450
Umpula, 450, 456
Vanhullebusch, M., 333
Varolei, D., 33
Vázquez, 33, 381, 404

Viljoen, 306
Wang, X., 34
Warbrick, 195
Warwick, B., 31
Weissbrodt, 456
Welch, C., 334
Werle, G., 34
White, 195
Wielenga, C., 333
Wildenthal, L., 32
Wuerth, I., 405
Yakaré-Oulé, 309
Yoo, 403
Zayas, A., 428
Zysset, 195

INTERNATIONAL HUMAN RIGHTS
IN A NUTSHELL®

SIXTH EDITION

CHAPTER 1

THE ORIGINS AND EVOLUTION OF INTERNATIONAL HUMAN RIGHTS LAW

I. INTRODUCTION

The international law of human rights may be defined as the law concerned with the protection of individuals against violations of their internationally guaranteed rights, and with the definition and promotion of these rights. This branch of international law has sometimes also been referred to as the international protection of human rights or international human rights law. Although scholars might disagree over whether one or the other of these labels is more appropriate, they are used interchangeably in this book.

The emergence of this field is typically linked to the UN Charter (1945), article 1(3) of which proclaimed that "promoting and encouraging respect for human rights and for fundamental freedoms for all without distinction as to race, sex, language, or religion" is a legitimate matter for international concern and regulation and thus one of the core purposes of the Organization. Until that time, the general view was that individuals were not properly considered "subjects" of international law, so that how a sovereign (or national government) treated its own citizens within its own territory was a domestic matter, not appropriate for international evaluation, regulation or "intervention." Similarly, how that sovereign treated foreign citizens was not a matter of general concern but rather to be resolved between the respective governments.

As revolutionary as the proclamation in Article 1(3) of the Charter was, it rested on several important historical antecedents. An appreciation of that history is essential to a clear understanding of the development of the contemporary human rights system.

II. PRE-WORLD WAR II LAW

§ 1–1. INTRODUCTION

The international law of human rights has firm roots in several international legal doctrines and institutions whose origins extend well back into the 19th century. The most important of these are state responsibility for injuries to aliens, the protection of minorities, the anti-slavery movement, the Mandates and Minorities Systems of the League of Nations, international humanitarian law, the protection of workers' rights, and the concept of humanitarian intervention. To the extent that these doctrines and institutions survive today, they may be said to form an integral part of contemporary international human rights law.

§ 1–2. HUMAN RIGHTS AND TRADITIONAL INTERNATIONAL LAW

International law (sometimes referred to as "public international law") was traditionally defined as the law governing relations between nation-states exclusively. That meant that only sovereign States were the "subjects" of—and therefore had legal rights and duties under—international law. That classic definition was expanded somewhat after World War I to include various newly created intergovernmental organizations (such as the League of Nations), which were acknowledged to have a limited degree of "international legal personality." However, individual human beings were not deemed to have internationally recognized legal rights as such; they were said to be *objects* rather than *subjects* of international law.

Under this "classical" approach, the authority of a particular State over individuals and activities within its own territory was considered nearly absolute. How a given State treated its *own* nationals was simply not regulated by international law, because it did not affect the rights of other States (or "sovereigns"). The entire subject matter was deemed to fall within the exclusive domestic jurisdiction of each State. Moreover, how a State treated *foreign* nationals within its own territory was considered a matter solely between the two sovereigns. To the extent that States had any obligations under international law towards foreigners within their territory, they were considered to be owed to the States whose nationality those individuals possessed (or, classically, to their "sovereigns"), rather than to the individuals themselves, and therefore a matter to be resolved between the respective governments.

Even while early international law was understood to only cover State-to-State relations, natural law theorists did posit certain limitations on the absolute nature of sovereignty. Hugo Grotius' conception of international law, for instance, was based on the natural law theory. *See* Grotius, *The Rights of War and Peace (2005 ed.) vol. 1 (Book I)* [1625]. John Locke later maintained that a sovereign who violated natural law could be justifiably overthrown. *See* Locke, *Two Treatises of Government* (1689), Chapter 13, § 149. The influence of natural law is reflected in many foundational documents asserting individual rights, such as the Magna Carta (1215), the French Declaration on the Rights of Man and Citizen (1789), and the American Declaration of Independence (1776), each of which rejected the absolute power of the sovereign on the basis of certain unalienable rights belonging to every individual, the existence of which was declared to be self-evident.

§ 1–3. HUMANITARIAN INTERVENTION

Another important doctrinal limitation on the exclusive power of the State was reflected in the idea of "humanitarian intervention." As expounded by some early international legal scholars, including Hugo Grotius in the 17th century, this principle recognized as lawful the use of force by one or more States to stop the maltreatment of individuals by another State—even of *its own* nationals within *its own* territory—when that conduct was so brutal and large-scale as to shock the conscience of the community of nations. In theory, it applied only to States and only when such intervention was necessary to maintain the stability and order of the international community. The doctrine was greatly misused, however, and frequently served as a pretext for the invasion of or intervention in weaker countries. Nevertheless, the doctrine of humanitarian intervention gave early expression to the proposition that international law imposes at least some limits on the discretion States enjoy in the treatment of individuals, whether foreigners or their own nationals, within their own territory.

More recently, the assertion that international organizations or groups of States have the right under international law to use force, if necessary, to put an end to massive violations of human rights has been justified at times by reference to this doctrine. The NATO military action in Kosovo in 1999, for example, revived debates over the legality of unilateral and multilateral humanitarian intervention. Despite the on-going controversy, State practice in some regions supports the doctrine. For instance, the Constitutive Act of the African Union, adopted July 11, 2000 (entered into force May 26, 2001), explicitly recognizes the right of the Union to intervene in a member State pursuant to a decision of the Assembly in respect of "grave circumstances, namely: war crimes, genocide and crimes against humanity." Constitutive Act of the African Union, art. 4(h).

Since the end of the so-called "Cold War" (a period of intense international confrontation and political rivalry between the United States and the former Soviet Union and their respective allies that began in 1945 and continued until the collapse of the Soviet Union in 1991), the United Nations Security Council has increasingly acted to respond to large-scale violations of human rights by authorizing enforcement measures pursuant to its powers under Chapter VII of the UN Charter. That Chapter applies to situations involving a "threat to the peace, breach of the peace, or act of aggression," as determined by the Security Council. UN Charter, art. 39. The Security Council has adopted decisions relating to the Kurds and other civilians in Iraq, the former Yugoslavia, Haiti, Sierra Leone, East Timor, and the Darfur region of the Sudan, as well as Afghanistan, Libya, Côte d'Ivoire and the Central African Republic. Although the resolutions authorizing these measures have often been ambiguous in terms of the legal norms and factual considerations giving rise to them, recent decisions contain important characteristics traditionally associated with the classic international law doctrine of collective humanitarian intervention. For more on the Responsibility to Protect, *see infra* § 2–22(2).

The UN Security Council's establishment of various *ad hoc* international tribunals, including the International Tribunals for the Former Yugoslavia (1993) and for Rwanda (1994) and the mixed war crimes tribunals for Sierra Leone (2002) and Cambodia (2003), to punish those responsible for crimes against humanity, genocide and war crimes committed in those regions, as well as the establishment of the International Criminal Court by the so-called Rome Statute (1988), may also be seen as reflecting aspects of a collective response to massive human rights violations.

§ 1–4. EARLY HUMAN RIGHTS TREATIES

It is a well-established principle of international law that a State may agree to limit its sovereignty by treaty and thus internationalize a subject that would otherwise be unregulated by international law. For example, if one State concludes a treaty with another State in which they agree to treat their respective nationals in a humane manner and to accord them certain human rights, they have, to the extent of the agreement, internationalized that particular subject. Neither of the two States can thenceforth lawfully assert that the treatment of its own nationals is a subject exclusively within its domestic jurisdiction or that criticism of such treatment by the other government constitutes an impermissible "interference" in domestic affairs. That principle was in fact acknowledged by the Permanent Court of International Justice (part of the League of Nations) in its Advisory Opinion on Nationality Decrees Issued in Tunis and Morocco, P.C.I.J., Ser. B, No. 4 (1923). Over time, the principle has been embraced in numerous treaties of amity, friendship, commerce or establishment.

This principle has been extremely important in the development of international human rights law and the gradual internationalization of human rights. That process began in the 19th century with the conclusion of treaties to ban the slave trade and international agreements to protect Christian minorities in the Ottoman (Turkish) Empire. *See, e.g.*, Treaty of Paris (1856) and the Treaty of Berlin (1878). Those treaties were relied upon by the States comprising the Concert of Europe to intercede diplomatically and at times even to intervene militarily on behalf of the Christian populations in the Turkish Empire. The Treaty of Berlin is of particular interest because of the special legal status it accorded to some religious groups; it also served as a model for the League of Nation's Minorities System.

§ 1–5. THE LEAGUE OF NATIONS

However, the Covenant of the League of Nations, the 1920 treaty that established the League and served as its constitution, contained no general provisions dealing with human rights. The notion that human rights should be internationally protected had not yet gained acceptance by the community of nations, nor was it seriously contemplated by those who drafted that treaty, despite efforts by Japan to have the principle of equality and non-discrimination included in the text. The Covenant did, however, contain two provisions (Articles 22 and 23) that bear on the development of international human rights law.

1. The Mandates System

Article 22 of the Covenant established the Mandates System of the League. This provision applied only to the former colonies of the States that had lost the First World War. It transformed these colonies into Mandates to be administered by the victorious powers pursuant to "the principle that the well-being and development of [the native] peoples form a sacred trust of civilization. . . ." The

Mandatory Powers undertook to provide the League with annual reports bearing on the discharge of their responsibilities. These reports were reviewed by a Mandates Commission, which gradually acquired more power in supervising the administration of the Mandates and the manner in which the native populations were treated. The League's dissolution in 1946 ended this arrangement.

In its stead, the United Nations established the UN Trusteeship System, which was entrusted with supervisory power over the remaining eleven Mandates and other non-self-governing territories. Among the last of these territories to gain independence (in 1990) was Namibia. It had been administered by South Africa under the South-West Africa Mandate. South Africa had for many years refused to comply with U.N. General Assembly and Security Council resolutions calling on it to relinquish control over Namibia. The bitter dispute between the U.N. and South Africa concerning Namibia generated considerable litigation before the International Court of Justice. *See* Advisory Opinion on the International Status of South-West Africa, 1950 I.C.J. Rep. 128; Advisory Opinion on Voting Procedure, 1955 I.C.J. Rep. 67; Advisory Opinion on Hearings of Petitioners, 1956 I.C.J. Rep. 23; Ethiopia and Liberia v. South Africa (Preliminary Objections), 1962 I.C.J. Rep. 319; Ethiopia and Liberia v. South Africa (Judgment), 1966 I.C.J. Rep. 6; Advisory Opinion on the Legal Consequences for States of the Continued Presence of South Africa in Namibia, 1971 I.C.J. Rep. 16.

By 1994, all Trust Territories had attained self-governing status or independence, either as separate States or by joining neighboring independent countries.

2. International Labor Standards

Article 23 of the Covenant concerned human rights in that it dealt, *inter alia*, with questions relating to the "fair and humane conditions of labour for men, women, and children." It also envisaged the establishment of an international organization to promote this objective. That function was assumed by the International Labor Organization, which came into being at about the same time as the League. The ILO survived the League and is now one of the Specialized Agencies of the United Nations. *See* § 2–29, *infra*. The legislative activities and the supervisory machinery established by the ILO to promote and monitor compliance with international labor standards have made important contributions over the years to the improvement of conditions of work and the development of international human rights law.

3. The Minorities System

The League of Nations also played a very important role in developing an international system for the protection of minorities, even though the subject was not directly regulated by the Covenant. Instead, the League derived its powers in this field from a series of treaties concluded after World War I. One consequence of that war was a substantial redrawing of the political map of Europe and the Middle East. A number of new States came into being and others regained their independence. Some of these countries, notably Poland, Czechoslovakia, Hungary, Yugoslavia, Bulgaria, Albania and Romania, included pockets of ethnic, linguistic and religious minorities. These minorities had good historical reasons for fearing that the new political order would threaten their cultural survival. The governments of the victor nations—the so-called Principal Allied and Associated Powers—insisted therefore that the new States conclude special treaties for the protection of their ethnic, linguistic and religious minorities.

The first treaty to establish this protective regime was the Treaty between the Principal Allied and Associated Powers and Poland, signed at Versailles on June 29, 1919. It served as a model for the other treaties. In these treaties, the States to which the minorities system applied undertook not to discriminate against members of the protected minorities and to grant them the rights necessary for the preservation of their ethnic, religious or linguistic integrity, including the right to the official use of their languages, the right to maintain their schools, and the right to practice their religions. To ensure compliance, the treaties contained provisions similar to Article 12 of the Polish treaty, which declared that "Poland agrees that the stipulations in the foregoing Articles, so far as they affect persons belonging to racial, religious or linguistic minorities, constitute obligations of international concern and shall be placed under the guarantee of the League of Nations."

The League of Nations agreed to serve as guarantor of the obligations the parties assumed in these treaties. It exercised that function by developing a system for dealing with petitions by minorities charging violations of their rights. That system was relatively effective and quite advanced for its time. Petitions were reviewed by a Committee of Three of the League Council, the States concerned were given an opportunity to present their views and, when appropriate, the Permanent Court of International Justice was asked to render advisory opinions on disputed questions of law. *See, e.g.*, Advisory Opinion on Minority Schools in Albania, P.C.I.J., Ser. A/B, No. 64 (1935); Advisory Opinion on Access to German Minority Schools in Upper Silesia, P.C.I.J., Ser. A/B, No. 40 (1931); Advisory Opinion on Greco-Bulgarian "Communities," P.C.I.J., Ser. B, No. 17 (1930). In addition, the League served as guarantor for certain special political arrangements that also provided for the protection of the rights of minorities. *See, e.g.*, Advisory Opinion on the Consistency of Certain Danzig Legislative Decrees with the Constitution of the Free City, P.C.I.J., Ser. A/B, No. 65 (1935), an important case that examines the meaning of "law" in the context of the Nazi takeover of Danzig.

Although some isolated minorities arrangements of the League era survive to this day, the minorities system as such died with the League. Nonetheless, some modern international human rights institutions bear considerable resemblance to the institutions first developed by the League for the administration of the minorities system.

For many years after their establishment, the United Nations and other international organizations showed little interest in the protection of minorities, focusing instead on individual rights, non-discrimination and equal protection. With the end of the Cold War and the rise of nationalism in various parts of the world, the international community began again to focus on the development of international norms and institutions designed to protect the rights of members of minorities. Efforts to lay the normative foundation for a system that would accomplish this objective were initiated in the United Nations with the adoption by the General Assembly of the 1992 Declaration on the Rights of Persons Belonging to National or Ethnic, Religious and Linguistic Minorities (A/RES/47/135), available at *https://www.ohchr.org/en/instruments-mechanisms/instruments/declaration-rights-persons-belonging-national-or-ethnic.* Within Europe, the Organization on Security and Cooperation in Europe (OSCE) pioneered in taking measures to protect minorities with the 1990 Copenhagen Concluding Document and a number of later OSCE instruments on the subject, culminating in 1992 with the establishment of the office of the High Commissioner for National Minorities. The Council of Europe followed with the adoption in 1994 of the Framework Convention for the Protection of National Minorities. Some of the actions taken in this regard within the framework of the United Nations, the Council of Europe, and the OSCE are discussed in § 3–30, *infra.*

§ 1–6. STATE RESPONSIBILITY FOR INJURY TO ALIENS

Over time, traditional international law came to recognize that States also have an obligation to treat foreign nationals in a manner that conformed to certain minimum standards of civilization or justice. Initially, however, because human beings as such were not recognized as holders of rights under international law, this obligation was deemed to be owed to the State of the individual's nationality. Thus, when individuals were subjected by a foreign government to treatment falling short of the minimum standards, the State of their nationality was considered to have a cause of action under international law against the offending State. *See, e.g.,* Mavrommatis Palestine Concessions (Jurisdiction), P.C.I.J., Ser. A, No. 2 (1934). It could therefore choose to "espouse" the claim of its national and assert it directly against the offending State. When damages were awarded, the successful State usually compensated its nationals for the damage they had sustained, although international law did not require such payment.

Disputes involving claims under the law of "state responsibility for injuries to aliens" were commonly resolved through diplomatic negotiations between the governments concerned. Sometimes the failure of the offending State to comply with demands for satisfaction, usually the payment of compensation, led to the use of force. More often than not, however, the disputes were resolved by diplomatic means, international arbitration or adjudication.

The principle that an injury suffered by the alien abroad was an injury to the State of the alien's nationality reflected the notion that only States were subjects of international law. It also had the negative consequence of leaving stateless persons and those who possessed the nationality of the offending State without protection. If no State could validly claim that its rights were affected when these human beings were injured, then (under the traditional approach) no State had standing to espouse their claims.

The substantive law applicable to claims by States on behalf of their nationals was largely derived from so-called "general principles of law recognized by civilized nations." *See* I.C.J. Statute, art. 38(1)(c). These principles had their source in natural law and various domestic legal doctrines applicable to the treatment of individuals. International arbitrators and tribunals drew on this body of law and doctrine to give substance to concepts such as "denial of justice" and "minimum standards of justice." When modern international law came to recognize that individuals, irrespective of their nationality, should enjoy certain basic human rights, the substantive principles of the law of State responsibility provided a reservoir of norms that could be drawn upon in codifying international human rights law. Today, because of the dramatic evolution and extensive codification of human rights law, human rights law nourishes the law of State responsibility. As the *Restatement (Third) of the Foreign Relations Law of the United States* (1987) aptly noted at Part VII, vol. 2, at 1058, "as the law of human rights developed, the law of responsibility for injury to aliens, as applied to natural persons, began to refer to violations of their 'fundamental human rights,' and States began to invoke contemporary norms of human rights as the basis for claims for injury to their nationals."

The law of State responsibility for injuries to aliens continues to play a key role in contemporary diplomatic relations. In 2001, for instance, the International Law Commission (ILC) adopted a set of articles on the Responsibility of States for Internationally Wrongful Acts. The text of those articles can be found at *https://legal.un.org/ilc/texts/instruments/english/draft_articles/9_6_2001.pdf*. The UN General Assembly took note of the articles and commended them to the attention of governments. G.A. Res. 56/83, U.N. Doc. A/RES/56/83 (Dec. 12, 2001). The ILC also adopted draft articles on diplomatic protection in 2006, article 3(1) of which stated that "[t]he state entitled to exercise diplomatic protection is the state of nationality." *See* Report of the International Commission, GAOR, Supp. No. 10 (A/61/10) at 16 (2006), at *https://legal.un.org/ilc/texts/instruments/english/draft_articles/9_8_2006.pdf*.

The subject remains on the UN General Assembly's agenda. In contemporary practice, States still "espouse" the claims of their nationals, be they natural persons or corporations, and settle them directly though bilateral negotiations, by submitting them to arbitration, or even by bringing claims to the International Court of Justice. *See*, for example, Elettronica Sicula S.p.A. (ELSI) (United States of America v. Italy), 1989 I.C.J. Rep. (July 20). The Case Concerning Ahmadou Sadio Diallo (Rep. of Guinea v. DRC), 2010 I.C.J. Rep. (Nov. 30), was based in part on customary international norms of State responsibility. In contrast, the Case Concerning Application of the International Convention on the Elimination of All Forms of Racial Discrimination (Georgia v. Russian Federation), 2011 I.C.J. Rep 70 (April 1), was based on one of the core UN human rights treaties. *See infra* § 2–14.

State responsibility and diplomatic protection claims are based on the growing number of bilateral and multilateral investment treaties ("BITs") and on so-called treaties of friendship, commerce and navigation ("FCNs"). These treaties frequently confer jurisdiction on existing or *ad hoc* international tribunals to resolve disputes relating to the application or interpretation of these agreements and thus provide an international remedy which may in some cases be more effective than available human rights procedures.

More recently, cases of diplomatic protection have been filed with human rights bodies. *See, e.g.*, Nicaragua v. Costa Rica, Rep. No. 11/07, Interstate Case 01/06, Inter-Am. Comm. H.R., March 8, 2006. Interestingly, the Inter-American Court of Human Rights has held that a bilateral investment treaty could not serve as a defense to violations of human rights. *See* Case of the Sawhoyamaxa Indigenous Community v. Paraguay, Judgment, Inter-Am. Ct. H.R. (ser. C) No. 146 (Mar. 29, 2006) at para.140.

§ 1–7. RESPONSIBILITY OF NON-GOVERNMENTAL INDIVIDUALS AND ENTITIES

In the past, international efforts to protect human rights focused on holding governments and governmental entities internationally responsible for human rights violations. Over time, however, there has been increased appreciation that non-governmental (private) actors can also commit such violations (including acts of genocide, crimes against humanity, involuntary servitude, etc.).

Initial efforts sought accountability of terrorist groups, criminal organizations and, in certain countries, paramilitary groups. Individuals belonging to these groups have often been able to engage in large-scale violations of human rights while enjoying *de facto* immunity (impunity) from prosecution for what in theory at least are criminal acts under the law of the State where these acts take place. While various principles of international criminal law permitted the imposition of individual responsibility for international crimes, no international tribunals with jurisdiction to apply that law existed following the dissolution of the Nuremberg and Tokyo War Crimes Tribunals.

This situation began to change in 1993 and 1994 with the establishment by the UN Security Council of the International Criminal Tribunals for the

Former Yugoslavia (ICTY) and for Rwanda (ICTR), which were granted jurisdiction over crimes against humanity, genocide, and war crimes committed in those territories. *See https://www.icty.org* and *https://unictr.irmct.org*. In 1998, a diplomatic conference convened by the United Nations adopted the so-called Rome Statute of the permanent International Criminal Court (ICC). The Statute entered into force on July 1, 2002 and the prosecutor's office began investigating allegations of international criminal conduct in Uganda, the Democratic Republic of the Congo, the Central African Republic and Sudan. Generally, *see https://www.icc-cpi.int*.

The question whether other non-State actors such as armed insurrectionists, intergovernmental organizations or private business entities can commit human rights violations broadly defined has gained importance as these actors have become more active and powerful. While only States are party to human rights treaties, the obligations contained in these agreements have usually been interpreted to require the parties to act with due diligence to protect human rights not only against State action, but also against private conduct that undermines the enjoyment of the guaranteed rights. *Cf.* Velásquez Rodríguez v. Honduras, 4 IA Ct.H.R. (Ser. C)(1988). In 2011, the UN Human Rights Council endorsed the "Guiding Principles on Business and Human Rights," which were developed by John Ruggie, the Special Representative of the Secretary General on the issue of human rights and transnational corporations. While recognizing that States have the primary duty to protect against human rights abuses by private parties, the Guiding Principles also recognize that business enterprises have a responsibility to respect human rights wherever they operate, a responsibility over and above that imposed by national law, and which exists independently of the States' ability or willingness to fulfill their own human rights obligations.

For more on the role of private corporations and non-governmental organizations, *see* Chapter 7, *infra.*

§ 1–8. INTERNATIONAL HUMANITARIAN LAW

International humanitarian law, which applies only in the context of armed conflict, significantly predates contemporary human rights law. It provides rules to regulate the use of armed force ("combat") primarily to protect individuals who are not (or are no longer) taking direct part in hostilities (i.e., civilians and combatants *hors de combat* such as the wounded, the sick and the shipwrecked or prisoners of war). Humanitarian law generally binds all parties in armed conflict, while human rights law primarily regulates States (governments) in their relations with individuals. Human rights law, developed primarily for peacetime, applies to all persons within the jurisdiction of a State. Unlike IHL, it does not distinguish between combatants and civilians or provide for categories of 'protected person'.

The origins of IHL can be traced to agreements between ancient Egyptians and Sumerians concerning the treatment of prisoners, circa 1400 B.C. In 200 B.C., the Hindu Code of Manu detailed numerous rules applicable during war, such as the prohibition of use of poisoned weapons, the prohibition against killing an enemy attempting to surrender, and the prohibition against attacking those who are badly wounded. Rules governing armed conflict were also found in Sun Tzu's 6th Century B.C. teachings and in the Roman text *Strategica*. The trial of Peter Von Hagenbach in Austria, in 1474, was the first recorded international war crimes prosecution.

The modern development of humanitarian law is usually linked to a series of initiatives undertaken in the 19th century by a number of Swiss individuals, who advocated the conclusion of international agreements making certain humanitarian rules applicable in the conduct of war. These initiatives produced the Geneva Convention of 1864, which was designed to protect medical personnel and hospital installations. It also provided that "wounded or sick combatants, to whatever nation they may belong, shall be collected and cared for." (Article 6(1).) For the text of this and other relevant instruments, *see International Red Cross Handbook*, published and periodically updated by the International Committee of the Red Cross. The Geneva Convention of 1864 was followed by the Hague Convention No. III of 1899, which established comparable humanitarian rules applicable to naval warfare. Several provisions in these treaties reflect State practice as it existed before and after their adoption.

These treaties have been revised, amplified and modernized from time to time and now comprise a vast body of law addressing almost all aspects of modern armed conflict. Much of that law is today codified in the four Geneva Conventions of 1949 and the two 1977 Protocols Additional to these Conventions. For background, *see https://www.icrc.org/en/document/what-international-humanitarian-law*. Although humanitarian law predates the development of international human rights law and had some influence on it, *see, e.g.*, common Article 3 of the Geneva Conventions of 1949, various provisions of the most recent Protocols mirror the principles underlying modern international human rights instruments. It is also worth noting that the derogation clauses of the principal international human rights treaties incorporate by reference the humanitarian law treaties and obligations of the State parties thereto. *See* International Covenant on Civil and Political Rights, art. 4; European Convention of Human Rights, art. 15; American Convention on Human Rights, art. 27.

§ 1–9. CONTEMPORARY INTERNATIONAL HUMAN RIGHTS LAW

As the foregoing illustrates, the international community has over time developed particular doctrines, adopted specialized treaties, and created specific institutions largely designed to protect discrete groups of human beings in need of particularized protection: slaves, minorities, certain indigenous populations, foreign nationals, victims of massive violations, combatants, etc. That law and practice provided the conceptual and institutional underpinnings for the development of contemporary international human rights law. Many of the older institutions and doctrines continue to exist side-by-side with, or form an inherent part of, the modern international law of human rights. For certain matters, that law has been profoundly influenced by its antecedents.

Contemporary international human rights law differs most clearly from these historical antecedents by recognizing that all human beings have internationally guaranteed rights as individuals, which they can exercise in their own right rather than the States of which they are nationals. A growing number of international institutions, for instance, now have jurisdiction to consider claims of individuals for human rights violations committed by any State (not just their own government). Although the remedies often remain inadequate or ineffective, the vast body of international human rights law now in existence—as well as the great increase in the number of international institutions designed to implement that law—have truly internationalized the subject of human rights.

This development has in turn produced a political climate in which the protection of human rights is broadly accepted as one of the most important items on the agenda of contemporary international political discourse involving governments, inter-governmental organizations, a vast international network of non-governmental organizations (and, to an increasing extent, private entities such as corporations).

The end of the "Cold War" brought renewed emphasis on the importance of human rights compliance. It also broadened international political acceptance of the proposition that electoral democracy is a precondition for the effective protection of human rights, as reflected in, *inter alia*, article 25 of the International Covenant on Civil and Political Rights, *discussed infra* § 2–7, and the Inter-American Democratic Charter, *discussed infra* § 4–18. Generally, *see https://www.un.org/en/global-issues/democracy*.

In the long run, the most important developments in the international human rights field can be attributed to the fact that human beings around the world have increasingly come to believe that individual States (including their governments and component agencies) as well as the international community as a whole have an obligation to protect their human rights, be they civil and political rights or economic, social and cultural rights. The expectations that this belief creates make it politically ever more difficult for States to deny the existence of this obligation. That, in turn, facilitates efforts to promote and protect human rights on the international plane. In other words, over the past decades the world has witnessed a true human rights revolution.

The gains, while many, remain to be consolidated. Much of the needed law has been enacted, but in many respects the national and international institutions to enforce the law remain rather weak. In many countries progress is constrained by authoritarian regimes as well as issues such as endemic poverty, illiteracy, corruption and various forms of discrimination and entrenched cultural practices that prevent large segments of the population from enjoying their internationally recognized human rights. These scourges cannot be eradicated by law and legal enforcement mechanisms alone. They require international cooperation and assistance geared to the needs of the people in those countries, educational programs that focus on the promotion of a culture of human rights, on inter-personal and inter-group tolerance, and on the creation of national and local institutions capable of translating international human rights norms into reality.

International lending and development institutions, such as the World Bank, the International Monetary Fund and regional development banks as well as bilateral governmental assistance agencies and non-governmental aid agencies can play an important role. Some of these agencies have in the past shied away from the adoption of a "human rights policy," fearing that they would be accused of politicizing their mandates. This view changed with the end of the Cold War and the gradual recognition that economic development without democracy and human rights cannot succeed in the long run.

Recognition of that interdependence has led to the recognition of a new "Right to Development" as "an inalienable human right by virtue of which every human person and all peoples are entitled to participate in, contribute to, and enjoy economic, social, cultural and political development, in which all human rights and fundamental freedoms can be fully realized." *See* UN GA Res. 41/128 (Dec. 4, 1986), para. 1(1), available at *https://www.ohchr.org/en/instruments-mechanisms/instruments/declaration-right-development*. In 2016, the UN Human Rights Council tasked a Special Rapporteur to prepare practical guidance for realizing this goal at local, national, regional, and international levels.

It should be noted that recognition of this new "right to development" remains a matter of some controversy, including with the United States generally voting against its recognition, arguing that the concept lacks both definition and jurisprudential roots in human rights law and seems to protect governments more than individuals. *See, e.g.*, Explanation of Vote on a Third Committee Resolution on the Right to Development—U.S. Mission to the United Nations (Nov. 13, 2024) at *https://usun.usmission.gov/explanation-of-vote-on-a-third-committee-resolution-on-the-right-to-development-3/*.

In 2018, the Human Rights Council voted to develop "a draft legally binding instrument on the right to development" and established an Intergovernmental Working Group for that purpose. *See* UNHRC Res. 39/9 (Oct. 5, 2018). In 2020, the Working Group published a draft multilateral Convention on the Right to Development, which it subsequently revised in 2022. *See* UN doc. A/HRC/WG.2/23/2 (April 2022). Article 4(1) of the revised text of this convention would recognize that "[e]very individual and all peoples have the inalienable right to development, by virtue of which they are entitled to participate in, contribute to and enjoy civil, cultural, economic, environmental, political and social development that is indivisible from and interdependent and interrelated with all other human rights and fundamental freedoms." For the text and background, *see https://www.ohchr.org/en/events/events/2023/24th-session-working-group-right-development*.

For many, that formulation reflects the broad evolution of contemporary approaches to international human rights law over the past century, from the limited (but still revolutionary) concept that it is a legitimate concern of the international community how a State treats individuals (not just in wartime but more generally, and not just foreigners but its own citizens), through the articulation that individuals themselves have rights that can be asserted against their own governments (first, civil and political rights, then economic social and cultural rights), to the proposition that States in fact owe broad, collective affirmative obligations to their citizens, including a "right to development." We hope you will keep such perspectives in mind as you read the following more detailed descriptions of these specific areas.

§ 1–10. A NOTE ABOUT CATEGORIZATIONS AND TERMINOLOGY

In human rights discourse and analysis, it has become common to differentiate among (and give different emphasis to) various categories of rights. Because such distinctions often reflect varying orientations, priorities and preferences, we have chosen to avoid using them in this volume. We offer the following brief discussion because students and practitioners alike should be aware of their use and the issues they can present.

Negative vs. Positive Rights. Perhaps the most frequent distinction is between civil and political rights on the one hand and economic, social and cultural rights on the other. In some instances the former are described as "negative" rights and the latter as "positive" rights, reflecting the fact that—in significant part—governments can ensure the former by not interfering with an individual's exercise of the right in question, while guaranteeing the latter typically requires affirmative steps and the application of resources. For example, consider the difference between (a) respecting freedoms of speech, association or religion, and (b) ensuring an adequate standard of living: the first are respected if the government takes no action, while the second can only be achieved by government action (including funding). In actuality, of course, the two "set" of rights are inter-dependent and both require government action; for example, one cannot have either "fair trials" or economic prosperity without both a system of justice and a functioning economy.

Individual vs. Group Rights. To describe something as a "human right" indicates that it applies inclusively to all people and the right is held and exercised by individuals. For instance, the preamble to the 1948 Universal Declaration of Human Rights (UDHR) refers broadly to the "inherent dignity and of the equal and inalienable rights of all *members* of the human family." A distinction is often made between (i) the rights of individuals as opposed to (ii) those addressed to "groups" or "collectives." Most of the UDHR's substantive provisions are in fact framed as individual rights: for instance, art. 3 proclaims that "Everyone has the right to life, liberty and security of person" and art. 7 states that "[n]o one shall be subjected to torture or to cruel, inhuman or degrading treatment or punishment." While the International Covenant on Civil and Political Rights (ICCPR) also speaks primarily to the rights of individuals (*see, e.g.,* art. 6(1) stating that "[e]very human being has the inherent right to life"), it does explicitly embrace a "collective" approach with respect to the right to self-determination in art. 1 in saying that "[a]]l peoples have the right of self-determination" and may "freely determine their political status and freely pursue their economic, social and cultural development." The African Charter on Human and Peoples' Rights contains both individual and group rights with an extensive guarantee of group rights in Articles 19–24. One challenge posed by the concept of group or collectively held rights is who (or what) is entitled to assert the rights in question on behalf of the group.

Generations of Rights. The term "generations" is sometimes used to make similar distinctions. For instance, civil and political rights are typically said to constitute the "first generation," while economic, social and cultural rights fall into the "second generation" (the latter may include norms related to the fulfillment of basic needs, such as food, water, shelter, or healthcare). Some view the distinction as a reflection of the relative importance placed on the rights by different legal/political systems of governance (with liberal democracies prioritizing the first "generation" and the socialist/communist systems prioritizing the second). A "third generation" covers what is often referred to as "solidarity rights" such as development, peace and decent environment, although it is also sometimes said to encompass the rights of specific groups or classes of people in need of special protection because of their origins, beliefs or characteristics (for instance, racial, ethnic and religious minorities, the disabled, indigenous groups, etc.). More recently, a "fourth" generation has been identified, focused on emergent developments affecting the human community as a whole and aimed at protecting human life and dignity from emerging challenges such as extreme poverty, climate change, pollution, and the abuse of technology.

§ 1–11. A NOTE ABOUT REFERENCES AND CITATIONS

Over the past decades, the body of primary sources (treaties, conventions and declarations, judicial decisions, etc.) and secondary materials (explanatory notes, learned treatises, textbooks, etc.) in the field of international human rights law has expanded exponentially. Given the introductory nature of this volume, and for ease of reading and clarity, we have chosen to limit the number of citations and references to primary sources in the text and to collect only a few (hopefully helpful) secondary references at the end of the relevant sections or chapters, often organized by major themes or subjects. Admittedly, we have been selective in our choices, giving priority to the more recent publications that we think might be most helpful to those encountering the topics for the first time (but on occasion including some of our 'favorite' books, articles, and other documents) in the hope they will be most useful to readers encountering the issues for the first time.

Selected References and Further Reading

Textbooks and Readers: I. Bantekas & L. Oette, *International Human Rights Law and Practice* (4th ed. 2024); H. Hannum, S.J. Anaya, D. Shelton & R. Celario, *International Human Rights: Problems of Law, Policy, and Practice* (7th ed. 2023); M. Ishay, *The Human Rights Reader* (3d ed. 2022); D. Harris, D. Moeckli, S. Shah & S. Sivakumaran (eds.), *International Human Rights Law* (4th ed. 2022); R. Murray (ed.) & D. Long (eds.), *Research Handbook on Implementation of Human Rights in Practice* (2022).

History, Background, Perspectives: P. Stearns, *Human Rights in World History* (2d ed. 2023); P. Kollontai & F. Lohmann, *On the Significance of Religion for Human Rights* (2023); K. McNeilly, B. Warwick, C. Harvey (eds.), *The Times and*

Temporalities of International Human Rights Law (2022); *The Cambridge Handbook of New Human Rights* (2020); A. Neier, *The International Human Rights Movement: A History* (2020); J. Quataert and L. Wildenthal, *The Routledge History of Human Rights* (2019); D. Shelton, *Remedies in International Human Rights Law* (3rd ed. 2015); S. Moyn, *Human Rights and the Uses of History* (2014); D. Shelton, *The Oxford Handbook of International Human Rights Law* (2013); Paul Gordon Lauren, *The Evolution of International Human Rights: Visions Seen* (3rd ed 2011); T. Buergenthal, "The Evolving International Human Rights System," 100 Am J. Int'l L. 783 (2006); L. Henkin, *The Age of Rights* 13 (1990).

Humanitarian Intervention: C. Henderson, *The Use of Force and International Law* (2d ed. 2023); T. Peak, *Westphalia from Below: Humanitarian Intervention and the Myth of 1648* (2021); M.P. Marchak, *No Easy Fix: Global Responses to Internal Wars and Crimes Against Humanity* (2008); F. Teson, *Humanitarian Intervention: An Inquiry into Law and Morality* (3d ed. 2005).

Humanitarian Law: E. Crawford and A. Pert, *International Humanitarian Law* (2024); Y. Dinstein, *The Conduct of Hostilities Under the Law of International Armed Conflict* (4th ed. 2022); G. Solis, *The Law of Armed Conflict: International Humanitarian Law in War* (3rd ed. 2021); B. Saul and D. Akande, *The Oxford Guide to International Humanitarian Law* (2020).

Diplomatic Protection, State Responsibility and Responsibility to Protect: M. Butler, *Reconstructing the Responsibility to Protect: From Humanitarian Intervention to Human Security* (Global Politics and the Responsibility to Protect) (2024); R. Illingworth, *Strengthening the Responsibility to Protect: A Transitional Cosmopolitan Approach* (2023); Jeffrey S. Bachman, *The Politics of Genocide: From the Genocide Convention to the Responsibility to Protect (Genocide, Political Violence, Human Rights)* (2022); E. Borchard, *The Diplomatic Protection of Citizens Abroad* (2022); G. Evans, *The Responsibility to Protect: Ending Mass Atrocity Crimes Once and For All* (2020); S. Breau, *The Responsibility to Protect in International Law: An Emerging Paradigm Shift* (2018); A. Bellamy and T. Dunne, *The Oxford Handbook of the Responsibility to Protect* (2016); J. Crawford, *State Responsibility: The General Part* (2014).

NGOs, Individuals and Non-State Actors: D. Varolei, *Non-Governmental Organizations and the Law* (2023); A. Clapham, *Human Rights Obligations of Non-State Actors* (2006); Knox, "Horizontal Human Rights Law," 102 Am. J. Int'l L. 1 (2008); Vázquez, "Direct Vs. Indirect Obligations of Corporations Under International Law," 43 Colum. J. Transnat'l L 927 (2005).

Right to Democracy: Khalifa A. Alfadhel, *The Right to Democracy in International Law: Between Procedure, Substance and the Philosophy of John Rawls* (Routledge 2022); A. Horn, *The Right to Democracy in International Law: A Critical Evaluation* (2020).

Right to Development: A. Jabri & R. G. Teshome, "The Draft Convention on the Right to Development: A New Dawn to the Recognition of the Right to Development as a Human Right?" 22 Hum Rts L. Rev. 1 (2022); A. Jabri, *The Right to Development in International Law: A Developing Countries' Perspective* (2022); Xigen Wang, *The Right to Development (Chinese Perspectives on Human Rights and Good Governance* (2019).

International Criminal Law: Luban, O'Sullivan, Stewart & Jain, *International and Transnational Criminal Law* (Aspen, 4th ed. 2023); K. Ambos, *Rome Statute of the International Criminal Court: Article-by-Article Commentary* (2022); Dittrich & A. Heinze, *The Past, Present and Future of the International Criminal Court* (2021); G. Werle & F. Jessberger, *Principles of International Criminal Law* (4th ed. 2020); W. Schabas, *An Introduction to the International Criminal Court* (2020).

CHAPTER 2

THE UNITED NATIONS HUMAN RIGHTS SYSTEM

I. INTRODUCTION

This chapter examines the human rights provisions of the Charter of the United Nations and provides an overview of the relevant norms and institutions that have since emerged within the UN framework. In many ways they constitute the "backbone" of the international human rights system. They derive from the Charter itself, the Universal Declaration of Human Rights, and the various human rights treaties subsequently adopted under the auspices of the UN or its specialized agencies. Generally, *see https://www.un.org/en/our-work/protect-human-rights.* Familiarity with this UN human rights history and structure is essential for anyone working in the field.

II. THE UN CHARTER

§ 2–1. INTRODUCTION

While modern international human rights law has clear roots going back well before the 20th century (*see* ch. 1), it is largely a post-World War II development. Its emergence and incorporation into the UN system can largely be attributed to the monstrous violations of human rights committed during the Nazi era in Western Europe and to the belief that those violations—and possibly the war itself - might have been prevented had an effective international system for the protection of human rights existed in the days of the League of Nations. In other words, the protection and promotion of human rights was considered (and continues to be) central to the establishment and maintenance of international peace and security.

U.S. President Franklin D. Roosevelt eloquently espoused the international human rights cause as early as 1941. In his famous "Four Freedoms" speech, he called for "a world founded upon four essential human freedoms." These he identified as "freedom of speech and expression," "freedom of every person to worship God in his own way," "freedom from want," and "freedom from fear." *See https://www.fdrlibrary.org/four-freedoms.* Roosevelt's vision of "the moral order," as he characterized it, became the clarion call of the nations that fought the Axis in the Second World War and founded the United Nations. Eleanor Roosevelt, the President's wife, was in her own right a strong supporter of (and advocate for) the idea of universal rights. Following the President's death in April 1945, she served as one of the first U.S. delegates to the new United Nations and played a central role in the drafting and adoption of the 1948 Universal Declaration. *See http://www.roosevelthouse.hunter.cuny.edu/exhibits/my-most-important-task/.*

§ 2–2. THE SAN FRANCISCO CONFERENCE AND HUMAN RIGHTS

The UN Charter (together with the Statute of an International Court of Justice) was adopted at a conference in San Francisco between April 25 and June 26, 1945. The human rights provisions that ultimately found their way into the Charter fell far short, however, of the expectations created by the Roosevelts' vision and the Allies' wartime rhetoric. Perhaps that was to be expected, for each of the principal victorious powers had troublesome human rights problems of its own. The Soviet Union had its *Gulag*, the United States its *de jure* racial discrimination, France and Great Britain their colonial empires. Given their own gaps in respect for human rights, it was not in the political interest of these countries to draft a Charter that established an effective international system for the articulation and protection of human rights, as a number of smaller democratic nations and non-governmental organizations advocated. Although the big powers prevailed to the extent that the San Francisco Conference itself produced no protective system as such, the UN Charter nevertheless established the legal and conceptual foundation for the development of contemporary international human rights law over the following decades.

§ 2–3. HUMAN RIGHTS IN THE UN CHARTER

Article 1(3) of the Charter of the United Nations proclaims the following goal as one of the three "purposes" of the UN:

> To achieve international co-operation in solving international problems of an economic, social, cultural, or humanitarian character, and in promoting and encouraging respect for human

rights and for fundamental freedoms for all without distinction as to race, sex, language, or religion.

The basic obligations of the UN and its Member States in achieving this goal are set out in Articles 55 and 56 of the Charter. These provisions read as follows:

ARTICLE 55

With a view to the creation of conditions of stability and well-being which are necessary for peaceful and friendly relations among nations based on respect for the principle of equal rights and self-determination of peoples, the United Nations shall promote:

(a) higher standards of living, full employment, and conditions of economic and social progress and development;

(b) solutions of international economic, social, health, and related problems; and international cultural and educational cooperation; and

(c) universal respect for, and observance of, human rights and fundamental freedoms for all without distinction as to race, sex, language, or religion.

ARTICLE 56

All Members pledge themselves to take joint and separate action in co-operation with the

Organization for the achievement of the purposes set forth in Article 55.

Although the substantive mandate spelled out in Article 55 is broad, it actually confers only limited powers on the UN itself as an organization. The precise charge is to "promote" human rights. Elsewhere the Charter assigns that responsibility to the UN General Assembly and the Economic and Social Council, organs whose resolutions on this subject are not legally binding. Textually, the "pledge" of the Member States under Article 56 is limited to promoting the "achievement of the purposes set forth in Article 55," that is, "universal respect for, and observance of, human rights and fundamental freedoms. . . ." Art. 55(c).

Moreover, the UN Charter itself does not define exactly what is meant by "human rights and fundamental freedoms." Article 55(c) does, however, contain an unambiguous non-discrimination clause which, when read together with Article 56, makes clear that the Member States and the Organization have a binding obligation to promote human rights and fundamental freedoms "without distinction as to race, sex, language, or religion." Moreover, Article 56 requires Member States "to take joint and separate action in co-operation with the Organization" to accomplish the objectives spelled out in Article 55. To facilitate this cooperation, Article 13(1) of the Charter provides that the General Assembly "shall initiate studies and make recommendations for the purpose of . . . (b) promoting international co-operation in the economic, social, cultural, educational, and health fields, and assisting in the realization of human rights and fundamental freedoms for all without distinction as to race, sex, language, or religion."

The Charter authorizes the UN Economic and Social Council (ECOSOC) to "make recommendations for the purpose of promoting respect for, and observance of, human rights and fundamental freedoms for all" and requires it to "set up commissions in economic and social fields and for the promotion of human rights. . . ." (Arts. 62(2) and 68.) Throughout its history the General Assembly, in particular, has been active in standard-setting and raising issues of human rights violations taking place in Member States. For its part, the UN Security Council is authorized to take up any dispute or matter that could lead to a threat to peace or a breach of peace (Chapter VI) and to take action whenever it determines the existence of such threat or breach, or an act of aggression (Chapter VII).

Despite their vagueness, the Charter's human rights provisions have had a number of important consequences. First, they "internationalized" human rights. That is to say, by adhering to the Charter, which is a multilateral treaty, the States Parties recognize that the "human rights" referred to in it are a proper subject of international concern and, to that extent, no longer fall within their exclusive domestic jurisdiction. Although the validity of this proposition was frequently challenged by some States in the early years of the United Nations, the issue is today no longer open to doubt.

That fact—that a State that has ratified the Charter cannot assert that human rights as a subject falls within its exclusive domestic jurisdiction or that criticism of its human rights practices constitutes illegitimate "interference" in its domestic affairs—does not necessarily mean that every infringement of human rights by a UN Member State is a matter of international concern. What it does mean is that even in the absence of any other treaty obligations, a State today can no longer assert that the maltreatment of its own nationals, regardless of how massive or systematic, is a matter within its exclusive domestic jurisdiction.

Second, the obligation of all UN Member States to cooperate in the promotion of human rights and fundamental freedoms has provided the UN with the requisite legal authority to undertake a massive effort to define and codify these rights. That effort is reflected primarily in the adoption of what is often referred to as the "International Bill of Human Rights" and the other core human rights instruments in force today, as discussed below. This critical body of legal and other norms constitutes a veritable human rights code that gives meaning to the phrase "human rights and fundamental freedoms" and clarifies the obligations imposed by Articles 55 and 56 of the Charter. The UN texts were reproduced in a two-volume United Nations publication, entitled *Human Rights: A Compilation of International Instruments* (2006).

Third, the Organization has over the years succeeded in clarifying and elaborating the scope of the Member States' obligation to "promote" human rights and creating UN Charter-based institutions designed to ensure compliance by governments with their human rights obligations. Today it is generally recognized, for example, that a UN Member State that engages in practices amounting to a "consistent pattern of gross violations" of internationally guaranteed human rights is not in compliance with its obligation to "promote . . . universal respect for, and observance of . . ." these rights and that, consequently, it is in violation of the UN Charter. *See* § 2–23 and § 2–25, *infra*. *See also* RESTATEMENT (THIRD) FOREIGN RELATIONS LAW OF THE UNITED STATES §§ 701 and 702, and the accompanying notes. The UN has sought to enforce this obligation with resolutions calling on specific states to stop such violations and by empowering its human rights bodies to establish procedures to review allegations of violations.

III. THE INTERNATIONAL BILL OF HUMAN RIGHTS

§ 2–4. INTRODUCTION

The human rights provisions of the UN Charter (arts. 55 and 56) were initially elaborated in three subsequent instruments—namely, the 1948 Universal Declaration of Human Rights and the two International Covenants on Human Rights adopted in 1966. Together, these instruments are often referred to as the "International Bill of Human Rights." These instruments are analyzed in the sections that follow.

By way of background, proposals to append an actual "Bill of Rights" or "Declaration of the Essential Rights of Man" to the UN Charter were in fact made but not acted upon at the San Francisco Conference. Those efforts were revived at the very first meeting of the United Nations, and shortly thereafter, its newly created Commission on Human Rights was charged with drafting "an international bill of human rights." The Commission soon recognized that it would be relatively easy to adopt the text of a hortatory declaration, but that it would prove much more difficult to reach agreement on the wording of a legally binding treaty. The Commission decided, therefore, to work first on a declaration and to take up immediately afterwards the preparation of one or more draft treaties. This approach produced the Universal Declaration of Human Rights, which was adopted by the UN General Assembly on December 10, 1948. *See* UN Gen.Ass.Res. 217A (III). It took 18 more years, however, before the treaties—the two Covenants and the (First) Optional Protocol—were adopted by the General Assembly and opened for signature. Another ten years elapsed before the two Covenants entered into force in 1976.

§ 2–5. THE UNIVERSAL DECLARATION OF HUMAN RIGHTS

The Universal Declaration of Human Rights (UDHR) is the first comprehensive human rights instrument to be proclaimed by a global international organization. Because of the moral status and legal and political importance it has acquired over the years, the Declaration ranks with the Magna Carta, the French Declaration of the Rights of Man and the American Declaration of Independence as a milestone in mankind's struggle for freedom and human dignity. Its debt to these great historic documents is unmistakable. "All human beings are born free and equal in dignity and rights," proclaims Article 1 of the Universal Declaration, and Article 28 adds "everyone is entitled to a social and international order in which the rights and freedoms set forth in this Declaration can be fully realized." *See https://www.un.org/en/about-us/universal-declaration-of-human-rights.*

1. The Rights and Freedoms

The Universal Declaration proclaims a broad range of civil, political, economic, social and cultural rights.

Its catalog of civil and political rights includes the right to life, liberty, and security of the person; the prohibition of slavery, torture, and cruel, inhuman or degrading treatment; the right not to be subjected to arbitrary arrest, detention or exile; the right to a fair trial in both civil and criminal matters, the presumption of innocence and the prohibition against the application of *ex post facto* laws and penalties. The Declaration recognizes the right to privacy and the right to own property. It proclaims freedom of speech, religion, assembly and freedom of movement, which embraces the right of everyone "to leave any country, including his own, and to return to his country." Also guaranteed are the right "to seek and to enjoy in other countries asylum from persecution" and the right to a nationality. Important political rights are proclaimed in Article 21 of the Declaration, including the individual's right "to take part in the government of his country, directly or through freely chosen representatives." That provision also declares that the "will of the people shall be the basis of the authority of government" and recognizes the right to "periodic and genuine elections" by universal suffrage.

The catalog of economic, social and cultural rights proclaimed in the Declaration starts with the proposition, expressed in Article 22, that:

> Everyone, as a member of society . . . is entitled to realization, through national effort and international co-operation and in accordance with the organization and resources of each State, of the economic, social and cultural rights indispensable for his dignity and the free development of his personality.

The Declaration then proclaims the individual's right to social security, to work, and to "protection against unemployment," to "equal pay for equal work," and to "just and favourable remuneration ensuring for himself and his family an existence worthy of human dignity, and supplemented, if necessary, by other means of social protection." Article 24 recognizes the right "to rest and leisure, including reasonable limitation of working hours and periodic holidays with pay." Article 25 states that everyone has the right "to a standard of living adequate for the health and well-being of himself and of his family." It also recognizes the individual's right "to security in the event of unemployment, sickness, disability, widowhood, old age or other lack of livelihood in circumstances beyond his control."

The right to education is addressed in Article 26 of the Declaration, which provides, among other things, that education shall be free "at least in the elementary and fundamental stages." Article 26 also declares that:

> Education shall be directed to the full development of the human personality and to the strengthening of respect for human rights and fundamental freedoms. It shall promote understanding, tolerance, and friendship among all nations, racial or religious groups, and shall further the activities of the United Nations for the maintenance of peace.

Article 27 of the Declaration specifies cultural rights and states, *inter alia,* that every human being has "the right freely to participate in the cultural life of the community, to enjoy the arts and to share in scientific advancement and its benefits."

The UDHR recognizes that the rights it proclaims are not absolute. It permits a State to enact laws limiting the exercise of these rights, provided their sole purpose is to secure "due recognition and respect for the rights and freedoms of others and of meeting the just requirements of morality, public order and the general welfare in a democratic society." Art. 29(2). A government's authority to impose such restrictions is further limited by Article 30, which provides that "nothing in this Declaration may be interpreted as implying for any State, group or person any right to engage in any activity or to perform any act aimed at the destruction of any of the rights and freedoms" proclaimed in the Declaration. This means, inter alia, that a government would violate its obligations if its reliance on the power to impose lawful restrictions or limitations on the exercise of certain human rights was a mere pretext for denying these rights.

2. Legal Effect and Political Importance

The Universal Declaration is not a treaty. It was adopted by the UN General Assembly by means of a non-binding resolution (G.A. Res. 217 A, Dec. 10, 1948). Its purpose, as stated in its preamble, is to provide "a common understanding" of the human rights and fundamental freedoms referred to in the UN Charter and to serve "as a common standard of achievement for all peoples and all nations. . . ."

Over the decades since its adoption, however, that appreciation has undergone a dramatic transformation. Today few international lawyers would deny that the Declaration is in fact a normative instrument that reflects some foundational legal obligations of all UN Member States. The ongoing discussion about its legal character concerns not so much claims that it lacks all legal significance but rather whether all the rights it proclaims are binding and under what circumstances, and whether its obligatory character derives from its status as an authoritative interpretation of the human rights obligations contained in the UN Charter, its status as customary international law, or its status as reflecting general principles of law.

The process that transformed the Universal Declaration from merely a non-binding recommendation to an instrument having a normative character came about, in part at least, because the effort to draft and adopt the two Covenants remained stalled in the UN for almost two decades. During that time the need for authoritative standards defining the human rights obligations of UN Member States became ever more urgent. As time passed, the Declaration came to be utilized with ever greater frequency for that purpose. Whenever governments, the UN or other international organizations wished to invoke human rights norms or condemn their violations, they would refer to and draw on the Declaration as the applicable standard. The Declaration thus came to symbolize what the international community means by "human rights," reinforcing the conviction that all governments have an "obligation" to ensure the enjoyment of the rights the Declaration proclaims.

The legal significance of this process has been analyzed in at least three ways. Some international lawyers and governments have contended that the UN's consistent reliance on the Universal Declaration when applying the human rights provisions of the UN Charter compels the conclusion that the Declaration has been accepted as an authoritative interpretation (or articulation) of these provisions. According to this view, UN Member

States have agreed that they have an obligation under the Charter to promote "universal respect for, and observance of" the rights which the Declaration proclaims. Whether a State will be deemed to have violated this obligation when it denies all, some or even only one of these rights will then depend upon the interpretation given to the undertaking contained in Article 55(c) of the Charter read together with Article 56.

Another view with substantial support considers that the repeated reliance on and resort to the UDHR by governments and intergovernmental organizations constitutes the requisite state practice which is capable of giving rise to customary international law. Under this theory, the Declaration or, at least, some of its provisions, have in fact become binding legal norms. A careful analysis of the relevant state practice suggests, however, that not all the rights proclaimed in the Declaration have acquired this status. That is why the RESTATEMENT (THIRD) FOREIGN RELATIONS LAW OF THE UNITED STATES (1987) characterized only *some* rights proclaimed in the UDHR as customary international law. Without claiming to be exhaustive, it lists the following governmental practices as violating customary international law: genocide, slavery, murder or causing the disappearance of individuals, torture or other cruel, inhuman or degrading treatment or punishment, prolonged arbitrary detention, systematic racial discrimination, and consistent patterns of gross violations of internationally recognized human rights. RESTATEMENT (THIRD) FOREIGN RELATIONS § 702.

One distinguished commentator combined these two theories by advancing the following view:

> The Declaration . . . is now considered to be an authoritative interpretation of the U.N. Charter, spelling out in considerable detail the meaning of the phrase "human rights and fundamental freedoms," which Member States agreed in the Charter to promote and observe. The Universal Declaration has joined the Charter . . . as part of the constitutional structure of the world community. The Declaration, as an authoritative listing of human rights, has become a basic component of international customary law, binding all states, not only members of the United Nations.

Sohn, "The New International Law: Protection of the Rights of Individuals Rather than States," 32 Am. U. L. Rev. 1, at 16–17 (1982).

Some commentators have put forth a third theory, characterizing the international human rights norms contained in the UDHR as being reflective of a dynamic modern aspect of general principles of law. This theory is supported by the adoption of the Universal Declaration verbatim or by reference into the constitutions of many states throughout the world. The UDHR is also referred to in all regional human rights treaties. Whatever the theory, it is clear that the international community today attributes a very special moral and normative status to the Universal Declaration that no other instrument of its kind has acquired.

§ 2–6. THE INTERNATIONAL COVENANTS ON HUMAN RIGHTS

Nearly two decades after the UDHR was adopted, two other foundational instruments—the International Covenant on Economic, Social and Cultural Rights (ICESCR) and the International Covenant on Civil and Political Rights (ICCPR)—were approved by the UN General Assembly and opened for signature by states in December 1966. Another decade passed before thirty-five states—the number required to bring the Covenants into force—had ratified both instruments. This number has increased steadily in recent years and by 2024 had grown to 174 States Parties to the Covenant on Civil and Political Rights and 173 to the Covenant on Economic, Social, and Cultural Rights. *See https://treaties.un.org/*. As treaties, the Covenants create binding legal obligations for their States Parties. Therefore, as between them, issues relating to compliance with and the enjoyment of the rights guaranteed by the Covenants are matters of international concern and not exclusively within the domestic jurisdiction of the States Parties.

The Covenants have a number of common substantive provisions. Two of these provisions address what might be described as "peoples" or "collective" rights. Article 1(1) of both Covenants proclaims that "all peoples have the right of self-determination." Both instruments recognize in Article 1(2) that "all peoples" have the right to freely dispose of their natural resources and that "in no case may a people be deprived of its own means of subsistence." They also bar discrimination based on race, color, sex, language, religion, political or other opinion, national or social origin, property or birth. *See* ICCPR, art. 2(1); ICESR, art. 2(2).

Each Covenant establishes a distinct international enforcement system designed to ensure that the States Parties comply with their obligations. These monitoring mechanisms are amplified by Optional Protocols permitting individuals to file petitions charging violations of their rights under the Covenants. All of the core U.N. human rights treaties include self-reporting by States Parties, as well as inter-state and individual communications procedures, among their monitoring mechanisms.

§ 2–7. INTERNATIONAL COVENANT ON CIVIL AND POLITICAL RIGHTS (ICCPR)

Like the UDHR, the catalog of civil and political rights enumerated in this Covenant is broad and includes, inter alia, the rights to life, freedom of speech, freedom of thought, conscience and religion, equality before the law, and to take part in the conduct of public affairs, directly or through freely chosen representatives. However, the Covenant is drafted with greater juridical specificity and lists more rights than the Universal Declaration. One important addition is the undertaking by states not to deny members of ethnic, religious or linguistic minorities the right, "in community with other members of their group, to enjoy their own culture, to profess and practice their own religion, or to use their own language." ICCPR, art. 27. That provision in turn inspired the Declaration on the Rights of Persons Belonging to National or Ethnic Religious and Linguistic Minorities, UNGA Res. 47/135, adopted 18 Dec. 1992, available at *https://www.ohchr.org/en/instruments-mechanisms/instruments/declaration-rights-persons-belonging-national-or-ethnic.*

Other rights in the ICCPR that are not expressly mentioned in the Universal Declaration include freedom from imprisonment for debt, the right of all persons deprived of their liberty to be treated with humanity and with respect for the inherent dignity of the human person, and the right of every child "to acquire a nationality" and to be accorded "such measures of protection as are required by his status as a minor."

By contrast, some important rights proclaimed in the Universal Declaration do *not* appear in the ICCPR, including the right to own property, the right to seek and enjoy asylum, and the right to a nationality. The right to own property was not included because the various ideological and political blocs represented in the UN at the time could not agree on its scope and definition. The right to seek and enjoy asylum had already been addressed in the 1951 Convention Relating to the Status of Refugees, which built on article 14 of the UDHR, and a related protocol was already under negotiation. The right to a nationality remains a contentious topic and, to this day, has not been elaborated in a "universal" treaty.

Moreover, the ICCPR contains a "derogation clause," which permits the States Parties "in time of public emergency that threatens the life of the nation" to suspend their obligations under the Covenant "to the extent strictly required by the exigencies of the situation." ICCPR, art. 4. However, the clause goes on to list seven specific rights that are non-derogable, and the Human Rights Committee has made clear that, in its opinion, this list is not exhaustive. *See* General Comment 29, para. 13, UN Doc. CCPR/CR/21/Add. 11 (2001), available at *https://digitallibrary.un.org/record/451555? ln=en*.

In addition, the Covenant permits States Parties to limit and restrict the exercise of some of the rights it proclaims, but these "limitations clauses" are themselves subject to limitations. A good example is found in Article 18, which guarantees freedom of religion but declares that "freedom to manifest one's religion or beliefs may be subject . . . to . . . limitations" and that such limitations must be "prescribed by law" and "necessary to protect public safety, order, health, or morals or the fundamental rights and freedoms of others." Similarly, Article 19 provides that freedom of expression (though not freedom of opinion) "may . . . be subject to certain restrictions," but states that such restrictions must be "provided by law" and "necessary . . . [f]or respect of the rights and reputation of others" or "[f]or the protection of national security or of public order *(ordre public)*, or of public health or morals." For the Human Rights Committee's interpretation of these provisions, *see* General Comment 34, CCPR/C/GC/34 (2011), available at *https://www2.ohchr.org/english/bodies/hrc/docs/gc34.pdf*. Including such limitations clauses in only some rights was a substantial step forward from the UDHR, which permits all of its rights to be limited.

These provisions are additionally qualified by ICCPR Article 5(1), which prohibits the imposition of restrictions or limitations aimed at the destruction of the rights or "their limitation to a greater extent than is provided for in the present Covenant." In practice, particularly in states that lack a strong and independent judiciary, the provisions that permit derogations and other restrictions are frequently invoked to justify non-compliance by governments violating their human rights obligations.

The obligations that the States Parties assume by ratifying the ICCPR are set out in Article 2. Paragraph 1 of that provision reads as follows:

> Each State Party to the present Covenant undertakes to respect and to ensure to all individuals within its territory and subject to its jurisdiction the rights recognized in the present Covenant, without distinction of any kind, such as race, colour, sex, language, religion, political or other opinion, national or social origin, property, birth or other status.

Article 2(2) requires the States Parties "to adopt such legislative or other measures as may be necessary to give effect to the rights" guaranteed in the Covenant whenever such provisions do not already exist in its domestic law. Unlike the ICESCR, which ties progressive implementation to available resources, the ICCPR imposes an immediate obligation "to respect and to ensure" the rights it proclaims and to take whatever other measures are necessary to bring about that result. *See* Human Rights Committee, General Comment 31, "The Nature of the Legal Obligation Imposed on States Parties to the Covenant," CCPR/C/21/Rev.1/Add.13 (2004), available at *https://digitallibrary.un.org/record/533996?ln=en*.

§ 2–8. THE HUMAN RIGHTS COMMITTEE

The ICCPR also established a Human Rights Committee and confers on it various functions designed to ensure that the States Parties comply with the obligations they have assumed by ratifying the treaty. *See https://www.ohchr.org/en/treaty-bodies/ccpr*. Not to be confused with the former UN Commission on Human Rights (composed of 53 elected individuals) which replaced in 2006 by the UN Human Rights Council), the Committee consists of 18 individuals, who are nominated and elected by the States Parties but serve in a personal capacity and not as government representatives. ICCPR art. 28. Their main responsibilities are to monitor implementation of the Covenant by States Parties and thereby to promote respect for civil and political rights. They do so by overseeing (i) the reports of States Parties, (ii) the inter-state complaint mechanism, and (iii) the system of "individual petitions" established by the First Optional Protocol to the ICCPR, which was adopted at same time as the Covenant itself. The Committee meets in three annual sessions of three or four weeks each. The Committee's annual reports are available at *https://tbinternet.ohchr.org/_layouts/15/TreatyBody*

External/TBSearch.aspx?Lang=en&TreatyID=8&DocTypeID=27.

1. The Reporting Procedure

ICCPR Article 40(1) requires States Parties "to submit reports on the measures they have adopted which give effect to the rights recognized [in the Covenant] and on the progress made in the enjoyment of those rights." The Covenant specifies that the reports should indicate any factors or difficulties affecting their ability to implement the Covenant. The Covenant requires all States Parties to submit their initial report within one year of the entry into force of the Covenant for them and thereafter whenever the Committee so requests. In practice, the Committee requests the submission of periodic reports every four to seven years.

While this obligation is now widely accepted, its adoption marked an important (even revolutionary) development in international law: that a state could be required to provide detailed information to, and to submit to review by, an international body about how it treats people—its own citizens as well as foreigners—within its own territory. Granted, the obligation was based on the state's own decision to ratify or accede to the Covenant, yet the departure from the classical Westphalian approach should not be underestimated. These reports are often useful resources with respect to country conditions of human rights concern and can stimulate corrective action by the government concerned.

The evolution of the reporting system has accelerated in recent years, transforming it into an increasingly more effective instrument for monitoring implementation of the Covenant. For instance, the Covenant does not expressly empower the Committee to verify the state reports by undertaking its own investigations, but in practice Committee members may - and do - draw on their own knowledge and experience as human rights experts. In addition, although this power was once disputed, the Committee may consider information from other sources—including other UN treaty bodies and the work of special rapporteurs, field offices, and specialized agencies as well as non-governmental human rights organizations (NGOs), national human rights institutions (NHRIs), and other stakeholders such as trade unions. Moreover, representatives of the reporting State are required to be present when their reports are examined and can be asked for explanations and supplemental information.

Over the years, the Human Rights Committee has developed a comprehensive set of reporting guidelines and procedures. *See* "Guidelines for the treaty-specific document to be submitted by States Parties under article 40 of the International Covenant on Civil and Political Rights," CCPR/C/2009/1 (2010), and supplemental information available on the Committee's web site, *https://www.ohchr.org/en/treaty-bodies/ccpr*. These guidelines are designed to prod the States Parties into compliance with their treaty obligations and to assist them in overcoming difficulties in doing so. In 2009, the Committee adopted an optional "simplified reporting" procedure under which the Committee transmits a list of issues to States Parties *before* submission of a periodic report, to which the State Party provides written responses *in lieu* of its periodic report. *See https://www.ohchr.org/en/treaty-bodies/ccpr/reporting-procedure.* This procedure eases the burden on States Parties by eliminating the need to provide both a periodic report and written responses to the list of issues. In 2019, the Committee changed that procedure to apply to all States Parties (unless they choose to "opt out") and shifted to an eight year review cycle. *See* UN Human Rights Committee, UN Doc. A/74/256 (July 30, 2019), *https://www.ohchr.org/en/treaty-bodies/ccpr/predictable-review-cycle.*

After a report has been received by the Committee, it is studied by a "country rapporteur" (a Committee Member who focuses on a particular country under review) and a Country Report Task Force of four to six members. The former presents a draft list of issues for discussion to the Task Force, which makes observations and adopts the final list of issues. The list is then transmitted to the State Party, which is expected to provide written responses. In examining State reports, the Committee can also draw on information from specialized agencies of the UN and studies by other UN bodies including reports of UN country and thematic rapporteurs. In addition, the Committee invites NGOs and other stakeholders to submit "alternative" or "shadow" reports. NGOs and other stakeholders are also given the opportunity to address the Committee in public session before the Committee reviews the State Party.

The Committee examines the States Parties' periodic reports in public session. Following the oral presentation by the State's representative, the country rapporteur and members of the Country Task Force pose questions to the delegation, after which other members may pose additional questions and comments. Once the public hearing is complete, the Committee meets in private and adopts its "Concluding Observations." The Concluding Observations consist of an assessment of the State's human rights situation as well as recommendations in light of the information provided in the State report, the answers the Committee received to the questions posed by its members during the examination of the report, and information available to the members from other sources, generally analyzed in terms of the country's obligations under the Covenant. Concluding Observations are adopted by the Committee in closed meetings (after a discussion of a draft text prepared by a country rapporteur) and then transmitted to the State Party and published on the Committee's web site. Under the Committee's "follow-up" procedure, a State Party may be requested to submit an additional report within one year regarding its implementation of these recommendations. NGOs and other stakeholders may also be invited to submit "alternative" follow-up reports. Based on those submissions, the Committee's Special Rapporteur for Follow-Up on Concluding Observations prepares a follow-up progress report.

Over time some States have declined to submit their reports to the Committee in a timely fashion. Some have been motivated by a desire to avoid public scrutiny of their failure to comply with their obligations under the Covenant; others lack the necessary resources or professional staff to prepare their reports within a reasonable period of time. Occasionally civil wars or internal turmoil have played a role, as has bureaucratic inertia. Public and private reminders, designed to shame States into complying with their reporting obligations, have eventually produced the desired result in most, but not all, cases.

Recognizing that the reporting system is the fundamental mechanism by which the Committee discharges its obligation to monitor the observance of obligations under the Convention, the Committee has adopted special procedures for considering the situation of States Parties that fail to report, beginning with the most overdue reports. The Committee notifies the State Party of the date on which the Committee proposes to examine the measures taken by the State Party to implement the rights guaranteed under the Covenant, providing it with a list of issues for review in the absence of a report. Some States Parties have answered the list of issues but not appeared for the review; others have both answered the list of issues and appeared. The Committee may proceed whether or not representatives of the State Party appear at the meeting. If the consideration goes forward, the Committee prepares Concluding Observations and transmits them to the State Party.

Over the years, the Committee's success in publicly examining reports and adopting concluding observations, recommendations and General Comments reflect its purposeful and dynamic interpretation of the Covenant.

2. General Comments

Building on its practice in dealing with individual petitions and in examining state reports, the Committee has adopted an increasing number of General Comments that elaborate its views on the meaning of various provisions of the Covenant and offer guidance to States Parties. Some have been addressed to the States Parties as a whole and are designed to provide guidance on implementing and complying with the Covenant. Although not legally binding, General Comments can be considered sources of nonbinding norms reflecting the Committee's interpretation of the Covenant's provisions. They are often derived from the Committee's prior decisions on individual communications and its Concluding Observations, and are relied upon by the Committee in evaluating compliance by States with their obligations under the Covenant. Over time, General Comments have become important guideposts for the interpretation and application of the Covenant. They are collected at *https://www.ohchr.org/en/treaty-bodies/ccpr/general-comments*.

The Committee's procedure for adopting General Comments has evolved over time. Under the current procedure, once a draft has been prepared and initially considered by the Committee, it is posted on the Committee's web site and States Parties and non-state actors are invited to submit written comments. The rapporteur takes these comments into account in further revising the draft General Comment. For example, with respect to General Comment 33, the Committee received comments from 21 States Parties and six NGOs, which resulted in significant revisions. *See* General Comment No. 33, Obligations of States Parties under the Optional Protocol to the Civil and Political Covenant, CCPR/C/GC/33, Nov.5, 2008, available at *https://www2.ohchr.org/english/bodies/hrc/docs/ccpr.c.gc.33.pdf*.

However, one in particular - General Comment 24, which sets out the Committee's position on reservations to the Covenant, elicited a number of highly critical observations challenging the Committee's position. The text is available at *https://digitallibrary.un.org/record/200963?ln=en*. The United States and United Kingdom observations are reprinted in [1994–95] HRC Report, GAOR, Supp. No.40 (A/50/40), Vol. I, at 131 and 135, respectively (1995); *see also https://www.iilj.org/wp-content/uploads/2016/08/US-and-UK-Responses-to-the-General-Comment.pdf*. For the observations of the French Government, *see* [1995–96] HRC Report, GAOR, Supp. No. 40 (A/51/40) (1996).

3. Inter-State Disputes

The Covenant also provides for an inter-state complaint procedure that enables one State Party to charge another with a violation of the treaty. ICCPR, arts. 41 and 42. This procedure can be resorted to only by and against States Parties that have made a separate declaration recognizing the Committee's jurisdiction to receive such complaints. ICCPR, art. 41(2). The ICCPR procedure provides neither for adjudication nor quasi-adjudication but instead establishes little more than an ad hoc conciliation procedure. To date, however, it has never been invoked.

By contrast, Article 44 expressly permits States Parties to have "recourse to other procedures for settling a dispute in accordance with general or special international agreements in force between them." That provision would enable States Parties, for example, to take a dispute relating to the interpretation or application of the Covenant to the International Court of Justice, provided they have accepted the Court's jurisdiction. For example, the Congo alleged violations of the ICCPR in its ICJ litigation against Rwanda, Burundi and Uganda. *See Armed Activities on the Territory of the Congo (DRC v. Uganda)*, 2005 I.C.J. Rep. 168 (Dec. 19). And in *Case Concerning Ahmadou Sadio Diallo* (Rep. of Guinea v. DRC), 2010 I.C.J. Rep. 639 (Nov. 30), Guinea alleged violations of the ICCPR by the Congo, and the Court found that the Congo had committed violations of Articles 13 (recognizing the right of lawfully admitted aliens not to be arbitrarily expelled) and Article 9 (recognizing the right of persons not to be arbitrarily arrested or detained).

§ 2–9. THE (FIRST) OPTIONAL PROTOCOL TO THE COVENANT ON CIVIL AND POLITICAL RIGHTS

The First Optional Protocol (OP1), adopted as a separate instrument at the same time as the Covenant, supplements the ICCPR's implementation provisions by enabling private parties claiming to be victims of a violation of the Covenant to file individual complaints (known as "communications") with the Human Rights Committee. These complaints may be filed only against States Parties to the Covenant that have also ratified the Protocol. At the time of its adoption, it was even more remarkable than the Covenant itself, since it permits individuals to challenge—on the international level—the internal (domestic) actions of States. Of the 174 parties to the Covenant in 2024, 116 had ratified the Optional Protocol; 3 others had signed but not ratified. Generally, *see https://www.ohchr.org/en/instruments-mechanisms/instruments/optional-protocol-international-covenant-civil-and-political.*

This individual petition system resembles a quasi-judicial system, allowing victims to file communications with the Committee if they have exhausted available and effective domestic remedies. To be admissible, the communications must not be anonymous, abusive of the "right of submission" or "incompatible with any provision of the Covenant." Optional Protocol, art. 3. The Committee may not consider a communication if "the same matter is . . . being examined under another procedure of international investigation or settlement." Optional Protocol, art. 5(2)(a).

Individual communications are initially reviewed by the Committee's Special Rapporteur on New Communications, who determines whether it should be referred to the State Party concerned for its observations on issues of admissibility and merits. The Special Rapporteur may recommend to the Committee that a communication be declared inadmissible, but the power to decide the issue is vested in the Committee. Ordinarily, the question of admissibility is considered at the same time as the merits. A pre-sessional Working Group makes non-binding recommendations to the Committee, whose decisions on the merits are designated as "Views." The Committee includes information on follow-up activities in its annual report to the UN General Assembly.

Since OP1's entry into force in 1976, the Human Rights Committee has dealt with an ever-increasing number of individual communications. Many of these were found inadmissible, in large part because domestic remedies had not been exhausted or because they involved "the same matter" that was "being examined under another procedure of international investigation or settlement." Protocol, art. 5(2). In recent years, the number of admissible communications has grown significantly, and in consequence the number of substantive issues addressed by the Committee has also increased. Generally, *see https://www.ohchr.org/en/treaty-bodies/ccpr/individual-communications.* The "jurisprudence" of the Human Rights Committee - and of the other UN treaty bodies that have similar mechanisms) is extensive and rich. Much is available online for an overview, and links to the annual reports, individual and inter-state communications, and general comments, *see https://www.ohchr.org/en/treaty-bodies.*

§ 2–10. SECOND OPTIONAL PROTOCOL TO THE INTERNATIONAL COVENANT ON CIVIL AND POLITICAL RIGHTS

The objective of the Second Optional Protocol (OP2) is the abolition of the death penalty. To that end it provides, first, that once a State has ratified the Protocol, "no one within [its] jurisdiction . . . shall be executed," and, second, that each State Party must take whatever measures are necessary to abolish the death penalty within its jurisdiction. Second Optional Protocol, art. 1. The only reservation that may be made to the Protocol would allow "for the application of the death penalty in time of war pursuant to a conviction for a most serious crime of a military nature committed during wartime." *Id.*, art. 2. The Protocol also makes the right it guarantees non-derogable under Article 4 of the Covenant. *Id.*, art. 6(2). *See https://www.ohchr.org/en/instruments-mechanisms/instruments/second-optional-protocol-international-covenant-civil-and.*

The Protocol also extends the jurisdiction of the Human Rights Committee under ICCPR Article 40 regarding State Party reporting. It also does so for inter-state complaints with regard to states that have recognized the Committee's jurisdiction under Article 41 of the Covenant and for individual complaints in cases involving States Parties to the First Optional Protocol. *See* OP2 arts. 3–5.

The Second Optional Protocol was opened for signature on December 15, 1989 and entered into force on July 11, 1991. The text is reprinted in 6 ILM 360 (1966). As of 2024, 91 of the 174 States Parties to the Covenant had accepted the Protocol. Pursuant to its terms, it is deemed to be an additional provision of the Covenant.

§ 2–11. THE INTERNATIONAL COVENANT ON ECONOMIC, SOCIAL AND CULTURAL RIGHTS

The International Covenant on Economic, Social and Cultural Rights (ICESCR), adopted by the UN General Assembly at the same time as the ICCPR, contains a longer and much more comprehensive catalog of economic, social and cultural rights than the Universal Declaration. It recognizes the following rights: the right to work; the right to the enjoyment of just and favorable conditions of work; the right to form and join trade unions; the right to social security, including social insurance; the right to the protection of the family; the right to an adequate standard of living; the right to the enjoyment of the highest attainable standard of physical and mental health; the right of everyone to education; and the right to take part in cultural life.

The ICESCR does not merely list these rights; it describes and defines them in considerable detail and frequently sets out the steps that should be taken to achieve their realization. Typical of this approach is Article 7, which reads as follows:

> The States Parties to the present Covenant recognize the right of everyone to the enjoyment of just and favourable conditions of work, which ensure, in particular:
>
> (a) Remuneration which provides all workers as a minimum with:
>
> (i) Fair wages and equal remuneration for work of equal value without distinction of any kind, in particular women being guaranteed conditions of work not inferior to those enjoyed by men, with equal pay for equal work;
>
> (ii) A decent living for themselves and their families in accordance with the provisions of the present Covenant;
>
> (b) Safe and healthy working conditions;
>
> (c) Equal opportunity for everyone to be promoted in his employment to an appropriate higher level, subject to no considerations other than those of seniority and competence;
>
> (d) Rest, leisure and reasonable limitation of working hours and periodic holidays with pay, as well as remuneration for public holidays.

As of 2024 the ICESCR had been ratified by 171 States Parties (the United States, Palau, Cuba, and the Comoros had signed but not ratified.)

1. Nature of the Obligations

By ratifying the ICESCR, a State Party does not undertake to give immediate effect to all of the rights it enumerates, as is the case with the ICCPR. The ICESCR adopts a different approach, which finds expression in Article 2(1):

> Each State Party to the present Covenant undertakes to take steps, individually and through international assistance and co-operation, especially economic and technical, to the maximum of its available resources, with a view to achieving progressively the full realization of the rights recognized in the present Covenant by all appropriate means, including particularly the adoption of legislative measures.

As this language indicates, a State Party obligates itself to take steps "to the maximum of its available resources" in order to achieve "progressively the full realization" of these rights. Also, unlike the ICCPR, the ICESCR includes a transnational dimension in its reference to international assistance and co-operation.

The different approaches taken in the texts of the two Covenants towards implementation stems from the understanding that, as a general matter, the protection of most civil and political rights vis-à-vis the state requires few, if any, economic resources. With some exceptions, such as the requirement of an independent judiciary and access to justice, little more is required of a government than legislation and a decision not to engage in certain illegal practices—not to torture people, not to imprison them arbitrarily, not to interfere with freedom of speech, etc. By contrast, when economic, social or cultural rights are involved, the burden on government tends to be heavier and the task more complicated because, in general, their enjoyment cannot be fully ensured without the affirmative commitment of economic and technical resources, education and planning, the gradual reordering of social priorities and, in many cases, international cooperation.

These differences between the two categories of rights are more a matter of degree than of kind, however. As discussed below, the Committee on Economic, Social and Cultural Rights (CESCR) (the body established to supervise the implementation of this Covenant) has recognized that some ESC rights are of an immediate and absolute nature. For its part, the Human Rights Committee (which interprets the ICCPR) has come to recognize an obligation of states to use due diligence to protect individuals from violations of their rights by non-state actors, thus recognizing that the ICCPR does impose some affirmative (not just negative) obligations on States Parties. Moreover, it is widely accepted and oft-repeated that all human rights are universal, inalienable, indivisible and interdependent. *See, e.g., https://www.ohchr.org/en/what-are-human-rights.*

Nevertheless, the affirmative character of most economic social and cultural rights underlies the "progressive" or "programmatic" nature of most of the obligations assumed by States Parties to the ICESCR. It would be unrealistic to require immediate compliance with all of these rights, given the nature of these rights and the specific problems each state must deal with to ensure their full enjoyment.

These considerations also explain why, as a practical matter, the standards by which to measure compliance under the ICESCR will differ from those that apply to treaties dealing with civil and political rights. Different criteria will have to be applied to different states in determining whether they are living up to their treaty obligations, because each state will invariably face different problems and no two states are likely to have the same "available resources."

This is not to say, however, that no rights guaranteed in this Covenant can be enforced by legislation or that judicial remedies will always be inappropriate. Indeed, the constitutional courts of some states have recognized such rights to be justiciable. *See, e.g.,* Gov't of South Africa v. Grootboom, Case CCT 11/00, 4 Oct. 2000) (South Africa); Olga Tellis v. Bombay Municipal Corp., AIR 1986 SC 18 (India). The assumption that the ICESCR creates no immediate obligations for the States Parties was rejected by the ICESCR in its General

Comment No. 3 (1990), available at *https://www.ohchr.org/en/resources/educators/human-rights-education-training/general-comment-no-3-nature-states-parties-obligations-article-2-para-1-1990*. *See* also Report of the Committee on Economic, Social and Cultural Rights, Fifth Session, U.N. Doc. E/199/23, E/C.12/1990/8, at 83 (1991). In its analysis of Article 2(1), the Committee points out that "while the Covenant provides for progressive realization and acknowledges the constraints due to limits of available resources, it also imposes various obligations, which are of immediate effect." Among these, the Committee singles out two in particular: the undertaking of the States Parties to guarantee that the rights set out in the Covenant will be exercised without discrimination; and the undertaking in Article 2(1) "to take steps."

Regarding the non-discrimination undertaking, the Committee notes that legislation and the provision of judicial remedies can often appropriately promote compliance with this obligation. It insists that although "the full realization of the relevant rights may be achieved progressively, steps towards that goal must be taken within a reasonably short time after the Covenant's entry into force for the States concerned." The Committee also emphasizes "that a minimum core obligation to ensure the satisfaction of, at the very least, minimum essential levels of each of the rights is incumbent upon every State Party." *Id.*, at 86.

2. Overseeing Implementation

The ICESCR requires the States Parties to submit "reports on the measures which they have adopted and the progress made in achieving the observance of the rights recognized herein." ICESCR, art. 16(1). Unlike the ICCPR, however, the ICESCR itself did not establish a special committee to review those reports; it stipulated merely that the reports must be submitted to the UN Economic and Social Council (ECOSOC). Neither did it establish any inter-state or individual complaints system.

Initially, ECOSOC had delegated the task of reviewing the state reports to a working group of its members, known as the Sessional Working Group on the Implementation of the International Covenant on Economic, Social and Cultural Rights. That body reported its general findings to ECOSOC, the UN Commission on Human Rights and various Specialized Agencies of the UN. Eventually, ECOSOC established a Committee on Economic, Social and Cultural Rights (CESCR), composed of 18 experts elected by the States Parties but serving in their personal capacities. The Committee first met in March 1987. Despite various obstacles, it gradually devised a sound and creative approach for pressing states to live up to their treaty obligations. It has also used its General Comments and analyses of state reports to clarify the meaning of the many ambiguous provisions of the Covenant, thus providing the international community with an analytically helpful interpretative gloss on the normative character of economic, social and cultural rights. *See* generally *https://www.ohchr.org/en/treaty-bodies/cescr*.

As early as 1990, the CESCR began discussing the advisability of an optional protocol to create an individual complaints mechanism for the ICESCR (paralleling the ICCPR's first optional protocol). The proposal was controversial but after more than a decade of work, the Protocol was adopted on December 10, 2008. The Protocol entered into force in May 2013 and the Committee issued its first views under the Protocol in 2016. As of 2024, 30 States were parties to the Optional Protocol; 24 others had signed but not ratified.

Some of the procedures set forth in the Protocol are innovative, reflecting the distinct character of some economic, social and cultural rights. For example, Article 2 provides that communications may be submitted by or on behalf of individuals or groups of individuals claiming to be victims of a violation of any of the rights set forth in Parts II and III of the Covenant by that State Party. Communications submitted on behalf of individuals or groups of individuals must have their consent unless the author can justify acting on their behalf without such consent. Article 8 authorizes the Committee to consult, in addition to the parties' submissions, "relevant documentation emanating from other United Nations bodies, specialized agencies, funds, programmes and mechanisms, and other international organizations, including from regional human rights systems." Although NGOs are not mentioned in the article, the Committee has issued a

"Guidance on Third-Party Interventions," setting forth guidelines for "individuals or entities seeking to submit interventions as a third party." *See https://www.ohchr.org/sites/default/files/Documents/HRBodies/CRC/GuidelinesTPI.pdf.*

The Committee's consideration of communications is to take place in closed session. Unusually, Art. 8(4) of the Protocol gives guidance on the standard to be applied by the Committee in judging whether or not a violation has been shown:

> When examining communications under the present Protocol, the Committee shall consider the reasonableness of the steps taken by the State Party in accordance with Part II of the Covenant. In doing so, the Committee shall bear in mind that the State Party may adopt a range of possible policy measures for the implementation of the rights set forth in the Covenant.

The State Party concerned must report within six months on the measures it takes in response to the views of the Committee (art. 6(2)). The Protocol also establishes an optional inter-state procedure (art. 10) and an optional inquiry procedure to respond to allegations of grave and systematic violations (art. 11). Article 14 contains measures designed to provide technical and financial assistance when appropriate, including through the establishment of a United Nations trust fund to aid in the further implementation of the relevant rights.

IV. OTHER CORE UN HUMAN RIGHTS TREATIES

§ 2–12. INTRODUCTION

In addition to the two Covenants and their protocols, the UN has over the years adopted a large number of treaties addressing specific types of human rights violations, including genocide, racial discrimination, apartheid, discrimination against women, torture and children's rights, among others. Many of the treaties define terms, such as "genocide," "torture" and "racial discrimination," that are not clearly defined in the more general treaties, thereby providing more precise legal norms. Each of these treaties (directly or by protocol) provides for the establishment of a committee of independent experts to monitor implementation of the treaty provisions by States Parties (except for the Apartheid Convention, which is overseen by the UN Human Rights Council, and the 1948 Genocide Convention, which does not require reporting). These committees are referred to by their acronyms, i.e., "CEDAW" for the Committee on Discrimination Against Women, "CAT" for the Committee Against Torture, "CERD" for the Committee on the Elimination of Racial Discrimination, "CRC" for the Committee on the Rights of the Child, CPRD for the Committee on the Rights of Persons with Disabilities, etc. Generally, *see https://www.ohchr.org/en/core-international-human-rights-instruments-and-their-monitoring-bodies.*

Each treaty body is directed to consider periodic state reports containing information on steps taken to implement the provisions of the relevant treaty (and in the case of the CRC its substantive protocols). Most of the treaties establish a timetable for the submission of initial and periodic reports, although the Covenants discussed above do not do so. Harmonized reporting guidelines on reporting, including guidelines for a common core document and treaty-specific documents, have been adopted. *See https://digitallibrary.un.org/record/574830?ln=en*. As noted above, the General Assembly has encouraged the treaty bodies to adopt the simplified reporting procedure described in § 2–8, and most have begun employing that procedure. Generally, *see https://www.ohchr.org/en/treaty-bodies*.

Over time, the committees have adopted a common framework for reviewing the reports and adoption of Concluding Observations based on those reports. The main feature of the procedure is the "constructive dialogue" in which the committees engage with representatives from the State Party whose report is under consideration. All treaty bodies may consider reports in the absence of a delegation, but this rarely happens, as the Committees use every means at their disposal to ensure that the State Party sends a delegation.

In addition, all committees follow the practice initiated by CERD in 1991 of undertaking a "review procedure" in the absence of a report to examine implementation of the relevant treaty by a State Party whose report is at least five years overdue. The notification that a treaty body plans to do so has been sufficient in many instances to encourage the state to submit the missing report. In a number of cases, however, States Parties have been considered under the review procedure in the absence of a report. For further discussion, *see* Report on the Working Methods of the Human Rights Treaty Bodies relating to the State Party Reporting Process, HRI/MC/2010/2, May 10, 2010, at *https://digitallibrary.un.org/record/682616?ln=en.*

All of the treaty bodies except the Committee on Migrant Workers (CMW) have the authority to consider individual communications with respect to States Parties that have accepted this procedure. In addition, the Committee Against Torture (CAT), the Committee for the Elimination of Discrimination Against Women (CEDAW), the Committee on the Rights of the Child (CRC), the Committee on the Rights of Persons with Disabilities (CRPD), and the Committee on Enforced Disappearances (CED) (as well as the CESCR, as discussed above) may conduct inquiries into alleged violations if this procedure has been accepted by the State Party in question. The CED also has the authority to consider requests for "urgent action" on behalf of disappeared persons at the behest of the person's relative or another person having a legitimate interest. *See* Convention for the Protection of All Persons from Enforced Disappearance, art. 30. Although not provided for in the Convention, CERD has established an early warning and urgent action procedure for the prevention of serious violations of its Convention.

All of the treaty bodies also adopt General Comments which set forth their recommendations for clarifying the States parties' obligations under their respective Conventions and otherwise elaborating the Committees' interpretations of the Conventions. CERD and CEDAW denominate these "General Recommendations," in line with the terminology employed in those Conventions.

The treaties designated by the United Nations as "core" agreements are summarized in the sections that follow, along with the first human rights treaty adopted by the United Nations, the Convention against Genocide.

§ 2–13. THE CONVENTION ON THE PREVENTION AND PUNISHMENT OF THE CRIME OF GENOCIDE

The Genocide Convention was adopted by the UN General Assembly on December 9, 1948 and entered into force on January 12, 1951. The extermination of millions of Jews and members of other national, ethnic and religious groups during the Nazi Holocaust prompted the adoption of the Convention, which explicitly outlaws this crime. As of 2024, 153 States had ratified the Convention. For background, *see https://www.un.org/en/genocideprevention/genocide-convention.shtml.*

Article 1 declares that "genocide, whether committed in time of peace or time of war, is a crime under international law which [the parties] undertake to prevent and punish." A "crime under international law" is a grave offense against the law of nations for which the individual perpetrator is punishable. It differs from a mere violation of international law, which makes a government liable for the resulting damages without imposing criminal responsibility on individuals. Article IV of the Genocide Convention accordingly provides that "persons committing genocide . . . shall be punished, whether they are constitutionally responsible rulers, public officials or private individuals."

The Convention defines "genocide" as the commission of certain enumerated acts "with intent to destroy, in whole or in part, a national, ethnic, racial or religious group, as such." (Art. II.) Other groups, e.g., political or economic ones, are not included, nor is widespread killing of persons because of their gender, although such deliberate attacks would be considered a crime against humanity. The acts constituting genocide are: (a) killing members of the group; (b) causing serious bodily or mental harm to members of the group; (c) deliberately inflicting on the group conditions of life calculated to bring about its physical destruction in whole or in part; (d) imposing measures intended to prevent births within the group; and (e) forcibly transferring children of the group to another group. To be guilty of the crime of genocide, an individual must have committed one of the foregoing acts with the specific intent of destroying, in whole or in part, a national, ethnic, racial or religious group. The killing of some members of a group could consequently amount to genocide if carried out with the intent of destroying the group or a substantial part thereof.

By outlawing the destruction of national, ethnic, racial and religious groups, the Genocide Convention formally recognizes the right of these groups to exist as groups. Viewed in this light, the Convention must be considered the centerpiece of the international law that applies to the protection of groups, be they minorities or majorities.

The Genocide Convention takes account of the possibility that those charged with genocide might be tried by an international criminal court, but it does not establish such a tribunal. The Statutes of the *ad hoc* Tribunals for the former Yugoslavia and Rwanda adopt the definition contained in the Genocide Convention as a basis in conferring jurisdiction over genocide on these tribunals. The same is true of Article 6 of the "Rome Statute," which created the International Criminal Court.

Disputes between two or more States Parties relating to the interpretation of the Convention may be submitted by either of them to the International Court of Justice. Genocide Convention, art. IX. The armed conflict in the Former Yugoslavia produced the first such cases in the ICJ. *See, e.g.*, Application of the Convention on the Prevention and Punishment of the Crime of Genocide (Bosnia and Herzegovina v. Yugoslavia), Order of 17 December 1997, 1997 ICJ Rep. 243 and the subsequent 2007 judgment, *supra*. National prosecutions for genocide are also contemplated. Article VI of the Genocide Convention speaks of "a competent tribunal of the State in the territory of which the act [of genocide] was committed." It is clear that the courts of other states, particularly those of the perpetrator's nationality, would also have jurisdiction under international law generally.

Today universal jurisdiction appears to be increasingly accepted with respect to the crime of genocide and a number of states have adopted legislation asserting jurisdiction over the offense no matter where it is committed or by whom.

§ 2–14. INTERNATIONAL CONVENTION ON THE ELIMINATION OF ALL FORMS OF RACIAL DISCRIMINATION

Adopted by the UN General Assembly in 1965, this treaty entered into force in 1969 (before either of the Covenants). As of 2024 it had been ratified by 182 states (3 others had signed but not ratified). The text is available at *https://www.ohchr.org/en/instruments-mechanisms/instruments/international-convention-elimination-all-forms-racial.*

The Convention prohibits "racial discrimination," which is defined broadly in Art. 1(1) as "any distinction, exclusion, restriction or preference based on race, colour, descent, or national or ethnic origin" having the purpose or effect of "nullifying or impairing the recognition, enjoyment or exercise, on an equal footing, of human rights and fundamental freedoms in the political, economic, social, cultural or any other field of public life." The obligation of States Parties imposed by Art. 2 is similarly broad: to eliminate racial discrimination "in all its forms" and to enact whatever laws are necessary to ensure non-discrimination in the exercise and enjoyment of various human rights.

More specifically, Article 2(1)(d) requires State Parties to "prohibit and bring to an end, by all appropriate means, including legislation as required by circumstances, racial discrimination by any person, group or organization." When circumstances warrant, States Parties to take "special and concrete measures to ensure the adequate development and protection of certain racial groups or individuals belonging to them, for the purpose of guaranteeing them the full and equal enjoyment of human rights and fundamental freedoms. Art. 2(2). *See* General Recommendation 32, The Meaning and Scope of Special Measures in the International Convention for the Elimination of Racial Discrimination, CERD/C/GC/32 (2009), available at *https://www.refworld.org/docid/4adc30382.html.*

The monitoring of the Convention is conducted by the Committee on the Elimination of Racial Discrimination (CERD), which is composed of 18 members who are elected by the States Parties but serve in their individual capacities. CERD was the first UN human rights treaty body to be established and has been functioning since 1970. It has a number of functions, including review of the periodic reports the States Parties have an obligation to prepare "on the legislative, judicial, administrative or other measures which they have adopted to give effect to the provisions" of the Convention, and addressing inter-state and individual communications. By ratifying the Convention, a state submits to the

Committee's jurisdiction to deal with inter-state communications directed against it by any other State Party. By distinction, the individual petition system established by the Convention is optional, since Article 14 requires a separate declaration recognizing the jurisdiction of the Committee to receive such communications. Not all States Parties have done so. Article 22 gives the ICJ jurisdiction to deal with disputes between the States Parties, although a number of States have reserved to that provision. *See https://www.ohchr.org/en/treaty-bodies/cerd/inter-state-communications.*

Since 1993, the Committee's agenda has regularly included consideration of preventive measures ("early-warning" and "urgent procedures") to respond to problems requiring immediate attention to prevent existing problems from escalating into a conflict and to prevent or limit the scale or number of serious violations of the Convention. Its decisions, statement and communications in this area can be found at *https://www.ohchr.org/en/treaty-bodies/cerd/decisions-statements-and-letters.*

§ 2–15. CONVENTION ON THE ELIMINATION OF ALL FORMS OF DISCRIMINATION AGAINST WOMEN

Adopted by the UN General Assembly in 1979, the CEDAW entered into force in 1981 and, as of 2024, it had 189 States Party (Palau and the United States had signed but not ratified). For the text and other information, *see https://www.un.org/womenwatch/daw/cedaw/*. In addition to being one of the most widely ratified treaties, it is also one of the most ambitious.

Article 1 defines "discrimination against women" broadly as "any distinction, exclusion, or restriction made on the basis of sex" that impairs the enjoyment by women of "human rights and fundamental freedoms in the political, economic, social, cultural, civil or any other field." In addition to condemning discrimination against women "in all its forms," it requires States Parties "to embody the principle of equality of men and women in their national constitutions or other appropriate legislation," "to adopt laws or other measures, including sanctions where appropriate, prohibiting all discrimination against women," "to take all appropriate measures to eliminate discrimination against women by any person, organization or enterprise," and "to take all appropriate measures, including legislation, to modify or abolish existing laws, regulations, customs and practices which constitute discrimination against women." Article 2.

Under Article 5, States Parties must take "all appropriate measures" to "modify the social and cultural patterns of conduct of men and women, with a view to achieving the elimination of prejudices and customary and all other practices which are based on the idea of the inferiority or the superiority of either of the sexes or on stereotyped roles for men and women" and "to ensure that family education includes a proper understanding of maternity as a social function. . . ." Other articles specify affirmative steps to be taken in the "political and public life of the country," in the fields of education, employment, health care, and in the social, economic and cultural realms to advance the enjoyment of equal rights by women.

Article 28(2) expressly permits States Parties to take reservations that are not "incompatible with the object and purpose" of the Convention (the standard contained in the Vienna Convention on the Law of Treaties), and indeed a number of States have in fact taken reservations in an effort to preserve various national or religious institutions that are not consistent with its provisions. In 1993, the Vienna World Conference on Human Rights urged the states "to withdraw reservations that are contrary to the object and purpose of the Convention or which are otherwise incompatible with international treaty law." Vienna Declaration and Programme of Action, U.N. Doc. A/Conf. 157/23, Art. II, para. 39, available at *https://www.ohchr.org/en/instruments-mechanisms/instruments/vienna-declaration-and-programme-action*. Since then, a number have done so. *See https://www.un.org/womenwatch/daw/cedaw/*.

As with other human rights treaties, States Party must submit periodic reports indicating "the legislative, judicial, administrative or other measures they have adopted to give effect to the provisions of the Convention." Art. 18(1). These reports are reviewed by the CEDAW Committee, which follows procedures and guidelines similar to the other treaty bodies. *See https://www.un.org/womenwatch/daw/cedaw/reports.htm*. For a time, the Committee was something of a stepchild among UN human rights treaty bodies because Article 20 (1) of the Convention provides that "the Committee shall normally meet for a period of not more than two weeks annually." This soon proved to be totally insufficient time to fulfill its duties under the Convention. In 1996, pending the entry into force of an amendment to Article 20(1), the General Assembly authorized CEDAW, on an interim basis, to hold two annual sessions of three weeks each. In 2005, General Assembly resolution 60/230 (23 December 2005) expanded the meeting time further, allowing the Committee to meet for the coming two years for three sessions. As of mid-2024, the amendment had not been ratified by the required two-thirds of States Party. *See https://treaties.un.org/Pages/ViewDetails.aspx?src=TREATY&mtdsg_no=IV-8-a&chapter=4&clang=_en.*

The powers of the Committee were expanded in 2002 by an optional protocol giving the Committee the power to accept and consider communications from individuals or groups claiming to be victims of violations of the Convention, when states have consented to this procedure. As of mid-2024, 115 States were Parties to the Convention. *See https://treaties.un.org/pages/ViewDetails.aspx?src=IND&mtdsg_no=IV-8-b&chapter=4&clang=_en.* For information on the procedure, *see https://www.ohchr.org/en/treaty-bodies/cedaw/individual-communications.* Article 8 of the Protocol authorizes the Committee to conduct an inquiry into the alleged violations.

§ 2–16. CONVENTION AGAINST TORTURE AND OTHER CRUEL, INHUMAN OR DEGRADING TREATMENT

The UN Torture Convention, adopted in 1984, entered into force in 1987. As of 2024, it had been ratified by 175 States; 4 others had signed but not ratified. *See https://treaties.un.org/pages/ViewDetails.aspx?src=IND&mtdsg_no=IV-9&chapter=4&clang=_en.*

The Convention is designed to prevent and punish torture committed "by or at the instigation of or with the consent or acquiescence of a public official or other person acting in an official capacity." Art. 1(1). In other words, it covers not only torture inflicted by government officials but also torture by private individuals or groups whose conduct such officials encourage or tolerate. The same provision defines torture broadly as "any act by which severe pain or suffering, whether physical or mental, is intentionally inflicted on a person" for the purpose, *inter alia,* of "obtaining from him or a third person information or a confession." Arts. 2(2) and 2(3) make clear that there are "no exceptional circumstances whatsoever" to justify torture and in particular that no orders from superior officers or a public authority may be invoked as a justification.

Under Art. 2(1), States Parties undertake to adopt "effective legislative, administrative, judicial or other measures to prevent" torture in any territory under their jurisdiction. Articles 4(1) and 5 require a State Party to ensure that all acts of torture (as defined in the treaty) are offenses under its criminal law, and that their courts have jurisdiction if the offense occurred within its territory, if the alleged offender is its national, and if the victim is its national (as each State considers appropriate). In the event that an alleged torturer is found in the territory of a State Party which does not have jurisdiction under those provisions, that State must either extradite him for prosecution elsewhere or submit the case for prosecution under its own law (a principle known as *aut dedere aut judicare*). Art. 7(1). The Convention declares torture to be an extraditable offense (Art. 8) but prohibits States Parties from extraditing a person to a country where he or she "would be in danger of being subjected to torture." Art. 3(1).

The Convention establishes the Committee Against Torture (CAT) to monitor States Parties' compliance with their obligations. *See https://www.ohchr.org/en/treaty-bodies/cat/background-convention.* As with other human rights monitoring measures, the Convention creates consist of an obligatory reporting system as well as optional inter-state and individual complaint mechanisms (Arts. 19, 21, 22). Under Article 20, the CAT can undertake certain investigatory actions on its own initiative. Generally, *see https://www.ohchr.org/en/treaty-bodies/cat.*

The Optional Protocol for the Prevention of Torture (OPCAT), which entered into force in 2006 and by 2024 had been ratified by 94 States, establishes an additional monitoring mechanism by requiring States Parties to establish a domestic body empowered to visit and report on places of detention (called "national preventive mechanisms") It also establishes a separate treaty body, the Subcommittee for the Prevention of Torture (SPT), consisting of twenty-five members serving in their individual capacities (arts. 2, 5(1), 5(6)). The OPCAT requires States Parties to give both the national preventive mechanism and the SPT unrestricted access to all places of detention under its jurisdiction and control (arts. 4, 14(1), 20). These may include police stations, prisons, immigration detention centers and juvenile justice centers. The SPT conducts visits to places of detention pursuant to a program of regular visits established by the Subcommittee (art. 13(1)). The visits are carried out by two or more members, assisted by one or more experts selected from a roster prepared on the basis of proposals by States Parties, the Office of the High Commissioner for Human Rights, and the UN Centre for International Crime Prevention (art. 13(3)). The SPT's report and recommendations are to be communicated to the State Party concerned confidentially (art. 16(1)), although the Subcommittee may make its report public if the State Party refused to cooperate with the SPT as required by the Convention (art. 16(4)). Generally, *see https://www.ohchr.org/en/treaty-bodies/spt*.

§ 2–17. CONVENTION ON THE RIGHTS OF THE CHILD AND ITS PROTOCOLS

Adopted by the UN General Assembly in 1989, the Convention on the Rights of the Child (CRC) entered into force in less than a year and by mid-2024 had been ratified by virtually every UN Member State (save the United States, which had signed in 1995). Although many of the rights the Convention proclaims are set out in one form or another in existing international human rights treaties, the Convention is the first treaty that singles out children as subjects of international rights and protection. It defines a child as "every human being below the age of eighteen unless under the law applicable to the child, majority is attained earlier." Art. 1. Under Art. 2(1), States Parties assume the obligation to accord children within their jurisdiction an extensive catalog of civil, political, economic, social and cultural rights "irrespective of the child's or his or her parent's or legal guardian's race, colour, sex, language, religion, political or other opinion, national, ethnic or social origin, property, disability, birth or other status." Article 3(1) declares that "in all actions concerning children, whether undertaken by public or private social welfare institutions, courts of law, administrative authorities or legislative bodies, the best interests of the child shall be a primary consideration." *See https://www.ohchr.org/en/instruments-mechanisms/instruments/convention-rights-child.*

The Convention establishes a Committee on the Rights of the Child (CRC), which is charged with the task of "examining the progress made by the States Parties in achieving the realization of the obligations undertaken in the present Convention." Art. 43(1). The Committee is composed of eighteen members who serve in their personal capacities. Its principal task is to review the reports which the States Parties are required to submit to the Committee on the measures they have taken in implementing the Convention. Art. 44. For an overview of the work of the CRC, *see https://www.ohchr.org/en/treaty-bodies/crc.*

Two optional protocols to the Convention, adopted by the UNGA in 2000, are designed to strengthen the protections afforded children. Both came into force in 2002. Under the first, which by 2024 had been ratified by 173 States (including the United States), States Parties must take all feasible measures to ensure that members of their armed forces under the age of 18 do not take a direct part in hostilities; they are also required to ensure that persons who have not attained the age of 18 are not forced to serve in their armed forces. Article 4 provides that armed groups that are distinct from the armed forces of a State should not, under any circumstances, recruit or use in hostilities persons under the age of 18 years. States Parties are to take measures to prevent such recruitment and use, including the adoption of legal measures necessary to prohibit and criminalize such practices.

The Second Optional Protocol, which as of 2024 had been ratified by 178 States (again including the United States), obligates States Party to criminalize the sale of children, child prostitution and child pornography, whether or not such offences are committed within their territory or are committed on an individual or organized basis. It establishes extensive enforcement jurisdiction based on the territory where the offense is committed, the nationality of the perpetrator, and nationality of the victim. Further, States must either prosecute or extradite offenders found on their territory.

A third Optional Protocol was adopted in 2011 and came into force in 2014. It enhances the CRC's monitoring powers by empowering it to receive and decide individual complaints and to conduct inquiries with respect to grave or systematic violations of the Convention or the Optional Protocols. It also empowers the Committee to received inter-state communications as between states that have accepted the Committee's jurisdiction over such complaints (art. 12). By 2024, 50 states had become parties, many of which had accepted the CRC's jurisdiction over inter-state communications.

§ 2–18. INTERNATIONAL CONVENTION ON THE PROTECTION OF THE RIGHTS OF ALL MIGRANT WORKERS AND MEMBERS OF THEIR FAMILIES

The International Migrant Workers Convention, adopted by the UN General Assembly in 1990, came into force in 2003 but has since been slow to gain adherents: according to the UN depositary, only 60 States Party by 2024, including none of the UN Security Council's Permanent Members and relatively few labor-receiving states. It was adopted outside the framework of the International Labor Organization, whose earlier work on the topic included the Migrant Workers (Supplementary Provisions) Convention 1975 (No. 143). For background, *see https://www.ohchr.org/en/treaty-bodies/cmw/background-convention*.

The Convention reflects the competing interests of sending and receiving states and the considerable concern states have about controlling entry into their territory. Art. 2(1) defines the term "migrant worker" as "a person who is to be engaged or has been engaged in a remunerated activity in a State of which he or she is not a national." Included are "frontier workers; seasonal workers; seafarers; workers on offshore installations; itinerant workers; migrants employed for a specific project; and self-employed workers." Part II consists of a single article which provides that the rights in the Convention are to be made available to all migrants without discrimination.

Among its key provisions, Article 25(1) calls for national treatment of migrant workers, establishing that they shall enjoy "treatment not less favorable than that which applies to nationals of the State of employment" in respect of terms and conditions of work. Article 33 requires States Parties to take the measures they deem appropriate to ensure that migrant workers and members of their families are informed of their rights under the Convention upon request without charge and, as far as possible, in a language they are able to understand.

The Convention establishes a Committee on Migrant Workers (CMW), empowered to receive and consider reports of States Party regarding their implementation of the Convention, to provide comments and recommendations in the form of Concluding Observations thereon as well as General Comments to provide guidance on the implementation of the Convention. Articles 76 and 77 establish inter-state and individual complaints procedures. Similarly, Article 77 establishes an individual complaint procedure, to come into effect once ten states have declared their consent. For information on the Committee's work, *see https://www.ohchr.org/en/treaty-bodies/cmw*.

§ 2–19. CONVENTION ON THE RIGHTS OF PERSONS WITH DISABILITIES

Adopted in 2006 and in force two years later, this Convention aims to combat discrimination against persons with disabilities and to guarantee them the exercise of human rights. States Parties commit broadly to develop and carry out policies, laws and administrative measures for securing the rights recognized in the Convention and abolish laws, regulations, customs and practices that constitute discrimination. They also agree to combat stereotypes and prejudices and promote awareness of the capabilities of persons with disabilities. For general background on the Convention (and its Optional Protocol, which establishes an individual complaint mechanism), *see https://www.ohchr.org/en/treaty-bodies/crpd*. As of 2024, there were 191 States Parties to the Convention, of which 107 had also ratified the Protocol.

The Convention requires States Parties to ensure persons with disabilities their right to enjoy the inherent right to life on an equal basis with others. Art. 10. Children with disabilities shall have equal rights, shall not be separated from their parents against their will, except when the authorities determine that this is in the child's best interests, and in no case shall be separated from their parents on the basis of a disability of either the child or the parents. Art. 23. States Parties are to recognize that all persons are equal before the law, to prohibit discrimination on the basis of disability and guarantee equal legal protection. Art. 5. Economic rights, the right of access to justice, the right to liberty and security, the right to physical and mental integrity, freedom from torture and from cruel, inhuman or degrading treatment or punishment, and from nonconsensual medical or scientific experiments are also guaranteed.

States Party are required inter alia to create a national mechanism to promote and monitor implementation. The Convention also creates a Committee on the Rights of Persons with Disabilities (CRPD), to receive and consider reports from States Parties regarding implementation of their obligations. Like other treaty bodies, the CRPD reviews State Party reports, adopts Concluding Observations and General Comments, and examines individual communications pursuant to the Optional Protocol. Generally, *see https://www.ohchr.org/en/treaty-bodies/crpd.*

§ 2–20. INTERNATIONAL CONVENTION FOR THE PROTECTION OF ALL PERSONS FROM ENFORCED DISAPPEARANCE

The most recent of the nine UN core human rights instruments, the 2006 Disappearances Convention entered into force in 2010. As of 2024 it had been ratified by 76 states party. Like the Genocide and Torture Conventions, the Disappearances Convention is not only a human rights instrument but is also concerned with criminal law, since Article 5 declares the widespread or systematic use of enforced disappearances to be a crime against humanity.

The Convention recognizes the non-derogable right of any person not to be subjected to enforced disappearance, which is defined in Article 2 as "the arrest, detention, abduction or any other form of deprivation of liberty by agents of the State or by persons or groups of persons acting with the authorization, support or acquiescence of the State, followed by a refusal to acknowledge the deprivation of liberty or by concealment of the fate or whereabouts of the disappeared person, which place such a person outside the protection of the law." States Parties must criminalize such acts in domestic law and bring to justice those responsible for them. The Convention prohibits secret detentions, sets forth a variety of remedies that a State Party must provide, and contains an extradite-or-prosecute provision.

It also establishes an expert Committee on Enforced Disappearances (CED), to which States Party must submit periodic reports. As with other treaty bodies, the Committee is tasked to review the reports, adopt Concluding Observations and General Comments, and consider individual and inter-state communications. It can conduct inquiries if it receives well-founded information that enforced disappearances are occurring on a widespread or systematic basis in the territory of a State Party. Article 30 of the Convention establishes an innovative "urgent action" procedure. Generally, *see https://www.ohchr.org/en/treaty-bodies/ced.*

V. UN CHARTER-BASED INSTITUTIONS

§ 2–21. INTRODUCTION

Aside from the 'treaty bodies" described above, various human rights institutions and procedures which have their constitutional basis in the UN Charter itself also play important roles in the global human rights system, especially with respect to "gross violations" of human rights. In actual practice, all the main UN organs deal with human rights matters today, one way or another, in accordance with the mandates conferred on them by the Charter.

§ 2–22. PRINCIPAL UN ORGANS

1. The General Assembly

As the plenary UN body, the General Assembly discusses, often modifies, and adopts human rights treaties and declarations drafted by subsidiary organs. In 2007, for example, it approved the Declaration on the Rights of Indigenous Peoples, a text negotiated over more than two decades by the Sub-Commission on Promotion and Protection of Human Rights and the Commission on Human Rights, in consultation with indigenous peoples. *See https://www.un.org/esa/socdev/unpfii/documents/DRIPS_en.pdf.* The General Assembly also receives the annual reports from the various human rights treaty bodies and Charter-based institutions, and it generally provides support for the treaty body system. In 2014 the General Assembly adopted a resolution on "Strengthening and enhancing the effective functioning of the human rights treaty body system," GA Res. 68/268, UN Doc. A/68/268 (April 9, 2014), available at *https://www.ohchr.org/sites/default/files/Documents/HRBodies/TB/HRTD/A-RES-68-268_E.pdf.*

2. The Security Council

Article 24 of the UN Charter entrusts the Security Council with primary responsibility for the maintenance of international peace and security. Article 34 authorizes it to "investigate any dispute, or any situation which might lead to international friction or give rise to a dispute, in order to determine whether the continuance of the dispute or situation is likely to endanger the maintenance of international peace and security." Such "situations" often emerge from, or lead to, gross and systematic human rights violations. If the Council determines that a situation constitutes a "threat to the peace" under Article 39 of the Charter, it may adopt binding measures to address the situation. In fact, the Council's first such actions concerned the apartheid regime in South Africa and the white minority government which declared independence in the former Rhodesia. Since then, the Council has addressed human rights violations in numerous crises.

In recent years, there has been increased discussion of the appropriate role of the Security Council in humanitarian crises and situations of massive violations of human rights. In 2001, an International Commission on Intervention and State Sovereignty, formed by the Canadian Government, issued a report entitled "Responsibility to Protect." *See https://www.globalr2p.org/resources/the-responsibility-to-protect-report-of-the-international-commission-on-intervention-and-state-sovereignty-2001/*. The Report emphasized the obligation of all governments to protect all persons from genocide, massive human rights abuses and other humanitarian crises, and concluded that when states "manifestly fail" to protect their populations, the international community shares a collective responsibility to respond through the United Nations. The "R2P" concept was embraced in the 2005 World Summit Outcome Document, and in December 2007 the UN Security Council approved the creation of a position of Special Advisor on the Responsibility to Protect. In the following years, the Security Council has repeatedly referred to the concept.

3. The High Commissioner for Human Rights

The Office of the High Commissioner for Human Rights (OHCHR), which was established in 1993 by UN General Assembly Res. 48/141, is the part of the UN Secretariat responsible for human rights matters. Appointed by the Secretary-General with the approval of the General Assembly, the High Commissioner (who has the rank of an Under

Secretary-General) is the "United Nations official with principal responsibility for United Nations human rights activities under the direction and responsibility of the Secretary-General." U.N. G.A. Res. 48/148(4). In discharging these responsibilities, the High Commissioner operates within the framework of the General Assembly, the Economic and Social Council and the Commission on Human Rights. For additional information, *see https://www.ohchr.org/en/about-us/high-commissioner* and *https://www.ohchr.org/en/ohchr_homepage*.

4. The International Court of Justice

The International Court of Justice (ICJ) is the principal judicial organ of the United Nations, established by the Charter and governed by a Statute which is annexed to the Charter. It consists of 15 independent judges elected by the General Assembly and the Security Council. Its jurisdiction is limited: under Art. 34(1) of the Statute, only States may be parties to "contentious" cases before the Court and only if they have affirmatively accepted the Court's' jurisdiction. The Court also has jurisdiction to issue "advisory opinions" at the request of the UN and its specialized agencies (and the IAEA). Generally, *see https://www.icj-cij.org/*.

A number of the ICJ's judgments over the past half century addressed questions relevant to international human rights, such as racial discrimination, political asylum, crimes against humanity, acts of genocide, and the right to consular assistance for detained foreign nationals. For example, one of the Court's early advisory opinions pronounced the impermissibility of States attaching reservations contrary to the object and purpose of a universal, humanitarian treaty like the Genocide Convention. *See* Reservations to the Convention on the Prevention and Punishment of the Crime of Genocide, 1951 ICJ Rep. 15 (May 28). Questions concerning apartheid in South Africa generated several advisory opinions and judgments. *See, e.g.*, International Status of South West Africa, 1950 ICJ Rep. (Advisory Opinion of July 11); South West Africa (Eth. v. S. Afr.), 1966 I.C.J. 16 (July 18); Legal Consequences for States of the Continued Presence of South Africa in Namibia (South West Africa). In its advisory opinion on the Legality of the Threat or Use of Nuclear Weapons, 1996 ICJ Rep. 226, the court determined that the ICCPR does not cease to apply in wartime, with the exception of provisions that may be derogated from in times of national emergency. In Legal Consequences of the Construction of a Wall in the Occupied Palestinian Territory, Advisory Opinion of 9 July 2004, 2004 ICJ Rep. 136, the ICJ explained that (1) some rights may be wholly regulated by international humanitarian law; (2) some rights may be governed entirely by international human rights law; (3) still other rights may be regulated by both humanitarian law and human rights law. *Id.* at para. 106. In the last circumstance, humanitarian law would be the *lex specialis* applicable in wartime.

§ 2–23. THE UN HUMAN RIGHTS COUNCIL

Since 2006, the main UN body responsible for human rights has been its Human Rights Council.

A bit of background is perhaps useful. Article 68 of the UN Charter gave the Economic, Social and Cultural Council (ECOSOC) responsibility for setting up various commissions, including on human rights. In 1947, acting under this authority, ECOSCO created a Sub-Commission on the Prevention of Discrimination and Protection of Minorities, later more simply called the Sub-Commission on Promotion and Protection of Human Rights, to undertake studies and to make recommendations to the previously-established Commission "concerning the prevention of discrimination of any kind relating to human rights and fundamental freedoms and the protection of racial, national, religious and linguistic minorities." Initially composed of independent experts in the field of human rights who were elected by ECOSOC with due regard to equitable geographical distribution but who acted in their personal capacity, the Sub-Commission was also empowered "to perform any other functions which may be entrusted to it by the Economic and Social Council or the Commission on Human Rights." ECOSOC Res. 9 (II) of June 21, 1946.

Reconfigured (and expanded) in 1999, this body undertook many useful programs to promote human rights, including creation of a number of working groups and special rapporteurs with thematic or country mandates such as those focusing on Enforced or Involuntary Disappearances, Extrajudicial,

Summary or Arbitrary Executions, Torture, Religious Intolerance, the Right to Food, Adequate Housing, and Indigenous Peoples.

The Commission was abolished in 2006 and replaced by the UN Human Rights Council, which is composed of 47 elected states. *See* GA Res. 60/251, UN Doc A/RES/60/251 (March 15, 2006), giving it responsibility for "promoting universal respect for the protection of all human rights and fundamental freedoms for all, without distinction of any kind and in a fair and equal manner. In making the change, the General Assembly aimed to address some of the widespread criticisms of the Commission and of the UN's human rights program in general. For instance, where members of the Commission (and its predecessor) had been individuals serving in their personal capacities, the new Council is composed of UN Member States elected by the General Assembly for three-year terms based on equitable geographical distribution among the different regions of the world. The new Council reports directly to the General Assembly (not to ECOSOC).

The Council's specific functions include to: (*a*) promote human rights education and advisory services, technical assistance and capacity-building; (*b*) discuss thematic issues on all human rights; (*c*) make recommendations to the General Assembly for the further development of international law in the field of human rights; (*d*) promote the implementation by States of their human rights obligations and commitments made at United Nations conferences and summits; (*e*) undertake a universal periodic review of each State's implementation of its human rights obligations and commitments; (*f*) act to prevent human rights violations and respond promptly to human rights emergencies; and (*g*) make recommendations with regard to the promotion and protection of human rights.

The Council's mandate also includes addressing and making recommendations on situations of violations of human rights, including gross and systematic violations, as well as promoting the effective coordination and the mainstreaming of human rights within the United Nations system. It holds at least three regular sessions a year and is allowed to hold special sessions if one-third of the members find a need. For detailed information about the Council and its activities, *see https://www.ohchr.org/en/hrbodies/hrc/home*.

§ 2–24. COMMISSION ON THE STATUS OF WOMEN

This Commission (the CSW) was established in 1946. It consists of 45 members elected as state representatives along geographic lines similar to those applicable to the former Commission on Human Rights. The Commission's mandate charges it with the preparation of studies, reports and recommendations on human rights and related issues affecting women. It has played an important role in initiating UN programs designed to eradicate *de jure* and *de facto* discrimination against women, including the drafting of the principal contemporary treaties dealing with women's rights. Generally, *see https://www.unwomen.org/en/csw.*

The first few decades of the Commission's existence were devoted to these normative activities. In recent years the Commission has focused more on issues relating to the role and needs of women in contemporary societies and on improving their political, economic, and social status. By serving as the preparatory committee for increasingly more important UN world conferences on the subject, the Commission gained political influence it needed but lacked in the past to make a significant impact. Following the 1995 Fourth World Conference on Women, for example, the General Assembly asked the Commission to integrate into its program a follow-up process to the Conference, regularly review the critical areas of concern in the Beijing Platform for Action.

In the early 1980's ECOSOC empowered the Commission to undertake a limited review of communications charging specific violations of women's rights. The Commission used these communications principally as a source of information for its studies rather than as an instrument designed to prod governments to address the specific complaints. The culmination of this work was the adoption of the Optional Protocol to the Convention on the Elimination of All Forms of Discrimination Against Women in 1999. *See https://www.un.org/womenwatch/daw/cedaw/protocol/.*

§ 2–25. PROCEDURES FOR DEALING WITH GROSS VIOLATIONS OF HUMAN RIGHTS

As soon as the UN came into being, it began to receive petitions from individuals and non-governmental organizations alleging human rights violations and seeking its intervention. However, the UN Human Rights Sub-Commission, logically the most appropriate body to deal with such petitions, decided in 1947 that it had "no power to take any action in regard to any complaints concerning human rights." This decision was confirmed by ECOSOC Res. 75(V) of August 5, 1947. Between 1947 and 1959, various (unsuccessful) efforts were made to persuade ECOSOC to reverse that decision. Eventually, they led to the adoption of Res. 744 (XXVIII) of July 30, 1959, which consolidated existing UN procedures for classifying communications while at the same time reaffirming the Commission's decision of the Commission that lacked authority to take any action in regard to any human rights complaints. Changes were finally adopted by ECOSOC in Resolutions 1235 (XLII) of June 6, 1967 and 1503 (XLVIII) of May 27, 1970. Resolution 1235 permitted the Commission at the time to examine publicly certain gross violations of human rights "as exemplified by the policy of *apartheid* as practised in the Republic of South Africa . . . and to racial discrimination as practised notably in Southern Rhodesia." Resolution 1503 established a limited, confidential procedure for the examination of communications received from individuals and other private groups with a view to identifying those that "appear to reveal a consistent pattern of gross and reliably attested violations of human rights and fundamental freedoms."

The 1503 procedure was not intended to establish an individual petition system as often understood: while individuals and non-governmental groups had standing to file petitions, those petitions had to be based on a showing of "a consistent pattern of gross and reliably attested violations." If a majority of the Working Group believed that the communication met that standard, it could be submitted together with the Working Group's report and recommendations to the Commission's Working Group on Situations. Resolution 1503 empowered the Commission to undertake a "thorough study" thereof in accordance with the provisions of paragraph 3 of Resolution 1235, *supra,* or to make it the "subject of an investigation by an *ad hoc* Committee to be appointed by the Commission which shall be undertaken only with the consent of the State concerned. . . ."

The Human Rights Council (which replaced the Commission in 2006) is similarly authorized to investigate specific country situations or thematic issues through mandates known collectively as "Special Procedures." *See https://www.ohchr.org/en/special-procedures-human-rights-council.* Some mandates are "thematic" and examine major phenomena of human rights violations worldwide, such as torture, summary executions and disappearances. Others are focused on specific countries.

The Council *has* adopted a "Complaint Procedure" to consider "communications" from individuals, groups, or non-governmental organizations claiming to be victims of human rights violations or that have direct, reliable knowledge of such violations. Like the former 1503 procedure, the process is confidential, to ensure that the procedure is impartial, objective, efficient, victims-oriented and conducted in a timely manner. *See https://www.ohchr.org/en/hr-bodies/hrc/complaint-procedure/hrc-complaint-procedure-index.* Submissions are reviewed by the Council's Working Group on Communications, consisting of five independent experts representative of the UN's five regional groups. *See https://www.ohchr.org/en/hr-bodies/hrc/complaint-procedure/wg-communications.*

These procedures are separate from those established by the various "treaty bodies" for considering individual complaints or communications from individuals or groups that rights protected by the relevant treaty are being violated, as discussed in Part IV above. *See also https://www.ohchr.org/en/treaty-bodies/complaints-about-human-rights-violations.*

§ 2–26. UN HUMAN RIGHTS CONFERENCES

United Nations global conferences on human rights offer an important means of reaffirming and strengthening aspects of international human rights law. Although the results of such conferences usually take the form of non-binding "declarations," they can nonetheless play an important role in shaping and developing the law and the programs of the United Nations in the field of human rights. Their "Final Acts" are a useful source of reference. *See https://www.un.org/en/development/devagenda/human rights.shtml.*

The first such conference was held in Teheran in 1968 and its Final Act affirmed the indivisibility and interdependence of all human rights. *See https://www.refworld.org/docid/3ae6b36f1b.html.* Another took place in Vienna in 1993, and the resulting Vienna Declaration and Program of Action of the World Conference on Human Rights adopted a common plan for strengthening human rights throughout the world including through creation of a new UN High Commissioner for Human Rights. *See https://www.ohchr.org/en/about-us/history/vienna-declaration* and *https://www.ohchr.org/en/about-us/history/vienna-declaration/teheran-vienna-timeline.*

Other significant conferences related to human rights include the World Conference to Combat Racism and Racial Discrimination (Geneva 1978), the International Conference on Population Development (Cairo 1994), the World Conference on Women (Beijing 1995), the World Summit on Social Development (Copenhagen 1995), the World Conference against Racism, Racial Discrimination, Xenophobia and Related Intolerance (Durban 2001), and the World Conference on Indigenous Peoples (New York 2014). Generally, *see https://www.un.org/en/conferences.*

VI. SPECIALIZED AGENCIES

§ 2–27. INTRODUCTION

The 17 Specialized Agencies of the United Nations are functional intergovernmental organizations affiliated with the UN. Although they are autonomous entities in the sense that they have their own constitutions and policy-making structure, they have a special institutional relationship with the UN and cooperate with it in areas of mutual concern, according to the specific mandate of each agency. Generally, *see https://www.un.org/en/about-us/specialized-agencies*. Over time, the goal of defining and promoting internationally-recognized human rights has been embraced by virtually all parts of the UN system, including the specialized agencies. We mention here only four: the ILO, UNESCO, WHO and FAO. For an overview, *see https://www.un.org/en/global-issues/human-rights*.

§ 2–28. THE INTERNATIONAL LABOR ORGANIZATION

The International Labor Organization (ILO) predates the UN. It was established in 1919 by the Treaty of Versailles, with a mandate to focus on the right to work and working conditions, including the rights to form trade unions, to strike, to be free from slavery and forced labor, equal employment and training opportunities, to safe and healthy working conditions, and to social security. It became a specialized agency of the UN in 1946. Its main aims are to promote rights at work, encourage decent employment opportunities, enhance social protection and strengthen dialogue on work-related issues. It does so through the adoption of binding conventions (now numbering 190) and recommendations containing core minimum standards (for example, on child labor, employment of women, migrant workers, and indigenous and tribal peoples, among others. Generally *see www.ilo.org*.

ILO Member States (which include all UN members (except Andorra, Bhutan, Liechtenstein, Micronesia, Monaco, Nauru, and North Korea) are required to submit all conventions to their appropriate national authorities for possible ratification (no reservations are permitted) and to report on the results. They must also regularly report on implementation. A committee of twenty independent experts monitors compliance. It meets annually to examine reports and may follow up with "Direct Requests" to governments and to organizations of workers and employers. If the Committee discovers more serious or persistent problems, it may make "Observations" to the government, which are published in the Committee's annual report to the Conference. A second supervisory body, the Committee on the Application of Conventions and Recommendations, established each year by the Conference with representatives of government, employers, and workers. On the basis of the Committee of Experts' Report, the Conference Committee selects specific important or persistent cases and asks the government to appear to discuss the situation. The Conference Committee then reports to the full Conference.

Under the ILO's Declaration of Fundamental Rights and Principles at Work, all ILO Member States have an obligation to ensure the protection of four specific areas of human rights or core labor standards: freedom of association and the right to collectively bargain; freedom from child labor; freedom from forced or compulsory labor; and non-discrimination in employment. All Member States must report annually if they have not ratified the relevant ILO conventions on these subjects and indicate the obstacles to ratification.

The ILO has developed several complaint procedures, two of which concern ratified conventions. A third procedure, restricted to complaints about freedom of association, applies whether or not the state has ratified any relevant ILO conventions. Under the most widely used procedure, the Committee on Freedom of Association considers complaints directly from workers' or employers' associations and, if it finds a violation, may ask the government concerned to continue reporting to it. It may also refer the case to the Committee of Experts, if it concerns a ratified Convention, or recommend referral to the Fact-Finding and Conciliation Commission on Freedom of Association (FFCC).

§ 2–29. UNESCO, WHO AND FAO

(1) UNESCO. The United Nations Educational, Scientific and Cultural Organization, created in 1945, includes human rights within its broad mandate to promote education, science and culture.

It promotes teaching and research on human rights and adopts conventions and recommendations on human rights related to its subject areas. It has also established a complaints procedure available to individuals and NGOs. Generally, *see https://www.unesco.org/en*.

Among UNESCO's best known conventions are the 1960 Convention against Discrimination in Education and the 1954 Convention for the Protection of Cultural Property in the Event of Armed Conflict (with a 1999 Protocol). In 1997 it adopted a Universal Declaration on the Human Genome and Human Rights, the first international instruments to address human rights and modern biotechnology and to reject the cloning of human beings, which was subsequently endorsed by the U.N. General Assembly. *See https://www.ohchr.org/en/instruments-mechanisms/instruments/universal-declaration-human-genome-and-human-rights*. In 2005 UNESCO adopted a Universal Declaration on Bioethics and Human Rights. *See https://www.unesco.org/en/ethics-science-technology/bioethics-and-human-rights*.

Under UNESCO's "104 Procedure," it may consider petitions from a victim or anyone with reliable knowledge about a human rights violation concerned with the rights to education, to share in scientific advancement, to participate freely in cultural life or to information (including freedom of opinion or expression). The communication is considered by a Committee on Conventions and Recommendations (C.R. Committee) and transmitted to the government concerned, which may submit a reply. Several actions may be taken on such communications: the Director-General may initiate consultations, even before a communication has been declared admissible, and the C.R. Committee may propose specific measures for the state to take. Although the procedure is confidential and non-judicial, it nevertheless appears to have been relatively successful. Generally, *see https://www.unesco.org/en/legal-affairs/cr-committee/104-procedure.*

(2) WHO. The Constitution of the World Health Organization affirms that the "enjoyment of the highest attainable standard of health is one of the fundamental rights of every human being without distinction of race, religion, political belief, economic or social condition." *See https://www.who.int/about/governance/constitution.* Member States thus have an obligation to ensure access to timely, acceptable, and affordable health care, including through the allocation of "maximum available resources" to progressively realize this goal, without discrimination on the grounds of race, age, ethnicity or any other factor but with particular focus on disadvantaged populations. In 2003, the WHO adopted the Framework Convention on Tobacco Control (FCTC). According to Article 3, the objective of the Convention is "to protect present and future generations from the devastating health, social, environmental and economic consequences of tobacco consumption and exposure to tobacco smoke." The FCTC entered into force in 2005, and as of 2023 had 182 States Parties, making it one of the most widely

ratified of all human rights treaties. States that have signed but not ratified include Argentina, Cuba, Haiti, Morocco, Switzerland and the United States. For an overview of the Convention, *see https://fctc.who.int/convention.* While it plays a fundamental role in developing and promoting human rights, the WHO does not itself provide for consideration of individual or state-to-states complaints.

(3) FAO. The right to food was explicitly recognized in article 25 of the 1948 Universal Declaration of Human Rights as part of the right to an adequate standard of living. *See https://www.un.org/en/about-us/universal-declaration-of-human-rights.* It is also enshrined in article 11 of the 1966 International Covenant on Economic, Social and Cultural Rights. *See* Committee on Economic, Social and Cultural Rights General Comment12 (1999), at *https://www.ohchr.org/en/documents/general-comments-and-recommendations/ec1219995-general-comment-no-12-right-adequate-food.* Generally *see https://www.ohchr.org/en/food.*

The goal of the Food and Agricultural Organization (FAO) is to achieve food security for all and make sure that people have regular access to enough high-quality food to lead active, healthy lives. With 195 members—194 countries and the European Union—FAO works in over 130 countries worldwide in an effort to develop national laws, strategies, policies and programs that aim at the fulfilment for all of the right to food. *See https://www.fao.org/home/en.* While the FAO as an organization is dedicated to promoting universal access to adequate food, it does not have specific mechanisms for receiving or acting upon individual or state-to-state complaints.

Selected References and Additional Reading

E. Abrusci, Judicial Convergence and Fragmentation in International Human Rights Law: The Regional Systems and the United Nations Human Rights Committee (2023)

H. Cantú Rivera, The Universal Declaration of Human Rights: A Commentary (2022)

F. McGaughey, Non-Governmental Organisations and the United Nations Human Rights System (2021)

A. Neier, The International Human Rights Movement: A History (2020)

P. Taylor, A Commentary on the International Covenant on Civil and Political Rights: The UN Human Rights Committee's Monitoring of ICCPR Rights (2020)

J. Dugard, B. Porter, et al. Research Handbook on Economic, Social and Cultural Rights as Human Rights (2020)

P. R. Ghandhi, The Human Rights Committee and the Right of Individual Communication: Law and Practice (2019)

S. Subedi, The Effectiveness of the UN Human Rights System: Reform and the Judicialisation of Human Rights (2017)

D. Shelton, The United Nations System for Protecting Human Rights (2016)

B. Saul, The International Covenant on Economic, Social and Cultural Rights: *Travaux Preparatoires* (2016)

S. Joseph and M. Castan, The International Covenant on Civil and Political Rights: Cases, Materials, and Commentary (2014)

B. Saul, D. Kinley, et al., The International Covenant on Economic, Social and Cultural Rights: Commentary, Cases, and Materials (2014)

L. Henkin, The International Bill of Rights: The Covenant on Civil and Political Rights (1981)

CHAPTER 3

THE EUROPEAN SYSTEM FOR THE PROTECTION OF HUMAN RIGHTS

I. INTRODUCTION

The European "system" for the protection of human rights consists of the human rights components of three separate but overlapping regional entities: the Council of Europe (COE), the European Union (EU), and the Organization of Security and Cooperation in Europe (OSCE). The human rights obligations, institutions, and activities of each are extensive; taken together, they constitute the most far-reaching of all the regional human rights approaches. We provide only an overview.

II. COUNCIL OF EUROPE

The protection and promotion of human rights was a fundamental goal—indeed, the *raison d'être* for the establishment—of the Council of Europe, a regional intergovernmental organization created in 1949 by ten Western European nations in the wake of World War II. Article 3 of its Statute provides that "every Member of the Council of Europe must accept the principles of the rule of law and of the enjoyment by all persons within its jurisdiction of human rights and fundamental freedoms. . . ." The end of the Cold War enabled Central and Eastern European nations to join the Council of Europe after declaring their acceptance of the principles spelled out in Article 3.

Today the COE comprises 46 Member States, 27 of which are also members of the European Union. *See generally, http://www.coe.int/en.* The Russian Federation was a member, but following its aggression against Ukraine, it was expelled from the COE and ceased to be a High Contracting Party to the European Convention on Human Rights in 2022. The Committee of Ministers (CM) continues to supervise the execution of existing judgments and friendly settlements involving Russia. In addition, there are five observer States: the Holy See, the United States of America, Canada, Japan and Mexico; these States must also accept these principles and adhere to the same human rights standards as Member States. Because of the importance of the European human rights system, not just for COE Member States but globally, we describe its structure, functions and substantive law in some detail.

The Council's human rights system began with the adoption of the Convention for the Protection of Human Rights and Fundamental Freedoms in 1950. Commonly referred to as the European Convention on Human Rights, it remains the centerpiece of the European human rights system. Sixteen protocols have lengthened the list of guaranteed rights and strengthened the institutional framework to supervise implementation and compliance by the Contracting Parties. In 1998 Protocol No. 11 replaced the original two-tier structure comprising the Court and the Commission on Human Rights with a single full-time Court. This change put an end to the Commission's filtering function and enabled applicants to bring their cases directly before the Court.

Protocol No. 15, adopted in 2013, inserted a reference to the principle of subsidiarity and the doctrine of the margin of appreciation to the Convention's preamble; it also reduced from 6 to 4 months the time within which an application must be lodged with the Court after a final national decision. Also adopted in 2013, Protocol No. 16 allows the highest domestic courts and tribunals to request the Court to give advisory opinions on questions of principle relating to the interpretation or application of the rights and freedoms defined in the Convention or the protocols thereto. Protocol No. 16 is optional. *See https://www.echr.coe.int/documents/d/echr/convention_ENG.*

In addition, the COE proclaimed economic and social rights in the 1961 European Social Charter and later protocols. Other specific human rights issues are dealt with in the European Convention for the Prevention of Torture and Inhuman or Degrading Treatment or Punishment (1987), the European Charter for Regional or Minority Languages (1992), the Framework Convention for the Protection of National Minorities (1995), the Convention for the Protection of Human Rights and Biomedicine (1997) and its Additional Protocol on the Prohibition of Cloning Human Beings (1998), the Convention on Action against Trafficking in Human Beings (2005) and the Convention on Preventing and Combating Violence Against Women and Domestic Violence (2011).

The Council also has promoted human rights through activities undertaken without the need to conclude additional treaties. It created the post of Commissioner for Human Rights in 1999. Elected by the Parliamentary Assembly for a non-renewable six-year term, the Commissioner serves as "a non-judicial institution to promote education in, awareness of and respect for human rights, as embodied in the human rights instruments of the Council of Europe." The functions of the Commissioner are thus primarily promotional and preventive; she cannot accept communications from individuals or groups. *See https://www.coe.int/en/web/commissioner/the-commissioner.*

The European Commission against Racism and Intolerance (ECRI), established in 1993, monitors the situation in Member States through an in-depth study of the situation in each country followed by specific proposals designed to solve problems and remedy deficiencies. It reviews Member States' legislation, policies and other measures to combat racism and intolerance and proposes action at local, national and European levels, and addresses General Policy Recommendations to the governments of all Member States; these Recommendations provide guidelines which policymakers are invited to use when drawing up national strategies and policies. *See https://www.coe.int/en/web/european-commission-against-racism-and-intolerance.*

The European Commission for Democracy through Law (commonly referred to as the "Venice Commission") is the Council of Europe's advisory body on constitutional matters and works to uphold democracy, constitutional justice, human rights, and the rule of law. Among other functions, it issues advisory opinions to national institutions concerning democratic institutions and fundamental rights, constitutional justice and ordinary justice, elections, referendums and political parties. In addition to the 46 COE member States, the Commission includes 15 non-European members: Algeria, Brazil, Canada, Chile, Costa Rica, Israel, Kazakhstan, the Republic of Korea, Kosovo, Kyrgyzstan, Morocco, Mexico, Peru, Tunisia and the United States. (Argentina, Japan, the Holy See and Uruguay are observers.) It also cooperates closely with the EU, OSCE/ODIHR and the OAS. *See https://www.venice.coe.int/webforms/events/*.

III. THE EUROPEAN CONVENTION ON HUMAN RIGHTS: AN OVERVIEW

§ 3–1. INTRODUCTION

The human rights system established by the Convention is the oldest and the most effective of those currently in existence. The decision to draft the European Convention was made shortly after the UN General Assembly adopted the Universal Declaration of Human Rights, when it became clear that it would take the UN many years to agree on the instruments to transform the Declaration into binding treaty obligations. *See* § 2–5, *supra*. The historical relationship between the Universal Declaration and the European Convention finds expression in the latter's preamble, where the signatories declare their resolve "as the Governments of European countries which are like-minded and have a common heritage of political traditions, ideals, freedom and the rule of law, to take the first steps for the collective enforcement of certain of the rights stated in the Universal Declaration."

The European Convention entered into force on September 3, 1953. Only Member States of the Council of Europe may become Contracting Parties to the European Convention. Convention, art. 59(1). Although the COE's Statute does not require its members to ratify the Convention, all Council members had ratified the Convention by the time the Cold War was over, and the Council decided that new applicant States would be required to ratify the Convention as a condition of membership. Today all COE member States have done so. Belarus has applied for Council of Europe membership but as of early 2004 had not been accepted due to concerns over its commitment to the requirements of the Council of Europe Statute art. 3.

§ 3–2. RIGHTS GUARANTEED

As originally adopted, the European Convention guaranteed the following rights: right to life; right not to be subjected to torture, inhuman or degrading treatment or punishment; freedom from slavery; right to liberty, security of person, and due process of law; freedom from *ex post facto* laws and punishment; right to private and family life; freedom of thought, conscience and religion; freedom of expression and of peaceful assembly; and the right to marry and found a family. A non-discrimination clause applies to the "enjoyment of the rights and freedoms" the Convention proclaims. Art. 14.

Contracting Parties are required to provide an "effective remedy before a national authority" to anyone whose rights have been violated. Art. 13. The beneficiary of the rights and freedoms which the Convention guarantees is "everyone" within the "jurisdiction" of the Contracting Parties to it (art. 1), meaning the nationality of the person does not matter and in some circumstances a Contracting Party may be responsible for violations of the Convention that occur outside its national territory. *See* Belozorov v. Russia and Ukraine, Judgment of October 15, 2015. The Court will not hear complaints, however, about extra-territorial acts of a Contracting Party taken under the authority of a U.N. Security Council peace-keeping operation. *See* Behrami and Behrami v. France and Saramati v. France, Germany and Norway, admissibility decision of May 31, 2007.

Over time, a number of Additional Protocols have expanded the catalogue of rights guaranteed by the Convention for those States that have ratified the later instruments. The first Protocol added a right to property, a right to education and an undertaking to hold free and secret elections at reasonable intervals. Protocol No. 4 prohibited deprivation of liberty for failure to comply with contractual obligations and guaranteed the right to liberty of movement. It also barred forced exile of nationals and the collective expulsion of aliens. Protocol No. 6 abolished the death penalty during peacetime, but Protocol No. 13

removed the exception to Protocol No. 6 that permitted executions during war, making the death penalty now illegal under all circumstances.

Protocol No. 7 requires States to accord aliens various due process safeguards before they may be expelled from a country where they reside. It also provides for a right of appeal in criminal proceedings, for compensation in cases of miscarriage of justice, for the right not to be subjected to double jeopardy, as well as for equality of rights and responsibilities between spouses. Protocol No. 12 augments the non-discrimination guarantee in Convention Art. 14 by providing that "the enjoyment of any right set forth by law shall be secured without discrimination on any ground . . ." and that no one shall be discriminated against by any public authority. Other Protocols have made institutional changes relating to the Convention organs and procedures, as discussed in the following section.

The ECHR's "decisional law," while vast, can be accessed at *https://hudoc.echr.coe.int/*.

§ 3–3. CONVENTION INSTITUTIONS

The Convention established two institutions "to ensure the observance of the engagements undertaken by the High Contracting Parties": the European Commission of Human Rights and the European Court of Human Rights. Art. 19. These entities were replaced on November 1, 1998, with the entry into force of Protocol No. 11 and the inauguration of a permanent, full-time Court.

The Convention also confers some supervisory functions relating to the enforcement of the rights it guarantees on the COE Committee of Ministers. Arts. 46(2) and 54. The Committee of Ministers may suspend or terminate a State's membership, as it did with Russia in 2022, and it has the critically important function of supervising the execution of judgments of the European Court of Human Rights. In addition, the Committee of Ministers undertakes thematic monitoring of human rights matters and gives approval to protocols to the Convention and other human rights treaties, which are then submitted to the Member States for ratification. *See* arts. 15(3), 22(1), 30(1), 52 and 58.

The Parliamentary Assembly is composed of national parliamentarians from COE Member States. It exercises important functions in verifying compliance by Members States with their human rights commitments and in selecting judges for the European Court. *See* § 3–13 *infra*.

The European Court of Human Rights has its seat in Strasbourg, which is also the seat of the Council of Europe. It is composed of "a number of judges equal to that of the High Contracting Parties" to the Convention. Art. 20. Elected for non-renewable nine-year terms by the Parliamentary Assembly, the judges serve in their individual capacities and must be persons of "high moral character," who "possess the qualifications required for appointment to high judicial office or be jurisconsults of recognized competence." Art. 21(1). The judges do not have to be nationals of COE Member States. Protocol 15 provides that Member States are no longer able to propose candidates over 65 years of age. Judges serve full-time during their term and may not undertake any activity incompatible with their judicial functions.

Before Protocol No. 11 abolished the European Commission of Human Rights and created the permanent Court, all cases were dealt with by the Commission, which established the facts, decided on admissibility and, in admissible cases, invited the applicant and the respondent States to reach a friendly settlement. Now the Court has sole compulsory jurisdiction over determinations of admissibility, fact-finding and the merits of cases. The Committee of Ministers continues to supervise compliance with the Court's judgments, assisted by the Council of Europe secretariat, which has established a Department for the Execution of Judgments within its Directorate of Monitoring, part of the Directorate General for Human Rights and Legal Affairs.

Although the Convention entered into force in 1953, the original Court was not established until 1959. The first case to reach the Court was the "Lawless" Case, Judgment of July 1, 1961 (Merits), 4 Yearbook of the European Convention of Human Rights [hereinafter cited as Y.B.] 438 (1961), which was referred to it by the Commission in 1960. That same year the Commission also filed the "De Becker" Case, Judgment of March 27, 1962, 5 Y.B. 321 (1962). Five years elapsed before another case reached the Court. *See* Case Relating to Certain Aspects of the

Laws on the Use of Languages in Education in Belgium, Judgment of July 23, 1968 (Merits), 11 Y.B. 833 (1968).

In the early 1980's, the caseload began to climb significantly, eventually leading to the restructuring provided by Protocol No. 11. However, the reforms have not significantly slowed the number of applications received: during 2022, for instance, the Court delivered judgments in respect of 4,168 applications (an increase of 33% over 2021).

However, the caseload has declined somewhat in recent years as a result of the various measures taken by the Court to strengthen admissibility and filing requirement. Protocol No. 14 instituted some of these changes, making a single judge competent to declare inadmissible or strike out an individual application. The Protocol also added a new admissibility criterion, empowering the Court to declare inadmissible applications where the applicant has not suffered a "significant disadvantage," provided respect for human rights does not otherwise require an examination on the merits by the Court. It also provided for three judge committees to decide both on admissibility and the merits of cases that are deemed repetitive, that is, those that raise no new issues of law different from those decided in prior cases.

Protocol No. 15 added further restrictions, shortening from six to four months the time limit within which an application must be made to the Court, amending the 'significant disadvantage' admissibility criterion, to remove the second safeguard preventing rejection of an application that has not been duly considered by a domestic tribunal, and removing the right of the parties to a case to object to relinquishment of a Chamber's jurisdiction in favor of the Grand Chamber. Protocol No. 16 further provides for the highest national court of Member States to request an advisory opinion of a Grand Chamber in pending cases "on questions of principle relating to the interpretation or application of the rights and freedoms defined in the Convention or the protocols thereto." Art. 1(1). The aim is to have more cases disposed of at the national level and further reduce the need to have recourse to the European Court.

In addition to the requirements added by Protocols, the Court has amended its rules of procedure to improve its case management and reduce the number of applications it receives. First, it has instituted the procedure of taking up "pilot" cases to address the existence of structural problems in countries that lead to numerous repetitive applications being filed. The Committee of Ministers invited this innovation, asking the Court to identify underlying systemic problems and their source, in particular when they are likely to give rise to numerous applications. Despite this innovation, in 2016, the Court reported that 30,500 of the pending 64,850 cases were repetitive ones—that is, nearly half of all cases stem from failing to cure a problem previously identified and judged against the State. Most of these cases concerned Russia, Turkey and Ukraine.

With a view to expediting the most urgent cases, the Court in 2009 established seven categories ranging from the most urgent cases to the clearly inadmissible cases. It placed inter-State cases outside the priority policy because they require special procedural treatment.

The operations of the Court are supported by a Registry, composed of lawyers and technical staff. Each of the Court's five judicial Sections is assisted by a Section Registrar and a Deputy Section Registrar. The same applies to the Filtering Section, which is responsible for sorting applications in order to direct them to the judicially appropriate formation. The principal functions of the Registry are to screen all cases when they first arrive, to eliminate all clearly inadmissible cases process, and to prepare for adjudication applications lodged by individuals with the Court.

Cases are assigned to the different divisions on the basis of knowledge of the language and legal system concerned, as applicants can address the Court, at the beginning of the proceedings, in any official language of the States Parties to the Convention. On the other hand, the documents prepared by the Registry for the Court are all drafted in one of its two official languages (English and French).

Protocol 14 resulted in the creation of a Filtering Section and a Single judge formation. This means that a Judge sitting alone, assisted by a Non-Judicial Rapporteur, can declare applications inadmissible, whereas previously three Judges had been required. The Filtering Section has centralized the handling of the incoming cases from five of the highest case-count countries: Russia, Turkey, Romania, Ukraine and Poland. These countries account for over half of the cases before the Court.

The Filtering Section has been in operation since the beginning of 2011. Its principal function is to carry out an accurate and immediate sifting of cases to ensure that all applications are placed on the appropriate procedural track, whether submitted to a Single Judge for prompt decision or sent to await examination by a Committee of three judges or Chamber in accordance with the Court's priority policy.

Most cases are decided by a seven-judge Chamber. The Convention provides a limited review procedure of Chamber decisions. Within three months of the date of the judgment, any party to the case may request that the case be referred to the Grand Chamber, which consists of 17 judges. A panel of five judges may decide to accept the request, but only "if the case raises a serious question affecting the interpretation or application of the Convention or the protocols thereto, or a serious issue of general importance." Convention, art. 43(2). The Chamber also may relinquish jurisdiction in favor of the Grand Chamber prior to issuing its judgment, for any of the same stated reasons, unless one of the parties to the case objects. Convention, art. 30. The Grand Chamber will then issue its own judgment, which is final.

Chamber decisions become final in any of the three following circumstances: when the parties declare that they will not ask for a review of the judgment by a Grand Chamber; three months from the date of the judgment if no request is made; or when the Grand Chamber panel rejects a referral request. A judgment of the Grand Chamber is final on the date it is issued.

IV. THE ENFORCEMENT MECHANISM OF THE CONVENTION

§ 3–4. INTRODUCTION

The rights guaranteed in the European Convention are enforced on both the national and international levels. In a substantial number of the Contracting Parties, the Convention enjoys the status of domestic law; it creates rights directly enforceable by individuals and may be invoked as law in the national courts of Member States. Where the Convention as such does not enjoy domestic law status, implementing legislation may be required to enforce the rights it guarantees unless existing national law already ensures the protection of comparable rights. Even in those countries the national courts frequently look to the Convention when interpreting and applying domestic law in order to avoid violating this treaty, if at all possible.

Only when domestic law does not provide relief capable of remedying a violation of the Convention may recourse be had to the European Court. This rule has its basis in the requirement found in all human rights treaties, including the Convention, that before international remedies may be invoked, available and effective domestic remedies must be exhausted. Convention, art. 35(1).

§ 3–5. JURISDICTION OF THE EUROPEAN COURT OF HUMAN RIGHTS

Initially the Convention conferred only contentious (State-to-State) jurisdiction on the Court. Protocol No. 2 added limited advisory jurisdiction, which was extended by the Convention on Human Rights and Biomedicine, and later by Protocol No. 16. That jurisdiction extends to all cases brought by a Contracting Party against another Party for breach of the Convention and to cases brought by victims alleging a violation by a Contracting Party of the rights guaranteed by the Convention or a Protocol. Convention, arts. 33 and 34. Complaints concerning other rights, such as those in the European Social Charter, fall outside the jurisdiction of the Court. All matters concerning the interpretation and application of the Convention and its protocols fall within the Court's jurisdiction. *See* § 3.7 *et seq.*, *infra*. Judgments of the Court are available at *www.echr.coe.int*.

§ 3–6. INTER-STATE COMPLAINTS

By ratifying the European Convention, a State is deemed to have accepted the jurisdiction of the Court to receive complaints from other States Parties alleging a violation of the treaty. Convention, art. 33. The Applicant State does not have to demonstrate any special interest in or relationship to the victim of the violation or its subject matter. The Court has said: ". . . the Convention allows Contracting States to require the observance of these obligations [contained in the Convention] without having to justify an interest deriving, for example, from the fact that a measure they complain of has prejudiced one of their nationals." Ireland v. United Kingdom, Judgment of January 18, 1978, 25 Publ. Eur. Court H.R. 1, at 91 (1978).

Inter-state complaints are not subject to the same admissibility requirements prescribed for individual petitions other than the obligation to exhaust domestic remedies. Convention, arts. 33 and 35. Nevertheless, between 1953 and 2005 fewer than two dozen inter-state cases were brought; in the past decade, however, seven cases have been filed against Russia by Georgia and Ukraine. Most of the earlier cases were filed against States that had not as yet recognized the right of individual petition and thus could be held internationally accountable for a breach of the Convention only by means of an inter-state proceeding.

The motivations for filing inter-state cases have sometimes been political and sometimes humanitarian. The latter was true, for example, of the proceedings instituted against Greece and Turkey by various Scandinavian nations. Increasingly, inter-state cases involve armed conflicts between States, as exemplified by the Russian invasion of Ukraine and the conflict between Armenia and Azerbaijan. Such conflicts also give rise to thousands of individual complaints, creating a complex situation for the Court. The processing of both types of cases in parallel raises questions regarding their prioritization as well as the need to avoid inconsistencies and duplications. The Convention does not specifically deal with how to coordinate interstate cases and individual applications.

§ 3–7. ADVISORY OPINIONS

Protocol No. 2 (1963) added limited advisory jurisdiction, which was extended by the Convention on Human Rights and Biomedicine and further expanded in 2013 by Protocol No. 16. Advisory opinions are given by a Grand Chamber of the Court and adopted by a majority vote. Under Convention Article 47, however, only the Committee of Ministers can request advisory opinions, and then only about "legal questions concerning the interpretation of the Convention and the protocols thereto." It may not interpret "the content or scope of the rights or freedoms" that are guaranteed by the Convention and its Protocols or deal with "any other question which the Court or the Committee of Ministers might have to consider in consequence of any such proceedings as could be instituted in accordance with the Convention." Convention, art. 47(2). Adopted in 2013, Protocol 16 added the ability of the highest court in each State to request an advisory opinion on questions of principle relating to the interpretation or application of the rights and freedoms defined in the Convention.

Given that narrow jurisdiction, it is not surprising that the Court has received only three requests for advisory opinions. The first request asked the Court to rule on the compatibility with the Convention of a human rights instrument adopted by the Commonwealth of Independent States. It was rejected because it concerned an issue that might come before the Court in a contentious case. *See* Decision on the Competence of the Court to Give an Advisory Opinion, June 2, 2004, available at *http://www.echr.coe.int*. The second, issued in 2008, concerned the composition of the Maltese list of candidates for the post of judge at the Court; the Court's opinion was that the Assembly could not add additional criteria for candidates to those set forth in the Convention. In the third, the Court opined that the Parliamentary Assembly could not add eligibility criteria for Member State nominations of candidates for election to the Court.

In January 2010, the Court issued its second formal Advisory Opinion, also involving legal questions concerning the lists of candidates for election of judges to the Court. In that case, Ukraine had withdrawn its list of three candidates, after one of the three indicated no further interest in being presented. It did so after the deadline set for submission of candidates by the Parliamentary Assembly. The Court's opinion was that such a withdrawal could take place only before the deadline set by the Parliamentary Assembly; therefore, Ukraine could only submit a new candidate to replace the person that had withdrawn but could not remove the other two names on the original list. Generally, *see https://www.echr.coe.int/advisory-opinions*.

§ 3–8. INDIVIDUAL PETITIONS

One of the European system's most important features is the individual petition. Under Convention art. 34, any "person, non-governmental organization or group of individuals claiming to be the victim of a violation . . . of the rights set forth in the Convention or the protocols thereto" may file an application with the European Court. The Court has interpreted the word "person" to include legal persons in cases where their rights have been violated. *See, e.g.*, The Sunday Times Case, Judgment of April 1979, 30 Publ. Eur. Court H.R. 5 (1979); Stran Greek Refineries and Stratis Andreadis v. Greece, Judgment of 9 December 1994, 301–B Publ. Eur. Court H.R. (1994),19 Eur. H.R. Rep. 293.

The notion of "victim" is interpreted autonomously and irrespective of domestic rules such as those concerning standing to institute litigation. The requirement that the petitioner be "a victim of a violation" has been interpreted to mean that "an individual applicant should claim to have been actually affected by the violation he alleges . . . . Article [34] does not institute for individuals a kind of *actio popularis* for the interpretation of the Convention. . . ." Case of Klass and Others, Judgment of September 6, 1978, 28 Publ. Eur. Court H.R. 5, at 17–18 (1979); Tănase v. Moldova, Judgment of April 27, 2010 [GC], § 104; Burden v. the United Kingdom, Judgment of April 29, 2008 [GC], § 33).

Indirect as well as direct victims may submit applications. The former generally are relatives or others with a close connection to the victim. If the applicant dies while the case is pending, the Court's practice generally is to strike the application in the absence of an heir or close relative who expresses the wish to pursue the case. However, if the main issue raised by the case transcends the person and the interests of the application, the Court may decide on public policy grounds in the common interest of protecting human rights to continue its consideration.

The acts in question must be attributable to a Contracting Party. Cases against States participating in NATO and UN activities in Kosovo were declared inadmissible on the ground that, because the UN Security Council retained ultimate authority, and because effective command of the relevant operational matters remained with NATO, the responsibility should be attributed to those organizations. Agim Behrami & Bekir Behrami v. France; Ruzhdi Saramati v. France, Germany & Norway, joined app. Nos. 71412/01 and 78166/01, European Court of Human Rights (Grand Chamber) May 2, 2007.

The admissibility of individual petitions is governed by the provisions of Article 35, which reads as follows:

> 1. The Court may only deal with the matter after all domestic remedies have been exhausted, according to the generally recognized rules of international law, and within a period of six months from the date on which the final decision was taken.

2. The Court shall not deal with any application submitted under Article 34 that

(a) is anonymous; or

(b) is substantially the same as a matter that has already been examined by the Court or has already been submitted to another procedure of international investigation or settlement and contains no relevant new information.

3. The Court shall declare inadmissible any individual application submitted under Article 34 if it considers that:

(a) the application is incompatible with the provisions of the Convention or the Protocols thereto, manifestly ill-founded, or an abuse of the right of individual application; or

(b) the applicant has not suffered a significant disadvantage, unless respect for human rights as defined in the Convention and the Protocols thereto requires an examination of the application on the merits.

4. The Court shall reject any application which it considers inadmissible under this Article. It may do so at any stage of the proceedings.

The question whether a petition is or is not admissible is first reviewed by the Registry. Article 35 provides that an application is inadmissible if it has already been the subject of a case before an international body, or is being examined by such a body, because the purpose of the requirement is to avoid the same case becoming the object of various international procedures. Assessment of similarity of the matters usually involves a comparison of the parties in the respective proceedings, the relevant legal provisions relied on by them, the scope of their claims and the types of redress sought. In addition, the relevant body must be one that is "international" and not domestic.

In another effort to avoid duplicate international procedures, some States Parties to the European Convention, in ratifying the Optional Protocol to the International Covenant on Civil and Political Rights, made reservations to prevent consideration of cases by the UN Human Rights Committee that had already been considered within the European system.

§ 3–9. ADMISSIBILITY: INCOMPATIBLE, ILL-FOUNDED, OR ABUSE OF THE RIGHT OF PETITION

The most common grounds for the inadmissibility of individual petitions are those set out in Article 35(2) and (3). For a detailed discussion of the admissibility criteria and case law, *see* the Court's *Practical Guide on Admissibility Criteria* (2023), available at *https://www.echr.coe.int/documents/d/echr/admissibility_guide_eng*.

Under Convention Article 35(3) an application must be considered inadmissible if it is "incompatible with the provisions of the . . . Convention or the protocols thereto, manifestly ill-founded, or an abuse of the right of application." The not "manifestly ill-founded" standard calls for a determination whether the application states a *prima facie* case. Airey Case, Judgment of October 9, 1979, 32 Publ. Eur. Court H.R. 4, 10 (1979). Any application will be considered "manifestly ill-founded" if a preliminary examination of its substance does not disclose any appearance of a violation of the rights guaranteed by the Convention. Case of Ferrazzini v. Italy, Judgment of 12 July 2001.

To conclude that an application is manifestly ill-founded, the Court sometimes invites observations from the parties and may issue a detailed reasoned decision. The term "manifestly ill-founded" may apply to the application as a whole or to a particular complaint within the broader context of an otherwise admissible case. The Court divides manifestly ill-founded complaints into four categories: "fourth instance" complaints seeking review of national judgments not presenting a human rights issue, complaints where there has clearly or apparently been no violation, unsubstantiated complaints and, finally, confused or far-fetched complaints. Gratzinger and Gratzingerova v. the Czech Republic (dec.) July 10, 2002 [GC] 2002–VII 399; Demopoulos and Others v. Turkey (dec.) March 1, 2010 [GC] 50 E.H.R.R. SE14.

"Abuse of the right of application" refers to conduct such as knowingly making false or groundless allegations, repeatedly using abusive and defamatory language about the Respondent Government, or intentionally breaching the rule of confidentiality applicable to the proceedings. The fact that an applicant may have political motives in filing the case does not necessarily constitute such an abuse of the right of application. Also, filing a petition after refusing to negotiate a friendly settlement at the national level is not construed as an abuse of the right of petition, at least when the proposed settlement contains no admission of the government's responsibility for the violation.

§ 3–10. EXHAUSTION OF DOMESTIC REMEDIES AND THE FOUR-MONTHS RULE

As adopted, Article 35(1) of the Convention provided that "the Court may only deal with the matter after all domestic remedies have been exhausted, according to the generally recognized rules of international law, and within a period of six months from the date on which the final decision was taken." That time-limit was reduced to four months by Article 4 of Protocol 15 (2013). This language does not distinguish between individual and inter-state applications.

The Court has explained the first requirement as follows: "the rule of exhaustion of domestic remedies . . . dispenses States from answering before an international body for their acts before they have had an opportunity to put matters right through their own legal system. . . ." De Wilde, Ooms and Versyp Cases, Judgment of June 18, 1971, 12 Publ. Eur. Court H.R. 12, 29 (1971). In short, it is not permitted to make an international case out of a matter that can be resolved on the local level. The rule emphasizes the primary role of national institutions and the subsidiary functions of the European Court. An application will, therefore, be dismissed for failure to exhaust domestic remedies when it appears that issues relevant to it were not brought to the attention of national bodies which could have resolved the matter. Generally, *see* Castells v. Spain, Judgment of April 23, 1992, 236 Publ. Eur. Court H.R. 1, 19–20 (1992).

The Court's case-law (like international law generally) indicates that applicants need not have recourse to remedies which are not effective or are unduly prolonged. Akdivar and others v. Turkey, Judgment of September 16, 1996, Reports 1996–IV, 1192 at para. 68. "The only remedies which . . . the Convention requires to be exhausted are those that relate to the breaches alleged and at the same time are available and sufficient. . . ." Van Oosterwijck Case, Judgment of November 6, 1980, 40 Publ. Eur. Court H.R. 5, at 13 (1981). A remedy is "sufficient" if it can redress the wrong allegedly committed. Stögmüller Case, Judgment of November 10, 1969, 12 Y.B. 364 (1969).

The failure of a petitioner to resort to a consistently unsuccessful domestic remedy will not result in a rejection of the petition. Neither will the failure to file an appeal against a law that prior judgments suggest will be upheld; this is so even in countries where the courts are free to depart from such precedents. However, if the domestic law on the subject is open to conflicting interpretations, a reasonable effort to exhaust potential remedies must be made.

If more than one potentially effective remedy is available, the applicant is only required to have used one of them. Indeed, when one remedy has been attempted, use of another remedy which has essentially the same purpose is not required. It is for the applicant to select the remedy that is most appropriate in his or her case.

Because it is deemed procedural in nature, the domestic remedies requirement may be waived by the State. According to the Court, "there is nothing to prevent States from waiving the benefit of the rule of exhaustion of domestic remedies, the essential aim of which is to protect their national legal order." De Wilde, Ooms and Versyp Cases, Judgment of June 18, 1971, 12 Publ. Eur. Court H.R. 12, 31 (1971). The waiver may be express, but more often it is inadvertent, for example, when the Respondent State fails to raise the issue in a timely manner and is thereafter estopped.

Under Rule 47 of the Rules of Court, a petitioner must include information about exhaustion of local remedies in its application to the Court. If it appears from the allegations contained in the application and the accompanying documents that the applicant has not exhausted available domestic remedies, the application may be rejected summarily.

After an application passes the preliminary examination, if the Respondent State pleads the non-exhaustion of domestic remedies, the State has the burden of proof to demonstrate the existence of an effective and accessible remedy capable of providing redress to the applicant. It then falls to the applicant to establish that the remedy indicated was in fact exhausted or was for some reason inadequate or ineffective in the particular circumstances of the case, or that there existed "special circumstances" absolving the applicant from the requirement. Such circumstances may include the inaction of national authorities in the face of serious allegations of misconduct or infliction of harm by state agents, for example where the authorities have failed to investigate or offer assistance in the face of evidence that violations occurred.

The Court also has indicated that the rule of exhaustion of remedies must make "due allowance" for the fact that the rule arises in the context of human rights proceedings and must be applied "with some degree of flexibility and without excessive formalism." Aksoy v. Turkey, Reports 1996–VI, 2260, para. 53 (1997). For example, a general situation of violence may create obstacles to the proper functioning of the system of the administration of justice, including the securing of probative evidence, and make the pursuit of judicial remedies futile. In such circumstances, the Court will make "a realistic assessment" of the general legal and political context in which the remedies operate and the personal circumstances of the applicant.

The rule spelled out in amended Article 35 requires the petition to be filed with the Court "within a period of four months from the date on which the final decision was taken." Its purpose is to ensure an end to litigation within a reasonable period of time or, put another way, "to prevent the past judgments being constantly called into question." DeBecker v. Belgium, Application No. 2/14/56, 2 Y.B. 214, at 244 (1958–59). In any given case, the final decision must be determined by reference to the last domestic remedy that must be exhausted pursuant to Article 35(1). If, for example, under the applicable domestic law all available remedies are exhausted with an appeal to the superior court of X, then the judgment of that tribunal is the "final decision" for purposes of the four-months rule.

A decision from an appeal to a domestic court which clearly lacks the power or jurisdiction to grant the relief sought under the Convention will not be taken into account for this purpose. Thus, if more than four months have passed after the "final decision," but the petitioner thereafter nevertheless appeals to a higher or special court which clearly lacks the power to affect that decision, the petition will be deemed inadmissible barring some very special circumstances.

§ 3–11. "SIGNIFICANT DISADVANTAGE"

With Protocol No. 14's entry into force in 2010, Art. 35(2)(b) of the Convention was amended to direct the Court to declare inadmissible any individual application submitted under Article 34 if it considers that "the applicant has not suffered a significant disadvantage, unless respect for human rights as defined in the Convention and the Protocols thereto requires an examination of the application on the merits." In 2013, Protocol No. 15 removed the concluding safeguard about domestic remedies from

Article 35(2)(b) and shortened the time to apply to the Court from six months to four months.

During 2013 and 2014, when single judges began evaluating cases for admissibility, the number of rejected applications grew considerably, perhaps suggesting a broad application of the new criterion. The jurisprudence during a one-year transition period of reported decisions suggested that the Court considered certain violations inherently to produce a significant disadvantage to the applicant. The decisions also made clear the distinction between victim status and significant disadvantage, and elaborated the factors that should determine whether the applicant has or has not experienced the requisite level of disadvantage due to the alleged violation.

In Korolev v. Russia, the Court established that the new criterion hinged "on the idea that a violation of a right, however real from a purely legal point of view, should attain a minimum level of severity to warrant consideration by an international court." The Court indicated that it would make a contextual assessment based on two factors: the subjective perception of the applicant and an objective assessment of what was at stake in the case. The subjective perception should be justified on objective grounds. The Court determined that the applicant's feelings, while relevant are by themselves insufficient to conclude that an applicant has suffered a significant disadvantage.

In a subsequent decision the Court indicated that in considering "significant disadvantage" it would take into account the nature of the allegedly violated right, the gravity of that alleged violation, and/or the possible consequences of the alleged violation on the personal situation of the applicant. These criteria may imply that violations of certain rights, including non-derogable rights, inherently cause a significant disadvantage to applicants. Giusti v. Italy, Application No. 13175/03, Merits, (18 October 2011).

§ 3–12. PRELIMINARY MATTERS

Since the reforms of Protocol No. 11, individual applicants have been able to bring complaints directly to the Court and participate in all the proceedings. Convention, art. 34. The individual must be represented by a lawyer licensed to practice law in one of the States Parties to the Convention once the communication is declared admissible and for any hearing that is held. Convention, art. 38(1) and Rules of Court, art. 36.

Before proceeding to the merits, the Court must place itself at the disposal of the parties concerned with a view to securing a friendly settlement of the matter. The friendly settlement can only be realized "on the basis of respect for human rights as defined in the Convention and the protocols thereto." Convention, art. 38(1)(b). If a friendly settlement is reached, the Court strikes the case from its list and issues a decision giving the facts and the solution reached. For an annual report on cases settled, *see* Eur. Court H.R., Statistical Information, available at *http://www.echr.coe.int*.

Cases can also be concluded by a "unilateral declaration," which is basically an extension of the friendly-settlement process. If at the conclusion of that stage, the applicant refuses without justification to accept a reasonable proposal made by the respondent State, the latter may file a unilateral declaration accompanied by a request for the application to be struck. Unlike friendly settlements, which are expressly referred to in the Convention, unilateral declarations originated in a practice based on Article 37(1)(c), which allows the Court to strike an application out of the list for "any other reason." Like friendly settlements, however, unilateral declarations, are deemed to be an effective means of resolving disputes on a non-contentious basis, allowing the Court to focus its resources on examining the most complex or "impact" cases.

In January 2019, the Court introduced a new compulsory stage in the procedure designed to encourage the parties to resolve their dispute by means of a friendly settlement or a unilateral declaration. The examination of a unilateral declaration is a public and adversarial phase in the proceedings. In some cases, the applicant accepts the Government's offer even if he or she has previously rejected it at the friendly-settlement stage. The application is then struck out on the basis of Article 39 of the Convention as a friendly settlement. The Court has had occasion to reject a unilateral declaration because the issue raised was a novel one on which it had not previously ruled. De Tommaso v. Italy [GC], 2017, §§ 133–139.

The existence of a structural problem may also prompt the Court to reject a unilateral declaration, whether it is a problem previously identified in its judgments which has not been addressed or a new issue which it has not yet had an opportunity to examine. Most commonly, where the Court rejects a unilateral declaration it is because the Government's proposal concerning individual measures is not adequate and sufficient, or because a strike-out would not allow the applicants access to a procedure for reopening the proceedings on the same basis as applicants who were victims of the same violation but had the benefit of a judgment. Strike-out decisions are not transmitted to the Committee of Ministers for supervision, unlike those taking note of a friendly settlement.

§ 3–13. PROCEEDINGS ON THE MERITS

In dealing with cases on the merits, the Court may hold hearings, receive written submissions, and examine witnesses either at its seat in Strasbourg or, if necessary, by interviewing them wherever they may be. It may ask any person or institution of its choice to obtain information, express an opinion or make a report on any specific point. It also may accept written or oral comments from *amicus curiae* and must allow the intervention of any State whose national is the applicant in the proceedings. Convention, art. 36. Hearings are open to the public unless the Court "in exceptional circumstances" decides otherwise, and submissions are publicly accessible unless the President of the Court closes the record.

Applicants, both private parties and States, must prove their allegations by "proof beyond a reasonable doubt." Ireland v. the United Kingdom, judgment of 18 Jan. 1978, 25 Pub. Eur. Ct. Hum. Rts., § 161. After criticism of this high standard, normally applied in criminal prosecutions, the Court clarified that the phrase does not have the same meaning as in domestic law and that "[s]uch proof may follow from the coexistence of sufficiently strong, clear and concordant inferences or of similar unrebutted presumptions of fact."

When the events in issue lie within the exclusive knowledge of the authorities, as in the case of persons within their control or custody, strong presumptions of fact will arise in respect of injuries occurring during such detention. In such cases the Court shifts the burden of proof to the authorities to provide a satisfactory and convincing explanation. In addition, where allegations are made under Articles 2 and 3 of the Convention, the Court applies "a particularly thorough scrutiny." Ribitsch v. Austria, Judgment of 4 Dec. 1995, 336 Pub. Eur. Ct. H.R., § 32; Avsar v. Turkey, Reports 2001–VII § 283.

§ 3–14. JUDGMENTS OF THE COURT

Under the Convention, the High Contracting Parties have undertaken to abide by the Court's decisions in any case to which they are parties. Art. 46(1). The Committee of Ministers supervises the execution of the Court's judgments. Art. 46(2). While judgments technically bind only the parties to the particular case, in practice the Court normally follows its case law and its reliance on prior decisions gives the judgments important precedential value for States parties and national courts.

In most cases, the Court awards "just satisfaction" in its judgment on the merits, but in complex cases it may hold separate proceedings on the subject. Just satisfaction may consist of a finding of the violation itself, which is seen by the Court as a form of remedy for moral harm. It may also include compensation for proven pecuniary and non-pecuniary injuries, as well as costs and attorneys' fees for representation that is not covered by the Court's legal aid program. The Court lacks the power to reverse domestic judicial decisions or to annul national laws, but it has called for restitution of property and liberty of detained persons. Brumarescu v. Romania (Article 41), Judgment of January 23, 2001, 33 Eur.H.R. Rep. 35 (2001); Assanidze v. Georgia, Judgment of 8 April 2004 (GC), Reports 2004–II.

In addition to affording remedies under Article 41, the Court has begun to indicate general measures that may help prevent repetitious cases. Scozzari and Giunta v. Italy, para. 249, ECHR 2000–VIII. The Court calls these "exceptional cases," but now frequently indicates the type of measure that might be taken in order to put an end to a situation it has found to exist, including legislative reforms.

§ 3–15. ENFORCEMENT OF JUDGMENTS

Article 46(2) of the Convention empowers the Committee of Minsters to ensure the enforcement of judgments of the European Court of Human Rights.

To discharge this obligation, the Committee has adopted "Rules Concerning the Application of Article [46] of the European Convention on Human Rights." The State concerned must inform the Committee of the steps it has taken to comply with the judgment. If the State has not taken the requisite action, the case is automatically placed on the Committee's agenda for consideration by it within the next six months. (Rule 2).

When the just satisfaction awarded consists of money damages, it is usually easy for the State to pay the injured party and to inform the Committee. When the Court's judgment declares that national laws or practices conflict with the Convention and that appropriate legislation needs to be adopted, the State may require more time, since the domestic legislative process moves at its own pace and compliance can be more difficult to monitor.

In recent years some States have challenged the authority of the Court's judgments with regard either to just satisfaction or the adoption of specific measures required by the judgments. In such cases, the Chairman of the Committee can make direct, usually confidential contacts with the respondent State.

In 1997, the Parliamentary Assembly created a monitoring mechanism to verify compliance with human rights obligations and commitments of all Council of Europe Member States. An Assembly Monitoring Committee is responsible for verifying the fulfillment of obligations assumed by Member States under the terms of the Council of Europe

Statute, the European Convention and all other Council of European human rights conventions, as well as the honoring of commitments entered into by the national authorities upon accession to the Council of Europe. The procedure permits the Assembly to sanction persistent non-compliance by adopting resolutions and recommendations, by non-approval of the credentials of a national parliamentary delegation, or ultimately by recommending action to the Committee of Ministers.

§ 3–16. ASSESSMENT

The European Court of Human Rights has for all practical purposes become the constitutional court for civil and political rights of Europe. It is one of the most respected voices for the recognition and protection of human rights generally. Its decisional law is vast and detailed. Over time, it has rendered more than 25,000 judgments addressing most of the rights guaranteed by the Convention. Generally, *see https://www.echr.coe.int/*.

The largest number of judgments have concerned due process issues, in particular the interpretation and application of Article 5 (right to liberty and security of person), Article 6 (right to a fair hearing, the obligations of States to afford adequate conditions of confinement, and Article 1 of Protocol No. 1 (protection of property). It has also ruled on a wide range of substantive and policy issues, including *inter alia* abortion, assisted suicide, body searches, domestic slavery, adoption by homosexuals, wearing religious symbols at school, the recognition of transsexuals, the protection of journalists' sources, environmental issues, conditions of gender reassignment surgery, the recognition of marriage to a minor, conditions of alien expulsions, limits on freedom of artistic expression, and climate change,

Other judgments have addressed the accountability of members of the security forces for acts of torture and other ill-treatment, a parent's right to contact his children, the conditions that may be imposed on an applicant seeking gender reassignment surgery, the protection of medical data concerning HIV-positive patient, a State's refusal to recognize marriage to a minor, protection against domestic violence, the prevention of terrorism, the right to receive and impart information, the right to the expulsion of aliens, legal recognition for homosexual couples, permissible limits on freedom of artistic expression, vaccinated-related issues, and disability rights.

The Grand Chamber's findings are final, and like all rulings of the ECtHR they are legally binding on States. The choice of measures for implementing a judgment have generally been left to the concerned government, under the supervision of the Council of Europe; this approach allows States to exercise a "margin of appreciation."

To guide States in complying with their Convention obligations, the *KlimaSeniorinnen* judgment provides a coherent roadmap for the Court's further climate cases. This is a powerful initial ruling, which both recognizes that climate change is an issue of great relevance for the protection of Convention rights and also declares Strasbourg's door open to relevant applications. In addition, it engages with fundamental underlying questions like the role of the Court and its method for interpreting human rights. It does so by creating a differentiated margin of appreciation, which is narrower for setting objectives than it is for the choice of means.

The judgment leaves some open questions (for example, the right to life is examined only tangentially), and will need to be examined further in follow-up cases, which are sure to come. In fact, half a dozen climate cases had been adjourned to await these judgments, and the examination of these cases will now be resumed by the Court. Overall, however, this judgment—in terms of its creativity, comprehensiveness, and willingness to engage with the claims—represents a landmark success not only for the Council of Europe, but for the ever-growing phenomenon of climate litigation around the world.

V. THE EUROPEAN SOCIAL CHARTER

§ 3–17. INTRODUCTION

The European Social Charter (ESC), like the ECHR, was drafted under the auspices of the Council of Europe. It complements the Convention by guaranteeing a broad range of human rights related to employment, housing, health, education, social protection and welfare rights. All forty-seven Member States of the Member States of the Council of Europe are parties (Russia was a party until it left the COE in 2022). An Additional Protocol to the Charter, concluded in 1988 and entered into force in 1992 (as of mid-2024 13 States were Parties), addresses the rights of workers to equal opportunities and equal treatment in matters of employment and occupation without discrimination on the ground of sex, to be informed and consulted within the undertaking, and to take part in the determination and improvement of working conditions and the working environment in the undertaking. It also gave the elderly the right to social protection.

In 1995, another Additional Protocol established a system of collective complaints; it entered into force in 1998 and as of mid-2024 had sixteen States Parties. In 1996, the Charter itself was revised to bring the earlier documents up-to-date and to add some new rights. For the text, see *https://rm.coe.int/168007cf93*. It entered into force in 1999 and as of mid-2024 had been ratified by 13 States. It is progressively replacing the original Charter. The consolidated text is the instrument described in the following sections.

§ 3–18. THE CATALOG OF RIGHTS

As revised, the Charter proclaims a list of 31 categories of "rights and principles," including the rights to work, to just conditions of work, to safe working conditions, to fair remuneration, to organize, and to bargain collectively. It addressed the right of children, of young people, and of employed women to protection. Also recognized are the right of the family to social, legal and economic protection, the right of mothers and children to social and economic protection, and the right of migrant workers and their families to protection and assistance. Additional rights listed in the Charter are the right to vocational guidance and training, to protection of health, to social security, to social and medical assistance, and to benefit from social welfare services.

It also establishes the right of disabled persons to training and rehabilitation, and the equal right to engage in gainful occupations in the territory of other Contracting Parties. The right of workers to equal treatment and non-discrimination on the grounds of sex, the right to be informed and consulted, and the right to take part in the determination and improvement of the working conditions and environment in their place of employment, are also included. It provides that "every elderly person has the right to social protection" and contains guarantees in case of termination of employment or employer insolvency. Protections also are afforded for dignity at work, against discrimination due to family responsibilities, and against poverty. Finally, it contains the right of everyone to housing.

Part II of the Revised Charter defines the meaning and elaborates on the "rights and principles" proclaimed in general terms in Part I. Thus, the right to safe and healthy working conditions, which is identified in paragraph 3 of Part I of the Charter, finds expression in the following undertaking contained in Article 3 of Part II:

1. to formulate, implement and periodically review a coherent national policy on occupational safety, occupational health and the working environment. The primary aim of this policy shall be to improve occupational safety and health and to prevent accidents and injury to health arising out of, linked with or occurring in the course of work, particularly by minimizing the causes of hazards inherent in the working environment;
2. to issue safety and health regulations;
3. provide for the enforcement of such regulations by measures of supervision;
4. to promote the progressive development of occupational health services for all workers with essentially preventive and advisory functions.

§ 3–19. LEGAL OBLIGATIONS OF CONTRACTING PARTIES

Part III of the Revised Charter specifies the obligations of States Parties. It gives the States Parties a set of options. While by becoming a party to the Charter a State undertakes "to consider Part I of this Charter as a declaration of the aims which it will pursue by all appropriate means. . ." (art. A(1)(a)), it must accept as binding the undertakings contained in at least six out of nine articles found in Part II.

This flexible system encourages States to ratify the Charter without forcing them either to accept all the rights it proclaims or to make complex reservations. It is also drafted to ensure that all States Parties will at the very least be bound to guarantee some of the most basic rights. Very few States have accepted all the rights the Charter proclaims.

§ 3–20. INTERNATIONAL MEASURES FOR ENFORCEMENT OF CHARTER RIGHTS

The Charter establishes a reporting system to monitor the compliance by States Parties with their obligations as well as a system of collective complaints. States Party present a report on part of the provisions annually, with the result that each provision of the Charter will be reported on once every four years. The reports are examined by the European Committee of Social Rights (ECSR), which consists of 15 experts "of the highest integrity and recognized competence in international social questions," elected by the Committee of Ministers for a term of six years, renewable once. Art. 25. The Committee assesses whether the States have respected their undertakings and publishes its conclusions and decisions in an annual report. If a State takes no action on a Committee decision of non-compliance, the Committee of Ministers may address a recommendation to that State, asking it to change the situation in law and/or in practice.

The Additional Protocol provides for a system of collective complaints about "unsatisfactory application of the Charter" (art. 1). Such complaints can originate with international organizations of employers and trade unions, non-governmental organizations having consultative status with the Council of Europe; and national organizations of employers and trade unions from the Contracting Party concerned.

Collective complaints are examined by the ECSR. The Committee's report and conclusions are submitted to the Committee of Ministers, which may adopt a resolution and contain recommendations. The Parliamentary Assembly also receives the report, which is then made public. The State concerned must submit information on its measures to comply with the recommendations made. Art. 10.

The ESC complaint procedure is increasingly utilized and has made the European Committee on Social Rights an increasingly judicialized body. The adversarial process received more than 65 complaints in the first decade after the entry into force of the Additional Protocol of the ESC in 1998, and the ECSR has addressed many of the rights in the ESC. Many of the discrimination cases concern the Roma.

In September 2022, the Committee of Ministers adopted a reform package aimed at modernizing the European Social Charter system. The goal is to assist States Parties in ensuring respect for social rights in line with their commitments. For this purpose, emphasis is placed on the need for enhanced dialogue between the Charter organs and national bodies. Information about the Committee's reporting system, including summaries of its reports, can be found at *https://www.coe.int/en/web/european-social-charter/national-reports.*

§ 3–21. THE EUROPEAN CONVENTION AGAINST TORTURE

In 1987, the Council of Europe adopted the European Convention for the Prevention of Torture and Inhuman or Degrading Treatment or Punishment. It has since been ratified by all COE Member States (and a number of non-COE States, since under Protocol No. 1 it is open to other States by invitation). The aim of the Convention is to strengthen the protection of persons deprived of their liberty by establishing non-judicial machinery of a preventive character; hence it makes no attempt to define its subject matter and contains no substantive provisions concerning torture and inhuman or degrading treatment or punishment.

The Convention creates a Committee for the Prevention of Torture (CPT), composed of independent and impartial experts "to examine the treatment of persons deprived of their liberty with a view to strengthening, if necessary, the protection of such persons from torture and from inhuman or degrading treatment or punishment." Art. 1. The CPT has the power to visit places of detention of any kind, such as prisons, police cells, military barracks, and mental hospitals; to examine the treatment of detainees; and, if appropriate, to make recommendations to the state concerned with a view to strengthening the protection of the detainees.

A principle of "cooperation" governs relations between the Committee and the competent national authorities, leading the Committee to exercise its functions in strict confidentiality. The Committee will publicize proceedings only if a State Party fails to cooperate with it or refuses to make improvements following the Committee's recommendations. The State itself may request publication of the Committee's report, together with its comments. Some 84 reports have been published in this way. In addition, the Committee's annual report to the Committee of Ministers is made available as a public document.

The Committee also carries out periodic visits to all Contracting Parties and may organize such *ad hoc* visits "as appear to it to be required in the circumstances." *See https://www.coe.int/en/web/cpt*.

§ 3–22. PROTECTION OF NATIONAL MINORITIES

Over time, the Council of Europe has devoted substantial attention to the problems of national minorities.

Languages Charter. The 1992 European Charter for Regional or Minority Languages was a first effort by the COE to afford protection to such groups. Adopted in 1992 and in force as of March 1, 1998, the Languages Convention has been accepted by about half the COE Member States (25 as of mid-2024). *See https://www.coe.int/en/web/european-charter-regional-or-minority-languages*.

The aims of the Languages Charter are to protect and promote the historical regional or minority languages of Europe and to respect the right to use a regional or minority language in private and public life. It is structured much like the European Social Charter. It first enunciates the objectives and principles that Parties undertake to apply, including respect for the geographical area of each language and promotion, facilitation and/or encouragement of the use of regional or minority languages in speech and writing, in public and private life. It also sets out a number of specific measures to promote the use of regional or minority languages in public life. Each State Party undertakes to apply a minimum of thirty-five paragraphs or sub-paragraphs chosen from among these measures. The measures selected must include three paragraphs or sub-paragraphs chosen from each of Articles 8 (education) and 12 (cultural activities and facilities) and one from each of Articles 9 (judicial authorities), 10 (administrative authorities and public services), 11 (media) and 13 (economic and social life).

Each Party must also specify in its instrument of ratification, acceptance or approval, each regional or minority language, or official language which is less widely used in the whole or part of its territory, to which the paragraphs chosen shall apply. States Parties must submit periodic reports that are examined by a committee of experts; groups or associations within a State may submit information or comments to the committee relating to the undertakings of the State in respect to Part III of the Charter. On the basis of the State report and the information received, the Committee prepares a report for the Committee of Ministers which may make recommendations. The Committee of Ministers also appoints the committee of experts, one for each Member State.

Framework Convention. In 1994 the Council of Europe adopted the Framework Convention for the Protection of National Minorities. The Convention entered into force in thirty-nine States Parties (Andorra, France, Monaco and Turkey have neither signed not ratified). The text is available at *https://rm.coe.int/168007cdac.*

Section I sets out general principles on the protection of national minorities, even though the term is not defined in the text. Section II refers to more specific principles: non-discrimination; promotion of effective equality; promotion of conditions to preserve and develop culture and religion, language, and traditions; freedom of assembly, association, expression, thought, conscience and religion; access to and use of media; language rights; education; international and trans-frontier contacts and cooperation; participation in economic, cultural and social life; participation in public life; and prohibition of forced assimilation. Section IV concerns monitoring of state compliance and confers supervisory authority on the Committee of Ministers, assisted by an Advisory Committee.

States must file periodic reports on the legislative and other measures they take to give effect to the principles of the Framework Convention. The reports are examined by the Advisory Committee, which prepares an opinion on the measures taken. The Committee of Ministers then issues its conclusions concerning the adequacy of the measures taken by the State Party and may make recommendations to the state. The opinion of the Advisory Committee, any comments on it by the State Party, and the conclusions and recommendations of the Committee of Ministers are made public.

§ 3–23. HUMAN RIGHTS AND BIOMEDICINE

The 1997 Convention on Human Rights and Biomedicine, in force from December 1, 1999, is the first legally-binding international text adopted to preserve human rights through a series of principles and prohibitions concerning bioethics, medical research, prior informed consent, rights to private life and information, organ transplantation, and public debate on all these issues. The Convention declares (in Art. 2) that "the interests and welfare of the human being shall prevail over the sole interest of society or science." It bans all forms of discrimination based on the grounds of a person's genetic make-up (art. 11) and allows the carrying out of predictive genetic tests only for medical purposes (arts. 11 and 12). For the text, *see https://www.coe.int/en/web/impact-convention-human-rights/convention-on-human-rights-and-biomedicine#/*.

The Convention allows genetic engineering, but only for preventive, diagnostic or therapeutic reasons and only where it does not aim to change the genetic make-up of a person's descendants. It prohibits the use of techniques of medically assisted procreation to help choose the sex of a child, except where it would avoid a serious hereditary condition. It also sets out rules related to medical research by including detailed and precise conditions, especially for people who cannot give their consent. It prohibits the creation of human embryos for research purposes and requires protection of embryos where countries allow in-vitro research.

The Convention embraces the principle of prior informed consent for treatment, except in emergencies (art. 5). Consent may be freely withdrawn at any time. The treatment of persons unable to give their consent, such as children and people with mental illnesses, may be carried out only if it could produce real and direct benefit to the individual's health (art. 6). The Convention stipulates that all patients have a right to be informed about their health, including the results of predictive genetic tests, but also recognizes the patient's right not to know (art. 11). The Convention prohibits the removal of organs and other tissues which cannot be regenerated from people not able to give consent (art. 19). The only exception is, under certain conditions, for regenerative tissue (especially marrow) between siblings (art. 20).

Four Protocols to the Biomedicine Convention have been adopted, covering (i) the Prohibition of Cloning Human Beings, (ii) the Transplantation of Organs and Tissues of Human Origin, (iii) Biomedical Research and (iv) Genetic Testing for Health Purposes.

§ 3–24. CONVENTION ON ACTION AGAINST TRAFFICKING IN HUMAN BEINGS

The COE Convention on Action against Trafficking in Human Beings focuses on the protection of victims of trafficking in human beings and aims to prevent trafficking and to prosecute traffickers. Concluded in 2005, the Convention entered into force on February 1, 2008. It applies to all victims of trafficking (women, men and children alike), to all forms of exploitation (including sexual exploitation, forced labour, servitude, and removal of organs) and it covers all forms of trafficking: national and transnational, related or not to organized crime.

States Parties are obligated to work towards raising awareness of persons vulnerable to trafficking and actions aimed at discouraging "consumers." They must prevent trafficking in human beings and recognize victims of trafficking as such rather than treating them as illegal migrants or criminals. Victims of trafficking are to be granted physical and psychological assistance and support for their reintegration into society. Medical treatment, counseling and information as well as appropriate accommodation are all among the measures provided. Victims are also entitled to receive compensation, time to recover and escape from the influence of the traffickers and to take a decision regarding their possible cooperation with the authorities. A renewable residence permit may be granted if the victims' personal situation so requires or if they need to stay in order to cooperate in a criminal investigation.

Trafficking is to be considered a criminal offence and traffickers and their accomplices are to be prosecuted. The private life and the safety of victims of trafficking must be protected throughout the course of judicial proceedings. The Convention also recognizes the possibility of punishing those who use the services of a victim if they are aware that the person is a victim of trafficking in human beings.

§ 3–25. CONVENTION ON PREVENTING AND COMBATING VIOLENCE AGAINST WOMEN AND DOMESTIC VIOLENCE

The COE Convention on Preventing and Combating Violence against Women and Domestic Violence (the "Istanbul Convention") was adopted in 2011 and entered into force in 2014. The text is available at *https://www.coe.int/en/web/istanbul-convention*. It recognizes gender-based violence against women as a violation of human rights and a form of discrimination and obliges States parties to take measures to eliminate such acts.

The Convention defines and criminalizes various forms of violence against women, including domestic violence. States parties must introduce new offences where they do not already exist, such as for example, psychological and physical violence, sexual violence and rape, stalking, female genital mutilation, forced marriage, forced abortion and forced sterilization. In addition, States parties need to ensure that culture, tradition or so-called "honour" are not regarded as a justification for any of the listed conduct.

In terms of prevention, States party must run awareness-raising campaigns, train professionals, include within teaching materials issues such as gender equality and non-violent conflict resolution in interpersonal relationships, set up treatment programs for perpetrators of domestic violence and for sex offenders, work closely with NGOs, and involve the media and the private sector in eradicating gender stereotypes and promoting mutual respect.

Protection measures include granting the police power to remove perpetrators of domestic violence from their home, ensuring people's access to adequate information on available services in a language they understand, setting up easily accessible shelters in sufficient numbers and in adequate geographic distribution, making available state-wide 24/7 telephone helplines free-of-charge, and setting up easily accessible rape crisis or sexual violence referral centers.

Compliance monitoring is the responsibility of two bodies. First, the Group of Experts on Action Against Violence Against Women and Domestic Violence ("GREVIO"), a body of independent and impartial experts known for their expertise in relevant fields prepares and publishes reports on legislative and other measures taken by countries that have ratified the Convention, designed to give effect to its provisions (evaluation procedure). Second, the Committee of Parties (composed of representatives of States) may adopt recommendations on measures to be taken to implement conclusions contained in

GREVIO's reports. The Committee also supervises the implementation of its own recommendations, examines the findings of any inquiry conducted by GREVIO members, and considers any necessary measures pursuant to these findings.

VI. THE EUROPEAN UNION

§ 3–26. ABSORBING THE EUROPEAN CONVENTION ON HUMAN RIGHTS

Shortly after the creation of the Council of Europe in 1950, three separate regional institutions (focused primarily on economic activity) were created: the European Coal and Steel Community (1952), the European Atomic Energy Community (1958), and the European Economic Community (1958). The EEC was transformed into the European Union (EU) by the Maastricht Treaty in 1993. The EU is a supranational organization distinct from the Council of Europe and its institutions, which are described above. Given the existence of the COE's human rights system, it was not given a specific human rights mandate by its foundational instruments.

Although the European Court of Justice (ECJ) was tasked with ensuring the observance of law in the interpretation and application of the foundational treaties, a specific separate (or parallel) role was not created for the ECJ with respect to human rights issues.

In 1964 the ECJ enunciated the principle of the supremacy of Community law over the domestic law of the Member States in Costa v. ENEL, Case 6/64,

1964 ECR 585. The Supremacy Doctrine was resisted by some States on human rights grounds. Following challenges by various domestic courts, the ECJ held in a series of cases that fundamental rights of individuals are enshrined in the general principles of Community law protected by the Court and form part of Community law, inspired by the constitutional traditions of Member States. Stauder v. Ulm, Case 29/69, 1969 ECR 419 and Handelsgesellschaft v. Einfuhr-und Vorratsstelle fur Getreide und Futtermittel, Case 11/70, 1070 ECR 1125. The Single European Act of 1987, O.J. L. 169/1 (1987) adopted this view and explicitly referred to the ECHR.

The 1992 Treaty of European Union made human rights an obligation of the Union. The 1999 Treaty of Amsterdam formally incorporated human rights by requiring that the "union shall respect fundamental rights, as guaranteed by the European Convention. . .as general principles of Community law." Treaty of Amsterdam, O.J. C 340/1 (1997), art. 6. In addition, human rights clauses are included in over fifty community trade or aid agreements with foreign states.

The ECJ has in fact decided cases addressing non-discrimination and freedom of religion, association and expression. The main impact of ECJ jurisprudence has been in the area of equality and non-discrimination, which is treaty based. It has stated that the principle of non-discrimination on the grounds of age must be regarded as "a general principle of Community law." Mangold v. Helm, Case C–144/04, 2005 ECR I–998, para. 75. In the French

Farmers case, the European Court of Justice decided that national authorities and courts have a duty to protect rights given by Community law against interference from other private parties as well as against interference from state authorities. Commission v. France, Case C–265/95, 1997 E.C.R. I–6959. *See also* Defrene v. Sabena, Case 43/75, 1976 E.C.R. 455; Prais v. Council, Case 130/75 1976 ECR 1589; Union Syndicale-Amalgamated European Pub. Serv. Union v. Council, Case 175/73, 1974 ECR 917; VBBB & VBVB v. Commission, Joined Cases 43 and 63/82, 1984 ECR 19.

This interactive process has been facilitated by the fact that all Member States of the European Union have also ratified the European Convention of Human Rights and have accepted the jurisdiction of the European Court of Human Rights. (Note, however, that not all parties to the European Convention are members of the European Union.)

Attempts have been made over the years to work out some form of association agreement between the European Union and the Council of Europe, which would enable the former to join the European Convention of Human Rights. The preamble to the Maastricht Treaty, which transformed the European Community into the European Union, declared that "the Union shall respect fundamental rights, as guaranteed by the European Convention [of] . . . Human Rights . . . and as they result from the constitutional traditions common to the Member States, as general principles of Community law." Treaty on European Union, Preamble, para. F (2). 36

Int'l Legal Mat. 253, at 256 (1992). Moreover, the treaty establishes a procedure that can be used to suspend certain membership rights if a "serious and persistent" breach of human rights occurs in a Member State (art. 7).

§ 3–27. THE CHARTER OF FUNDAMENTAL RIGHTS OF THE EUROPEAN UNION

In December 2002, the EU Council approved the European Charter of Fundamental Rights recognizing all rights that pertain to the Union's citizens and in effect combining the guarantees of the European Convention on Human Rights, the European Social Charter, and other human rights instruments. That Charter was not adopted as a treaty due to lack of agreement among the Member States. It was, however, subsequently incorporated into the Treaty of Lisbon, which entered into force on 1 December 2009, making it binding on all EU Member States pursuant to Article 6. Accordingly, it has become one of the foundational instruments for the overall European human rights system.

The Charter's Preamble expresses that its aim is "to strengthen the protection of fundamental rights in the light of changes in society, social progress and scientific and technological developments by making those rights more visible in a Charter" and by reaffirming those rights deriving "from the constitutional traditions and international obligations common to the Member States, the Treaty on European Union, the Community Treaties, the European Convention for the Protection of

Human Rights and Fundamental Freedoms, the Social Charters adopted by the Community and by the Council of Europe and the case-law of the Court of Justice of the European Communities and of the European Court of Human Rights."

The rights guaranteed in the Charter are divided into six categories or chapters: dignity, freedoms, equality, solidarity, citizens' rights, and justice. Chapters I–III and VI basically restate the rights found in the European Convention, but in some instances go beyond the Convention guarantees. That is the case, for example, with Charter Art. 10(2), which guarantees a right to conscientious objection to military service. Other rights expressly mentioned in these chapters of the Charter but not found in the Convention are: a prohibition on trafficking in human beings (art. 5(3)); protection of personal data (art. 8); respect for academic freedom (art. 13); freedom to conduct a business (art. 16); and rights of the child, elderly and disabled (arts. 24–26). Article 3 (right to integrity of the person) includes a restatement of the main provisions of the Convention on Biomedicine and its Protocol against Human Cloning. Chapter IV (Solidarity) encompasses the rights contained in the European Social Charter.

The most innovative aspect of the Charter is found in Chapter V. Entitled "Citizens Rights," it is a catalogue of political rights and principles of democratic governance: the rights to vote and to stand for office in internal and European Parliament elections (arts. 39–40); the right to good administration (art. 41); the right of access to documents (art. 42); the right to petition (arts. 43–44); and the right to diplomatic and consular protection (art. 45). A final chapter, entitled "General Provisions" declares in Article 51 that the Charter "is addressed to the institutions and leaders of the Union with due regard to the principle of subsidiarity and to the Member States only when they are implementing Union law."

The Treaty of Lisbon also provided that the European Union 'shall' accede to the European Convention on Human Rights. Negotiations on a draft agreement were concluded between the EU and the Council of Europe's 20 non-EU signatories in April 2013, and the Commission then asked the ECJ for its advice on the compatibility of the agreement with the EU treaties (under Article 218(11) TFEU). In Opinion 2/13 delivered on 18 December, the European Court of Justice ruled that the draft accession agreement between the European Union and the Council of Europe breaches EU law, placing in doubt the future adherence of the EU to the European Convention.

§ 3–28. NON-JUDICIAL EU HUMAN RIGHTS BODIES

The European Union Agency for Fundamental Rights (FRA) is a body of the European Union (EU), established through Council Regulation (EC) No. 168/2007 of 15 February 2007, OJ L 53, 22.2.2007, p. 1. *See https://fra.europa.eu/en*. It is based in Vienna and is built on the foundation of the European Monitoring Centre on Racism and Xenophobia

(EUMC). FRA is an independent body that cooperates with national and international bodies and organizations, in particular the Council of Europe. It also works closely with civil society organizations. Its objective is to provide the relevant institutions and authorities of the Community and its Member States, when implementing Community law, with assistance and expertise relating to fundamental rights in order to support them to fully respect fundamental rights. (Article 2 of the Regulation).

The Agency has no regulatory powers and cannot receive individual complaints. It publishes an annual report on fundamental rights in the EU, and thematic reports based on research and surveys, highlighting examples of good practice regarding fundamental rights. The European Parliament's subcommittee on human rights, which is charged with evaluating the implementation of EU instruments in the field of human rights and democracy and holding the Commission and Council accountable for their activities in this area, decided in 2001 to begin drafting annual reports on fundamental rights in the European Union.

Each report analyzes the degree of respect for each of the rights laid down in the Charter, making use of the work of the United Nations, Council of Europe, EU institutions, case law of the European Court of Human Rights and the Court of Justice of the European Communities, legislation, case law and practices in the Member States, and contributions by relevant NGOs. The annual reports facilitate the

EP's role in triggering the warning system introduced by Article 7 (1) of the EU Treaty in the case of a serious risk of violation of fundamental rights by a Member State. Also, since 1998, the EP has issued annual reports on human rights in the world. These reports help determine the EU's bilateral and multilateral policies and dialogues with non-member states. Respect for human rights is also one of the preconditions for any candidate country's accession to the Union.

A third EU institution is the European Ombudsman, established in 1995 pursuant to the Maastricht Treaty to deal with complaints about maladministration by the institutions and bodies of the European Community. Any citizen of a Member State of the European Union or person living in a Member State can complain to the Ombudsman. Businesses, associations or other bodies with a registered office in the Union can also complain. A complaint must be made within two years of the date when the complainant became aware of the facts on which the complaint is based and the person must already have contacted the institution or body concerned about the problem. *See https://www.ombudsman.europa.eu.*

Some of the most common problems submitted to the Ombudsman concern unnecessary delay, refusal of information, discrimination and abuse of power. The Ombudsman transmits the complaint to the relevant institution, which can take steps to resolve the problem. If maladministration is found and the case is not settled during the inquiry, the

Ombudsman seeks a friendly settlement. If this fails, he or she can make a draft recommendation to the relevant institution, calling on it to take the necessary steps to remedy the situation. If the institution does not accept his recommendation, he or she can make a special report to the European Parliament.

VII. ORGANIZATION FOR SECURITY AND COOPERATION IN EUROPE

§ 3–29. INTRODUCTION

As its name suggests, the Conference on Security and Cooperation in Europe (CSCE), initially created in 1972 and which in 1994 became the Organization for Security and Cooperation in Europe (OSCE), is not, strictly speaking, either a European organization or a human rights institution. Although its members now include all European nations, the United States and Canada have been members from its very inception. For an overview, *see https://www.osce.org/*. We have chosen to examine its human rights work in this chapter, as opposed to a separate one, because the OSCE works closely with the Council of Europe when it comes to the promotion of human rights. The CSCE was created by the Helsinki Final Act (HFA), signed in 1975 by 33 European nations, including the Soviet Union, plus the United States and Canada. At the time only Albania refused to join.

Since the end of the Cold War, the OSCE's membership has grown to 57 nations, spanning much of the Northern Hemisphere. Conceived as a compromise instrument to bridge the ideological chasm that divided East from West in the 1970's, the HFA is not itself legally-binding but established a negotiating process that included a highly imaginative linkage between human rights and security concerns. This linkage, which gave human rights an important place on the political agenda of East-West relations, did not lose its significance with the end of the Cold War. It has enabled the OSCE to continue to play a major role in today's Europe and to influence the human rights policies of many of its nations.

In its current form, the OSCE consists of a number of components, including (among others) a Parliamentary Assembly, High Commission on Minorities, Office for Democratic Institutions, and the Representative on Freedom on the Media. *See https://www.osce.org/institutions-and-structures.*

§ 3–30. THE HELSINKI FINAL ACT

The Helsinki Final Act, available at *https://www.osce.org/helsinki-final-act,* is a massive document, consisting of four chapters or so-called "baskets." Basket I, entitled "Questions Relating to Security in Europe," consists of two sections ("Principles Guiding Relations Between Participating States," and "Confidence-Building Measures and Certain Aspects of Security and Disarmament"). Basket II deals with "Cooperation in the Field of Economics, of Science and Technology and of the Environment." The subject of Basket III is

"Cooperation in Humanitarian and Other Fields." Basket IV, the final chapter of the instrument, spells out the so-called "follow-up" process.

Human rights issues are addressed primarily in the Guiding Principles proclaimed in Basket I and to some extent in Basket III, although over time the latter has become less important because the subjects it deals with—human contacts, family reunification, etc.—no longer have the importance they had during the Cold War. Of the ten Guiding Principles set out in the HFA, two relate to human rights. The remaining principles concern sovereignty, the use of force, inviolability of frontiers, territorial integrity, peaceful settlement of disputes, non-intervention in internal affairs, cooperation of states, and fulfillment in good faith of international legal obligations.

Principle VII ("Respect for human rights and fundamental freedoms") consists of eight unnumbered paragraphs. In the first two, the participating States undertake to "respect human rights and fundamental freedoms" and to "promote and encourage the effective exercise of civil, political, economic, social, cultural and other rights and freedoms. . . ." This principle also addresses freedom of religion, rights of individuals belonging to national minorities, and the "right of the individual to know and act upon his rights and duties in this field." The last paragraph reads as follows:

In the field of human rights and fundamental freedoms, the participating States will act in conformity with the purposes and principles of the Charter of the United Nations and with the

Universal Declaration of Human Rights. They will also fulfil their obligations as set forth in the international declarations and agreements in this field, including inter alia the International Covenants on Human Rights, by which they may be bound.

The significance of this paragraph, at the time it was adopted, lay in the fact that until then some of the participating States, including the Soviet Union, had never formally acknowledged an obligation to conform their conduct to the Universal Declaration of Human Rights. (The Soviet Union had abstained when the UN General Assembly adopted the Universal Declaration, and its adherence to Principle VII appears to have been its first unambiguous recognition of the "normative" character of this instrument.)

Principle VIII articulates "Equal rights and self-determination of peoples." After undertaking to respect the equal rights of peoples and their right to self-determination, the participating States recognize that "all peoples always have the right, in full freedom, to determine, when and as they wish, their internal and external political status, without external interference. . . ." They also reaffirm "the universal significance of respect for and effective exercise of equal rights and self-determination of peoples for the development of friendly relations among themselves as among all States; they also recall the importance of the elimination of any form of violation of this principle."

It took quite a while before the Soviet Union and its allies fully acknowledged that these two Guiding Principles had in fact placed human rights issues on the agenda of the on-going East-West political dialogue. Their efforts to silence that debate by the invocation of the doctrine of non-intervention in internal affairs, enshrined in Principle VI, at times threatened to break up the CSCE. They relented gradually and by the latter part of the 1980's the discussion of specific human rights violations had become routine during CSCE follow-up meetings. Moreover, as we shall see, these meetings also dramatically expanded the human rights catalog of the HFA. *See* § 3–33, *infra*.

§ 3–31. THE OSCE PROCESS

The OSCE's impact in the human rights area is partially attributable to the follow-up process provided for by Basket IV, which has come to be known as the "OSCE process." It consists of the convening by the participating States of periodic intergovernmental conferences for the purpose of achieving "a thorough exchange of views both on the implementation of the provisions of the Final Act . . . as well as . . . on the deepening of their mutual relations, the improvement of security and the development of co-operation in Europe, and the development of the process of détente in the future." These follow-up conferences have been used for the dual purpose of providing a conference forum to review compliance with human rights commitments and a mechanism for the expansion of the human rights catalog.

The existence of this process has permitted the HFA to be amplified, reinterpreted, and extensively revised at successive conferences. These meetings have of course also been used to focus public attention on the failure of certain states to live up to their human rights commitments.

This normative evolution is accomplished by the so-called "concluding documents" adopted by consensus at these conferences. These documents are used to proclaim new OSCE commitments or to expand, modify or interpret the scope and meaning of existing ones. The result is a dynamic and creative process that has produced a growing body of OSCE human rights commitments.

§ 3–32. THE NON-BINDING CHARACTER OF OSCE COMMITMENTS

The HFA is not a treaty nor was it intended by the participating States to create binding legal obligations. Instead, they conceived it as a non-binding instrument proclaiming political commitments. A State's failure to comply with any of these commitments thus has political but not legal consequences. Put another way, non-compliance does not give rise to a cause of action under international law, but it could have very serious political repercussions. Subsequent OSCE concluding documents are also not intended to be legally binding unless the contrary intent is stated expressly.

The non-binding character of the HFA and subsequent instruments has not been detrimental to the objectives they were designed to achieve.

National governments and legislatures, domestic courts and administrative bodies have frequently looked to them in making, interpreting and applying national laws and regulations. They have also proved to be a useful tool for national and international non-governmental organizations seeking to promote the observance of human rights.

§ 3–33. THE OSCE CATALOG OF RIGHTS

What distinguishes the OSCE's rights catalog from that of traditional human rights treaties is that, in addition to proclaiming basic individual human rights, it also addresses the rights of minorities, rule of law issues, democratic values, elections, etc. The OSCE in fact pioneered a comprehensive approach to human rights, which proceeds on the assumption that individual rights are best protected in States that adhere to the rule of law and democratic values and are so constituted as to permit these concepts to flourish.

The breakthrough came with the adoption of the Copenhagen Concluding Document in 1990. This instrument contains chapters dealing with human rights, the rule of law, free elections and democratic values. It also expanded upon prior OSCE commitments on the rights of minorities. *See https://www.osce.org/odihr/elections/14304.*

Subsequent OSCE documents, from the Charter of Paris for a New Europe (1990), the Moscow Concluding Document (1991), the 1992 Helsinki Document ("Challenges for Change"), through the 1994 Budapest Document ("Towards a Genuine

Partnership in a New Era") refined, reinforced and expanded upon these commitments, which today also include commitments relating to international humanitarian law and the rights of refugees, migrant workers, and indigenous populations, among others. The essence of this expansive human rights catalogue is captured in Chapter VIII, para. 2, of the Budapest Document, which reads in part as follows:

> Human rights and fundamental freedoms, the rule of law and democratic institutions are the foundation of peace and security, representing a crucial contribution to conflict prevention. The protection of human rights, including the rights of persons belonging to national minorities, is an essential foundation of democratic civil society.

The OSCE has thus moved from traditional international human rights concerns to the articulation of those basic democratic constitutional principles and legal remedies which seek to ensure that all instrumentalities of the state exercise their powers in conformity with laws adopted by the people through their democratically elected representatives. *Generally, see OSCE Handbook* (2007), at *https://www.osce.org/human-rights.*

§ 3–34. THE OSCE'S HUMAN DIMENSION MECHANISM

The Vienna Concluding Document (1989) consolidated the subject of human rights, previously addressed as a "Basket I" item, with the human contact and related humanitarian topics set out in Basket II. It subsumed both topics under the heading of the "Human Dimension of the CSCE" and established the Human Dimension Mechanism for dealing with the non-observance by States with their human dimension commitments. Subsequent OSCE conferences, among them the Copenhagen (1990), Moscow (1991) and Helsinki (1992) Concluding Documents, have expanded the scope of the Mechanism in order to make it more effective. *See https://www.osce.org/odihr/human-dimension-mechanisms.*

The OSCE today monitors and reports on the human rights situation in each of its 57 participating States, particularly in the areas of freedom of assembly and association, the right to liberty and to a fair trial, and in the use of the death penalty. It provides training and education across the field of human rights, including for government officials, law-enforcement officers, rights defenders and students.

The Mechanism consists of a multi-stage process of negotiations, mediation, and fact-finding, involving bilateral and multilateral negotiations, OSCE missions of experts and rapporteurs assisted by the OSCE Office for Democratic Institutions and Human Rights (ODIHR). The process usually begins with claims by one or more states that another State is not living up to its OSCE Human Dimension commitments. There follows a diplomatic exchange between the States concerned for which specific time limits are provided. If the matter is not resolved between them, the States may bring it to the attention of all OSCE members and place the matter on the agenda of OSCE follow-up or Human Dimension conferences.

If this process does not produce results, OSCE expert missions or rapporteur missions may be appointed to investigate the charges. These perform the role of third-party factfinders and mediators. As a rule, the missions are established by mutual consent of the states concerned, although such consent is not necessary in serious situations. In such cases a mission may be convoked whenever a group of states or the OSCE Senior Council considers it necessary.

The OSCE has taken up the issue of human trafficking as a priority matter. Permanent Council Decision 557 of July 24, 2003, adopted an Action Plan to Combat Trafficking in Human Beings based on the 2000 UN Convention on the topic. The Office of the Special Representative and Coordinator for Combating Trafficking in Human Beings, set up in 2006, supports the development and implementation of anti-trafficking policies in OSCE participating States. The Office of the Special Representative coordinates cooperation among relevant OSCE institutions, structures and field operations mandated to combat trafficking. The OSCE programs and policies reflect a strong regional effort to implement and enforce the global laws on the topic.

§ 3–35. THE HIGH COMMISSIONER ON NATIONAL MINORITIES

Although the HFA makes a passing reference to the rights of individuals belonging to national minorities, the subsequent Copenhagen Concluding Document (1990), the Report of the Geneva Meeting of Experts on National Minorities (1991), and the Moscow Concluding Document (1991) laid the normative foundation for a system to protect national minorities. Based on these, the OSCE in 1992 established the office of the High Commissioner on National Minorities (HCNM). *See CSCE Helsinki Document: The Challenges of Change,* ch. II, at 7 (1992) (spelling out the mandate of the HCNM). Concern with the potential for violent conflicts arising from ethnic tensions is reflected in the mandate of the HCNM, which reads in part as follows:

> The High Commissioner will provide "early warning" and, as appropriate, "early action" at the earliest possible stage in regard to tensions involving national minority issues which have not yet developed beyond an early warning stage, but, in the judgement of the High Commissioner, have the potential to develop into a conflict within the CSCE area, affecting peace, stability or relations between participating States, requiring the attention of and action by the Council [of Ministers of Foreign Affairs] or the CSO [Committee of Senior Officials].

As this language indicates, the HCNM's principal function of the is to address problems of minorities before they escalate into serious conflicts. In discharging this mandate, the High Commissioner is to be guided by "CSCE principles and commitments."

He or she is to "work in confidence and . . . act independently of all parties involved in the tensions."

By formulating a catalog of basic OSCE commitments relating to the rights of national minorities, the Copenhagen CSCE Conference (1990) tackled a subject that had attracted only sporadic interest on the part of the international community after the demise of the League of Nations minorities system. *See* § 1–5, *supra*. Shortly thereafter, the tragic events in the former Yugoslavia and elsewhere led to a renewed interest in international norms and institutions for the protection of minorities. As a result, in 1992, the United Nations adopted the "Declaration on the Rights of Persons Belonging to National or Ethnic, Religious and Linguistic Minorities," (UN General Assembly Res. 47/135 of December 18, 1992). In 1994, the Council of Europe adopted and opened for signature the Framework Convention for the Protection of National Minorities, discussed *supra* § 3–22. These new instruments strengthen the normative framework within which the High Commissioner on National Minorities discharges his or her mandate.

§ 3–36. REPRESENTATIVE ON FREEDOM OF THE MEDIA

The useful work of the High Commissioner on National Minorities led the OSCE to establish a similar post of Representative on Freedom of the Media. Created in November 1997, the Representative "address[es] serious problems caused by, *inter alia*, obstruction of media activities and unfavorable working conditions for journalists." Mandate of the OSCE Representative on Freedom of the Media (November 5, 1997), PC Journal No. 137, Decision No. 193, para. 2. *See https://www.osce.org/hcnm.*

Unlike the High Commissioner, the Media Representative is not a mediator, but acts as an advocate, observing relevant media developments in OSCE participating States and promoting compliance with OSCE principles and commitments regarding freedom of expression and free media. The Representative also aims to provide early warning on violations of freedom of expression, concentrating on rapid response to serious non-compliance with OSCE principles and commitments by participating States. Where there are serious problems, the Representative seeks direct contacts with the participating State and other parties involved, assesses the facts and seeks to resolve the issue. The Representative collects and receives information on the situation of the media from participating States, organizations or institutions, media and their representatives, and relevant NGOs including information about hate speech. The Representative reports to the Permanent Council, recommending further action where appropriate.

Selected References and Further Reading

Angeleri, et al. The European Social Charter: A Commentary: Articles 11 to 19 (2024)

Lukas, Nowak, Overleitner, Heschle, Czech, eds., European Yearbook on Human Rights 2023 (2024)

Harris, O'Boyle & Warbrick: Law of the European Convention on Human Rights (2023)

Remezaite, Brett, et al, Compliance with Judgments of the European Court of Human Rights (International Studies in Human Rights) (2023)

Gerards, Fundamental Rights: The European and International Dimension (2023)

Reid, A Practitioner's Guide to the European Convention on Human Rights (7th ed. 2023)

Peers, Hervey, et al., The EU Charter of Fundamental Rights: A Commentary (2022)

Jacobs, White, and Ovey: The European Convention on Human Rights (8th ed. 2021)

Nussberger, The European Court of Human Rights (Oxford 2020)

Lukas, The Revised European Social Charter: An Article by Article Commentary, Elgar Commentaries in Human Rights series (2021)

William A. Schabas, The European Convention on Human Rights: A Commentary (2015)

Council of Europe, *Collected Edition of the 'Travaux Préparatoires' of the European Convention on Human Rights* (8 vols., 1975–85).

Tripkovic and Zysset, Uncovering the Nature of ECHR Rights: An Analytical and Methodological Framework, 24 Hum. Rts. L. Rev. 1 (2024).

CHAPTER 4

THE INTER-AMERICAN HUMAN RIGHTS SYSTEM

I. INTRODUCTION

This chapter examines the law and institutions of the Organization of American States created to promote and protect human rights.

The OAS is a regional inter-governmental organization, whose 34 members comprise most sovereign states of the Americas. These states are: Antigua and Barbuda, Argentina, The Bahamas, Barbados, Belize, Bolivia, Brazil, Canada, Chile, Colombia, Costa Rica, Cuba, Dominica, Dominican Republic, Ecuador, El Salvador, Grenada, Guatemala, Guyana, Haiti, Honduras, Jamaica, Mexico, Panama, Paraguay, Perú, St. Kitts and Nevis, St. Lucia, St. Vincent and the Grenadines, Suriname, Trinidad and Tobago, United States, Uruguay, and Venezuela.

Cuba's Castro government was suspended from participation in the Organization in 1962, by an OAS resolution whose effects were terminated by another resolution unanimously adopted in 2009, allowing the government to request resumption of its participation. The government had not made such a request as of mid-2024. Despite non-participation of the government, throughout the entire period Cuba has remained a Member State subject to the OAS human rights system. Nicaragua's formal withdrawal from the OAS was effective in 2023. It withdrew over criticism of its human rights record though the OAS decided to continue to monitor human rights issues in the country.

The OAS discharges its functions through its organs, including the General Assembly and Permanent Council. The General Assembly meets once a year in regular session and in special ones as necessary. It is the supreme policy-setting organ of the Organization. Each Member State has one vote in the Assembly. The Permanent Council is composed of the permanent representatives of each Member State to the OAS. The Council serves as the Organization's decision-making organ between Assembly sessions and performs other functions bearing on the resolution of disputes and peacekeeping. Both organs have jurisdiction to deal with human rights matters.

The Inter-American human rights system has two distinct legal sources: in part it has evolved from the Charter of the Organization of the OAS ("Charter"), while the other part is based on the American Convention on Human Rights ("Convention") and related treaties. The Charter-based system applies to all 34 Member States of the OAS, while the Convention and other treaties are legally binding only on the States Parties. The sources overlap and interact in a variety of ways. In some instances, the legal mechanisms or norms of several instruments apply to different aspects of the same human rights situation. *See, e.g.*, Advisory Opinion OC–10/89, IA Ct.H.R., Series A: Judgments and Opinions, No. 10 (1990) (interpreting the normative effect of the

American Declaration of the Rights and Duties of Man). Hence, although this chapter presents the Charter evolution separately from the Convention and other treaties because it is conceptually clearer to do so, as a practical matter, the two systems often function as one.

Two official publications of the Inter-American system, one entitled *Basic Documents Pertaining to Human Rights in the Inter-American System* [hereinafter cited as *Basic Documents*], available at *http://www.oas.org/en/iachr/mandate/basic_documents.asp* and the other, *Inter-American Yearbook on Human Rights,* are indispensable research tools on the Inter-American system.

II. THE OAS CHARTER-BASED SYSTEM

§ 4–1. INTRODUCTION

The Charter-based human rights norms and institutions of the Inter-American system have evolved over nearly seventy years. Legal and political events contributed to its evolution. The major legal developments include the promulgation of the American Declaration of the Rights and Duties of Man ("Declaration"), the establishment of the Inter-American Commission on Human Rights ("Commission"), the 1970 amendment of the OAS Charter, and the entry into force of the American Convention on Human Rights.

The political factors that have played an important role include the Cuban revolution and the hemispheric reaction to it. Also important has been the attitude of the U.S. Government, which initially showed little interest in, if not outright hostility to, the development of an inter-American human rights system, and then championed it at different times and for different reasons. The fall of the Latin American dictatorships that were so prevalent in the 1980s has also had a significant political impact.

§ 4–2. THE OAS CHARTER

The Charter, a multilateral treaty that is the constitution of the OAS, was opened for signature in Bogotá, Colombia, in 1948 and entered into force in 1951. The Charter (sometimes referred to as "the Pact of San José") was amended by the Protocol of Buenos Aires, which came into effect in 1970, followed by the Protocol of Cartagena de Indias, the Protocol of Managua, and the Protocol of Washington, in force since 1988, 1996 and 1997, respectively.

The 1948 Charter made few references to human rights. One provision of importance was Article 3(j), now Article 3(*l*), wherein "the American States proclaim the fundamental rights of the individual without distinction as to race, nationality, creed, or sex" among the principles to which they are committed. Another important reference to human rights appears in Article 13, now Article 17. After declaring that "each State has the right to develop its cultural, political and economic life freely and naturally," this provision prescribes that "in this free development, the State shall respect the rights of the individual and the principles of universal morality."

The 1948 Charter did not define "the fundamental rights of the individual" to which Article 3 referred, nor did it create any institution to promote their observance. However, the same diplomatic conference which adopted the 1948 Charter also proclaimed the American Declaration of the Rights and Duties of Man. Promulgated in the form of a conference resolution, this instrument proclaims an extensive catalog of human rights. *See* § 4–3, *infra*.

In amending the OAS Charter, the Protocol of Buenos Aires introduced some important changes bearing on human rights: it established the Inter-American Commission on Human Rights as an OAS Charter organ and prescribed that the Commission's principal function should be "to promote the observance and protection of human rights. . . ." OAS Charter, as amended, arts. 51(e) and 112, now arts. 53(e) and 106. With these amendments, the Commission acquired the constitutional legitimacy it previously lacked. *See* § 4–4, *infra*. These changes also significantly strengthened the normative character of the American Declaration. *See* § 4–3, *infra*.

§ 4–3. THE AMERICAN DECLARATION OF THE RIGHTS AND DUTIES OF MAN

The Ninth International Conference of American States proclaimed the Declaration on May 2, 1948, antedating by a few months the UN's Universal Declaration of Human Rights, with which it has much in common. The preamble of the American Declaration emphasizes that "the international protection of the rights of man should be the principal guide of an evolving American law."

The American Declaration includes a list of some 27 human rights and ten duties. The catalog of rights embraces civil and political as well as economic, social and cultural rights. These include the right to life, liberty and security of person, to equality before the law, to residence and movement, to a fair trial, to protection from arbitrary arrest to due process of law, and to nationality and asylum. Freedom of religion, expression, assembly and association are proclaimed.

Protected, too, is the right to privacy, to property, to health, to education, to the benefits of culture, to work, to leisure time, and to social security. The list of duties includes a duty to society, toward children and parents, to receive instruction, to vote, to obey the law, to serve the community and the nation, to pay taxes, and to work. Also proclaimed are duties with respect to social security and welfare, as well as the duty to refrain from political activities in a foreign country.

The Declaration was adopted as a non-binding conference resolution that was deemed by those who drafted it to have no legal effect. Gradually, however, the legal status of the American Declaration began to change. Today it is deemed by many to be the normative instrument that embodies the authoritative interpretation of "the fundamental rights of the individual," which Article 3(*l*) of the OAS Charter proclaims.

On this subject, the Inter-American Court of Human Rights has found that "for the member states of the Organization, the Declaration is the text that defines the human rights referred to in the Charter. . . . [T]he Declaration is for these States a source of international obligations related to the Charter of the Organization." Advisory Opinion OC–10/89, IA Ct.H.R., Series A: Judgments and Opinions, No. 10, para. 45 (1989). As such, the Court will apply the Declaration as appropriate to construe the articles of the American Convention. *See* Case of Bueno-Alves v. Argentina, Judgment of May 11, 2007, IA Ct.H.R., Series C: Judgments and Opinions No. 164 (2007), paras. 54–60; *but see* Case of La Cantuta, IA Ct.H.R., Series C: Judgments and Opinions No. 162, para. 119. This conclusion finds support in the human rights practice of the OAS and of its Member States, which the Court reviewed in considerable detail in that advisory opinion. Advisory Opinion OC–10/89, *supra* at para. 43.

§ 4–4. COMMISSION AS CHARTER ORGAN: ITS INSTITUTIONAL EVOLUTION

The establishment of the Inter-American Commission on Human Rights (IACHR) was mandated in 1959 by the Fifth Meeting of Consultation of Ministers of Foreign Affairs. The OAS Council complied with that mandate in 1960 by adopting the Statute of the Commission and electing the first seven Commission members. Because the 1948 OAS Charter did not provide for the establishment of the Commission, the Council designated it as an "autonomous entity" of the OAS, "the function of which it is to promote respect for human rights." 1960 Commission Statute, art. 1. These rights were defined as follows in Article 2 of the Statute (now article 1(2)): "For the purpose of this Statute, human rights are understood to be those set forth in the American Declaration of the Rights and Duties of Man." The adoption of the Statute of the Commission and the language it employed set in motion the long process that transformed the Declaration into the important normative instrument it has become.

Article 9 of the 1960 Statute gave the IACHR various powers to promote the observance and protection of human rights, including the power to prepare studies and reports and "to make recommendations to the governments of the member states in general . . . for the adoption of progressive measures in favor of human rights within the framework of their domestic legislation. . . ." The Commission, in its first session, interpreted this language to authorize it to address general recommendations to individual states. In reliance on this interpretation and on its power to prepare studies, the Commission ushered in the practice of undertaking so-called country studies, a practice it continues; it has issued at least one report on well over half of the OAS Member States. All reports undertaken by the Commission and published since 1962 are available at *http://www.oas.org/en/iachr/reports/country.asp*.

The Commission later began issuing thematic reports as well on problems common throughout the region. It has published numerous such thematic reports on human rights issues including access to justice, human rights defenders, rights of migrant workers, the status of women, and terrorism and human rights. Some of the reports address institutional issues, such as the friendly settlement procedure, and achieving universal ratification of the Convention.

The Second Special Inter-American Conference authorized the IACHR in 1965 to receive and act on individual petitions charging OAS Member States with violations of some, but not all, rights proclaimed in the American Declaration. The new powers, which the Commission incorporated into its Statute in 1966 as Article 9(*bis*), applied to the following "preferred" rights: the right to life, liberty and security of person (Article I), equality before the law (Article II), freedom of religion (Article III), freedom of expression (Article IV), freedom from arbitrary arrest (Article XXV), and the right to due process of law (Article XXVI). In this fashion, Article 9(*bis*) authorized the Commission to establish a limited individual petition system. That system had its legal source in powers implied in the OAS Charter, rather than in any specific human rights treaty.

The status of the Commission changed in 1970 with the entry into force of the Protocol of Buenos Aires. It amended the 1948 OAS Charter and transformed the IACHR into a formal organ of the OAS, whose "principal function shall be to promote the observance and protection of human rights and to serve as a consultative organ of the Organization in these matters." OAS Charter, as amended, arts. 51 and 112(1), now arts. 53 and 106(1). The Protocol added two other provisions applicable to the new Charter organ it created. The first was Article 112(2), now 106, which provides that "an inter-American convention on human rights shall determine the structure, competence and procedures of this Commission. . . ." The other was Article 150, now 145, which reads as follows: "Until the inter-American convention on human rights, referred to in . . . [Article 111, now 106], enters into force, the present Inter-American Commission on Human Rights shall keep vigilance over the observance of human rights."

By becoming an OAS Charter organ, the IACHR acquired an institutional and constitutional legitimacy it had not previously enjoyed. The reference in Article 150, now 145, to "the present" Commission, read in conjunction with Article 112, now Article 106, can also be deemed to have legitimated the practices and procedures the Commission developed under Articles 9 and 9(*bis*) of its prior Statute.

In 1969, the OAS adopted the "inter-American convention" to which the amended OAS Charter referred; it entered into force in 1978. Those who drafted the Convention, aware of the Commission's status in the amended OAS Charter, assigned two distinct functions to it: the functions it had previously performed in relation to all Member States of the OAS, spelled out in Article 41(a)–(e) and (g) of the Convention, on the one hand, and the functions applicable only to States Parties to the Convention, on the other. Convention, arts. 41(f), 44–51.

The entry into force of the Convention required the OAS General Assembly to adopt a new Statute for the Commission, incorporating these new functions. Convention, art. 39. This it did in 1979. That Statute remains in force today, despite the efforts of some States to amend it to reduce the Commission's powers. The Statute takes account of the distinct roles the IACHR performs as an OAS Charter organ and as a Convention organ. It thus spells out the Commission's powers as they apply (a) to all OAS Member States (Article 18); (b) to the States Parties to the Convention (Article 19); and (c) to OAS Member States that are not parties to the Convention (Article 20). Articles 18 and 20 of the Statute in effect preserve for the Commission the powers it had under Articles 9 and 9(*bis*) of its old Statute.

Article 1(2) of the new Statute defines "human rights" as follows:

> (a) The rights set forth in the American Convention on Human Rights, in relation to the States Parties thereto;
>
> (b) The rights set forth in the American Declaration of the Rights and Duties of Man, in relation to the other Member States.

This reference to the Declaration reinforces its normative character and legitimates the authority of the Commission in relation to states that are not parties to the Convention. For these states, the OAS Charter and the Declaration impose human rights obligations which the Commission has the authority to enforce under its Statute. Inter-American Commission on Human Rights, Rep. No. 31/93 (Case No. 10.573/United States), Decision of October 14, 1993, IACHR, *Annual Report 1993*, OEA/Ser.L/V/II.85, Doc. 9 rev., at 312 (1993).

§ 4–5. THE COMMISSION AS CHARTER ORGAN: ITS PRACTICE

As a Charter organ, the Commission (IACHR) performs a variety of functions, including promotional and consultative activities. It has helped draft OAS human rights instruments, including the American Convention on Human Rights, and it is regularly consulted by the OAS Permanent Council and the General Assembly on human rights issues. It also sponsors conferences and publishes human rights documents and pamphlets.

On different occasions during its existence, the Commission has played an important role in mediating and protecting human rights during internal and international armed conflicts and hostage seizures. However, country and thematic studies and the examination of individual petitions, including litigation at the Inter-American Court, have occupied most of its time.

1. Country Studies and On-Site Investigations

A country study is an investigation of all or some of the human rights conditions in a state. The Commission usually initiates such a study when it receives individual communications or other credible evidence, often from non-governmental human rights organizations, suggesting that a government is engaging in large-scale violations of human rights or has a serious specific problem that needs to be addressed. The first country reports were prepared in the early 1960's and dealt with Cuba, Haiti and the Dominican Republic. Cuba and Haiti refused to allow the Commission to visit their countries; the Dominican Republic gave entry permission and became the first country to be the subject of an on-site investigation.

In its initial country study concerning Cuba, the Commission established the precedent of hearing witnesses and receiving evidence. In that instance, it held hearings in Miami and interviewed many refugees. During its visits to the Dominican Republic, the Commission crisscrossed the country, held hearings, met with government and opposition leaders, and interviewed representatives of various church, business and union groups as well as private individuals; it also set up offices in the country for the receipt of written and oral complaints.

The *modus operandi* adopted by the Commission during its visits to the Dominican Republic in the 1960's became a model which it has followed with minor variations to this day in its on-site investigations. On-site investigations are usually arranged by communications between the chairman of the Commission and the government concerned. As a rule, the Commission requests permission to visit a particular country, but some governments have extended invitations for such visits on their own initiative.

Prior to 1977, the rules governing on-site visits were negotiated on an *ad hoc* basis. Thereafter the Commission adopted a set of rules on the subject. These are now codified in Articles 53 through 57 of the IACHR's 2013 Rules of Procedure. Article 56 of the Rules requires the host government to put at the disposal of the Commission all facilities necessary for the accomplishment of its mission and to pledge that it will impose no punitive measures against individuals who cooperate with or supply information to the Commission.

The right of members of the Commission and its staff to travel freely in the host country, to meet with any individuals whatsoever, and to visit prisons is provided for in Article 57 of the Rules. This provision also establishes the government's obligation to ensure the safety of the Commission and its staff, and to provide the Commission with whatever documents or other information it may request.

On-site investigations are now generally carried out by a so-called "Special Commission" of the IACHR but, in particularly serious situations, the entire Commission may undertake the visit. To avoid conflict-of-interest problems, Article 54 of the Rules provides that members of the Commission who are nationals of or reside in a country in which the investigation is to be carried out shall be ineligible to serve on the "Special Commission."

In preparing its country studies, whether or not on-site investigations are involved, the Commission proceeds in stages. Initially, after the relevant information has been gathered, it prepares a draft report. That document examines the conditions in the country by reference to the human rights standards set out in the American Declaration of the Rights and Duties of Man or the American Convention on Human Rights, depending upon whether or not the state is a party to the Convention. The draft report is then submitted to that country's government for its comments. The government's response is analyzed by the Commission to determine whether the report should be amended in light of the information brought to its attention by the government.

After reassessing its findings, the Commission decides whether to publish the report. Its Rules require the publication of the report if the government does not respond to the request for observations (Art. 60). The Commission does not have to publish the report, however, if the government either agrees to comply with the recommendations or demonstrates that it is not committing any violations.

In addition to publishing the report, the IACHR may also transmit it to the OAS General Assembly. Because debates in the Assembly attract considerable public attention, reference to and discussion by the Assembly of a country report, followed by an appropriate resolution, can have a significant impact on the behavior of a government that has been charged by the Commission with human rights violations.

Although OAS General Assembly resolutions are not legally binding, they are acts emanating from the highest political organ of the Organization and, consequently, carry considerable moral and political weight. Governments tend to take these considerations into account before they decide how to react to recommendations made by the Commission in its country studies. Ultimately, as in all efforts to enforce internationally guaranteed human rights, the effectiveness of the Commission's country-study practice depends on the Commission's prestige and credibility, on the public opinion pressure its recommendations are likely to generate, and on the resolutions that the OAS General Assembly is willing to adopt in support of the Commission.

The General Assembly has tended to adopt "boilerplate" resolutions that fail to fully address the recommendations of the Commission based on its country reports. These resolutions are often drafted in such a way as either to disguise the names of the countries that were the subjects of these reports or to name them without taking note of the charges against them. *See, e.g.*, AG/Res. 1269 (XXIV–O/94), OAS Gen. Ass. Doc. OEA/Ser.P./XX.O.2, vol. 1, at 75 (1994); AG/Res. 1213 (XXIII–O/93), OAS Gen. Ass. Doc. OEA/Ser.P/XXIII.O.2, vol. 1, at 31 (1993).

2. Individual Petitions

Prior to the entry into force of the American Convention, the Commission examined and acted formally on only those private communications that alleged a violation of one of the "preferred" freedoms enumerated in Article 9(*bis*) of its old Statute. *See* § 4–4, *supra*. This practice changed with the promulgation of its current Statute. The Commission's Rules no longer distinguish between the "preferred freedoms" and other rights proclaimed in the American Declaration. Instead, they establish a procedure, based on Article 20 of the Statute, that allows the IACHR to receive and act on individual petitions charging a violation of any of the rights enumerated in the Declaration. *See* the Commission's 2013 Rules, arts. 51–52.

The Commission processes these petitions in the same way as the private communications it receives under the Convention. *See* § 4–9, *infra*. The two types of petitions are treated differently only after the conclusion of the proceedings before the Commission, because petitions brought under the Charter-based system cannot be referred to the Court. The petition process applicable to states not parties to the Convention concludes with a "final report." This report usually contains findings of facts and the Commission's conclusions and recommendations. The Commission may publish the report as a separate document and/or include it in the Commission's annual report to the OAS General Assembly.

This Charter-based individual petition system is plagued by several weaknesses. The first has to do with the multiple functions the IACHR must perform coupled with its sitting as a part-time body. In 2023, it reported receiving over 2,500 complaints but only met in person for about six weeks during the year. Many petitions remain in the system for many years before a decision is reached on the merits. The second problem has to do with the fact that, because the petitions are directed against states which are not parties to the Convention, the Court has no contentious jurisdiction to address them. Third, although the Commission transmits its decisions in these cases to the General Assembly, this body has shown little interest in dealing with individual petitions. Non-compliance by states with the decisions of the Commission in these cases consequently attracts little notice and thus deprives the system of effectiveness.

In order to mitigate these problems, the Commission has instituted a follow-up procedure. Commission Rules, art. 48. After the Commission has adopted recommendations or achieved a friendly settlement in a case, it may adopt the follow-up measures it deems appropriate, including holding hearings, to verify compliance with the recommendations or the terms of the settlement. Reports on compliance are included in each Annual Report of the Commission.

3. Precautionary Measures

Like all other human rights bodies, the IACHR has exercised an implied power to request states to take measures to protect those threatened with imminent and irreparable harm. It has established a mechanism to decide on such precautionary measures in Article 25 of its Rules of Procedure. Article 25 provides that, in serious and urgent situations, the Commission may, on its own initiative or at the request of a party, request that a state adopt precautionary measures to prevent irreparable harm to persons or to the subject matter of the proceedings in connection with a pending petition or case, as well as to persons under the jurisdiction of the State concerned, independently of any pending petition or case.

The number of precautionary measures granted does not reflect the number of persons protected by their adoption; as can be seen below, many of the precautionary measures issued by the Commission protect more than one person and, in certain cases, groups of persons such as communities of indigenous peoples.

The Rules of Procedure establish that the granting of such measures and their adoption by the state shall not constitute a prejudgment on any alleged violation of human rights. The 2013 amendments added that "the decisions granting, extending, modifying or lifting precautionary measures shall be adopted through reasoned resolutions. . . ."

Precautionary or interim measures have proven controversial in some instances for several reasons. First, the power to request them is implied rather than expressly mentioned by the treaties. Second, such measures have sometimes extended to large groups of people in the context of an armed conflict, making compliance with them difficult; other measures have been issued to halt large development projects the state has approved and have been politically unpopular. Third, the Commission, like other human rights bodies, takes the position that at least some requests are legally binding. Many states disagree and some have sought to restrict the power of the Commission to issue such measures.

For example, when the Commission in 2011 requested precautionary measures for the members of 11 indigenous communities believed to be at risk from the construction of the Belo Monte ("Kararaô") hydroelectric power project on the Xingu River in the state of Pará, Brazil called the request "precipitous and unwarranted," severed formal relations with the Commission, recalled its OAS ambassador, and froze its annual $800,000 contribution to the IACHR in protest. PM382/10—Indigenous Communities of the Xingu River Basin, Para, Brazil.

However, it is noteworthy that states have acceded to the Commission's power to issue precautionary measures in some cases, such as in cases of forced disappearance. *See* IA Convention on Forced Disappearance of Persons, art. XIII. The Commission also has the express power under the Convention to request the Court to grant provisional measures. *See* § 4–13 below.

III. THE CONVENTION-BASED SYSTEM

§ 4–6. INTRODUCTION

The American Convention on Human Rights was opened for signature on November 20, 1969, at an Inter-American diplomatic conference held in San

José, Costa Rica. It entered into force on July 18, 1978, and as of 2024 has 24 OAS Member States as parties: Argentina, Barbados, Bolivia, Brazil, Chile, Colombia, Costa Rica, Dominica, Dominican Republic, Ecuador, El Salvador, Grenada, Guatemala, Haiti, Honduras, Jamaica, Mexico, Nicaragua, Panama, Paraguay, Perú, Suriname, and Uruguay. Missing from the list are Canada, the United States, and most of the English-speaking Caribbean nations. Trinidad and Tobago denounced the Convention effective in 1999 and Venezuela did so in 2012 but re-joined in 2019. The United States has signed the Convention and President Jimmy Carter referred it to the Senate for its advice and consent to ratification, but the Senate did not act on the request and subsequent administrations have failed to renew it. *See* § 6–3, *infra*.

The ratification record of OAS Member States reveals the cultural, linguistic and juridical split that exists in the OAS between Latin America, where all countries except Venezuela and Cuba are parties to the Convention, and the English-speaking north, where few countries have adhered. This record (and the division between civil-law and common-law systems) has affected the composition of the Court and its resulting jurisprudence. It also has brought criticism of the non-party states, with some Convention States Parties submitting proposals to move the headquarters of the Commission away from Washington, D.C., or to ban non-parties from nominating individuals for election to the Commission.

Two protocols supplement the Convention: the Additional Protocol to the American Convention on Human Rights in the Area of Economic, Social and Cultural Rights ("Protocol of San Salvador"), which entered into force in 1999, and the Protocol to the American Convention on Human Rights to Abolish the Death Penalty, which entered into force in 1993. As of 2024, the 18 parties to the San Salvador Protocol are: Argentina, Bolivia, Brazil, Chile, Colombia, Costa Rica, Ecuador, El Salvador, Guatemala, Honduras, Mexico, Nicaragua, Panama, Paraguay, Perú, Suriname, Uruguay, and Venezuela. The latter protocol has been ratified by Argentina, Brazil, Chile, Costa Rica, Ecuador, Honduras, Mexico, Nicaragua, Panama, Paraguay, Dominican Republic, Uruguay and Venezuela.

§ 4–7. THE CONVENTION AND ITS GUARANTEES

The Convention recognizes some two dozen categories of civil and political rights. These include the following: the right to juridical personality, right to life, right to humane treatment, freedom from slavery, right to personal liberty, right to a fair trial, freedom from ex post facto laws, right to compensation for miscarriage of justice, right to privacy, freedom of conscience and religion, freedom of thought and expression, right of reply, right of assembly, freedom of association, rights of the family, right to a name, rights of the child, right to nationality, right to property, freedom of movement and residence, right to participate in government, right to equal protection of the law, and right to judicial protection.

While article 4 of the Convention permits a state to retain capital punishment for the most serious crimes, the Inter-American Court has held that a law which provides for a mandatory death penalty without a judicial determination of mitigating or aggravating circumstances is contrary to the Convention. Case of Hilaire, Constantine and Benjamin et al. v. Trinidad and Tobago, Judgment of June 21, 2002, IA Ct.H.R., Series C: Judgments and Decisions, No. 94 (2002); Case of Raxcaco Reyes v. Guatemala, Judgement of September 15, 2005, *id.* No. 133; Case of Boyce et al. v. Barbados, Judgment of November 20, 2007, *id.* No. 169 (2007). The Commission and Court both take a strict view of the guarantees afforded in sentencing and the Commission in particular has promoted abolition of the death penalty. *See* IACHR, The Death Penalty in the Inter-American Human Rights System: From Restrictions to Abolition, OEA/Ser.L/V/II, Doc. 68 (2011).

The Convention's protections are reinforced by a broad non-discrimination clause and by the obligation of the States Parties to adjust their domestic laws to guarantee the rights enshrined in the Convention and to make the laws effective. This means repealing rules and practices that violate the Convention or hamper the exercise of the rights recognized therein, as well as developing new rules and practices to ensure effective observance of the rights.

The Convention also contains an undertaking by the States Parties to take progressive measures for "the full realization of the rights implicit in the economic, social, educational, scientific, and cultural standards set forth in the Charter of the Organization of American States as amended by the Protocol of Buenos Aires." (Art. 26.) This pledge is amplified by the additional catalog of rights set out in the Protocol of San Salvador, which proclaims the right to work, to unionize and to strike, the right to social security and to health, and the right to a healthy environment, to food and to education. The Protocol sets out additional rights, including the right to the benefits of culture and to the protection of the family, as well as the rights of children, the elderly and the handicapped. However, only trade union freedoms and the right to education are explicitly subject to the petition procedure.

Whether Convention art. 26 allows complaints to be brought alleging violations of economic, social and cultural rights is a matter of considerable debate, resulting from the uncertain interaction of the American Declaration, Convention arts. 26 and 29, and the Protocol on Economic and Social Rights. The Court itself has been cautious but has addressed social and economic rights where these have been presented in the context of cases involving discrimination, indigenous peoples, and property. *See* Acevedo Buendía v. Perú, IA Ct.H.R., Judgment of July 1, 2009, Series C No. 198 (2009), paras. 92–107 (right to social security).

Article 1(2) declares that the term "person" as used in the Convention means "human being." Corporations and other juridical persons are thus not the intended beneficiaries of the rights the Convention guarantees. The States Parties to the Convention have an obligation not only "to respect" the rights guaranteed in the Convention, but also "to ensure" their free and full exercise. Art.1(1). They consequently have both positive and negative duties, that is, they have the obligation not to violate the rights which the Convention guarantees and are required to adopt whatever measures may be necessary and reasonable under the circumstances "to ensure" their full enjoyment. For an extensive interpretation of the obligations states have under Article 1 of the Convention, *see* Velásquez Rodríguez Case, IA Ct.H.R., Judgment of July 29, 1988, Series C: Decisions and Judgments, No. 4, paras. 159 *et seq.* (1988).

Article 27 of the Convention allows the States Parties to derogate from their obligations "in time of war, public danger, or other emergency that threatens [their] independence or security." Derogation is not permitted, however, from the protections of the more basic human rights which the Convention guarantees. The catalog of non-derogable rights is longer than that of the European Convention of Human Rights and the International Covenant on Civil and Political Rights. Unlike these treaties, the American Convention also declares that "the judicial guarantees essential for the protection" of the non-derogable rights may not be suspended. On this subject, *see* Advisory Opinion OC–8/87, IA

Ct.H.R., Series A: Judgments and Opinions, No. 8 (1987); Advisory Opinion, OC–1987, IA Ct.H.R., Series A: Judgments and Decisions, No. 9 (1987).

The rights proclaimed in the Protocol of San Salvador may however be restricted "by means of laws promulgated for the purpose of preserving the general welfare in a democratic society only to the extent that they are not incompatible with the purpose and reason underlying these rights." Art. 5. The Protocol Abolishing the Death Penalty does not contain a derogation clause. It bars general reservations but provides that "at the time of ratification or accession, the States Parties to this instrument may declare that they reserve the right to apply the death penalty in wartime in accordance with international law, for extremely serious crimes of a military nature." Art. 2.1.

The Convention also contains a so-called "federal state clause," which enables a federal state to assume more limited obligations by binding itself only in relation to matters over which it "exercises legislative and judicial jurisdiction." Art. 28. This provision was included in the Convention at the urging of the U.S. delegation to the San José Conference, which argued that the clause was needed to enable the U.S. to become a party to the Convention.

§ 4–8. THE CONVENTION ORGANS

The Convention provides for the establishment of the Inter-American Commission on Human Rights (IACHR) and the Inter-American Court of Human

Rights (IA Ct.H.R.) and confers on them "competence with respect to matters relating to the fulfillment of the commitments made by the States Parties" thereto. Art. 33. In addition, the Protocol of San Salvador empowers the Commission to formulate observations and make recommendations on economic, social, and cultural rights in the States Parties. Art.19(7).

The Commission and the Court consist of seven members each, elected in their personal capacities. The members of the Commission are elected by all OAS Member States, but only the States Parties to the Convention may nominate the judges of the Court and vote on their election. Since the Commission, unlike the Court, is both a Convention and an OAS Charter organ, *see* § 4–4, *supra,* all OAS Member States, whether or not they have ratified the Convention, have a right to vote in the selection of the Commissioners. The Commission has its seat at the headquarters of the OAS in Washington, D.C.; the Court sits in San José, Costa Rica. Membership on the Court and Commission is not a full-time position; both institutions have small permanent professional staffs.

IV. THE INTER-AMERICAN COMMISSION ON HUMAN RIGHTS

§ 4–9. THE COMMISSION AS CONVENTION ORGAN

The functions of the Inter-American Human Rights Commission (IACHR) are spelled out in

Article 41 of the Convention, which codifies the Commission's preexisting functions as an OAS organ, *see* § 4–4, *supra,* and mandates it "to take action on petitions and other communications pursuant to its authority under the provisions of Articles 44 through 51 of this Convention." Art. 41(f). These provisions apply only to the States Parties to the Convention and relate to the petition system it establishes. It should not be confused with the petition system the Commission administers as an OAS Charter organ. *See* § 4–5, *supra.*

1. Examination of Petitions

The Convention empowers the Commission to deal with individual petitions and inter-state communications. Arts. 44 and 45. By becoming a party to the Convention, a state is deemed to have accepted the IACHR's jurisdiction to examine private complaints lodged against that state. Art. 44. The Commission may also address inter-state complaints—complaints filed by one State Party against another—but only if both states, in addition to ratifying the Convention, have also recognized the inter-state jurisdiction of the Commission. Art. 45.

In adopting this approach, the American Convention departs from the more traditional scheme utilized by the European Convention, for example, which initially established an optional individual petition system and a mandatory inter-state complaint procedure. *See* Chapter 3, *supra.* Moreover, unlike some other human rights treaties, the American Convention does not limit the right to file private petitions to victims only; any person or group of persons and nongovernmental organizations may also do so. Art. 44.

The admissibility of a petition is conditioned, *inter alia,* on (1) the exhaustion of domestic remedies "in accordance with the generally recognized principles of international law;" and (2) the requirement that the petition be submitted to the Commission within a period of six months from the date on which the victim of the alleged violation was notified of the final domestic judgment in his case. Art. 46(1). These requirements do not defeat the admissibility of a petition, however, if (1) there exist no domestic remedies to protect against the violation of the rights at issue; (2) there has been a denial of access to or interference with recourse to the applicable domestic remedies; or (3) the domestic remedies have been subjected to unwarranted delay. Art. 46(2).

The Inter-American Court of Human Rights interpreted the requirement for the exhaustion of domestic remedies in a number of its early cases and advisory opinions, including *inter alia,* Godínez (Preliminary Exceptions), IA Ct.H.R., Series C: Judgments and Decisions, No. 3, paras. 81 et seq. (1987); Advisory Opinion OC–11/90, *id.*, Series A: Judgments and Opinions (1992). The Commission's rules of procedure provide, moreover, that the respondent government has the burden of demonstrating the non-exhaustion of domestic remedies if it invokes that objection and if the complaint alleges that compliance with that requirement was impossible. Commission Rules, art.

31(3). This proposition is consistent with the Court's case law on the subject. *See, e.g.*, Fairen Garbi Case (Preliminary Objections), IA Ct.H.R., Series C: Decisions and Judgments, No. 2, para. 87 (1987).

A complaint will also be held inadmissible if it does not state a *prima facie* case under the Convention or if it is otherwise "manifestly groundless or obviously out of order." Art. 47(b) and (c). The petition must provide an account of the fact or situation that is denounced, specifying the place and date of the alleged violations and, if possible, the name of the victim and of any public authority who has taken cognizance of the fact or situation alleged. Commission Rules, art. 28. These facts are the basis for assessment of admissibility; the petitioner does not need to characterize the consequences by specifying which provisions of the American Convention on Human Rights or another applicable instrument has been violated. The Commission and Court both determine which rights are implicated by the facts alleged, using the principle *jura novit curia* (according to which courts have authority to find different violations from those alleged by the applicants).

Article 47(d) of the Convention requires the Commission to reject a petition that "is substantially the same as one previously studied by the Commission or by another international organization." This provision complements Article 46(1)(c), which conditions admissibility on the requirement "that the subject of the petition or communication is not pending in another international proceeding of settlement." The Commission and Court interpret these last two requirements in a manner designed to ensure that a complaint will not be rejected when the other international organization, although seized of the matter in general, is or was in no position to grant petitioners the specific relief they seek from the Commission. Commission Rules, art. 32(2); Case of the Saramaka People v. Suriname, Judgment of November 28, 2007, IA Ct.H. R., Series C: Judgments and Opinions, No. 172 (2007).

For the manner in which the Court has resolved various admissibility issues, *see* Velásquez Rodríguez Case (Preliminary Objections), IA Ct.H. R., Series C: Decisions and Judgments, No. 1 (1987); Neira Alegría Case (Preliminary Objections), IA Ct.H.R., Series C: Decisions and Judgments, No. 13 (1991); Cayara Case (Preliminary Objections), IA Ct.H.R., Series C: Decisions and Judgments, No. 14 (1993); Caballero Delgado Case (Preliminary Objections), IA Ct.H.R., Series C: Decisions and Judgments, No. 17 (1994).

When the Commission receives a petition which meets, in principle, the requirements established in the Convention, the Commission assigns a number to that petition and begins to process it as a case, without prejudice to the Commission's eventual decision on admissibility. The pertinent parts of the petition are sent to the Government with a request for relevant information. Each party submits pleadings, but the Commission also may carry out its own investigations, including conducting on-site visits, or holding a hearing in which the government and the petitioners participate.

The Commission must also offer to "place itself at the disposal of the parties concerned with a view to reaching a friendly settlement of the matter on the basis of respect for the human rights recognized" in the Convention. Art. 48(1)(f). If a friendly settlement is reached, the Commission prepares a report that describes the facts of the case and the settlement. Art. 49. For a precedent-setting friendly settlement that the Commission negotiated with the Government of Argentina, *see* Report No. 1/93, IACHR, *Annual Report 1992–93*, OAS/Ser.L.V./II.83, Doc. 14, at 35 (1993).

If the parties are unable to reach a friendly settlement, the Commission draws up a report, setting out the facts and the conclusions it has reached about the case. Art. 50. For a finding that no violation of the Convention was committed, *see* Report No. 2/92 (Case 10.289/Costa Rica), IACHR, *Annual Report 1991*, OEA/Ser.L/V/II.8 Doc. 6 rev. 1, at 73 (1992). A report containing a finding that a violation has been committed normally includes whatever recommendations the Commission wishes to make and is transmitted to the state concerned. The state has three months within which to comply with or react to the recommendations of the Commission.

The Convention provides that during that period, the case may also be referred to the Inter-American Court of Human Rights by the Commission or the interested states. *See* § 4–11, *infra*. In the past, the

Commission made that decision on a case-by-case basis, but its Rules of Procedure since 2001 have required the Commission to refer to the Court all cases of non-compliance by States that have accepted the Court's jurisdiction unless the Commission decides otherwise by an absolute majority vote. Commission Rules, art. 45.

Although individuals do not have standing to refer cases to the Court, the Commission's Rules of Procedure give the petitioner the right to be heard on that subject by the Commission. Art.44(3). *See* § 4–11, *infra*. An addition to the 2013 Rules of Procedure now governs the increasingly frequent requests from states to allow more time for compliance with the Commission's recommendations before a decision is taken to refer the case to the Court. Commission Rules, art. 46. The state must show its willingness and ability to implement the recommendations included in the merits report through the adoption of concrete and adequate measures of compliance and must irrevocably waive any right to file a preliminary objection with the Court about the failure to submit the case within three months.

In dealing with a case that has not been referred to the Court or settled by the parties, the Convention provides that "the Commission may, by the vote of an absolute majority of its members, set forth its opinion and conclusions concerning the question submitted for its consideration." Art. 51(1). If it has concluded that the Convention was violated, the Commission must set out its "recommendations," if any, and "prescribe a period within which the state is to take the measures that are incumbent upon it to remedy the situation examined." Art. 51(2). Once this period has expired it "shall decide by a vote of an absolute majority of its members whether the state has taken adequate measures and whether to publish its report." Art. 51(3). *See, e.g.*, Report No. 32/92 (Case 10.454/Colombia), IACHR, *Annual Report 1992–93*, OEA/Ser.L/V/II.83/Doc. 14, at 52 (1993). For a discussion of the relationship between Articles 50 and 51, *see* Advisory Opinion OC–13, IA Ct.H.R., Series A: Judgments and Opinions, No. 13 (1993); Caballero Delgado Case (Preliminary Objections), IA Ct.H.R., Series C: Decisions and Judgments, No. 17 (1994).

The Commission may deal with inter-state communications only if the applicant and respondent states have recognized its jurisdiction to receive such complaints. Art. 45. Jurisdiction may be accepted on an *ad hoc* basis for a specific case or in general. A number of States Parties to the Convention have made the requisite general declaration. The admissibility requirements and procedures for addressing inter-state applications are in all respects the same as those that are prescribed for individual petitions.

A ruling by the Commission that a petition is inadmissible is a quasi-judicial decision, which is final and not subject to appeal. The Convention is silent on the legal effect of an opinion of the Commission rendered pursuant to Article 51 holding that a state has violated the Convention. Although this decision is not formally binding (as is a judgment of the Court), it is a legal determination by a body to which the Convention assigns "competence . . . relating to the fulfillment" of the obligations assumed by the States Parties. The Commission's findings under Article 51 may thus be regarded as an authoritative ruling that a State Party has violated its treaty obligation.

2. Role Before the Court

The Convention gives the Commission standing to refer cases to the Court and provides, in addition, that "the Commission shall appear in all cases before the Court." Arts. 61 and 57. The quoted language mandates the participation of the Commission in all contentious proceedings before the Court, whether or not they originated as private petitions or as actions by one state against another. The Commission is thus more than a mere party in proceedings before the Court. Even when the Commission refers a case to the Court, it is deemed to do so not on its own behalf, but on behalf of an individual or a state.

The Commission need not, moreover, adopt the contentions of the victim or state whose case it has referred to the Court. When the Commission appears before the Court, it does so not as "party" but as "the 'Ministerio Público' of the inter-American system." In the Matter of Viviana Gallardo, Case No. G 101/81, Decision of Nov. 13, 1981, IA Ct.H.R., Series A: Judgments and Opinions 77, at para. 22 (1984). The Court's reference to the Latin American legal institution known as "ministerio público" was designed to make clear that the Commission appears before the Court as protector of the legal order established by the Convention. Its function before the Court, in short, is to promote the legal and institutional integrity of the Convention system.

The Commission also has standing to request advisory opinions from the Court. *See* § 4–14, *infra*. Moreover, the provisional measures that the Court has power to enter, § 4–13, *infra,* may be granted only "at the request of the Commission." Convention, art. 63(2). Thus, in addition to the multitude of promotional and protective functions the Commission performs, it also plays an important role in assisting the Court in discharging its judicial responsibilities. The Commission's Annual Reports as a rule include a chapter or subchapter entitled "Activities of the IACHR in connection with the Inter-American Court of Human Rights," which reports on pending cases, requests for provisional measures, advisory opinion requests, and the Commission's role relating thereto.

V. THE INTER-AMERICAN COURT OF HUMAN RIGHTS

§ 4–10. JURISDICTION OF THE COURT

The Court has contentious jurisdiction, that is, jurisdiction to adjudicate cases involving charges that a State Party has violated the Convention. It also has jurisdiction to render advisory opinions interpreting the Convention and certain other human rights treaties. Although the Convention is silent on the topic of participation in cases, the Court

Rules provide in article 19 that a judge may not sit on an individual case coming from the state of which the judge is a national. The Convention and Rules provide for the appointment of an *ad hoc* judge in inter-state cases if no national of a party to the case is a judge on the Court. Convention art. 45; Rules, art. 20.

§ 4–11. CONTENTIOUS JURISDICTION

Article 62 of the Convention delimits the Court's contentious jurisdiction as follows:

> 1. A State Party may, upon depositing its instruments of ratification or adherence to this Convention, or at any subsequent time, declare that it recognizes as binding, *ipso facto,* and not requiring special agreement, the jurisdiction of the Court on all matters relating to the interpretation or application of this Convention.
>
> 2. Such declaration may be made unconditionally, on the condition of reciprocity, for a specified period, or for specific cases. It shall be presented to the Secretary General of the Organization, who shall transmit copies thereof to the other member states of the Organization and to the Secretary of the Court.
>
> 3. The jurisdiction of the Court shall comprise all cases concerning the interpretation and application of the provisions of this Convention that are submitted to it, provided that the States Parties to the case recognize or have recognized such jurisdiction, whether by special declaration

pursuant to the preceding paragraphs, or by a special agreement.

This provision indicates that a State Party does not accept the contentious jurisdiction of the Court merely by ratifying the Convention. To do so, it must either have filed the declarations referred to in paragraphs 1 and 2 of Article 62 or have concluded the special agreement mentioned in paragraph 3. General declarations accepting the Court's jurisdiction have been made by a majority of the States Parties to the Convention. *See https://www.oas.org/dil/treaties_B-32_American_Convention_on_Human_Rights_sign.htm#Dominican%20 Republic.*

The Convention specifies in Article 61(1) that "only the States Parties and the Commission shall have the right to submit a case to the Court." Individuals consequently do not have the right to refer a case to the Court. However, the Court's Rules of Procedure give alleged victims and their representatives standing to participate in their own right in the proceedings once the case has been submitted to the Court. Arts. 2 and 25. The victims or their next of kin thus can file briefs, submit arguments and evidence independently of those filed by the Commission and even present claims inconsistent with those of the Commission. They may not, however, allege new facts distinct from those presented in the application to the Court, unless they are supervening facts. *See* Five Pensioners v. Perú, Judgment of February 28, 2003, IA Ct.H.R., Series C No. 98, para. 150–157. In 2010, the Court established a Legal Assistance Fund of the Inter-American Human Rights System to assist victims with the costs of litigation.

Before a case may be referred to the Court, the relevant Commission proceedings applicable to it must be "completed." Art. 61(2). In the Gallardo case, the first contentious case to come before the Court, the government of Costa Rica sought to waive the proceedings before the Commission and take the matter directly to the tribunal. The Court held that it lacked jurisdiction to entertain the case until the Commission had dealt with it, emphasizing that the proceedings before the Commission "have not been created for the sole benefit of the States, but also in order to allow for the exercise of important individual rights, especially those of the victims." In the Matter of Viviana Gallardo, Case No. Gl/01/81, Decision of Nov. 13, 1981, IA Ct.H.R., Series A: Judgments and Opinions, at para. 25 (1984). The Court's concern here was that individuals, unlike a State Party, had no formal standing in the Court, whereas they do in proceedings before the Commission. This consideration would give the state a significant advantage if it were to be permitted to bypass the Commission.

The rule set forth in Article 61(1) that "only the States Parties and the Commission shall have the right to submit a case to the Court," requires further explanation. First, Article 62(3) indicates that a case may only be taken to the Court by one state against another state if both have accepted the Court's jurisdiction. Second, Article 62(2) permits the States Parties to accept that jurisdiction "on the condition of reciprocity," and a number of states have done so. A state that has made such a declaration cannot be taken to the Court by a State Party that has not accepted the tribunal's jurisdiction. However, even if a state has accepted the Court's jurisdiction subject to reciprocity, this reservation cannot deprive the Commission of the right to take the matter to the Court if the case grew out of an individual petition rather than an inter-state complaint. This conclusion finds support in the Court's holding regarding the limited applicability of the principle of reciprocity to human rights treaties. Advisory Opinion OC–2, IA Ct.H.R., Series A: Judgments and Opinions, No. 2 (1982). Finally, Article 61(1) does not say whether it permits all States Parties to refer any case to the Court or only the cases in which the applicant states were parties in the proceedings before the Commission.

§ 4–12. THE COURT'S POWERS IN CONTENTIOUS CASES

Once a case has been referred to the Court, it has the power to fully review the Commission's findings of fact and law. *See, e.g.*, Velásquez Rodríguez v. Honduras (Preliminary Objections), IA Ct.H.R., Series C: Decisions and Judgments No. 1, para. 84; Ituango Massacres v. Colombia, *supra*, No. 148 (2006) (determination of victims). The Court has the power also to hear any challenges to its jurisdiction based on non-compliance by the Commission with the procedures set out in Articles 48 to 50 of the Convention and any other relevant provisions thereof. *See, e.g.*, Godínez Cruz Case (Preliminary

Objections), *supra,* No. 3 (1987). This means, for example, that the Commission's finding that the petitioner has exhausted all available domestic remedies, as required by Article 46 of the Convention, may also be reviewed. Fairen Garbi Case (Preliminary Objections), *supra*, No. 2 (1987); Neira Alegría Case (Preliminary Objections), *supra*, No. 13 (1991).

The Inter-American Court liberally applies the doctrine *jura novit curia,* according to which courts have authority to find different violations from those alleged by the applicants. *See* Ituango Massacres Case, *supra*, para. 191; Case of Bueno-Alves v. Argentina, Judgment of May 11, 2007, *supra*, No. 164 (2007), para. 70. Also, the Inter-American Court will often find violations of several rights based on the same facts. *See* Ricardo Canese Case, Judgment of August 31, 2004, IA Ct.H.R., Series C: Decisions and Judgments, No. 111 (2004) (holding that restrictions on a politician's travel abroad resulting from a slander conviction violated both freedom of expression and freedom of movement). *But see* García Asto and Ramirez Rojas Case, Judgment of November 25, 2005, IA Ct.H.R., Series C: Decisions and Judgments, No. 137 (2005).

Article 67 of the Convention provides that the judgment rendered by the Court is "final and not subject to appeal." *See* Castillo Petruzzi Case, Order of November 17, 1999 (Compliance with Judgment), IA Ct.H.R., Series C: Decisions and Judgments, No. 59 (2000). The same provision also authorizes the Court to interpret its judgments if there is a disagreement as to its "meaning or scope." As the Court's judgments and reparations orders have become more complex, states are increasingly filing requests for interpretation. The "States Parties to the Convention undertake to comply with the judgment of the Court in any case to which they are parties." Art. 68(1). For an interpretation of this provision, *see* Castillo Petruzzi Case (Compliance with Judgment), *supra*.

The types of judgments that the Court may render and the manner in which they are to be enforced are spelled out in two provisions of the Convention. The first is Article 63(1), which reads as follows:

> If the Court finds that there has been a violation of a right or freedom protected by this Convention, the Court shall rule that the injured party be ensured the enjoyment of his right or freedom that was violated. It shall also rule, if appropriate, that the consequences of the measure or situation that constituted the breach of such right or freedom be remedied, and that fair compensation be paid to the injured party.

The Court is, consequently, empowered to award money damages and render declaratory judgments. The latter may specify not only what rights have been violated, but also how the state should remedy the violation. *See* Loayza Tamayo Case (Reparations), Judgment of November 27, 1998, IA Ct.H.R., Series C: Decisions and Judgments, No.42 (2000), as well as the concurring opinion thereto by Judge Oliver Jackman. Over time, the Court has moved towards ordering various structural reforms of domestic institutions in order to prevent repetition of the violations found and has insisted on the obligation of domestic courts to apply the Convention.

The second provision is Article 68(2), which deals with money damages. It provides that the "part of a judgment that stipulates compensatory damages may be executed in the country concerned in accordance with domestic procedures governing the execution of judgments against the state." The language of Article 68(2) suggests that the States Parties are not required to establish a mechanism for the domestic execution of the Court's money judgments; it merely permits them to do so.

By contrast, Article 27 of the headquarters agreement between the Court and the Government of Costa Rica provides that the Court's judgments shall be enforced in Costa Rica as if they were domestic judgments. For the text, IA Ct.H.R., *Annual Report 1981*, OEA/Ser.L/III.5, Doc. 13, at 16 (1981). Some OAS Member States have legislation on their books that provide for the domestic enforcement of money judgments rendered against them by international human rights institutions whose jurisdiction these states have accepted. It is unclear how and to what extent these laws have been given effect.

The Convention does not establish any specific mechanism to supervise the enforcement of the Court's judgments. The Court itself has taken on compliance monitoring as an inherent exercise of its jurisdictional powers supported by Convention arts. 33, 62(1), 62(3) and 65 as well as Article 30 of the Court's Statute. The procedure is regulated in Article

69 of the Court's Rules. Its purpose is to ensure that the reparations ordered by the Court in each specific case are implemented.

Monitoring compliance involves periodic requests for information from each state on the measures taken to comply with the judgments against it, along with the observations of the Commission and of the victims or their representatives. The Court makes an assessment of the information and may provide further guidance to the state and, if appropriate, convenes a monitoring hearing. During such hearings, the Court seeks collaboration between the parties to suggest options to resolve difficulties, calls attention to any perceived lack of willingness to comply, and promotes the establishment of timetables for compliance.

The recourse to hearings has been supported by the OAS General Assembly in a resolution which recognized "that the private hearings held on the monitoring of compliance with the Court's judgments have been important and constructive and have yielded positive results." OAS General Assembly Resolution No. AG/RES.2759 (XLII–0/12). The Court has gone further and adopted the practice of holding joint hearings to monitor compliance with the judgments in several cases against the same state, when similar reparations have been ordered, or in cases in which it has verified the existence of structural difficulties or problems that could hinder implementation of reparations measures.

In 2015, the Court began holding hearings on monitoring compliance in the territory of the states and making on-site visits. On August 28, 2015, the Court held a hearing in Honduras on monitoring compliance with the judgments in the cases of Juan Humberto Sánchez, López Álvarez, Servellón García et al., Kawas Fernández, Pacheco Teruel et al., and Luna López, IA Ct.H.R., Series C: Decisions and Judgments No. 102 (2003). Later, the Court held a hearing in Panama on monitoring compliance in the case of the Kuna Indigenous Peoples of Madungandí and the Emberá Indigenous Peoples of Bayano and their members v. Panama, IA Ct.H.R., Series C: Decisions and Judgments No. 284 (2014). In addition, the Court conducted its first on-site visit to Panamanian territory in the context of the compliance monitoring in this case.

Article 65 of the Convention also has a bearing on the subject of compliance. It reads as follows:

> To each regular session of the General Assembly of the Organization of American States the Court shall submit, for the Assembly's consideration, a report on its work during the previous year. It shall specify, in particular, the cases in which a state has not complied with its judgments, making any pertinent recommendations.

This provision requires the Court to inform the OAS General Assembly of situations involving non-compliance with its decisions, thus permitting the Assembly to discuss the matter and to take whatever political measures it deems appropriate. Although the Assembly lacks the power to adopt resolutions that are legally binding on the Member States, condemnatory OAS resolutions do carry considerable political weight, which can translate into public opinion pressure.

§ 4–13. PROVISIONAL MEASURES

The American Convention is the only major human rights treaty that expressly authorizes the issuance of provisional or protective measures during or even prior to cases being submitted to it. Article 63(2) of the Convention addresses these so-called provisional measures. It provides that:

> In case of extreme gravity and urgency, and when necessary to avoid irreparable damage to persons, the Court shall adopt such provisional measures as it deems pertinent in matters it has under consideration. With respect to a case not yet submitted to the Court, it may act at the request of the Commission.

This provision permits the Court to grant temporary restraining orders in cases pending before it and in cases that have been lodged with the Commission but not yet referred to the Court.

In the two types of cases that may be brought to it under Article 63(2), the Court has to determine, if only in a preliminary manner, whether it has jurisdiction over the parties. In cases that are already pending before it, this issue will as a practical matter arise only when the request for the order is made before the question of the Court's jurisdiction to hear the case has been settled. But the jurisdictional issue will always have to be examined in those cases that are still being considered by the Commission.

The Court has granted some requests for provisional measures submitted by the parties. The Commission has also requested such measures in matters under its consideration and the Court has granted some, but not all of them.

Three requirements—extreme gravity, urgency and the risk of irreparable harm—have to be demonstrated satisfactorily for the Court to grant these measures. Although the Convention does not expressly address the subject, the Court's practice indicates that it considers the provisional measures issued pursuant to Article 63(3) of the Convention to be binding on the States to which they are addressed. *See, e.g.,* Constitutional Court Case (Provisional Measures), Order of the Inter-American Court of Human Rights of August 14, 2000.

§ 4–14. ADVISORY JURISDICTION

The scope of the Court's advisory jurisdiction is very broad. This power is spelled out in Article 64 of the Convention, which provides:

> 1. The member states of the Organization may consult the Court regarding the interpretation of this Convention or of other treaties concerning the protection of human rights in the American states. Within their spheres of competence, the organs listed in Chapter X [now Chapter VIII] of the Charter of the Organization of American

> States, as amended by the Protocol of Buenos Aires, may in like manner consult the Court.
>
> 2. The Court, at the request of a member state of the Organization, may provide that state with opinions regarding the compatibility of any of its domestic laws with the aforesaid international instruments.

Thus, any OAS Member State, and not only the States Parties to the Convention, have standing to request an advisory opinion. Moreover, the Court's advisory jurisdiction is not limited to interpretations of the Convention; it extends to any other treaty "concerning the protection of human rights in the American states." All OAS organs "within their sphere of competence," including the Inter-American Commission on Human Rights, have standing to request advisory opinions. Under Article 64(2) the Court is also empowered, at the request of any Member State of the OAS, to render advisory opinions determining whether the state's domestic laws are compatible with the Convention or the aforementioned human rights treaties.

Since its establishment in 1979, the Court has rendered a substantial number of advisory opinions, extensively interpreting Article 64. For example, the Court has held that, to satisfy the requirement that an advisory opinion request fall "within their spheres of competence," OAS organs must demonstrate a "legitimate institutional interest" in the subject matter of the request. Advisory Opinion OC–2/82 of Sept. 24, 1982, IA Ct.H.R., Series A: Judgments and Opinions, No. 2 (1982). The Court has also ruled that the phrase "other treaties concerning the protection of human rights in the American states" to which Article 64 refers applies not only to OAS or inter-American treaties, but to any treaty bearing on the enjoyment or enforcement of human rights in a state belonging to the Inter-American system. Advisory Opinion OC–1/82, IA Ct.H.R., Series A: Judgments and Opinions, No. 1 (1982); Advisory Opinion OC–16/99, IA Ct.H.R., Series A: Judgments and Opinions, No.16 (2000).

In interpreting Article 64(2), the Court has held that the reference to "domestic laws" may in certain circumstances be deemed to apply also to proposed or pending legislation and not only to laws already in force. Advisory Opinion OC–4/84, IA Ct.H.R., Series A: Judgments and Opinions, No. 4 (1984). The mere fact that a request for an advisory opinion concerns a matter that is or was once the subject of a contentious proceeding before the Commission will not necessarily result in its rejection by the Court. *See* Advisory Opinion OC–15/97, IA Ct.H.R., Series A: Judgments and Opinions, No.15 (1999).

But where a state appears to have asked for an advisory opinion in order to delay pending contentious proceedings before the Commission, or otherwise to gain an unfair advantage over the private parties in such proceedings, the Court will decline to render the requested advisory opinion. Advisory Opinion OC–12/91, IA Ct.H.R., Series A: Judgments and Opinions, No. 12 (1992). The Court has also held that a state's decision to withdraw its request for an advisory opinion does not divest the

Court of jurisdiction to render the opinion. Advisory Opinion, OC–15/97, *supra*.

In recent years, the pace of requests for advisory opinions has accelerated. In the last few years, the Court has rendered advisory opinions on a variety of issues, notably human rights and the environment, indefinite presidential re-election (triggered by states such as Nicaragua, Honduras, and Bolivia seeking to undermine domestic law barring indefinite election), and denunciation of the OAS Charter (which was animated by Nicaragua's denunciation).

As of mid-2024, two notable advisory opinion requests that were pending involve the climate emergency and human rights as well as the responsibility of firearms companies for interference with the right to life. For a compilation of advisory opinions, *see https://www.corteidh.or.cr/opiniones_consultivas.cfm?lang=en*. This uptick in requests for advisory opinions, which is also happening before the International Court of Justice, may be due to the fact that it is less diplomatically contentious to receive an authoritative judicial opinion by seeking an advisory opinion rather than suing another country.

§ 4–15. LEGAL EFFECT OF ADVISORY OPINIONS

Advisory opinions are not, as such, legally binding. That conclusion is inherent in the concept of advisory opinions. *See* Advisory Opinion OC–3/83, IA Ct.H.R., Series A: Judgments and Opinions, No. 3 (1983). Moreover, the Convention nowhere states that these opinions are binding. Nevertheless, the Court is a "judicial institution whose purpose is the application and interpretation of the American Convention on Human Rights," Statute of the Court, art. 1, and it is an organ having "competence with respect to matters relating to the fulfillment of the commitments by the States Parties to this Convention." Convention, art. 33.

The Court's pronouncements, whether made in a contentious case or advisory opinion, derive their value as legal authority from the Court's character as a judicial institution empowered to interpret and apply that instrument. In short, advisory opinions are not academic exercises; they are judicial pronouncements that could be regarded as authoritative on the legal principles enunciated by them.

What then is the difference between an advisory opinion and a judgment in a contentious case? Since a judgment is binding on the parties to the dispute (Convention, art. 68), a state which does not comply with it in a case to which it was a party violates the specific obligation set out in Article 68. It is also in breach of whatever other provisions of the Convention the Court determined was violated by the state. An advisory opinion, on the other hand, is not binding.

Consequently, the failure of a state to comply with the opinion does not constitute a breach of the Convention. But if a state engages in activities determined by the Court in an advisory opinion to be incompatible with the Convention, the state is on notice of the Court's view that its conduct violates its treaty obligations. This fact will seriously undermine the legitimacy of any legal arguments in conflict with those pronounced in the Court's advisory opinion that the states might assert to justify its position. The Court's Advisory Opinions can also impact international diplomacy when they are cited in diplomatic negotiations. In addition, domestic courts may be influenced by or even cite to the Court's advisory opinions.

§ 4–16. CASE LAW

In recent years, the policy of the Commission has been to refer all contentious cases to the Court that are within its jurisdiction, unless there are compelling reasons not to forward the case. In these judgments, the Court consistently cites to its own precedents, but also often refers to the investigations and decisions of other human rights bodies, including the UN treaty bodies and special procedures, as well as the jurisprudence of the European Court of Human Rights and sometimes the African Commission on Human and Peoples' Rights.

The Court has pronounced some human rights violations to constitute crimes against humanity and some rights to constitute part of *jus cogens*. Case of La Cantuta, Judgment of November 29, 2006, IA Ct.H.R., Series C: Decisions and Judgments, No. 162 (2006) (a systematic pattern or practice of extra-legal executions and forced disappearances a crime against humanity and violation of *jus cogens*); Case of Bueno-Alves v. Argentina, *supra* (prohibition of torture *jus cogens*). The Court has also articulated the "right to know the truth" as a right implicit in the right to justice, guaranteed by Article 8 of the American Convention. Bamaca Velásquez v. Guatemala, IA Ct.H.R., Series C: Decisions and Judgments, No. 70 (2000), paras. 197–202.

During the first decade and a half of its existence, very few contentious cases were referred to the Court. Much of its jurisprudence during that period consisted of a series of important advisory opinions bearing on the interpretation and application of the Convention and international human rights law in general. In one of its first opinions, for example, the Court declared that "modern human rights treaties, in general, and the American Convention in particular, are not multilateral treaties of the traditional type concluded to accomplish the reciprocal exchange of rights for the mutual benefit of the contracting States." Advisory Opinion, OC–2/82, IA Ct.H.R., Series A: Judgments and Opinions, No. 2, para. 29 (1982).

Since the object and purpose of these treaties "is the protection of the basic rights of individual human beings, irrespective of their nationality, both against the State of their nationality and all other contracting States," *id.,* the concept of reciprocity, which plays an important role in the application of traditional treaties, loses much of its relevance in the application of human rights treaties. The Court consequently determined that a state which had ratified the Convention with a reservation did not have to await the acceptance of the reservation by other contracting parties before it could be considered to be a party to the Convention. *Id.,* at para. 40. *See also* The Right to Information on Consular Assistance in the Framework of the Guarantees of the Due Process of Law, Advisory Opinion OC–16/99, IA Ct.H.R., Series A, No. 16 (1999), paras. 114–115. The Court has also insisted that the terms in human rights instruments have an autonomous meaning. The Word "Laws" in Article 30 of the American Convention on Human Rights, Advisory Opinion OC–6/86, IA Ct.H.R. Series A, no. 6 (1986) paras. 19–21; Mayagna (Sumo) Awas Tingni Community v. Nicaragua, IA Ct.H.R., Series C: Decisions and Judgments, No. 79 (2001).

Article 27 of the Convention permits the States Parties, "in time of war, public danger, or other emergency that threatens the independence or security of a State Party," to derogate from some of their treaty obligations. The second paragraph of Article 27 lists the rights which may not be suspended even during such emergencies. The European Convention on Human Rights and the ICCPR have comparable derogation clauses, and the Court has sometimes referred to the jurisprudence of the European Court and Human Rights Committee on the requirements for a lawful derogation and measures taken pursuant thereto. Case of Zambrano Vélez et al. v. Ecuador, Judgment of July 4, 2007, IA Ct.H.R., Series C: Judgments and Decision, No. 166 (2007).

In its Advisory Opinion OC–3/83, IA Ct.H.R., Series A; Judgments and Opinions, No. 3 (1983), the

Court had to interpret the scope of a reservation to Article 4 of the Convention, which addresses the right to life and is one of the non-derogable rights listed in Article 27(2). Although it eventually found that the reservation did not authorize the measures the reserving state had taken, the Court took the position that its inquiry had to start with the question whether the reservation was compatible with the object and purpose of the treaty, which is the test for the validity of reservations under Vienna Convention on the Law of Treaties. Art. 19(c).

Article 27 of the Convention allows the States Parties to suspend, in time of war, public danger, or other emergency that threatens their independence or security, the obligations they assumed by ratifying the Convention, provided that in doing so they do not suspend or derogate from certain basic or essential rights, among them the right to life guaranteed by Article 4. For the Court, it would follow therefrom that a reservation designed to enable a State to suspend any of the non-derogable fundamental rights must be deemed to be incompatible with the object and purpose of the Convention and, consequently, not permitted by it.

The situation would be different if the reservation sought merely to restrict certain aspects of a non-derogable right without depriving the right as a whole of its basic purpose. Since the reservation referred to by the Commission in its submission did not appear to be of a type that is designed to deny the right to life as such, the Court concluded that, to that extent, it could be considered, in principle, as not being incompatible with the object and purpose of the Convention. *Id.*, at para. 61. Apart from its specific holding, the real importance of this opinion derives from the fact that it is the first unambiguous international judicial articulation of the principle that incompatibility and non-derogability are conceptually interrelated.

In another opinion, the Court was asked to interpret the scope of the last phrase of Article 27(2), which prohibits the suspension "of the judicial guarantees essential for the protection" of the rights that are non-derogable. Here, the Court ruled that the right to a writ of habeas corpus and related remedies may not be suspended in emergency situations, even though these rights are not defined as non-derogable rights under Article 27(2). Advisory Opinion OC–8/87, IA Ct.H.R., Series A: Judgments and Opinions, No. 8 (1987).

The Court has also rendered several important opinions dealing with the right to freedom of expression. It ruled that a Costa Rican law, which required journalists to belong to a professional association in order to be licensed to practice their profession, violated the right to freedom of expression guaranteed in Article 13 of the Convention. Advisory Opinion OC–5/85 IA Ct.H.R., Series A: Judgments and Opinions, No. 5 (1985). A second advisory opinion dealt with the scope and nature of the right of reply, which is guaranteed in Article 14 of the Convention. Here the Court explored the delicate balance between the right of reply and freedom of expression. Advisory Opinion OC–7/86, IA Ct.H.R.,

Series A: Judgments and Opinions, No.7, at paras. 24–25 (1986).

In these two opinions as well as in Advisory Opinion OC–6/86, IA Ct.H.R., Series A: Judgments and Opinions, No. 6 (1986), the Court analyzed the interrelationship between representative democracy, the protection of human rights, and the inter-American system. Contentious cases have upheld the Convention's unique provision prohibiting prior censorship as well as condemned blasphemy and defamation laws that unduly restrict criticism of public officials. Case of "The Last Temptation of Christ" (Olmedo-Bustos et al.), *supra*; Case of Kimel v. Argentina, Judgment of May 2, 2008, IA Ct.H.R., Series C: Judgments and Opinions, No. 177 (2007); Case of Moya Chacon et. al v. Costa Rica, Judgment of May 23, 2022, IA Ct. H.R, Series C: Judgments and Opinions, No. 451(2022).

In an advisory opinion rendered in December 1994, the Court ruled that government officials who enforce national laws that violate the Convention themselves incur international responsibility if the execution of these laws also constitutes an international crime. Advisory Opinion OC–14, IA Ct.H.R., Series A; Judgments and Opinions, No. 14 (1995). Though the Court does not have criminal jurisdiction, there is nothing in international law as such that would prevent the States Parties to the Convention from conferring such jurisdiction on the Court by appropriate protocols to that instrument.

In the meantime, the Court has made clear that each State Party to the Convention has a duty to investigate and prosecute individuals who commit human rights violations that are crimes. Any law proclaiming amnesty for perpetrators of international crimes is incompatible with the American Convention and without effect. Barrios Altos Case, IA Ct.H.R., Series C: Judgments and Opinions, No. 75 (2001); La Cantuta Case, *supra*; Almonacid Arellano et. al., IA Ct.H.R., Series C: Judgments and Decisions No. 154 (2006). The Court has also concluded that the principle against double jeopardy would not preclude a second prosecution if the first was dismissed in violation of international law or if the proceeding was not conducted independently or impartially pursuant to due process of law. *See, e.g.,* Case of Gutierrez-Soler, Judgement of September 12, 2005, IA Ct.H.R., Series C: Judgments and Decisions, No. 132 (2005).

Another important pronouncement by the Court is to be found in its Advisory Opinion OC–16/99, IA Ct.H.R., Series A: Judgments and Opinions, No. 16 (2000). Here the Court was asked by Mexico to interpret Article 36 of the Vienna Convention on Consular Relations, which addresses the rights of nationals of the States Parties to the Convention who are detained in the territory of another State Party. The Court ruled, *inter alia*, that the right of the detained aliens to be informed "without delay" of their rights under the Consular Convention was a human right complementing the due process provisions of international human rights treaties, including the ICCPR. The Court also concluded that the right to be informed "without delay" must be understood to mean that the information is to be provided at the time of the alien's arrest or, in any case, before the detainee is required to make a first statement to the authorities. *See also* Case of Chaparro Alvarez and Lap Iníguez v. Ecuador, IA Ct.H.R., Series C: Judgments and Opinions, No. 170 (2007).

Among the most important decisions are the so-called Honduran Disappearance Cases, which constituted the first ever international adjudication of charges implicating a state in a policy of forced disappearances. In the first two of these cases, the Court held Honduras responsible for the disappearances of two Honduran nationals after finding that in the early 1980's there existed in that country a policy of forced disappearances that was tolerated by and imputable to its government. Velásquez Rodríguez Case (Merits), IA Ct.H.R., Series C: Decisions and Judgments, No. 4 (1988); Godínez-Cruz Case (Merits), IA Ct.H.R., Series C: Decisions and Judgments, No. 5 (1989). In the third case, Fairen Garbi and Solis Corrales Case (Merits), IA Ct.H.R., Series C: Decisions and Judgments, No. 6 (1989), the Court found that Honduras' responsibility for the disappearance of two Costa Rican nationals had not been proved.

The abduction, torture and murder of street children by the police and the failure of the respondent state to properly investigate these crimes was dealt with by the Court in the Villagran Morales ("Street Children") Case, Judgment of November 19, 1999, *id.*, No. 63 (2000). In this decision, the Court found the respondent state's conduct in violation not only of the Convention but also of the Inter-American Convention to Prevent and Punish Torture, even though the latter treaty makes no express reference to the Court. In another case, the Court was called upon to address the legal effect of Perú's purported withdrawal of its acceptance of the Court's contentious jurisdiction. It held that Perú could not validly withdraw the acceptance without also denouncing the Convention. Constitutional Court Case (Competence), Judgment of September 24, 1999, *id.*, No. 55 (2000).

The majority of contentious cases considered by the Court have involved forced disappearances, arbitrary executions, and denials of due process. *See, e.g.*, Cesti Hurtado Case, Judgment of September 29, 1999, IA Ct. H.R., Series C: Decisions and Judgments, No. 56 (2000) (military justice, failure to comply with writ of habeas corpus); Castillo Petruzzi Case, Judgment of May 1999, *id.*, No. 52 (2000), and Suárez Rosero Case, Judgment of November 12, 1997, *id.* No. 35 (1999) (numerous due process violations); Blake Case, Judgment of January 24, 1998, *id.*, No. 36 (2000) (forced disappearance and related violations); La Cantuta, *supra* (kidnapping, killings and disappearances).

In such cases, states increasingly admit the facts alleged by claimants or found by the Commission, acquiescing in the claims while continuing to contest some of the legal consequences of the findings. La Cantuta, *supra*; Case of Bueno-Alves v. Argentina, *supra*. In many instances, it appears that the state is seeking to avoid having the court set forth the facts in detail in its judgment, which gives the findings greater credence and visibility. The Court has said that a state's acceptance of responsibility for human rights violations "constitutes an important step" towards concluding the case before it and "for the enforcement of the principles that are consecrated by the American Convention." La Cantuta, *supra*, para. 57; Servellón García et al., para. 77. However, the Court generally finds that the "best protection of human rights" requires a judgment adjudicating issues of fact and all the elements of the merits of the case and the corresponding consequences thereof, as a way of contributing to the preservation of historical memory and as part of the redress of damages suffered by the victims. La Cantuta, *supra*.

A review of the Court's contentious practice indicates that the Court has increasingly had an opportunity to interpret and apply the full range of the due process guarantees the Convention proclaims, making important contributions to the law on that subject. *See, e.g.,* Case of Chaparro Álvarez & Lap Iníguez v. Ecuador, *supra*. While some of the Court's advisory opinions have in the past dealt with various political freedoms set out in the Convention, the Court has more recently had the same opportunity to address these issues in contentious cases. Case of Yvon Neptune v. Haiti, Judgment of May 6, 2008, IA Ct.H.R. Series C: Judgments and Opinions No. 180 (2008).

A series of cases involving the rights of indigenous and tribal peoples to their lands and resources have resulted not only in recognition of collective property rights to the territories in question, but also orders that the respective states ensure the rights of indigenous and tribal peoples to be informed about and to participate in decisions about the use and benefits derived from the resources on their lands, including the right of prior informed consent about any major development project that would affect their lands and resources. The Court has reiterated in these cases that indigenous and tribal peoples, sharing similar characteristics, are entitled to special measures under international law to guarantee the full exercise of their rights. Case of the Mayagna (Sumo) Awas Tingni Community v. Nicaragua, Judgment of August 31, 2001, IA Ct.H.R., Series C: Judgments and Opinions, No. 79 (2001); Case of the Indigenous Community Sawhoyamaxa v. Paraguay, Judgment of March 29, 2006, *id.,* No. 146; Case of the Indigenous Community Yakye Axa v. Paraguay, Judgment of June 17, 2005, *id.*, No. 125; Case of the Saramaka People v. Suriname, Judgment of November 28, 2007, *id.,* No. 172; Case of the Indigenous Communities of the Lhaka Honhat (Our Land) Association v. Argentina, Judgment of February 6, 2020, Series C: Judgments and Opinions, No. 400 (2020).

The early focus on the positive obligations of the state to ensure human rights has led to a growing number of cases concerned with private violence, including domestic violence and gender-based violence in general. The most significant of the series of cases addressing these issues are González et al. (Cotton Field) v. Mexico, IA Ct.H.R., Series C: Judgments and Decisions No. 205 (discussion of femicide); Veliz Franco et al. v. Guatemala, IA Ct.H.R., Series C: Judgments and Decisions No. 277 (2014) (gender discrimination in investigating killings of women and girls); and Maria da Penha Maia Fernandes v. Brazil, a Commission report on domestic violence that led to legislative reform in Brazil. IACHR, Case No. 12.051, Report No. 54/01, Maria da Penha Maia Fernandes v. Brazil (2001). With regard to the Court's jurisprudence involving the harm by private actors, it should be noted that it recently provided its views on the human rights responsibilities of companies for the first time. Miskito Divers (Lemoth Morris et. al. v. Honduras, Judgment of August 31, 2021, Series C: Judgments and Decisions No. 432 (2021).

§ 4–17. OTHER INTER-AMERICAN HUMAN RIGHTS INSTRUMENTS

Like other global and regional systems, the Inter-American system has expanded its human rights protections over time. In addition to the two protocols to the Convention, it has adopted the 1985 Inter-American Convention for the Prevention and Punishment of Torture (entry into force Feb. 28, 1987); the Inter-American Convention on the Prevention, Punishment, and Eradication of Violence against Women (Belem do Para, 1994, entry into force Mar. 5, 1995); the Inter-American Convention on Forced Disappearance of Persons (1994, entry into force March 28, 1996), and the Convention on the Elimination of All Forms of Discrimination against Persons with Disabilities (1999, entry into force Sept. 14, 2001). Unlike the U.N., however, the OAS decided to confer monitoring responsibilities on the existing Commission and Court rather than create new treaty monitoring bodies. The exception is the disabilities convention, which creates a state reporting procedure and a committee to receive and review the reports.

On June 5, 2013, the OAS adopted two conventions on the topic of equality and non-discrimination: the Inter-American Convention against Racism, Racial Discrimination, and Related Forms of Intolerance (which entered into force in 2020) and the Inter-American Convention against All Forms of Discrimination and Intolerance (which entered into force in 2017).

The reason for adopting two agreements lies in the opposition of some states to including sexual orientation among the prohibited grounds of discrimination. Apart from this issue, some of the provisions of the two treaties have been criticized for inconsistency with the American Convention's provisions on freedom of expression. Important additional texts include the Inter-American Democratic Charter and the IACHR's Declaration of Principles on Freedom of Expression and the Principles and Best Practices on the Protection of Persons Deprived of Liberty in the Americas.

§ 4–18. DEMOCRACY AND HUMAN RIGHTS IN THE INTER-AMERICAN SYSTEM

In 1991, the OAS adopted Resolution 1080, or the Santiago Commitment, instructing the Secretary General to convoke the Permanent Council or the

General Assembly in the event of "a sudden or irregular interruption" of the democratic process in a Member State, and to act to resolve that conflict. *See* O.A.S. General Assembly, Representative Democracy, Res. 1080, Doc. No. AG/RES. 1080 (XXI–O/91) (June 5, 1991). A year later, on December 14, 1992, the OAS adopted the Washington Protocol to the OAS Charter, thereby becoming the first regional organization to allow suspension of a member state in the event that its democratically elected government is overthrown by force.

Before Resolution 1080 was superseded by the Washington Protocol, the OAS invoked it in four instances in which either a military coup, self-coup by an elected president, or severe civil-military crisis occurred: Haiti (1991), Perú (1992), Guatemala (1993), and Paraguay (1996). In the case of the coup d'état in Haiti in 1991, which overthrew a president elected in an internationally monitored election, the OAS relied on Resolution 1080 to deny recognition to coup leaders and to demand immediate reinstatement of the former government. The resolution urged Member States to "isolate" those holding power by imposing diplomatic and economic sanctions. *See* O.A.S. Meeting of Foreign Ministers, Support for the Democratic Government of Haiti, Res. 1, Doc. No. MRE/RES/1/91 (Oct. 3, 1991).

Subsequently, a Meeting of Foreign Ministers urged OAS member states to freeze the bank accounts of the coup members and to embargo the country except for humanitarian aid. In July 1993, the Haitian military leaders agreed to negotiations that led to the Governors Island Agreement; failure of the military to implement the agreement led to further UN and OAS action strengthening the sanctions.

On September 11, 2001, the OAS General Assembly meeting in a special session in Lima, Perú, strengthened Resolution 1080 by adopting the Inter-American Democratic Charter ("Democratic Charter"). Unlike the Washington Protocol, the Democratic Charter is a declaration, which is formally nonbinding. Nevertheless, since it was adopted unanimously, it could be considered an authoritative interpretation of the Washington Protocol. *See* Observations of the Inter-American Juridical Committee on the Draft Inter-American Democratic Charter, CJI/Doc. 76/01, paras. 35–40.

Substantively, the difference between the two is that the Washington Protocol applies when a "democratically constituted government has been overthrown by force" whereas the Democratic Charter applies "[i]n the event of an unconstitutional alteration of the constitutional regime that seriously impairs the democratic order in a member state." The difference in wording was urged by Perú to ensure that the Democratic Charter would apply in the event of an *auto-golpe* (i.e., a self-coup by a head of state using illicit means) such as Fujimori's.

The Democratic Charter proclaims that "[t]he peoples of the Americas have a right to democracy and their governments have an obligation to promote and defend it." It sets forth in detail the nature of democratic governance and the responsibilities of

Member States. It reaffirms "that the promotion and protection of human rights is a basic prerequisite for the existence of a democratic society, and recognize[s] the importance of the continuous development and strengthening of the inter-American human rights system for the consolidation of democracy."

Part IV of the Democratic Charter concerns the actions to be taken by the OAS in response to "an unconstitutional interruption of the democratic order or an unconstitutional alteration of the constitutional regime that seriously impairs the democratic order in a member state." Article 19 calls coups d'état and similar takeovers "an insurmountable obstacle" to a government's participation in the Organization. In the event of an extraconstitutional taking of power, any Member State or the Secretary General may request the immediate convocation of the Organization's Permanent Council to undertake a collective assessment of the situation and to take such decisions as it deems appropriate. The General Assembly may resolve, by a two-thirds vote of the Member States, to suspend the membership of the state in question. This Democratic Charter procedure has been invoked in 2002 concerning Venezuela and in 2009 after a coup d'état in Honduras.

In the case of Honduras, a Special OAS General Assembly convened to suspend immediately the right of the government to participate following the expulsion of President José Manuel Zelaya from power. The resolution instructed the OAS Secretary General "to reinforce all diplomatic initiatives and to promote other initiatives for the restoration of democracy and the rule of law in the Republic of Honduras and the reinstatement of President José Manuel Zelaya Rosales." "No such initiative will imply recognition of the regime that emerged from this interruption of the constitutional order." The resolution also reaffirmed that Honduras "must continue to fulfil its obligations as a member of the Organization, in particular with regard to human rights," and urged "the Inter-American Commission on Human Rights to continue to take all necessary measures to protect and defend human rights and fundamental freedoms in Honduras." O.A.S. Gen Assembly, Resolution on the Suspension of the Right of Honduras to Participate in the OAS, Res. 2, Doc. No. AG/RES. 2 (XXXVII–E/09) (July 16, 2009).

On June 1, 2011, the OAS General Assembly voted 32–1 to readmit Honduras, following actions by the government to address the problems identified by the OAS. Ecuador was the only country in opposition, expressing concern about the lack of investigation and punishment of human rights abuses committed during and after the coup. While other states agreed that more needed to be done to improve Honduras's human rights record, they also expressed the belief that they could more effectively assert pressure on Honduras and hold it accountable if Honduras were readmitted to the international community. Some fifty nongovernmental organizations wrote a letter to OAS member states to express their opposition to the readmission because of alleged human rights violations. Subsequently, Honduras continued to appear in Chapter IV of the 2011 Annual Report of the Inter-American Commission on Human Rights, a chapter where serious concerns about cohuman rights are discussed.

Selected References and Further Reading

Abramovic, "From Massive Violations to Structural Patterns: New Approaches and Classic Tensions in the Inter-American Human Rights System," 11 Sur. Int'l J. Hum. Rts. 7 (2009).

Antkowiak, "Remedial Approaches to Human Rights Violations: The Inter-American Court of Human Rights and Beyond," 46 Colum. J. Transnational L. 351 (2008).

Baluarte, "Strategizing for Compliance: The Evolution of a Compliance Phase of Inter-American Court Litigation and the Strategic Imperative for Victims' Representatives," 27 Am. U. Int'l L. Rev. 263 (2012).

Buergenthal, "The Revised OAS Charter and the Protection of Human Rights," 69 Am. J. Int'l L. 828 (1975).

Buergenthal & Norris, *Human Rights: The Inter-American System* (5 Loose-leaf volumes 1982–1994).

Buergenthal, "The Inter-American System for the Protection of Human Rights," *in* T. Meron (ed.), *Human Rights in International Law: Legal and Policy Issues* 438 (1984).

Buergenthal, "The Inter-American Court of Human Rights," 76 Am. J. Int'l L. 231 (1982).

Buergenthal, "Human Rights in the Americas: View from the Inter-American Court," 2 Conn. J. Int'l L. 303 (1987).

Buergenthal, "The Advisory Practice of the Inter-American Human Rights Court," 79 Am. J. Int'l L. 1 (1985).

Buergenthal, "Implementation in the Inter-American Human Rights System," *in* R. Bernhardt & J.A. Jolowicz (eds.), *International Enforcement of Human Rights* 57, 61 (1987).

Buergenthal, "Interim Measures in the Inter-American Court of Human Rights," *in* R. Bernhardt (ed.), *Interim Measures Indicated by International Courts* 69 (1994).

Burbano-Herrera, "The Inter-American Court of Human Rights and its Role in Preventing Violations of Human Rights through Provisional Measures," *in The Inter-American Court of Human Rights: Theory and Practice, Present and Future*, at 355 (Haeck, Ruiz-Chiriboga and Burbano-Herrera, eds. 2015).

Dulitzky, "An Inter-American Constitutional Court? The Invention of the Conventionality Control by the Inter-American Court of Human Rights," 50 Tex. Int'l L.J. 45 (2015).

Garcia-Sayan, "The Role of the Inter-American Court of Human Rights in the Americas," 19 U.C. Davis J. Int'l L. & Pol'y 103 (2012).

Grossman, "A Framework for the Examination of States of Emergency under the American Convention on Human Rights," 1 Am. U. J. Int'l L. & Pol. 35 (1986).

Hillebrecht, "The Domestic Mechanisms of Compliance with International Human Rights Law: Case Studies from the Inter-American Human Rights System," 34 Human Rts. Q. 959 (2012).

Horowitz, *The Transformation of the Organization of American States: A Multilateral Framework for Regional Governance* (2011).

Huneeus, "Reforming the State From Afar: Structural Reform Litigation at the Human Rights Courts," 40 Yale J. Int'l L. 1 (2015).

Mendez & Cone, "Human Rights Makes A Difference: Lessons from Latin America," in *Oxford Handbook of International Human Rights Law* 955 (D. Shelton ed., 2013).

Norris, Observations *In Loco:* Practice and Procedure of the Inter-American Commission on Human Rights, 1979–1983," 19 Tex. Int'l L. J. 285 (1984).

Neuman, "Bi-Level Remedies for Human Rights Violations," 55 Harv. Int'l L. J. 323 (2014).

Pinto, The Role of the Inter-American Commission and Court of Human Rights in the Protection of Human Rights: Achievements and Contemporary Challenges," 20 Human Rights Brief 34–38 (2013).

Popa, A Consistent Treaty Interpretation by the Inter-American Court of Human Rights in Light of Corpus Juris, 52 Denv. J. Int'l L. & Pol'y 207 (2024).

Pasqualucci, "Provisional Measures in the Inter-American Human Rights System: An Innovative Development in International Law," 26 Vand. J. Transnat'l L. 803 (1993).

Pasqualucci, "Victim Reparations in the Inter-American Human Rights System: A Critical Assessment of Current Practice and Procedure," 18 Mich. J. Int'l L. 1 (1996).

Pasqualucci, *The Practice and Procedure of the Inter-American Court of Human Rights* 37 (2nd ed. 2013).

Ramirez & Siri, Compliance with Advisory Opinions in the Inter-American System, 117 AJILUNB 298 (2023).

Shelton, "Implementation Procedures of the American Convention on Human Rights," 26 Germ. Y.B. Int'l L. 238 (1983).

Shelton & Carozza, *Regional Protection of Human Rights* (2nd ed. 2013).

Shelton, "The Inter-American Human Rights System," in H. Hannum (ed.), *Guide to International Human Rights Practice* 121 (4th ed. 2004)

Shelton, "Representative Democracy and Human Rights in the Western Hemisphere," 12 Hum. Rts. L. J. 353 (1991).

Shelton, *Remedies in International Human Rights Law* (3rd ed. 2015).

CHAPTER 5

THE AFRICAN AND OTHER REGIONAL SYSTEMS

Although the law and institutions of the European and Inter-American regional systems are the most advanced, others are developing, including in other regional and sub-regional organizations. This chapter discusses the African region and then presents the emergent mechanisms in the Arab and Asian regions.

I. OVERVIEW OF THE AFRICAN SYSTEM

The African Charter on Human and Peoples' Rights—sometimes referred to as the "Banjul Charter"—was adopted in 1981 and entered into force on October 21, 1986. It established a system for the protection and promotion of human and peoples' rights that was designed to function within the institutional framework of the Organization of African Union (OAU), a regional intergovernmental organization that came into being in 1963.

In particular, the Charter created the African Commission of Human and Peoples' Rights ("African Commission"), which since its inauguration in 1987 has served as the principal regional human rights mechanism. The eleven-member Commission sits in Banjul, The Gambia, and has responsibility for the protection and promotion of human and people's rights and the interpretation of the Charter. Generally, *see https://achpr.au.int*.

In 2001, the OAU was replaced by a successor organization, the African Union (AU). The new African Union assumed the responsibilities of the OAU, including the protection and promotion of human and peoples' rights in accordance with the African Charter. *See* Art. 3(h), Constitutive Act of the African Union, available at *https://au.int/en/Treaties/1157*.

While the Constitutive Act makes no explicit reference to the African Commission and contains no provision for any new human rights bodies, it does give a more prominent place to human rights. In its preambular considerations, Member States express that they are "determined to promote and protect human and peoples' rights, consolidate democratic institutions and culture and to ensure good governance and the rule of law." The AU Objectives (Article 3) and Principles (Article 4) include the need to "promote peace, security and stability on the continent" with a recognized need to "encourage international co-operation, taking due account of the Charter of the United Nations and the Universal Declaration of Human Rights" and to "promote and protect human and peoples' rights in accordance with the African Charter on Human and Peoples' Rights and other relevant human rights instruments." States should promote gender equality, have "respect for democratic principles, human rights, the rule of law and good governance, respect the sanctity of life and condemn unconstitutional changes of government."

The African Commission has continued to function in the role contemplated by the African Charter. A major institutional change in the African regional human rights system came with the adoption in 1998 of an Additional Protocol to the Charter on the establishment of an African Court on Human and Peoples' Rights (ACtHPR or African Court). The AU has sought to merge this human rights court with the AU Court of Justice, adopting in July 2008 a protocol of merger for the creation of an African Court of Justice and Human Rights (ACtJHRts). *See https://www.refworld.org/legal/constinstr/au/2008/en/64042*. The Protocol of Merger requires fifteen ratifications to enter into force; as of 2024, only eight States had approved it, and the ACtHPR continues as a separate entity. These developments are discussed in more detail at § 5–10, *infra*.

All but one of the 55 AU Member States are parties to the African Charter. Morocco had been an AU Member but left upon admission of Western Sahara in 1984; it subsequently rejoined the organization in 2017 but has not ratified the Charter. South Sudan, admitted as an AU member in July 2011, signed and ratified the African Charter in 2013.

The text of the African Charter is reprinted at 21 I.L.M. 59 (1982) and is retrievable at *https://au.int/en/treaties/african-charter-human-and-peoples-rights*. Details concerning the African Commission's activities may be found at *www.achpr.org*.

II. THE RIGHTS AND DUTIES

§ 5–1. INTRODUCTION

The African Charter differs from the European and American Conventions on Human Rights in a number of respects. First, the African Charter proclaims not only rights but also duties. Second, it codifies peoples' as well as individual rights. Third, in addition to guaranteeing civil and political rights, it gives equal emphasis to economic, social and cultural rights. Fourth, the Charter is drafted in a form that could permit the States Parties to impose extensive restrictions and limitations on the exercise of the rights it proclaims, often through what are referred to as "clawback clauses." Fifth, it establishes a periodic reporting system akin to procedures of U.N. treaty bodies.

The provisions of the Charter reflect the influence of UN human rights instruments as well as African traditions. Thus, it bears a stronger resemblance to the International Covenants of Human Rights than to the two other regional human rights treaties. The emphasis that the Charter places on African tradition finds expression in its preamble as well as in the form in which many of its rights and duties are articulated. The preamble speaks of "the virtues of [African] historical tradition and the values of African civilization which should inspire and characterize their reflection on the concept of human and peoples' rights." Other principles that inform the African Charter are referred to in the following provision of the preamble:

> *Convinced* that it is henceforth essential to pay particular attention to the right to development and that civil and political rights cannot be dissociated from economic, social and cultural rights in their conception as well as universality and that the satisfaction of economic, social and cultural rights is a guarantee for the enjoyment of civil and political rights.

The emphasis on the right to development, which is a "peoples" (or collective) right, and the linking together of different categories of individual rights has its conceptual source in the standard-setting practices of the UN. *See, e.g.,* U.N. Beijing Declaration and Platform for Action, Fourth World Conference on Women, 15 September 1995, A/CONF.177/20 (1995) and A/CONF.177/20/Add.1 (1995), at *https://www.unwomen.org/en/digital-library/publications/2015/01/beijing-declaration.*

§ 5–2. INDIVIDUAL RIGHTS

The African Charter contains both a broad non-discrimination clause and an equal protection clause. It guarantees the right to life and it prohibits slavery as well as torture, cruel, inhuman or degrading treatment and punishment. It bars arbitrary arrest and detention as well as *ex post facto* criminal legislation and punishment. It also contains provisions designed to ensure due process of law and fair hearings. It guarantees freedom of thought, conscience and religion, the right to receive information, to express one's opinions, and freedom of association and assembly. Arts. 2–8. In addition to recognizing the right to freedom of movement, the right to leave any country and to return to one's own, the Charter prohibits mass expulsions of non-nationals "aimed at national, racial, ethnic or religious groups." Art. 12(1), (2) and (5).

The Charter also guarantees the rights to property, work, equal remuneration for equal work, the enjoyment of "the best attainable state of physical and mental health" (Art. 16(1)), and the right to education. The provision which proclaims the rights to education and to take part in the cultural life of one's community also declares that "the promotion and protection of morals and traditional values recognized by the community shall be the duty of the State." Art. 17(3). A similar concept finds expression in Article 18, which characterizes the family as "the natural unit and basis of society" and declares, *inter alia,* that "the State shall have the duty to assist the family which is the custodian of morals and traditional values recognized by the community."

Besides providing that "the aged and the disabled shall . . . have the right to special measures of protection in keeping with their physical and moral needs," Article 18(3) also contains the following provision:

> The State shall ensure the elimination of every discrimination against women and also ensure the protection of the rights of the woman and the child as stipulated in international declarations and conventions.

Very few, if any, human rights treaties resort to this extremely liberal form of incorporation by reference to other international instruments.

The AU Member States have adopted several other significant regional human rights instruments, including (1) the 2003 Protocol to the African Charter on the Rights of Women in Africa, which entered into force in 2005, (2) the 1990 African Charter on the Rights and Welfare of the Child, which entered into force in 1999, (3) the 1969 Convention Governing the Specific Aspects of Refugee Problems in Africa, which entered into force in 1974, (4) the 2016 Protocol to the African Charter on Human and Peoples' Rights on the Rights of Older Persons, (5) the 2016 Statute on the Establishment of Legal Aid Fund for the African Union Human Rights Organs, and (6) the 2018 Protocol to the African Charter on Human and Peoples' Rights on the Rights of Persons with Disabilities in Africa.

As of 2024, the Protocol on the Rights of Women had been ratified by 44 of the 55 AU Member States, but observers have criticized the level of compliance with its provisions. Fifty Member States are parties to the 1990 children's convention, with only three countries having subsisting reservations, namely Egypt, Mauritania, and Sudan.

Although the aforementioned catalog of individual rights is very extensive, some of the rights contain qualifications that seem designed to deprive the guarantee of much meaning. Article 8 of the African Charter, for example, which proclaims "freedom of conscience, the profession and free practice of religion," declares that "no one may, *subject to law and order,* be submitted to measures restricting the exercise of these freedoms." (Emphasis added.) Article 10(1) provides that "every individual shall have the right to free association *provided that he abides by the law.*" (Emphasis added.)

Similarly, Article 9(2) articulates the right to freedom of expression by declaring that "every individual shall have the right to express and disseminate his opinions *within the law.*" (Emphasis added.) It should be noted, however, that other rights, particularly those which concern the physical integrity of the individual and due process, do not authorize the restrictions that are permitted with regard to the rights applicable to the exercise of political freedoms. The Commission has interpreted these clauses restrictively against the states, as discussed *infra* at § 5–9.

Noteworthy, too, is the fact that the African Charter does not contain a general derogation clause permitting the States Parties to suspend the enjoyment of certain rights during national emergencies or other exceptional circumstances. In Commission Nationale des Droits de l'Homme et des Libertes v. Chad, Comm. 74/92, 9th Annual Activities Rep. (1995), the African Commission declined to imply the right of States to derogate: "The African Charter . . . does not allow for States parties to derogate from their treaty obligations during emergency situations. Thus, even a civil war in Chad cannot be used as an excuse by the State violating or permitting violations of rights in the African

Charter." It reaffirmed this view in Article 19 v. Eritrea, Comm. 275/2003, 22nd Annual Activities Rep. Annex II, 15 IHRR 880 (2009) (no derogations are permissible even in time of war or emergency).

The Charter omits mention of several rights which have assumed importance in the European and Inter-American systems, including the right to privacy, the prohibition against forced or compulsory labor, and the right to vote and be elected to public office in periodic elections, although these rights have been implied by the Court as part of the "right to political participation" (*see* In the Consolidated Matter of Tanganyika Law Society and the Legal and Human Rights Centre v. Tanzania, App. No. 009/2011; Reverend Christopher R. Mtikila v. Tanzania, App. No. 011/2011, Judgment of June 14, 2013) and by the African Commission as part of the right of self-determination (*see* Kevin Mgwanga Gunme v. Cameroon, Afr. Comm'n HPR, Comm No 266/2003, EX.CL/529 (XV), 45th Ordinary Sess., Annex 4 (2009).

§ 5–3. PEOPLES' RIGHTS

The African Charter is unique in the scope it affords peoples' rights (sometimes called "solidarity rights") and in distinguishing these collective rights from those accorded to individuals. Among the peoples' rights it includes is the right of peoples to self-determination and to full sovereignty over their natural resources. This right is particularly significant in the African context, where control over natural resources has been a central issue in many conflicts and a critical factor in the pursuit of economic independence. Also on the list are the right to development, the right to peace and security, and "the right to a general satisfactory environment favourable to their development." Arts. 20, 23, and 24, respectively.

The right to development is formulated as follows: "All peoples shall have the right to their economic, social and cultural development with due regard to their freedom and identity and in the equal enjoyment of the common heritage of mankind." Art. 22(1). This and similar language found in the African Charter reinforces the AU's political agenda by giving it treaty status. Article 22(2) emphasizes that "States shall have the duty, individually or collectively, to ensure the exercise of the right to development." The African Commission has concluded that these rights, like all others in the Charter, are justiciable. *See* Social and Economic Rights Center v. Nigeria, Afr. Comm'n HPR Comm no. 155/96 (2001) AHRLR 60 (ACHPR 2001). For a detailed discussion of the right of self-determination, *see* Gunme v. Cameroon, *supra*; Shelton, "Self-Determination in Regional Human Rights Law: From Kosovo to Cameroon," 105 Am. J. Int'l L. 60 (2011). For detailed discussion on indigenous peoples' right to land and associated rights under the African Charter) *see* the "Ogiek" case—the African Commission on Human and Peoples' Rights v. Republic of Kenya, Merits Judgments, Application No. 006/2012 (2017). *See https://www.african-court.org/cpmt/storage/app/uploads/public/62fe2bb9a2274387959947.pdf (african-court.org).*

§ 5–4. DUTIES

A distinguished African jurist and former vice president of the International Court of Justice, who played an important role in drafting the African Charter, has pointed out that "in Africa, laws and duties are regarded as being two facets of the same reality: two inseparable realities." Kéba Mbaye, "*Keynote Address on the African Charter*", in Int'l Comm. of Jurists, *Human and Peoples Rights in Africa: Report of a Conference* (1985) at 27. *See, https://icj2.wpenginepowered.com/wp-content/uploads/1986/04/Africa-human-and-peoples-rights-conference-report-1986-eng.pdf*. This perspective reflects a broader philosophical view in many African cultures, where community responsibilities are deeply integrated with individual rights, creating a more holistic approach to social order. Mbaye suggests that it should therefore come as no surprise to anyone that the African Charter proclaims duties as well as rights. Here it is worth recalling that the American Declaration on the Rights and Duties of Man and the Universal Declaration of Human Rights adopted the same approach, but that the drafters of the OAS and UN human rights treaties did not follow that course.

The duties that the African Charter proclaims fall into two broad categories. In the first group are duties which can be characterized as correlatives of rights. The other category might be described as restrictions on the enjoyment of rights disguised as duties. Article 27(2), for example, which declares that "the rights and freedoms of each individual shall be exercised with due regard to the rights of others, collective security, morality and common interest," appears to codify both categories of duties. Here it is evident that the scope of these duties or their impact on the rights guaranteed in the Charter would differ significantly depending upon whether an individual's rights were to be limited by the rights of others or by considerations of collective security; the latter type of duties appear to be dangerously vague.

The contrast between these different types of duties is even more striking in Article 29, which imposes on the individual the duty "to respect his parents at all times, to maintain them in case of need" and "to preserve and strengthen social and national solidarity, particularly when the latter is threatened." Arts. 29(1) and 29(4). The first two duties differ very considerably from the third, which is an invitation to the imposition of unlimited restrictions on the enjoyment of rights.

Other types of duties reflect the African values which the Charter seeks to advance. Article 29(7) imposes the duty "to preserve and strengthen positive African cultural values in relation with other members of the society, in the spirit of tolerance, dialogue and consultation and, in general, to contribute to the promotion of the moral well-being of society." The catalog of duties which the Charter proclaims carries with it a risk of governmental abuse. For instance, governments might invoke these duties to justify censorship or other repressive measures under the guise of protecting cultural values or social order. The seriousness of this risk depends, in part, on the pace and success of the process of democratization in Africa, but also on the strength and independence of the regional human rights bodies.

III. STATE OBLIGATIONS AND MEASURES OF IMPLEMENTATION

§ 5–5. INTRODUCTION

The obligations assumed by the States Parties to the African Charter and the measures of implementation or international supervision it establishes are modeled more on the two UN Covenants than on the American or European Conventions. As pointed out in §§ 5–8 and 5–9, *infra,* unlike the international mechanisms of protection of the two other regional systems, the African system was designed to address massive denials of human rights as well as individual violations.

§ 5–6. STATE OBLIGATIONS

The basic obligation of the States Parties to the African Charter is spelled out in Article 1. It provides that they "shall recognize the rights, duties and freedoms enshrined in this Chapter and shall undertake to adopt legislative or other measures to give effect to them." This provision is supplemented by the obligations contained in Articles 25 and 26. Article 25 calls for promoting, ensuring and respecting the rights and freedoms contained in the Charter, while Article 26 requires the States Parties to guarantee the independence of the courts.

These obligations have proved important in limiting the ability of States to adopt broad restrictions on rights, as has Article 27(2). The latter, although written as an individual duty to exercise rights with due regard to the rights of others, collective security, morality and common interest, has instead been read to contain an exhaustive list of legitimate reasons for limiting guaranteed rights. *See* In the Mtikila v. Tanzania, *supra*, paras. 106–07. *See* further Sébastien Germain Ajavon v. Republic of Benin, Merits Judgment, Application 013/2017 *https://www.african-court.org/cpmt/storage/app/uploads/public/5f5/9ed/96b/5f59ed96b896891 3504265.pdf* wherein Benin had to demonstrate that limitations are necessary, proportionate, and justified in particular circumstances. The Court held that the Beninois government had violated the rights to freedom of association, the right to free participation in the government, and the right to non-discrimination under the African Charter of and the ICCPR.

Article 62 provides a technique of compliance monitoring, requiring the States Parties to report biennially "on the legislative or other measures" they have adopted to give effect to the rights recognized and guaranteed by the Charter. The task of reviewing these reports was assigned to the African Commission by the OAU Assembly in 1988, which examines them at public meetings. Although States began submitting reports in 1991, *see* § 5–7, *infra,* not all AU Member States have submitted the required reports and many are overdue. More details regarding reports reviewed by the African

Commission can be found at *https://achpr.au.int/index.php/en/states/reports*.

Although the process has not functioned as well as intended, this fact has had the beneficial impact of allowing the African Commission more time to deal with individual and interstate complaints. The process has also stimulated the creation and activities of local NGOs, who are invited to present shadow reports to the Commission. The Commission's Rules of Procedure enable the use of Shadow reports from National Human Rights Institutions and NGOs. Shadow reports play a critical role in providing alternative perspectives on a country's human rights situation, often highlighting issues that may be overlooked or downplayed in official state reports. *See* 2020 Rules of Procedure, under Rule 80(4).

§ 5–7. THE AFRICAN COMMISSION ON HUMAN AND PEOPLES' RIGHTS

As indicated above, the Charter provides for the Commission, established within the institutional framework of the OAU (now the AU), "to promote human and peoples' rights and ensure their protection in Africa." Art. 30. The Commission's 11 members are elected by the AU's Assembly of Heads of States and Governments from a list of names presented by the States Parties. They serve six-year terms in their individual capacities rather than as government representatives. Generally, *https://achpr.au.int/*.

As in other human rights systems, there have been concerns about ensuring the independence of commissioners, some of whom in the past held high political offices at the national level. The AU in April 2005 issued a *note verbale* to Member States prescribing guidelines for nomination of members to the Commission, calling for the exclusion of senior civil servants and diplomatic representatives. The Commission's Rules of Procedure were revised in 2020 and were approved and adopted by the African Commission during its 27th Extra-Ordinary Session held in Banjul, The Gambia from 19 February to 4 March 2020.

The Commission meets four times a year in "ordinary sessions" (Rule 28), which are convened either at the request of the majority of the members of the Commission, or at the request of the Chairperson of the African Union Commission. The Commission presents an "annual activity report" to the AU's Assembly. These reports are also available on the Commission's website. There are 577 African and non-African NGOs that have official observer status with the Commission. The Commission is perennially short of funds and staff.

The Commission has both promotional and quasi-judicial functions. Its promotional mandate is very broad and includes the power to undertake studies, convene conferences and workshops, initiate publication programs, disseminate information, consult with governments, and collaborate with national and local institutions concerned with human and peoples' rights. As part of this promotional effort, the Commission may "give its views or make recommendation to Governments." Art. 45(1)(a). This power enables the Commission to bring to the attention of individual governments "problem areas" revealed by its studies as well as by its review of States' implementation reports.

In recent years, the Commission has adopted a number of significant reports and resolutions regarding the human rights situations in particular regions or countries as well as in specific "thematic" areas. *See*, for example, Resolution 580 on Internet Shutdowns and Elections in Africa (2024), *https://achpr.au.int/en/adopted-resolutions/580-internet-shutdowns-elections-africa-achprres580-lxxvii*; Resolution 550 on Business and Human Rights in Africa (2023); Resolution 567 on the Human Rights Situation in Senegal (2023); see *https://achpr.au.int/en/adopted-resolutions/550-resolution-business-and-human-rights-africa-achprres550-lxxiv-2023; see, https://achpr.au.int/en/adopted-resolutions/567-resolution-human-rights-situation-senegal-achprres567-lxxvi-2023*); Resolution 554 on the Situation of Human Rights in the Kingdom of Eswatini (2023), *see, https://achpr.au.int/en/adopted-resolutions/554-resolution-situation-human-rights-kingdom-eswatini);* Resolution 544 on the Death Penalty and the prohibition of Torture and cruel, inhuman or degrading punishment or treatment (2022). *See https://achpr.au.int/en/adopted-resolutions/544-resolution-death-penalty-and-prohibition-torture-and-cruel*; Resolution 511 on the continuing Violation of Human Rights Situation in the Republic of Cameroon (2021). *See https://*

achpr.au.int/en/adopted-resolutions/511-resolution-continuing-violation-human-rights-situation-republic.

The Commission has increasingly relied on "special mechanisms" including "thematic rapporteurs" and Working Groups. Unlike in the UN system, the thematic rapporteurs are members of the Commission, while the Working Groups include commissioners, independent experts and NGO representatives. Thematic rapporteurs have been designated for such topics as death penalty and extra-judicial, summary or arbitrary killings in Africa; prisons and conditions of detention; the rights of women; freedom of expression and access to information; human rights defenders; and refugees, asylum seekers, migrants and internally displaced persons. Working Groups have been established, *inter alia,* for Indigenous Populations/Communities and Minorities in Africa; Economic, Social and Cultural Rights; and the Death Penalty, Extra-Judicial, Summary or Arbitrary Killings and Enforced Disappearances in Africa.

The Commission has also adopted a system of "country rapporteurs" and has carried out visits to individual countries (including, among others, Nigeria, Sudan, Burundi, Rwanda and Mauritania). *See,* for example, the Report on the Fact-Finding Mission to the Republic of Sudan (Darfur), 22nd Ann. Act. Rep. Annex III (2007). In the final communiqué of its 77th Ordinary Session (2023), it noted the adoption of one country resolution, addressed to the Human Rights Situation and Humanitarian Crisis caused by the ongoing Armed Conflict in the Republic of The Sudan.

The quasi-judicial powers of the African Commission may be divided into two parts: so-called interpretative powers and powers applicable to the resolution of disputes involving allegations of human rights violations. The Commission's interpretative powers are quite extensive and resemble the advisory jurisdiction of some international courts.

The Commission has jurisdiction to "interpret all the provisions of the present Charter at the request of a State Party, an institution of the OAU or an African Organization recognized by the OAU." Art. 45(3). The Commission is also empowered, in the context of its promotional activities, "to formulate and lay down, principles and rules aimed at solving legal problems relating to human and peoples' rights and fundamental freedoms upon which African Governments may base their legislations." Art. 45(1)(b). This grant of power combines quasi-legislative and quasi-judicial aspects, for it seems to permit the Commission to prepare draft legislation, to propose legal solutions to disputes and to articulate human rights standards by means of codification and interpretation. The Commission's other quasi-judicial powers—those relating to complaints charging violations of human rights—are discussed in § 5–8 and § 5–9, *infra*.

The powers conferred by Article 45 gain special importance because of the unusual lawmaking mandate embodied in Articles 60 and 61 of the Charter. Article 60 declares that "the Commission shall draw inspiration from international law on human and peoples' rights. . . ." It then lists, by way of illustration, the normative sources of that law, making specific mention of the UN and OAU Charters, the Universal Declaration of Human Rights, African instruments on human and peoples' rights and "other instruments adopted by the United Nations and by African countries in the field of human and peoples' rights as well as from the provisions of various instruments adopted within the Specialized Agencies of the United Nations of which the parties to the present Charter are members." This provision is amplified by Article 61, which permits the Commission "to take into consideration, as subsidiary measures to determine the principles of law," various other human rights agreements to which the Member States of the AU are parties, together with "African practices consistent with international norms on human and peoples' rights, customs generally accepted as law, general principles of law recognized by African States as well as legal precedents and doctrine."

Consequently, in interpreting and applying the African Charter, the Commission has a broad mandate to draw on a vast body of law which Articles 60 and 61 incorporate by reference into the African Charter. These provisions grant the Commission an invaluable tool capable of ensuring that the interpretation of the Charter will keep up with the growth of general international law of human and peoples' rights. In addition, the Commission has employed other interpretive tools such as General Comments and Studies to achieve the mandate of promotion and protection of human rights. *See* activity reports, studies, communique and statements published by the Commission at *https://achpr.au.int/en/documents*.

§ 5–8. INTERSTATE COMPLAINTS

The African Charter establishes an inter-state complaint mechanism that provides for two distinct methods of dispute resolution. *See* arts. 47–54.

The first method permits a State Party that believes that another State Party has violated the Charter to bring the matter to that State's attention in a formal communication which is copied to the Commission. The respondent State has three months within which to present its reply. Art. 47. Either State may submit the matter to the Commission if within three months from the date on which the original communication is received by the respondent State, "the issue is not settled to the satisfaction of the two States involved through bilateral negotiations or by any other peaceful procedure." Art. 48; revised Rules 87–88. The Commission plays no active role in these proceedings and, if the States decide not to take their dispute to it, the negotiations could go on for years without producing any solution.

The second option open to a State is set out in Article 49 of the Charter. It permits a State Party to file an interstate complaint directly with the Commission without going through the procedure outlined above.

Once an interstate complaint has been formally referred to the Commission under Article 48 or 49, it is treated in an identical fashion and the procedures applicable to it are the same. Here the complaint is subject to the requirement that "all local remedies, if they exist, have been exhausted, unless it is obvious to the Commission that the procedure of achieving these remedies would be unduly prolonged." Art. 50.

Once the admissibility requirement has been met, the Commission embarks on a fact-finding process, designed to obtain all relevant information bearing on the case. The Commission is not limited to the information provided by the parties and is free to draw on "other sources." Art. 52. These sources include reports from international organizations such as the United Nations, statements from NGOs, and evidence gathered from the media or independent observers on the ground. The report of the Commission's findings is transmitted to the States concerned and the AU Assembly. In it the Commission may also address to the Assembly whatever recommendations it "deems useful." Art. 53. The Charter contains no provisions requiring any further action by the Assembly on the Commission's report, although presumably any State represented in the Assembly is free to raise the matter at its annual meetings.

To date there have only been three inter-state complaints submitted to the Commission. The first was submitted in February 1999 by the Democratic Republic of the Congo, alleging that military forces from Burundi, Rwanda and Uganda had committed serious human rights abuses on Congolese territory. In 2006, the Commission found the respondent States in violation of the African Charter. Democratic Republic of Congo v. Burundi, Rwanda, Uganda, Comm. 227/1999, 20th Ann. Act. Rep. Annex IV, 98, *See https://achpr.au.int/en/documents/2006-01-01/20th-activity-report* (2006). Although the troops had withdrawn from DRC territory by the time of the decision, the Commission recommended payment of adequate compensation and reparation to the victims of human rights violations committed while those forces were in effective control of the provinces in question.

The second communication related to allegations, made by Sudan against South Sudan (*see* 34th Activity Report) at *https://archives.au.int/handle/123456789/6856*) of violations of human rights which took place primarily in southern Sudan since 1989. In February 2013, during its 13th Extra-ordinary Session, the Commission resolved not to be seized with the communication. While the reasoning behind this decision has not been made public, it can be assumed that this was due to the fact that South Sudan only became independent in July 2011.

The third communication in 2022 concerned a dispute submitted by Djibouti against Eritrea (*see, decision-communication-47814-withdrawal-eng.pdf*), regarding Eritrea's continued refusal to provide information about the fate of the 13 Djiboutian prisoners of war. *See* A/HRC/47/21, A/HRC/44/23 and A/HRC/41/53.

§ 5–9. INDIVIDUAL COMPLAINTS

The individual communications mechanism set forth in the Charter bears a striking textual resemblance to the relatively limited procedure established by the UN under ECOSOC Resolution 1503. *See* § 2–25, *supra*. As interpreted and applied by the Commission in practice, however, it has increasingly come to approximate the individual petition systems of the European and American Conventions. *See* The African Commission on Human and Peoples' Rights Information Sheet No. 3.

The African Charter originally outlined a limited role for the Commission in regard to individual communications, with Article 55 simply requiring the Secretariat of the Commission to compile "a list of communications other than those [from] States Parties to the present Charter and transmit them to the members of the Commission." Over the years, through Practice Directives and changes adopted in its 2020 Rules of Procedure, this mandate has expanded. For example, Practice Directive I clarifies that all Complaints and Communications received on or after the entry into force of the 2020 Rules of Procedure shall be processed, in their entirety and until finalization. Those received prior to that date shall be considered in accordance with the relevant provisions of the 2010 Rules of Procedure.

Practice Directive II provides that the Secretariat, through the Secretary, is now primarily responsible for the consideration of Complaints on behalf of the Commission. Practice Directive III details a strict format for Complaints to bring them in compliance with the requirements for seizure as stipulated under Rules 109 (2) and 115 (2) of the 2020 Rules of Procedure. While this language does not specify that the communications may originate with private individuals, non-governmental organizations, and various other entities, the Commission has accepted and considered several hundred such communications to date, whether or not submitted by victims or their representatives, including some whose authors were not nationals of a State Party to the Charter. No communications may be received, however, concerning a State that is not a party to the Charter. *See* Rule 115(2)(g) of the 2020 Rules of Procedure.

Article 58(1) of the Banjul Charter permits the Commission to act only in relation to "special cases which reveal the existence of a series of serious or massive violations of human and peoples' rights." Like the so-called 1503 procedure, this system was intended to allow the Commission to consider communications alerting it to situations involving large-scale and wide-spread abuses. The concept of a series of serious violations was probably introduced to ensure that the Commission would not deal with isolated violations of the Charter. Conversely, even if a State Party is not engaging in massive violations of human or peoples' rights, a showing that it regularly commits or tolerates serious individual violations, whether related or not, might nonetheless bring the matter within the jurisdiction of the Commission.

Two separate provisions of the 2020 Rules of Procedure make reference to the reporting of mass violations. Rule 85 and Rule 99. None of the provisions relating to serious or massive violations has been used frequently, but in December 2015, acting on the request from the Peace and Security Council of the African Union, a delegation of the Commission undertook a fact-finding mission to the Republic of Burundi to investigate human rights violations that had taken place since April of that year. Earlier, the Commission undertook a similar investigation of human rights violations on site in Mali. *See* Report of the Fact-Finding Mission to the Republic of Mali, Afr. Comm'n HPR, June 2013, available at *https://reliefweb.int/report/mali/fact-finding-mission-republic-mali*. *See also* Report of the African Union Commission of Inquiry on South Sudan, available at *https://www.peaceau.org/uploads/auciss.final.report.pdf*, and Final Communiqué on Fact-Finding Mission of the African Commission on Human and Peoples' Rights to Burundi, available at *https://www.peaceau.org/uploads/achpr-com-fact-finding-mission-burundi-13-12-2015.pdf*.

The Commission has expanded its role considerably by interpreting Article 55 to allow it to consider communications that do not meet the "special case" criteria of Article 58. Instead of considering such communications only to inform it about situations of large-scale and wide-spread abuses, the Commission considers them individually on their own merits. Communications are subject to the admissibility requirements of Article 56, including the obligation to exhaust domestic remedies, the requirement that the claim must not be "based exclusively on news disseminated through the mass media," and the requirement that they be submitted "within a reasonable time" either following exhaustion of local remedies or "the date when the Commission is seized of the matter." Art. 56(4), (5) and (6). Admissibility is determined separately from the merits, and if the concerned State Party fails to respond within three months of the date of notification, the Commission may decide the merits of the issue presented. *See* Rule 111 of the 2020 Rules of Procedure.

The Commission also has the general authority to recommend provisional measures in appropriate cases "in order to prevent irreparable harm to the victim or victims of the alleged violation as urgently as the situation demands." Revised Rule 100 (1).

The Commission has to date considered several hundred such cases and taken decisions on the merits in many of them, but relatively less than the number of judgments rendered by the European Court in a single year. Decisions made by the Commission are available at *https://achpr.au.int/en/category/decisions-communications*. Its jurisprudence is, however, much less extensive than that issuing from many UN bodies and special procedures. The relatively small number of cases to date means that each decision of the Commission usually contains new elements of law and for that reason carries substantial weight. In addition to raising questions about the scope of rights and duties, many cases have involved procedural issues, including in particular the requirements for admissibility. Several have addressed the issue of exhaustion of domestic remedies. *See, e.g.,* Zimbabwe Lawyers for Human Rights and the Institute for Human Rights and Development v. Republic of Zimbabwe, Comm. 293/2002, 24th Ann. Act. Rep. Annex II, 16 IHRR 253 (2009) (unduly prolonged domestic remedies do not require exhaustion).

The Commission's case law now covers the full range of rights in the Charter, including civil and political rights as well as economic, social and cultural rights. For instance, the Commission has held that annulment of free and fair elections violates the right of citizens to participate in the government of their country, as well as their right freely to determine their political status, guaranteed by Article 13 of the Charter. Constitutional Rights Project and Civil Liberties Organization v. Nigeria, Comm. 102/93, 12th Ann. Act. Rep. Annex V (1999).

With the adoption of the African Charter on Democracy, Elections and Governance by the Assembly in January 2007, it can be expected that the Commission will receive more cases involving fundamental civil and political rights. At its 42nd Ordinary Session in November 2007, the Commission called on AU Member States to ratify the new instrument, recalling that Article 13(1) of the African Charter on Human Rights provides that "every citizen shall have the right to participate freely in the government of his country, either directly or through freely chosen representatives in accordance with the provisions of the law." Res. 115 (XXXXII) 07. Promotion of "democratic principles and institutions, popular participation and good governance" is also among the specified goals of the AU under Article 3(g) of the Constitutive Act. By February 2023, the new Democracy Charter had been signed by 46 Member States and ratified by 38 of them.

A particular focus of the Commission's attention has been the conditions necessary for a fair trial. A series of decisions has condemned the trial of civilians as well as military personnel by special military courts martial without possibility of appeal (for example, pursuant to "ouster" clauses depriving the ordinary courts of jurisdiction). *See, e.g.*, Constitutional Rights Project (in respect of Wahab Akamu, G. Adeaga and others) v. Nigeria, Comm. 60/91, 8th Ann. Act. Rep. (1995), 18 Hum. Rts. L.J. 28 (1997); International Pen, Constitutional Rights Project, Interights on behalf of Ken Saro-Wiwa Jr. and Civil Liberties Organization v. Nigeria, Comms. 137/94, 139/94, 154/96 and 161/97, 12th Ann. Act. Rep. Annex V (1998), 7 IHRR 274 (2000); Forum of Conscience v. Sierra Leone, Comm. 223/98, 14th Ann. Act. Rep. Annex V (2000); Law Office of Ghazi Suleiman v. Sudan, Comms. 222/98 and 229/99 (2003), 16th Ann. Act. Rep. Annex VII, 11 IHRR 237 (2004) (military courts should not try civilians or deal with offenses under the purview of ordinary courts). More generally, in Malawi African Association v. Mauritania, Comm. 54/91, 13th Ann. Act. Rep. Addendum (2000), the Commission stated that for an appeal to be effective the appellate jurisdiction must objectively and impartially consider both the elements of fact and law that are brought before it and that failure to do so will constitute a violation of Article 7 of the Charter.

In Article 19 v. Eritrea, Comm. 275/2003, 22nd Ann. Act. Rept. Annex II (2007), 15 IHRR 880 (2008), the Commission held that the incommunicado detention of prisoners for over three years constituted a prima facie violation of due process and arbitrary deprivation of liberty. The decision builds on the Commission's earlier finding in Liesbeth Zegveld and Mussic Ephremr v. Eritrea, Comm. 250/2002, 17th Ann. Act Rep. Annex VII (2003), 12 IHRR 863 (2005), that "incommunicado detention is a gross human rights violation that can lead to other violations such as torture or ill-treatment or interrogation without due process safeguards. . . . The African Commission is of the view that all detentions must be subject to basic human rights standards." For a more detailed discussion *see* the Commission's Working Group on the Death Penalty at *https://achpr.au.int/index.php/en/mechanisms/working-group-death-penalty-extra-judicial-summary-or-arbitrary-killings-and-enforced.*

The Commission has also considered cases involving allegations of physical and mental torture and inhuman or degrading treatment, indefinite detention and arbitrary arrest. *See, e.g.,* Free Legal Assistance Group et al. v. Zaire, Comm. 25/89 et al., 9th Ann. Act. Rep. (1996), 4 IHRR 89 (1997), 18 Hum. Rts. L. J. 32 (1997). It has held that detention without charge or possibility of bail violates Article 6 of the Charter, as does deprivation of liberty under a retroactive law and detention beyond the expiration of one's criminal sentence. *See* Constitutional Rights Project and Civil Liberties Organization v. Nigeria, Comm. 102/93, 12th Ann. Act. Rep. (1998), 7 IHRR 259 (2000); Alhassan Abubakar v. Ghana, Comm. 103/93, 10th Ann. Act. Rep. (1996), 6 IHRR 823 (1999). *See also* the Commission's Resolution on Guidelines and Measures for the Prohibition and Prevention of Torture, Cruel, Inhuman or Degrading Treatment or Punishment in Africa, 16 Ann. Act. Rep. Annex VI (2002). It has also held that the politically motivated, summary deportation of long-term residents and long-term refugees violates Article 7. Amnesty International (on behalf of Banda and Chinula) v. Zambia, Comm. 212/98, 12th Ann. Act. Rep. (1999), 7 IHRR 286 (2000). More recently, the Commission condemned the mass expulsion of non-nationals in Institute for Human Rights Development in Africa v. Republic of Angola, Comm. 292/2004, 43rd Ord. Sess., 15 IHRR 180 (2008).

In several cases, the Commission has considered the procedural aspects of cases involving capital punishment. In its decision in Civil Liberties Organisation, Legal Defence Centre, Legal Defence and Assistance Project v. Nigeria, Comm. 218/98, 14th Ann. Act. Rep. (Annex V) (2001), it stated that "the foreclosure of any avenue of appeal to competent national organs in a criminal case attracting punishment as severe as the death penalty clearly violates" Article 7 of the African Charter. In Interights et al. (on behalf of Mariette Sonjaleen Bosch) v. Botswana, Comm. 240/2001, 17th Ann. Act. Rep. Annex VII (2003), 12 IHRR 856 (2005), it held that the death penalty should only be imposed after full consideration of all the circumstances, including those related to the offense as well as the offender. Nonetheless, it observed, no rule of international law prescribes the circumstances under which the death penalty may be imposed, although it pointedly referred to the "the evolution of international law and the trend towards abolition of the death penalty."

In November 2008, the Commission adopted Resolution 136, urging States Parties that still retain the death penalty to observe a moratorium on the execution of death sentences with a view to abolishing the death penalty (in conformity with its earlier Resolution 42 (XXVI) (1999)). It exhorted States Parties to the African Charter on Human and Peoples' Rights that still retain the death penalty to guarantee that every person accused of capital crimes benefits from all the guarantees of a fair trial included in the African Charter and in other relevant regional and international norms and treaties.

The Commission has also had occasion to address the question of self-determination under Article 20(1) of the Charter. The context involved a request by the Katangese Peoples' Congress for recognition as a liberation movement entitled to support and independence, and for an order requiring Zaire (as it was then known) to evacuate Katanga Province. The Commission concluded that the "case holds no evidence of violations of any rights under the African Charter." While recognizing that "all peoples have a right to self-determination," the Commission noted that there may be "controversy as to the definition of peoples and the content of the right" and acknowledged the relevance of the principles of sovereignty and territorial integrity.

> [S]elf-determination may be exercised in any of the following ways: independence, self-government, local government, federalism, confederalism, unitarism, or any other form of relations that accords with the wishes of the people but fully cognizant of other recognized principles such as sovereignty and territorial integrity.

Katangese Peoples' Congress v. Zaire, Comm. 75/92, 8th Ann. Activities Rep. (1995), at para. 4. Later, in the Gunme v. Cameroon case, *supra,* the Commission provided a lengthy discussion of self-determination, including the distinction between internal and external sovereignty.

The Commission has addressed the important question of permissible limitations on rights. As indicated above, the African Charter contains a number of provisions that permit rights to be limited or circumscribed by national law. Such "clawback clauses" have the clear potential for allowing governments to undermine the rights in question. In the eyes of the Commission, however, a narrow interpretation must be given to the clawback provisions. As stated in Media Rights Agenda, Constitutional Rights Project, et al. v. Nigeria, Comm. 105/93 et al., 12th Ann. Act. Rep. (1998), 7 IHRR at 271:

> International human rights standards must always prevail over contradictory national law. Any limitation on the rights of the Charter must be in conformity with the provisions of the Charter.
>
> In contrast to other international human rights instruments, the African Charter does not contain a derogation clause. Therefore limitations on the rights and freedoms enshrined in the Charter cannot be justified by emergencies or special circumstances.
>
> The only legitimate reasons for limitations to the rights and freedoms of the African Charter are found in Article 27.2, that is that the rights of the Charter 'shall be exercised with due regard to the rights of others, collective security, morality and common interest.'
>
> The reasons for possible limitations must be founded in a legitimate state interest and the evils of limitations of rights must be strictly proportionate with and absolutely necessary for the advantages which are to be obtained.
>
> Even more important, a limitation may never have as a consequence that the right itself becomes illusory.

Id. at paras. 66–70.

More generally with respect to the relationship between the Charter and domestic law, the Commission stated that its jurisdiction does not extend to the adjudication of the legality or constitutionality of national laws. Rather, its function is to examine the compatibility of domestic law and practice with the Charter. "Where the Commission finds a legislative measure to be incompatible with the Charter, this obliges the State to restore conformity in accordance with the provisions of Article 1." Legal Resources Foundation v. Zambia, Comm. 211/98, 14th Ann. Act. Rep. Annex V (2001).

In Lawyers for Human Rights v. Swaziland, Comm. 251/02, 18th Act. Rep. Annex III, 13 IHRR 887 (2006), it emphasized the obligation of States to bring their domestic laws into conformity with the Charter. The Commission has also held that the failure of a State Party to ensure respect for the rights contained in the Charter constitutes a violation even if neither the State nor its agents were the perpetrators of the acts that resulted in the violation. Mouvement Burkinabé des Droits de L'Homme v. Burkina Faso, Comm. 204/97, 14th Ann. Act. Rep. Annex V (2001). To the same effect is Zimbabwe Human Rights NGO Forum v. Zimbabwe, Comm. 245/2002, 21st Ann. Act. Rep. Annex III (2006), 15 IHRR 832 (2008), where the Commission underscored that States have a "positive obligation" to prevent human rights obligations and to protect all persons within their jurisdiction from harmful actions even by private (non-state) actors.

An increasing number of the Commission's decisions have addressed substantive issues concerning economic, social and cultural rights. In Free Legal Assistance Group et al. v. Zaire, *supra*, the Commission noted simply that the "failure of the Government to provide basic services such as safe drinking water and electricity and the shortage of medicines" constitutes a violation of Article 16, which guarantees every individual the best attainable states of physical and mental health. The same decision concluded that the government's closure of secondary schools and universities violated the right to education under Article 17. *Id.* In Angés Uwimana-Nkusi & Saidati Mukakibibi v. Rwanda, COMM 462/12, two Rwandan journalists (Angés and Saidati) were arrested and jailed for several articles they wrote. The Commission opined that "journalists ought to be offered a high level of protection under Article 9 of the charter given the important contribution of journalists to public debate." *Id.* at para 225. The Commission later held that Rwanda violated Art. 9(2) of the Charter

Open Society Justice Initiative v. Côte d'Ivoire, COMM 318/06, concerned the right to citizenship for minority groups when Côte d'Ivoire introduced new citizenship policies based on the concept of "*Ivoirité*," The Commission found that "failure to grant nationality as a legal recognition is an injurious infringement of human dignity. [. . .]. In the African context, where social recognition and belonging to the community are vital, denial or doubt of nationality can constitute the highest form of violation of dignity. *Id* at para 141. The Commission declared that the Republic of Côte d'Ivoire violated Articles 1, 2, 3, 5, 12, 13, 14, 15, 18 and 22 of the Charter.

Property rights were briefly addressed in Constitutional Rights Project et al. v. Nigeria, Comm. 105/93 et al., 12th Ann. Act. Rep. (1998) ("The right to property necessarily includes a right to have access to property of one's own and the right that one's property not be removed."). *See generally,* A. Sisay, The Justiciability of Economic, Social And Cultural Rights in The African Regional Human Rights System: Theory, Practice And Prospect (2013).

On linking civil and political rights with economic, social and cultural rights, *see* Ssenyonjo, "The Protection of Economic, Social and Cultural Rights under the African Charter," in The Protection of Economic, Social and Cultural Rights in Africa (Chirwa & Chenwi eds. 2016); Udombana, "Social Rights Are Human Rights: Actualizing the Rights to Work and Social Security in Africa," 39 Cornell Int'l L.J. 181 (2006); Mbazira, "Enforcing the Economic, Social and Cultural Rights in the African Charter on Human and Peoples' Rights: Twenty Years of Redundancy, Progression and Significant Strides," 6 Afr. Hum. Rts. L.J. 333 (2006); Odinkalu, "Analysis of Paralysis or Paralysis of Analysis? Implementing Economic, Social, and Cultural Rights Under the African Charter on Human and Peoples' Rights," 23 Hum. Rts. Q. 327 (2001).

Initially, neither the Charter nor the Rules set forth specific procedures to implement the Commission's recommendations, and no formal mechanisms exist to compel States to abide by them. However, Rule 125(5) of the 2020 Rules grants the Rapporteur for the Communication, or any other member of the Commission so designated, the authority to monitor the measures taken by the State Party to give effect to the Commission's decision. Still, the Commission's decisions and resolutions are included in its annual activity reports to the AU Assembly of Heads of State and Government, providing a measure of publicity and approbation. The last activity report was published in March of 2024. The issue of compliance with Commission decisions is garnering increased attention. *See* Murray & Long, The Implementation of the Findings of the African Commission on Human and Peoples Rights (2015); Viljoen and Louw, "State Compliance with the Recommendations of the African Commission on Human and Peoples' Rights," 101 Am. J. Int'l L. 1 (2007).

§ 5–10. THE AFRICAN COURT OF HUMAN AND PEOPLES' RIGHTS

The African Charter does not provide for a human rights court or any other judicial mechanism. In 1998, the Member States of the OAU agreed on a protocol to the Charter establishing an African Court of Human and Peoples' Rights (The African Court) to hear cases and resolve disputes concerning the interpretation and application of the Charter. *See* OAU/LEG/AFCHPR/Prot.III, *reprinted at* 12 Afr. J. Int'l & Comp. L. 187 (2000). That Protocol entered into force in January 2004 and the first set of eleven judges were elected in 2006. In 2003, the Member States of the African Union also agreed on the establishment of an African Court of Justice to serve as the main judicial organ of the organization, as provided in the Constitutive Act. *See* Protocol on the Court of Justice of the African Union, adopted July 9, 2003, at *https://au.int/web/en/treaties/protocol-court-justice-african-union.*

In July 2004, the AU Assembly decided to integrate the two courts, and in January 2005, recommended a new protocol for the merged court. *See* Protocol on the Statute of the African Court of Justice and Human Rights, adopted in July 2008 at the 11th Ordinary Session of the AU Assembly, text available at *https://au.int/en/treaties/protocol-african-charter-human-and-peoples-rights-establishment-african-court-human-and.* The Protocol will enter into force after approval by 15 Member States. As of 2024, only eight have ratified it, leaving the African Court to function independently for the present.

The judges of the existing African Court are elected, after nomination by their respective States, in their individual capacities and are expected to be African jurists of proven integrity and of recognized practical, judicial or academic competence and experience in the field of human rights. In practice, State Parties that have ratified the Protocol have opted for diversity and have elected the eleven members based on equitable representation of gender, the five major African regions, and the major legal systems.

The judges are elected for a six-year term renewable once. In turn, the judges elect a President and Vice-President to serve a two-year term. They can be re-elected only once. The President of the

Court resides and works on a full-time basis at the seat of the Court, while the other ten judges work on a part-time basis. The Court has complained that its part-time basis is a challenge to the effective discharge of its mandate. Its quarterly sessions are said to be the only time when effective judicial work can be done and this has resulted in delays in processing cases. *See* Afr. Ct., Annual Report 2012, AU Doc. EX.CL/825(XXIV).

The African Court is unique thus far among regional courts in electing a majority of judges with prior domestic judicial experience, a factor that could affect both the procedures and the outcome of cases, as well as compliance over time. Judges with judicial experience may be better equipped to decide issues of evidence, procedure, and case management. In addition, if domestic courts are held in high regard this could enhance the reputation of the regional court. The prior judicial experience of African judges could also facilitate their relations with other judges in the national systems and encourage incorporation and application of the regional norms and court decisions. It is difficult to evaluate the impact at present, however, given the relatively short period in which the African Court has been operating.

The African Court has broad jurisdiction, encompassing "all cases and disputes submitted to it concerning the interpretation and application of the Charter, this Protocol and any other relevant Human Rights instrument ratified by the States concerned" (1998 Protocol Art. 3), which will certainly include the Charter on the Rights and Welfare of the Child, the Protocol on the Rights of Women in Africa, and any other human right instruments. Thus far, Article 3 has allowed the Court to find a State in violation of its human rights obligations set forth in the International Covenant on Civil and Political Rights and the 1993 Revised Treaty of the Economic Community of West African States (ECOWAS). *See* Konate v. Burkina Faso, Afr. Court HPR, App. 4/2013, judgment of Dec. 5, 2014. In the case of Actions pour la Protection des Droits de l'Homme v. Côte d'Ivoire, (2016) 1 AfCLR 668, the Court engaged in a detailed discussion as to whether the African Charter on Democracy, Elections and Governance and the ECOWAS Protocol on Democracy and Good Governance could be considered human rights treaties as per Article 3 of the Protocol. The Court came to the conclusion that both agreements fell within the purview of Article 3. *Id* at paras 58–65. For a more detailed discussion of the Court's jurisdiction *see* Yakaré-Oulé (Nani) J. Reventlow & Rosa Curling, 'The Unique Jurisdiction of the African Court on Human and People's Rights: Protection of Human Rights Beyond the African Charter", 33 Emory Int'l L. Rev. 203 (2019).

The African system uniquely allows the possibility of either filing a communication at the African Commission or by-passing the Commission to file a case directly with the African Court. The latter is optional with State Parties, however, and by 2024, only eight of the thirty-four States Parties to the Protocol had made the declaration recognizing the competence of the Court to receive cases from NGOs and individuals. The eight States are Burkina Faso,

Gambia, Ghana, Guinea-Bissau, Mali, Malawi, Niger and Tunisia. The thirty-four States that have ratified the Protocol establishing the Court are Algeria, Benin, Burkina Faso, Burundi, Cameroon, Chad, Cote d'Ivoire, Comoros, Democratic Republic of Congo, Republic of the Congo, Gabon, Gambia, Ghana, Guinea-Bissau, Kenya, Libya, Lesotho, Madagascar, Mali, Malawi, Mozambique, Mauritania, Mauritius, Nigeria, Niger, Rwanda, Sahrawi Arab Democratic Republic, South Africa, Senegal, Tanzania, Togo, Tunisia, Uganda, and Zambia. The seat of the court is in Arusha, Tanzania.

The Court delivered its first judgment in 2009 following an application dated August 11, 2008 by Mr. Michelot Yogogombaye against the Republic of Senegal. As of 2024, the Court had received and considered 366 applications and finalized 253 cases. Many of the applicants represented themselves and most of the petitions were declared outside the jurisdiction of the Court because the States in question had not filed the requisite declaration accepting the right of individuals to sue. Other applicants had not exhausted local remedies and the matter was deemed inadmissible.

The Court issued its first judgment on the merits of a case in June 2013, a highly important case concerning political parties and elections in Tanzania. Mtikila v. Tanzania, *supra*. This is a sensitive issue in a region where States are still heavily committed to the doctrine of non-intervention in domestic matters. In the Mtikila case the government argued that the entire matter should be considered to raise political questions outside the Court's competence. The Court disagreed and gave little deference to Tanzania's arguments about the need to afford it broad discretion in organizing its political system, given its history and social values. The Court's ability and willingness to engage in this scrutiny may have been strengthened by the African Union's recent concern with building African democratic institutions, but the Court also invoked decisions of the African Commission and judgments of the other regional courts to support its reasoning. The second merits determination, Konate v. Burkina Faso, *supra*, concerned criminal defamation statutes and press freedoms, also a topic of concern throughout the region.

In its judgments, the African Court generally cites favorably and as persuasive decisions of the African Commission, invoking them before referring to judgments of other regional courts or to UN practice. *See* Case of Alex Thomas v. Tanzania, Afr. Court HPR, App. No. 005/2013, Judgment of Nov. 20, 2015. The African Court's unique practice in this respect may enhance the legitimacy and credibility of the African Commission, an important element in this system given the paucity of States that have accepted the Court's optional jurisdiction to receive individual communications. For most States in the region, the African Commission is the only regional venue available to victims alleging violations of their rights.

The African Court has perhaps the broadest remedial powers, being given the authority to "order any appropriate measures" to remedy a violation found. The African Court has issued a number of reparations judgments showing concern to provide redress and enhance compliance. As of March 2024, the Court has handed down 25 Merit judgments, 17 Reparations judgments, and 95 judgements that addressed both merits and reparations. *See* Mtikila v. Tanzania (Reparations), App. No. 011/2011, judgment of June 13, 2014; Zongo et al v. Burkina Faso, App. No. 013/2011 (Reparations) judgment of June 5, 2015, Houngue Eric Noudehouenou v. Republic of Benin, App. No. 028/2020 (Merits and Reparations) judgment of December 1, 2021; Kennedy Owino Onyachi & Another v. United Republic of Tanzania, App. No. 003/2015 (Merits) judgment of September 28, 2017 (Reparations) judgment of September 30, 2021; Kouadio Kobena Fory v. Republic of Coté d'Ivoire, App. No. 034/2017 (Merits and Reparations) judgment of December 2, 2021; Legal and Human Rights Centre and Human Rights and Tanzania Human Rights Defenders Coalition v. United Republic of Tanzania, App. No. 039/2020 (Merits and Reparations) judgment of June 13, 2023; Issiaka Keïta and Others v. Republic of Mali, App. No. 005/2019 (Merits and Reparations) judgment of September 5, 2023; Romward William v. United Republic of Tanzania, App. No. 030/2016 (Merits and Reparations) judgment of February 13, 2024.

Like other human rights bodies, the African Court has suffered from a lack of resources. It began operating with no registry, offices, equipment, resources, budget or rules of Court. By 2014, the operational budget from Member States was

US$6,607,632 with an additional US$2,362,315 for programs coming from external sources, including the European Union. The Court noted, however, that many staff members and judges continue to lack basic furniture and working equipment, necessitating a manual case management system. African Court HPR, Annual Report 2013, *supra*.

The Court has commented on the lack of action by the political bodies to promote compliance or to take action when there is non-compliance with its judgments by States Parties. For instance, the Court in Sébastien Germain Marie Aikoué Ajavon v. Republic of Benin, App. No. 062/2019, found that the Republic of Benin had violated various provisions of the African Charter and ordered, *inter alia* that Benin repeal all provisions prohibiting the right to embark on strike. The Republic of Benin failed to file any report on the measures taken. For more discussions around non-compliance with the African Court's judgments. *See* Activity Reports of the African Court at *https://www.african-court.org/wpafc/category/publications/activity-reports/*.

Article 31 of the Protocol provides that the Court's annual report "shall specify, in particular, the cases in which a State has not complied with the Court's judgment." Invoking "the spirit" of this provision, the Court decided not to wait for its annual report, but to notify the Executive Council of Libya's non-compliance with a March 15, 2013, order of provisional measures within two months of issuing the order. The Interim Report sent on May 17, 2013, noted the binding nature of provisional measures, extensions of time granted Libya to comply, and Libya's failure to do so. The Report went on to recommend action by the Assembly, including adoption of a decision calling upon all Member States to comply with and implement judgments and orders of the Court. The Court followed up by letter to the Executive Council on October 8, 2013, but no action was taken.

In its Annual Report for 2013, the Court was outspoken in seeing non-compliance as a threat to its future. (Annual Report 2013, para. 110). In its recent Activity Report the African Court detailed the status of implementation of a number of its judgments and orders. For example, in Guillaume Kigbafori Soro v. the Republic of Coté D'Ivoire, App. No. 012/2020. In John Lazaro v. United Republic of Tanzania, App. No. 003/2016, the Court ordered that Tanzania refrain from executing the death penalty against John Lazaro pending the determination of the application.

In Kennedy Gihana and Others v. the Republic of Rwanda, App. No. 017/2015 the Court held that Rwanda had violated Articles 12(2) and 13(1) and ordered it to pay each applicant in the matter 465,000 Rwandese Francs. Rwanda had informed the Court that it will not participate in the proceedings of the Court.

Recently, the discussions have widened to cover ways of improving on this. *See* Draft Framework For Reporting & Monitoring Execution Of Judgments And Other Decisions Of The African Court On Human And Peoples' Rights (EX.CL/1126(XXXIV)

Annex I. *See* further, *https://www.african-court.org/wpafc/the-dar-es-salaam-communique-conference-on-the-implementation-and-impact-of-decisions-of-the-african-court-on-human-and-peoples-rights/*.

§ 5–11. ECOWAS COURT OF JUSTICE

Human rights claims can now also be presented to the Court of Justice of the Economic Community of West African States (ECOWAS). As of 2024, fifteen nations are members of ECOWAS: Benin, Burkina Faso, Cape Verde, Côte d'Ivoire, The Gambia, Ghana, Guinea, Guinea-Bissau, Liberia, Mali, Niger, Nigeria, Senegal, Sierra Leone, and Togo. (Mauritania withdrew in 2000 but became an associate member in 2017).

ECOWAS was originally established under the Treaty of Lagos in 1975 to promote economic integration across the region. Over the years, the scope of ECOWAS has expanded to include political and security cooperation, recognizing that economic development cannot occur in a vacuum without peace and stability. A revised version of its constitutive treaty was agreed in 1993 and under the 2005 Protocol to that revised treaty, individuals can initiate proceedings before the Court. The Protocol's silence on the need to exhaust domestic remedies has been interpreted by the Court to mean the inapplicability of the principle and thus enabling individuals and NGOs to seek redress for human rights violations, bypassing national courts that might be compromised or ineffective. *See* Etim Moses

Essien v. The Republic of the Gambia and the University of Gambia (unreported) Suit No. ECW/CCJ/APP/05/05, delivered 14 March 2007; Hadijatou Mani Koraou v. The Republic of Niger, Judgement No. ECW/CCJ/JUD/06/08 of October 2008 at *https://caselaw.ihrda.org/api/files/15247466200936pmq64mcg518qtoxs3iejyvi.pdf.* In addition, the ECOWAS Council has empowered the Court to hear claims based on human rights principles. Generally, *see http://www.courtecowas.org/*.

One of the first such cases was brought by Nigerian politicians complaining of violations of their human rights in the determination of election outcomes. In 2008, the Court issued a judgment ordering the release from unlawful detention of a journalist in The Gambia, based on articles 6 and 7 of the Banjul Charter. ECW/CCJ/JUD03/08 (June 5, 2008). The ECOWAS Court considered its first case addressing grave human rights abuses in Dame Hadijatou Mani Koraou v. La République du Niger, (ECW/CCJ/APP/08/08; ECW/CCJ/JUD/06/08) [2008] ECOWASCJ 6 (27 October 2008). In 1996, at the age of 12, the applicant was sold to a local Chief, aged 46 for 240 000 CFA Francs to carry out domestic chores and 'cater' to the Chief. Niger's Supreme Court failed to convict her "owner" under Article 270 of the Penal Code of Niger, which made slavery illegal in 2003. The Court ruled that the applicant had been a slave under the definition in Article 1 (I) of the Slavery Convention of 1926 and that in failing to convict her former "owner," Niger failed to protect her from slavery under international law. *Id* at paras 84–86.

The judgment by the ECOWAS Court signalled that it, and possibly other regional economic tribunals, were to play a significant role in resolving human rights disputes.

The ECOWAS Court addressed various violations of socio-economic rights in The Registered Trustees of The Socio-Economic Rights and Accountability Project (SERAP) v. The Federal Republic of Nigeria and Universal Basic Education Commission (UBEC), ECW/CCJ/APP/12/07; ECW/CCJ/JUD/07/10 [2010] ECOWASCJ (30 November 2010). SERAP approached the EWOCWAS Court alleging violations of the human right to quality education, the right to human dignity, the right of peoples to their wealth and natural resources, as guaranteed by Articles 1, 2, 17, 21 and 22 of the African Charter. The Court affirmed that the right to education should not be undermined by corruption and that the government needs to ensure that the right to free and compulsory basic education is upheld. *Id.*, at para 28. The judgment marks a significant advancement for the progressive realisation of economic, social and cultural rights, in Nigeria and the West African region as a whole. *See generally, https://www.chr.up.ac.za/images/researchunits/bhr/files/extractive_industries_database/nigeria/national_case_law/SERAP%20v%20Nigeria.pdf.* *See*, Alter, Helfer & McAllister, "A New International Human Rights Court for West Africa: The ECOWAS Community Court of Justice," 107 Am. J. Int'l L. 737 (2013).

IV. ARAB AND ASEAN DEVELOPMENTS

§ 5–12. THE ARAB CHARTER ON HUMAN RIGHTS

The founding Charter of the League of Arab States, adopted on March 22, 1945 (available at *https://digitallibrary.un.org/record/551368?v=pdf*) does not mention human rights. There were six original members: Egypt, Iraq, Jordan, Lebanon, Saudi Arabia, and Syria. Yemen joined two months later. The League of Arab States, also known as the Arab League, was established primarily to promote political, economic, cultural, and social cooperation among its member states, with the initial focus being on political unity and collective defense. The Arab League at 2024 has twenty-two members and four observers. On September 12, 1966, the Council of the League of Arab States adopted its first resolution on human rights, calling for the establishment of a steering committee to elaborate a program for the celebration of Human Rights Year in 1968. The Committee recommended the establishment of a permanent Arab Committee on Human Rights and the convening of an Arab Conference on Human Rights. The latter was held in December 1968 in Beirut.

The League of Arab States initially approved an Arab Charter on Human Rights on September 15, 1994 (*see https://www.refworld.org/legal/agreements/las/1994/en/10672*), building on earlier texts adopted by regional non-governmental and inter-governmental organizations. This initial

Charter was criticized for falling short of international human rights standards, particularly in its vague provisions and lack of enforcement mechanisms. The text is reprinted in 18 Hum. Rts. L.J. 151 (1997). In 2001, by Resolution 6089 (March 12), the Council of the Arab League recommended that Arab States accelerate the process of signing and ratifying the 1994 Charter. Many Arab and international NGOs objected, however, complaining that the 1994 Charter did not correspond to international standards for human rights.

On March 24, 2003, the Council of the Arab League by Resolution 6032–129, encouraged the Permanent Arab Commission on Human Rights to "modernize" the Arab Charter on Human Rights. Amr Musa, Secretary General of the League, explained that the term "modernization" should be understood as the process to bring Charter provisions into compliance with international standards for human rights. The League adopted the revised Charter in May 2004, and it entered into force on March 15, 2008. *See, https://www.refworld.org/legal/constinstr/las/2004/en/123762.* However, the lack of consistency of some provisions in the revised Charter with other human rights instruments has been questioned. *See, e.g.*, the January 30, 2008 statement by former UN High Commissioner for Human Rights Louise Arbour, available at *http://www.cartercenter.org/resources/pdfs/peace/democracy/des/revised_Arab_charter_human_rights.pdf.*

The text of the revised 2004 Arab Charter is an improvement over the 1994 version, although it retains its condemnation of "Zionism" in Article 2 on the right of self-determination. In addition, Article 3 on equality and non-discrimination adds that "[m]en and women have equal human dignity and equal rights and obligations in the framework of the positive discrimination established in favor of women by the Islamic Shariah and other divine laws and by applicable laws and international instruments." Nonetheless, its Preamble refers directly to international standards including those in the UN Charter, the UDHR, the ICCPR and the ICESCR, and its first stated objective is "to place human rights at the centre of the key national concerns of the Arab States."

The Arab Charter has a relatively lengthy list of non-derogable rights and protects the core rights of physical integrity, including the right to life, although it permits imposition of the death penalty for serious offenses. It contains prohibitions of torture and cruel, inhuman and degrading treatment, slavery and forced labor, non-consensual medical and scientific experimentation, and trafficking in human beings. The guarantees of civil and political rights include the rights of access to justice and to due process, freedom from ex post facto laws, prohibition of imprisonment for debt, freedom from double jeopardy, rights to privacy, family and home life, the right to a remedy, the right to political participation, freedom of association and assembly, freedom of movement, freedom of thought conscience and religion, freedom of information and opinion, and rights to property, nationality, and cultural manifestations. Economic and social rights are also protected by the Charter, including the right to work and form trade unions, the rights to social security, health, an adequate standard of living, education, and the right to development. The Charter is the only regional instrument to contain an article specifically on the rights of persons with disabilities.

States Parties are obligated to implement the rights contained in the Charter. An Arab Human Rights Committee, consisting of seven independent human rights experts serving in their personal capacities for a four-year term, is given the mandate to review periodic State reports on the measures taken to give effect to the rights contained in the Charter. The Arab Human Rights Committee may request from a State Party "additional information relating to the implementation of the Charter" (Article 48(2)), but neither inter-state nor individual complaints are provided for.

Information on the non-governmental Arab Organization for Human Rights (AOHR) is available at *https://en.aohrarab.com/*.

The political changes and conflicts that have swept many countries in North Africa and the Eastern Mediterranean since 2010 have led the League of Arab States to take several new and stronger actions concerning human rights. On November 16, 2011, the League condemned the human rights violations of Syria's government. The League gave Syria three days to withdraw military forces from occupied cities, start talks between the government and opposition, and pave the way for an observer team of military peacekeepers and human rights experts. The government rejected the demand. Members then voted to suspend the State from participating in the League and overwhelmingly approved sanctions on November 28, 2011. The sanctions included freezing the assets of senior officials in the Syrian government, banning visits by those officials to other Arab nations, and ending transactions with the Syrian central bank.

The second major development was the decision of the League's Council in 2014 to adopt a Statute for an Arab Court of Human Rights, providing for the first time an institution to hear claims of human rights violations. *See* Decision of the Council of the League of Arab States, July 9, 2014, at *https://www.acihl.org/article.htm?article_id=44*. The Statute confirms "that Arab Conventions on human rights to which relevant States are party, including the Arab Charter on Human Rights, constitute the legal framework for the human being in the Arab States to enjoy and practice his/her rights," and that "the setting up of an Arab Court of Human Rights will help to achieve the purposes and objectives of the Arab Charter on Human Rights."

The Statute will enter into force after seven of the Member States have ratified it and deposited the instruments of ratification; the Statute will then be operative one year after it has entered into force. The headquarters of the Court will be in Bahrain, which has long promoted creation of the Court. An unofficial translation of the Statute by the Arab Centre for International Humanitarian Law and Human Rights

Education is available at *http://www.acihl.org/texts.htm?article_id=44.*

The Court is to have seven Judges, citizens of and elected by the States Parties for a four-year term renewable once. The Assembly of States Parties to the Statute can increase the number of judges to eleven if necessary. Perhaps for this reason, the Statute contains the unusual provision that the Assembly shall establish a list of reserve judges from among the candidates that were not elected as primary judges according to the number of votes that they received. The qualifications for the candidates nominated by the States Parties include integrity and commitment to high moral values, competence and experience in legal or judicial office, and having the qualifications required for appointment in the highest judicial or legal offices in their countries. Experience in the field of human rights is "preferred." The Court's president is to serve full time and appoint the registrar and other members of the registry.

The Court's jurisdiction is to extend to all "suits and conflicts" resulting from the implementation and interpretation of the Arab Charter of Human Rights, or any other Arab convention in the field of human rights involving a Member State (Statute, Art. 16). There will be no right of individual petition, however. The Statute provides that cases may be brought on the basis of diplomatic protection by the State of nationality of the victim of an alleged violation. In addition, State Parties can accept, when ratifying or acceding to the Statute or at any time later, that one or more NGOs that are accredited and working in the field of human rights in the State whose subject claims to be a victim of a human rights violation has access to the Court (Statute Art. 19).

Admissibility of cases will require exhaustion of local remedies, filing within six months of the alleged violation, and the absence of complaint to any other "regional human rights court" (Statute Art. 18). The last-mentioned criterion clearly includes the African Court of Human and Peoples' Rights, and might also be interpreted to include the ECOWAS Court. No other regional court has jurisdiction over Member States of the League.

Non-party States can accept jurisdiction for a particular case (Statute Art. 20). The Court will also have the power to issue advisory opinions regarding any legal issue related to the Charter or to any other Arab convention on human rights, but only upon request of the League of the Arab State's Assembly or any of its subsidiary organizations or authorities.

Several unique provisions are included in the Statute. First, the Court will be required to hold public hearings in every case, unless the parties request or the Court decides it is in the interest of justice to do otherwise. Second, the Court will have a mandatory sixty days in which to enter a judgment after the end of its deliberations. Third, Article 27 of the Statute provides a lengthy list of grounds to ask the Court to reconsideration a decision. Finally, and most problematic for the independence of the Court, its Rules of Court must be submitted to the Assembly of States Parties for approval.

§ 5–13. ASSOCIATION OF SOUTH EAST ASIAN NATIONS (ASEAN)

For the Asia-Pacific region as a whole, no human rights system exists, perhaps because of the lack of geographic, political and cultural proximity of the many countries that are located from the Caucasus Mountains to the eastern Pacific Ocean. Most efforts have been mounted, therefore, in organizations existing at the sub-regional level. One early non-governmental effort resulted in a 1983 document entitled "The Declaration of Basic Duties of ASEAN Peoples and Governments." The United Nations Center for Human Rights held annual government workshops during the 1990s for officials from countries in the Asia-Pacific region. *See, e.g.*, United Nations, Fourth Workshop on Regional Human Rights Arrangements in the Asian and Pacific Region, HR/PUB/96/3 (1996). The workshops produced National Action Plans and programs for human rights education.

The Association of Southeast Asian Nations (ASEAN) was established on August 8, 1967. It was initially formed as a political and economic organization with the primary aim of promoting peace, stability, and economic cooperation among its members. The 10 current Member States are Brunei Darussalam, Cambodia, Indonesia, Laos, Malaysia, Myanmar, Philippines, Singapore, Thailand, and Vietnam. The secretariat is based in Jakarta, Indonesia. For most of its history the organization lacked a constituting treaty. On the 40th Anniversary of the founding of ASEAN, July 30,

2007, a Charter was completed, establishing a legal and institutional framework for ASEAN. The Charter was ratified by all ten Member States and entered into force on December 15, 2008. *See, http://asean.org/asean/asean-charter/.*

The Charter provides the basis for human rights activities in this region. The Charter's Preamble specifies the States Parties' adherence "to the principles of democracy, the rule of law and good governance, respect for and protection of human rights and fundamental freedoms." Among the purposes of ASEAN, set forth in Article 1, are "to strengthen democracy, enhance good governance and the rule of law, and to promote and protect human rights and fundamental freedoms, with due regard to the rights and responsibilities of the Member States of ASEAN." Art. 1(7). Article 2's principles include respect for fundamental freedoms, the promotion and protection of human rights, and the promotion of social justice" (Art. 2(i)) as well as upholding the UN Charter and international law, including international humanitarian law, "subscribed to by ASEAN Member States." Art. 2(j). Respect for the different cultures, languages and religions is called for, while emphasizing common values in the spirit of unity in diversity. Art. 2(*l*).

ASEAN Charter Article 14, which calls for establishing an ASEAN human rights body, was implemented through the creation of the ASEAN Inter-Governmental Human Rights Commission (AICHR) whose Terms of Reference (TOR) were approved by the ASEAN Foreign Ministers. Terms of

Reference of the ASEAN Intergovernmental Human Rights Commission (AICHR), July 20, 2009, *http://www.refworld.org/docid/4a6d87f22.html.* Unlike individuals elected to other regional bodies, the AICHR members are not appointed in their personal capacities; instead, each serves at the pleasure of his or her government. AICHR, TOR, Article 5(2),(6). Member States are obliged to pay "due consideration to gender equality, integrity and competence in the field of human rights," but in practice most Commissioners have been current or former government officials. They must act by consensus and have limited powers conferred by the TOR. *See https://www.aseansec.org/.*

The TOR lists the purpose of AICHR as follows: "To promote and protect human rights and fundamental freedoms of the peoples of ASEAN." Another purpose is to uphold specific international standards contained in "international human rights instruments to which ASEAN Member States are parties." The promotion work is to be done "within the regional context, bearing in mind national and regional particularities and mutual respect for different historical, cultural and religious backgrounds, and taking into account the balance between rights and responsibilities." The 'promotional' mandate and functions include enhancing public awareness of human rights, promoting capacity building, encouraging Member States "to consider acceding to and ratifying international human rights instruments" and promoting implementation of "ASEAN instruments related to human rights." Although protection is mentioned, that mandate has not been spelled out through the grant of specific functions and powers. Notably, in late March 2010, during the AICHR's first formal session in Jakarta, efforts by families of journalists massacred in Maguindanao, Philippines, to have the Commission receive a formal complaint and investigate the incident were rejected, the Commission being unwilling to imply a power not formally granted in the TOR.

ASEAN also created a Commission on the Promotion and Protection of the Rights of Women and Children (ACWC) and a Committee on the Implementation of the Declaration on the Protection and Promotion of the Rights of Migrant Workers (ACMW). *See, http://www.asean.org/wp-content/uploads/images/2012/Social_cultural/ACW/TOR-ACWC.pdf and http://www.asean.org/wp-content/uploads/images/archive/23062.pdf.* Like the AICHR, these human rights bodies are composed of governmental representatives.

On November 18, 2012, the Heads of State of ASEAN adopted the ASEAN Human Rights Declaration clarifying the AICHR's mandate. *See https://asean.org/asean-human-rights-declaration/.* Although the AICHR was responsible for drafting the ASEAN Declaration, the actual drafting was done by a group of human rights experts appointed by the AICHR. The Working Group's terms of reference were not made public and drafts of the Declaration remained confidential, although some versions were leaked. AICHR held two regional consultations with civil society organizations late in the drafting process and some individual members of AICHR organized national consultations. Civil society organizations and the UN High Commissioner for Human Rights criticized the process for its lack of openness.

The 2012 ASEAN Declaration revived the question of regional diversity in part because of the methodology used for its drafting and in part because of critics' claims that some of its provisions fell below global standards. Nonetheless, the Preamble reaffirms adherence to the ASEAN Charter, in particular respect for and promotion and protection of human rights and fundamental freedoms "as well as in the principles of democracy, the rule of law and good governance," and a "commitment to the Universal Declaration of Human Rights, the Charter of the United Nations, the Vienna Declaration and Programme of Action, and other international human rights instruments to which ASEAN Member States are parties."

ASEAN Declaration Articles 10 and 26 affirm all of the civil and political rights and all of the economic, social and cultural rights in the UDHR, as well as the specific rights contained in the ASEAN Declaration itself. Several provisions are quoted verbatim from the UDHR, including Articles 3, 5 and 14, which mirror UDHR Articles 5, 6 and 8, concerning the right to recognition before the law, the right to an enforceable remedy and the prohibition of torture and cruel, inhuman and degrading treatment.

While acknowledging the positive development of adopting a regional instrument for ASEAN, this has however drawn critical assessment from important sources such as the Office of the United Nations High Commissioner for Human Rights, *see https://www.ohchr.org/ru/press-releases/2012/11/pillay-encourages-asean-ensure-human-rights-declaration-implemented,* the group of United Nations independent human rights experts, *see https://news.un.org/en/story/2012/11/425852*, and the U.S. State Department, *see, https://2009-2017.state.gov/r/pa/prs/ps/2012/11/200915.htm*).

Another sub-regional organization, the South Asian Association for Regional Cooperation (SAARC), was established in 1985 to promote regional cooperation between the Member States, but local conflicts have limited its ability to act. The Member States of SAARC are Bangladesh, Bhutan, India, Maldives, Nepal, Pakistan, Sri Lanka, and Afghanistan. Its Charter makes no mention of human rights and it currently does not have a human rights mechanism, but in 2002, the organization adopted two treaties linked with specific human rights issues: the SAARC Convention on Preventing and Combating Trafficking in Women and Children for Prostitution and the SAARC Convention on Regional Arrangements for the Promotion of Child Welfare in South Asia. Subsequently, in 2004, SAARC adopted the SAARC Social Charter which addresses many economic, social, and cultural rights.

Finally, on February 8, 2011, SAARC adopted a Charter of Democracy which expresses, inter alia, a "shared commitment to the rule of law, liberty and equal rights of all citizens" and "reaffirm[s] faith in fundamental human rights and in the dignity of the human person as enunciated in the Universal Declaration of Human Rights and as enshrined in the respective Constitutions of the SAARC Member States." For a commentary written before adoption of the Charter of Democracy, *see* Surya Deuja, Establishing a Robust Regional Human Rights Mechanism in South Asia, 6 Asian Hum.Rts. Defender 4 (2010).

Selected References and Further Reading

Misha Ariana Plagis and Lena Riemer, "From Context to Content of Human Rights: The Drafting History of the African Charter on Human and Peoples' Rights and the Enigma of Article 7," 23 Journal of the History of International Law 556–589 (2021).

Mujib Jimoh, "The Evolutive Interpretation of the African Charter," Indonesian J. Int'l & Comp. L. No. 37 at 43 (Jan. 2023), available at *https://international.vlex.com/vid/the-evolutive-interpretation-of-940208612.*

Annika Rudman, "The African Charter: Just One Treaty among Many? The Development of the Material Jurisdiction and Interpretive Mandate of the African Court on Human and Peoples' Rights," 21 African Human Rights L.J. 699 (2021).

Anneth Amin, "The Potential of African Philosophy in Interpreting Socio-Economic Rights in the African Charter on Human and Peoples' Rights," 5 African Human Rights Yearbook (AHRY) 23 (2021).

Solomon Dersso, "Forty Years of the African Charter and the Reform Issues Facing the Discourse and Practice of Human Rights," 21 African Human Rights L,J. 649 (2021).

Santino Ayuel Longar Dau, International Human Rights in Post-Colonial Africa: Universality in Perspective (2024).

Clément, Human Rights Protection in Africa (2024).

Isaac Mutelo and Domuni Press, Human in Southern Africa: Theory and Practice (2024).

Saidou Dogon Guida, The Life of Human Rights Legal Instruments: An African Experience (2024).

Nat Rudner, The African Charter on Human and Peoples' Rights (2023).

Nsongurua Udombana, Social and Economic Rights in Africa (2023).

Aderomola Adeola and Makau W. Mutua, *The Palgrave* Handbook of Democracy, Governance and Justice in Africa (2022).

Oyeniyi Abe, Implementing Business and Human Rights Norms in Africa: Law and Policy Interventions (2022).

Sören Stapel, Regional Organizations and Democracy, Human Rights, and the Rule of Law: The African Union, Organization of American States, and the Diffusion of Institutions (2022).

Christopher Roberts, Alternative Approaches to Human Rights: The Disparate Historical Paths of the European, Inter-American and African Regional Human Rights Systems (2022).

Aderomola Adeola, Compliance with International Human Rights Law in Africa: Essays in Honour of Frans Viljoen (2022).

Aloys Ntirushwamaboko, Accessibility of the African Court on Human and Peoples Rights: Individuals and NGOS (2022).

Bertrand G. Ramcharan, Africa and the Universality of Human Rights (2022).

Charles C. Jalloh, Kamari M. Clarke, et al., The African Court of Justice and Human and Peoples' Rights in Context: Development and Challenges (2019).

Cori Wielenga, African Feminisms and Women in the Context of Justice in Southern Africa (2021).

Arab and Asian Systems

M. Baderin, International Human Rights and Islamic Law (2003).

Al-Midani, "Human Rights Bodies in the League of Arab States," 3 Jinan Hum. Rts. J. 109–34 (2012).

Matthias Vanhullebusch, Steve Foster, et al., The Asian Yearbook of Human Rights and Humanitarian Law (Asian Yearbook of Human Rights and Humanitarian Law (2023).

Raphael Israeli, Human Rights and Human Development in the Arab and Islamic World (2022).

Claude Welch, Asian Perspectives on Human Rights (2021).

Rana Siu Inboden, China and the International Human Rights Regime (2021).

Mukhtar Ahmed, Human Rights in Islam and the UN Universal Declaration of Human Rights (2020).

Religion and Civil Society in the Arab World: In the Vortex of Globalization and Tradition (Ethics, Human Rights and Global Political Thought (2018).

Karla McKanders, Arabs at Home and in the World: Human Rights, Gender Politics, and Identity (2018).

Ahmed Mohamed El Demery and Prof M. Cherif Bassiouni, The Arab Charter of Human Rights: A Voice for Sharia in the Modern World (2015).

CHAPTER 6

INTERNATIONAL HUMAN RIGHTS LAW IN THE UNITED STATES

I. INTRODUCTION

This chapter reviews the laws and governmental policies of the United States as they relate to the domestic incorporation and application of international human rights law. It addresses questions relating to U.S. ratification and implementation of human rights treaties, congressional legislation designed to promote human rights abroad, and the application of international human rights law by U.S. courts.

Some background will be helpful. Different legal systems incorporate (or "domesticate") international law obligations in different ways. In some (the so-called "monist" systems), international law is treated as part of the domestic legal system and given direct effect; in others (the "dualist" systems), the two are considered separate so that, while international law may govern relations between States, international organizations, and other entities, it must affirmatively be "domesticated" or "internalized"—for instance, by legislation—before it can be applied domestically.

The distinction is not always clear. Indeed, the United States takes a "hybrid" approach. Generally speaking, some treaties are considered directly applicable ("self-executing") while others are not ("non-self-executing"). That distinction can even apply between different articles of a particular treaty. By contrast, customary international law is typically considered part of the "common law" and can therefore be directly applied by the courts in appropriate cases. However, the status of *jus cogens* in domestic U.S. courts remains contested.

In an increasing number of countries, the national government has established some type of organization (a ministry, department, commission, ombudsman, etc.) to coordinate its human rights policies and procedures and to oversee compliance with its international obligations. *See https://www.ohchr.org/sites/default/files/Documents/Publications/PTS-4Rev1-NHRI_en.pdf.* The United States, however, lacks such an entity (in either the executive or legislative branches of the federal government).

One reason is the federal structure of the U.S. government. Under the Constitution, the federal government is given specific (limited) powers and responsibilities, so that many areas addressed by contemporary human rights law fall within the purview of the individual states (consider, for example, family law and the rights of children, including primary and secondary education). An increasing number of states, counties and cities within the United States have established human rights bodies.

Overall, the U.S. position on giving domestic effect to international human rights obligations has been marked by several contradictions. On the one hand, the notion of limited government and the protection of individual rights and liberties have been guiding national principles since the nation's founding, and they are reflected in the U.S. Constitution itself. As indicated in Chapter 1, the United States was among the strongest proponents of the human rights movement and a leader in the formulation of the essential human rights instruments in the period following World War II. Over the following decades, it continued to promote human rights energetically at the international level.

Human rights advocacy has long been a fundamental element of the country's foreign policy; indeed, Congress adopted legislation in 1977 establishing a Bureau of Democracy, Human Rights and Labor within the Department of State for the purpose of promoting human rights compliance and advancing individual liberty and democratic freedoms, requiring it to publish annual reports on human rights compliance by countries around the world. For the 2023 report, *see https://www.state.gov/reports/2023-country-reports-on-human-rights-practices/*.

On the other hand, the United States declined for decades to ratify any major international human rights treaty and, although it has adhered to a number of them in recent years (including the Covenant on Civil and Political Rights, the Torture Convention, and the Convention Against All Forms of Racial Discrimination), it still lags behind most Western democracies. Moreover, it refused for some years to participate in the newly-established UN Human Rights Council (which replaced the UN Commission on Human Rights in 2006), finally standing for election in early 2009 (and again in 2012 and 2016), only to withdraw in 2018 and then to rejoin in 2021.

As a matter of law as well as policy, the United States has strongly endorsed civil and political rights while giving comparatively short shrift to economic, social and cultural rights as well as "group rights." It generally does not submit itself to treaty-based mechanisms permitting individual petitions but was among the first countries of the world to condition foreign aid on the recipients' compliance with human rights standards. Those laws continue to serve today as the legal foundation of the country's human rights foreign policy. Other nations have also looked to those laws as models for shaping their own legislation on the subject.

Even though the United States emerged from the Second World War as one of the strongest advocates of a treaty-based international system for the protection of human rights, official U.S. policy on the subject soon became one of complete non-participation, largely as the result of the Cold War and fears of an emergent "world government." That policy was formally reversed in the 1960's. The years 1973–74 marked the revival of U.S. interest in and commitment to an effective international human rights system. During that period, the U.S. Congress began to address the subject and laid the legislative foundation for America's current human rights policy. The Carter administration (1977–81) made human rights the centerpiece of its foreign policy. Although the Reagan administration (1981–89) initially showed little enthusiasm for the subject, it gradually recognized that it was in the national interest to maintain the promotion of human rights as an important item on its foreign policy agenda. Its human rights policy was amplified by President Reagan's Democracy Initiative, which focused on support for democratic institutions and elections.

That approach was strengthened in the administration of President George H.W. Bush (1989–93) and pursued by the Clinton administration (1993–2001). The latter expanded the policy to include, in addition to promoting human rights, bolstering the rule of law and democracy, strengthening the rights of labor, and emphasizing the protection of religious freedom.

The two administrations of President George W. Bush (2001–2009) exhibited considerably less enthusiasm for participating in human rights institutions (as well as for international law and organizations in general). While it vigorously promoted certain goals (such as religious freedom) as a matter of policy, the United States was widely criticized for having engaged in practices as part of its "war on terror" that were manifestly contrary to basic human rights principles, for example by conducting "extraordinary renditions," unlawful detentions, and treatment of detainees in violation of the proscriptions against torture and cruel, inhuman and degrading treatment or punishment.

For its part, the Obama administration (2009–17) proclaimed a renewed commitment to international human rights and succeeded in claiming a seat on the

UN Human Rights Council. It took a number of steps to reverse the policies and practices of its predecessor, including trying to close the detention camp at Guantanamo Bay, and indicated an intent to seek the Senate's advice and consent to pending human rights treaties, in particular the Convention on the Elimination of All Forms of Discrimination Against Women and the Convention on the Rights of Persons with Disabilities. However, neither goal was achieved by the end of the administration's second term.

More generally, the Obama administration gave special emphasis to advancing the rights of members of specific groups (including women, the LGBT community, persons with disabilities, and ethnic minorities), preventing mass atrocities, opposing gender-based violence and human trafficking, and promoting the freedom of religion, assembly and the press. Although the Obama administration often criticized human rights abuses committed by other governments, domestic critics frequently took issue with its emphasis on "soft power" and its failure to achieve concrete results.

In contrast, under the first Trump Administration (2017–21), the United States withdrew from the UN Human Rights Council and adopted more restrictive policies on immigration and asylum, minorities, diversity and inclusion, and affirmative action in various areas such as housing and employment. In 2017, however, it did adopt an executive order blocking the property of persons involved in serious human rights abuse or corruption.

Upon taking office in early 2021, the Biden Administration reaffirmed its commitment "to a world in which human rights are protected, their defenders are celebrated, and those who commit human rights abuses are held accountable" and "to a foreign policy that unites our democratic values with our diplomatic leadership, and one that is centered on the defense of democracy and the protection of human rights." The United States was re-elected to the UN Human Rights Council effective in January 2022 and pledged to be "a leading voice" in furthering international human rights efforts and promoting accountability for human rights violations and abuses. Despite the fact that these administrations all acknowledged (to varying degrees) the need to infuse human rights concerns into the foreign policy of the United States (and most in fact did just that), none escaped justified criticism for the manner in which they at times implemented or failed to implement that policy.

Current statements and documents related to administration policy can be found on the website of the U.S. State Department at *https://www.state.gov/bureaus-offices/under-secretary-for-civilian-security-democracy-and-human-rights/bureau-of-democracy-human-rights-and-labor/*.

II. THE UNITED STATES AND HUMAN RIGHTS TREATIES

§ 6–1. INTRODUCTION

Until 1988, the United States had not ratified any major international human rights treaty (although in 1968 it had acceded to the 1967 Protocol Relating to the Status of Refugees). In 1988 the Senate gave its advice and consent to the ratification of the Genocide Convention; President Reagan ratified it shortly thereafter. The Genocide Convention had in fact been submitted to the U.S. Senate by President Truman in 1949 and resubmitted by President Nixon more than two decades later. President Carter also signed and submitted to the Senate five human rights treaties but failed to obtain its advice and consent to their ratification. *See* § 6–3 *infra*.

The Senate's 1988 action on the Genocide Convention marked a turning point in U.S. policy towards human rights treaties. In 1992, the United States ratified the International Covenant on Civil and Political Rights. Two years later it ratified the International Convention on the Elimination of All Forms of Racial Discrimination and the Convention Against Torture and Other Cruel, Inhuman or Degrading Treatment or Punishment.

Of course, as a member of both the United Nations and the Organization of American States, the United States had earlier assumed various treaty-based human rights obligations enunciated in the respective Charters of those organizations. It is also a party to the 1949 Geneva Conventions on international humanitarian law (but not to the two 1977 Protocols Additional). In 1999, the United States signed and ratified ILO Convention 182 on the Worst Forms of Child Labor, and in 2002 it adhered to the two optional protocols to the Convention on the Rights of the Child (CRC), one on the involvement of children in armed conflict and the other the sale of children, child prostitution and child pornography. In 2005, it also ratified the third CRC Protocol to Prevent, Suppress and Punish Trafficking in Persons, Especially Women and Children.

Among the multilateral human rights treaties the United States has signed but not yet ratified are the International Covenant on Economic, Social and Cultural Rights, the Convention on the Elimination of All Forms of Discrimination Against Women, the American Convention on Human Rights, the Optional Protocols to the Covenant on Civil and Political Rights, the Convention on the Rights of the Child, and the Convention on the Rights of Persons with Disabilities.

Recent efforts to obtain the Senate's advice and consent to ratification of the Women's Convention and the Disabilities Convention proved unsuccessful. As of the end of 2024, it is unclear whether renewed efforts will be undertaken to ratify either of those treaties in the foreseeable future. Nonetheless, it is worth examining the U.S. position regarding domestic implementation of the human rights treaties which the U.S. has ratified and its practice of attaching a variety of reservations. The following sections put the main issues in their historical, constitutional and political contexts.

§ 6–2. TREATIES AND THE U.S. CONSTITUTION

Article VI, clause 2 of the U.S. Constitution provides, *inter alia*, that "this Constitution, and the Laws of the United States which shall be made in Pursuance thereof; and all Treaties made, or which shall be made, under the Authority of the United States, shall be the supreme Law of the Land. . . ."

This provision has been interpreted to mean that both enacted federal statutes and ratified treaties have the same normative rank under the Constitution, and both displace inconsistent state and local law. In the case of conflict between a federal statute and a ratified treaty provision (at least a treaty provision that is "self-executing" and therefore does not require additional implementing legislation), the later-in-time prevails as far as domestic law is concerned. *See* Whitney v. Robertson, 124 U.S. 190 (1888); Cook v. United States, 288 U.S. 102, 119 (1933); *cf.* Medellín v. Texas, 552 U.S. 491 at 518 (2008); RESTATEMENT (FOURTH) FOREIGN RELATIONS LAW OF THE UNITED STATES § 309 (2018). These issues are discussed in more detail in §§ 6–11 and 6–12 *infra*.

It is also clear that a treaty provision may not be given effect as U.S. domestic law if it conflicts with the Constitution, in particular individual constitutional rights. *Cf.* Geofroy v. Riggs, 133 U.S. 258 (1890); Reid v. Covert, 354 U.S. 1 (1957);

RESTATEMENT (FOURTH) FOREIGN RELATIONS LAW § 307 (2018). As federal law, self-executing treaties supersede all inconsistent state laws and, unless they contain provisions to the contrary, they may also federalize a subject that heretofore has been governed by state law. Missouri v. Holland, 252 U.S. 416 (1920); United States v. Pink, 315 U.S. 203 (1942). Whether legislation implementing non-self-executing treaties has that effect is a matter of legislative intent, at least in the first instance. *See* Bond v. United States, 572 U.S. 844 (2014).

As discussed in the following section, the place treaties have in U.S. law and the consequences flowing from it have in the past played a major role in determining the willingness of the U.S. Senate to approve the ratification of human rights treaties.

§ 6–3. THE U.S. SENATE AND HUMAN RIGHTS TREATIES

Some historical background is helpful for understanding implementation of human rights treaties in the United States. When World War II ended in 1945 and the United Nations was established, racial segregation and a variety of other forms of discrimination were either legally mandated or not unlawful in the United States. Much of the law codifying *de jure* racial discrimination was state law, most of it in the South. Segregation was practiced and enforced though a variety of means, including racially segregated schools, anti-miscegenation statutes, poll taxes, and segregated public services and accommodations. A coalition of Southern

Democrats and Conservative Republicans in the U.S. Congress made changing this situation by federal legislation extremely difficult.

Political groups dedicated to doing away with *de jure* racial segregation and other forms of discrimination recognized that the human rights provisions of the UN Charter and the UN treaties then being drafted might be used to strike down the laws that Congress was unwilling to repeal or nullify. Among the first judicial suggestions that the UN Charter, as a duly ratified treaty of the United States, was a federal law that outlawed racial discrimination, were the concurring opinions of Justices Black and Murphy in the U.S. Supreme Court decision in Oyama v. California, 332 U.S. 633, at 649–50 and 673 (1948). They relied on Articles 55 and 56 of the UN Charter, which impose on the Organization and its Member States the obligation to "promote . . . universal respect for, and observance of, human rights and fundamental freedoms for all without distinction as to race, sex, language or religion."

The domestic legal effect of this obligation was faced squarely in Sei Fujii v. California, 38 Cal.2d 718, 242 P.2d 617 (1952). In that case, an intermediate California state court had decided that California's Alien Land Law, by discriminating against aliens of Asian origin, was unenforceable because it violated the human rights provisions of the UN Charter. That court reasoned that the Charter, being a treaty of the United States, was equal in rank to a federal statute and thus superseded any inconsistent state legislation. The Supreme Court of California rejected that view. It ruled that the human rights provisions of the UN Charter were non-self-executing (by which it meant that the provisions did not "create rights and duties in individuals," *see* 38 Cal. at 722) and, as such, could not supersede state law unless and until they were implemented by Congressional legislation. (The Court went on to hold, however, that the challenged state law violated the Fourteenth Amendment of the U.S. Constitution.) Since no appeal was taken from this ruling, the holding on the applicability of the Charter's human rights provisions was not presented to the U.S. Supreme Court.

The Sei Fujii decision did not allay the fears of those who saw UN human rights treaty provisions as a threat to discriminatory state legislation, which had thus far withstood constitutional challenge. The clearest warning was sounded by Senator John W. Bricker of Ohio, who spelled out the danger to his conservative colleagues in the following terms: "if the [intermediate court opinion in the] Fujii case should eventually be affirmed by the United States Supreme Court, or if the principle announced therein should be sustained, literally thousands of Federal and State laws will automatically become invalid." To avert this danger, "something must be done to prevent treaties from having such far-reaching and unintended consequences." 98 Cong. Rec. 911 (1952). What needed to be done, according to Senator Bricker, was the adoption of an amendment to the U.S. Constitution that would limit the treaty-making power.

Although different versions of the so-called "Bricker Amendment" were introduced in the U.S. Senate between 1952 and 1957, all had three basic aims. The different versions are reproduced in "Report on the 1957 Bricker Amendment," 12 Rec. Bar Assoc. N.Y. 320, at 343–46 (1957). The three aims were: first, to make all international agreements non-self-executing under U.S. law, which means that they would require implementing legislation before they could be enforced in U.S. courts; second, to reverse Missouri v. Holland, 252 U.S. 416 (1920), which recognized that treaties could federalize subjects otherwise within the jurisdiction of the states; and third, to provide expressly what had always been implicit, namely, that under U.S. law, international agreements are subject to those restraints of the Constitution that limit all powers of the federal government. *Compare* De Geofroy v. Riggs, 133 U.S. 258 (1890) *with* Reid v. Covert, 354 U.S. 1 (1957).

The major targets of Senator Bricker's attack were the human rights treaties the United Nations had already adopted and the two proposed human rights covenants, which seemed to be nearing completion at the time. *See* Senator Bricker's testimony, Hearings on S.J. Res. 1 and S.J. Res. 43 Before a Subcomm. of the Senate Comm. on the Judiciary, 83d Cong., 1st Sess. 10–11 (1953). In the negotiations that eventually resulted in the defeat of the Bricker Amendment, Secretary of State John Foster Dulles had to make a policy commitment on behalf of the Eisenhower Administration that the U.S. Government did "not intend to become a party to any such covenant [on human rights] or present it as a treaty for consideration by the Senate." *Id.* at 825. This policy statement was officially communicated to the United Nations. 13 M. Whiteman, Digest of International Law 667–69 (1968). As a result, the proposed constitutional amendment failed of adoption by one vote.

The United States adhered to this policy until 1963. In that year, President John F. Kennedy transmitted three human rights treaties to the Senate for its advice and consent—the Supplementary Convention on the Abolition of Slavery and the Slave Trade, ILO Convention 105 on the Abolition of Forced Labor, and the Convention on the Political Rights of Women. *See* 49 Dept. State Bull. 23 (1963). It took four years for the Senate to schedule hearings on the treaties. Hearings on Executive J, K, and L, 88 Cong., 1st Sess., 90th Cong., 1st Sess. (Feb. 23 and March 8, 1967); *id.*, Part 2 (Sept. 13, 1967). These hearings produced consent to the ratification of only the Supplementary Slavery Convention. Later, the United States did ratify the Convention on the Political Rights of Women (1976) and the Forced Labor Convention (1991). U.S. adherence to the Protocol Relating to the Status of Refugees was easily authorized by the Senate in 1968, but it was not presented as a human rights treaty.

To demonstrate his Administration's strong commitment to human rights, President Jimmy Carter, in an unusual act for a head of state, personally signed three major human rights treaties during his first year in office. He signed the two International Covenants of Human Rights at UN Headquarters in New York and the American Convention on Human Rights at the seat of the Organization of American States in Washington, D.C. A year later, in 1978, President Carter transmitted these instruments, together with the International Convention on the Elimination of All Forms of Racial Discrimination, to the Senate for its advice and consent to ratification. Message from the President of the United States Transmitting Four Treaties Pertaining to Human Rights, Senate Ex. C, D, E, and F, 95th Congress, 2d Sess. (Feb. 23, 1978). In 1979, the Senate Foreign Relations Committee held extensive hearings on this request. Hearings before the [Senate] Committee on Foreign Relations on Ex. C, D, E, and F, 95–2—Four Treaties Relating to Human Rights, Nov. 14–16 and 19, 1979 (1980). Subsequently, at the end of his Administration, President Carter transmitted the Convention on the Elimination of All Forms of Discrimination Against Women. Message from the President of the United States Transmitting the Convention on the Elimination of All Forms of Discrimination Against Women, Senate Ex. R, 95th Congress, 2d Sess. (July 17, 1980).

As previously noted, the Senate took no further action on these treaties until 1992, when advice and consent was given to the ratification of the Covenant on Civil and Political Rights (ICCPR), and again in 1994, when it approved the Convention on the Elimination of All Forms of Racial Discrimination (as well as the Torture Convention). The big breakthrough, however, had come earlier, in 1988, with the U.S. ratification of the Genocide Convention, which after forty years was finally approved with the strong support of President Reagan.

§ 6–4. LEGAL AND POLICY CONSIDERATIONS AFFECTING RATIFICATION

In analyzing the views of those who have opposed U.S. ratification of human rights treaties or have insisted on imposing conditions on ratification, it is not always easy to distinguish the legal from the policy arguments. *See, e.g.,* Hearing before the Subcommittee on the Constitution of the Senate Committee on the Judiciary on the Constitutional Implications of the Proposed Genocide Convention, 99th Cong., 1st Sess., Feb. 26, 1985 (1985). Basically, three legal arguments have been advanced at different times by opponents of U.S. adherence to these treaties.

The first argument is that human rights are a matter of domestic jurisdiction and that the U.S. Constitution does not permit the use of the treaty-making power to regulate a matter that is not a proper subject of international negotiations. Whatever force this contention might have had during the era of the Bricker Amendment has long since disappeared. Even assuming that the treaty-making power applies only to matters that are of genuinely "international" concern, it cannot be seriously contended today that human rights fail to meet this test.

The huge number of international human rights agreements agreed to and in force today, some of which have been ratified by virtually the entire international community of States, attests to the internationalization of the human rights concern. *See also* United Nations, Human Rights: A Compilation of International Instruments, UN Doc. ST/HR/1/Rev.6, Vol. 1 (First Part) (2002); *cf*. Kadić v. Karadszić, 70 F.3d 232 (2d Cir.1995); Filártiga v. Peña-Irala, 630 F.2d 876 (2d Cir.1980); RESTATEMENT (FOURTH) FOREIGN RELATIONS LAW §§ 307 and 312 (2018). In short, the constitutional standard about what is or is not a matter of international concern for purposes of the treaty power, assuming there is in fact such a requirement, cannot be divorced from contemporary international realities and diplomatic practice.

The second argument against U.S. adherence to human rights treaties is that many of the rights these instruments protect are regulated domestically by state rather than federal law. Ratification of these treaties, it is contended, would improperly federalize these subjects. Given the manner in which this argument is often put, it is often unclear whether its proponents believe that this federalization would be unconstitutional or merely unwise. For example, in testifying in 1981 against U.S. ratification of the Genocide Convention, Senator Strom Thurmond, then Chairman of the Senate Judiciary Committee, declared:

> Matters concerning fundamental criminal conduct involving murder or conspiracy to

> commit murder should be primarily a matter of State domestic jurisdiction—I repeat, State domestic jurisdiction. The use of the treaty-making power in this area is inappropriate. In effect, the [Genocide] Convention would continue the policy made possible by the Supreme Court in its decision in Missouri v. Holland, 252 U.S. 416 [1920], in which the Court held that State powers could be transferred to the Federal Government through the treatymaking process as a de facto method of amending the Constitution.

Hearing before the [Senate] Committee on Foreign Relations on the Genocide Convention, 97 Cong., 1st Sess., Dec. 3, 1981, at 9 (1982).

In Missouri v. Holland, the U.S. Supreme Court held that the Tenth Amendment (which provides that "the powers not delegated to the United States by the Constitution, nor prohibited by it to the States, are reserved to the States respectively, or to the people") does not limit the treaty-making power of the federal government since that power was expressly delegated to the federal government. At the same time, the Court has also made clear that the treaty-making power is not without some constitutional limits. *See, e.g.,* De Geofroy v. Riggs, 133 U.S. 258 (1890); Reid v. Covert, 354 U.S. 1 (1957). Moreover, a number of recent Supreme Court decisions circumscribing federal authority have re-invigorated the concerns about "federalizing" issues or areas. *See, e.g.,* New York v. United States, 505 U.S. 144 (1992); Printz v. United States, 521 U.S. 898 (1997); United

States v. Lopez, 514 U.S. 549 (1995); *cf.* United States v. Morrison, 529 U.S. 598 (2000); Medellín v. Texas, 552 U.S. 491 (2008); Bond v. United States, 572 U.S. 844 (2014).

Nevertheless, in Bond v. United States, *supra*, a majority of the Court declined to reconsider the holding in Missouri v. Holland. *But cf.* dissenting opinion of Justice Scalia; *see also* RESTATEMENT (FOURTH) FOREIGN RELATIONS LAW OF THE UNITED STATES §§ 307 and 312 (2018).

In fact, some human rights treaties do contain provisions that would conflict with the U.S. Constitution. One such clause, for example, is Article 20(1) of the Covenant on Civil and Political Rights, which requires that "[a]ny propaganda for war shall be prohibited by law." Another is Article 20(2), which provides that "[a]ny advocacy of national, racial or religious hatred that constitutes incitement to discrimination . . . shall be prohibited by law." These prohibitions, if enacted into U.S. law, would run afoul of the First Amendment to the Constitution. Here and in similar cases appropriate reservations have been made upon ratification to ensure that the United States does not assume international obligations which it would be unable to discharge on the domestic plane because they violate the Constitution.

Some opponents of U.S. adherence to human rights treaties have argued that the U.S. Supreme Court might at some future time hold that treaties in general were not subject to any of the limitations the Constitution imposes on the exercise of all governmental power. However, the Court expressly rejected this interpretation in Reid v. Covert, *supra*. *See also* RESTATEMENT (FOURTH) § 307, which states that "[a] treaty provision will not be given effect as law in the United States to the extent that giving it this effect would violate any individual constitutional rights." Its predecessor, The RESTATEMENT (THIRD) § 302(2), declared that "no provision of an [international] agreement may contravene any of the prohibitions or limitations of the Constitution applicable to any exercise of authority by the United States."

Moreover, various human rights treaties contain a clause similar to that of Article 5(2) of the Covenant on Civil and Political Rights, which declares that:

> There shall be no restriction upon or derogation from any of the fundamental human rights recognized or existing in any States Party to the present Covenant pursuant to law, conventions, regulations or custom on the pretext that the present Covenant does not recognize such rights or that it recognizes them to a lesser extent.

See also American Convention on Human Rights, art. 29(b).

Still, concern that treaties should not impinge on the constitutional rights and protections of American citizens continues to resonate in the Congress. In giving its advice and consent to the ratification of the Genocide Convention, the Senate attached a reservation providing "that nothing in the Convention requires or authorizes legislation or other action by the United States of America prohibited by the Constitution of the United States as interpreted by the United States." For the full text of the resolution of ratification, *see* 132 Cong. Rec. S1377–78 (daily ed., Feb. 19, 1986). The Senate Foreign Relations Committee explained this reservation by pointing out that it had no doubt whatsoever that "no treaty can override or conflict with the Constitution. The Constitution is paramount. Reid v. Covert, 354 U.S. 1 (1957)." Report of the [Senate] Committee on Foreign Relations on the International Convention on the Prevention and Punishment of the Crime of Genocide, Exec. O, 81st Cong., 1st Sess., Exec. Rep. 99–2, 99th Cong., 1st Sess., at 20 (1985).

The Committee emphasized instead that the purpose of the reservation was to anticipate the possibility that the International Court of Justice might at some future time interpret the Genocide Convention to require the United States to adopt measures that would be unconstitutional. *Id.* at 20–21. Some members of the Senate Foreign Relations Committee opposed this reservation and argued that it was both unnecessary and unwise. They were unsuccessful in urging the full Senate to vote against it. *Id.* at 30–31. Similar language was adopted by the Senate in giving its advice and consent to other treaties ratified by the United States, but no longer in the form of a reservation. Instead, it is now formulated as a "proviso, which shall not be included in the instrument of ratification deposited by the President. . . ." *See, e.g.*, Report of the Senate Foreign Relations Committee on the International Covenant on Civil and Political Rights, Exec. Rep. 102–23, at 24 (March 24, 1992), approved by full Senate, 102 Cong. Rec. S4781–4784 (daily ed. April 2, 1992).

§ 6–5. THE CONDITIONAL APPROACH: RATIFICATION WITH RESERVATIONS, UNDERSTANDINGS AND DECLARATIONS

Over the past decades, the attitude of the United States to human rights treaties has changed from a policy of total non-participation to one that proceeds on a treaty-by-treaty basis in deciding whether to ratify (and how to implement) a particular instrument. This decision is made by taking account of various factors, including the national interest in U.S. participation, consistency with U.S. law and practice, and the likelihood that the Senate will give its advice and consent to ratification. Recent administrations have gradually reached the conclusion that, in general, it is in the U.S. national interest to join such treaties and that, in principle, there are no compelling constitutional objections to their ratification. There is general agreement, moreover, that almost all such treaties present some constitutional issues, but that these can be addressed by appropriate reservations.

To obtain the requisite political support of the Senate, which under Article II of the Constitution must give its advice and consent to the ratification of these treaties by a two-thirds majority, the Executive Branch has evolved a practice of addressing all real and potential objections relating to a particular treaty provision by proposing a number of reservations, understandings and declarations—so-called "RUDs"—designed to overcome these objections. The practice began in the Carter Administration and has continued since then. Driven by a combination of constitutional imperatives, legal considerations and political expediency, the practice is now insisted upon by the Senate and supported by the Executive Branch regardless of its political affiliation.

Before addressing the implementation of this practice, it is worth clarifying the nature and legal effect of RUDs as a matter of international treaty law. A reservation modifies the substantive terms of the treaty as between the reserving State and the States not objecting to the reservation. As such, a reservation changes the international obligation of these States *inter se*. By distinction, understandings and declarations are traditionally thought of as unilateral statements by a State regarding its interpretation or position with regard to a given provision of a treaty. As a rule, such statements will not modify a State's international obligations, but it is not always clear whether they will or will not have legal consequences because the label a State attaches to these statements is not determinative under the law of treaties. *See* Vienna Convention on the Law of Treaties, art. 2(1)(d); Belilos v. Switzerland, European Court of Human Rights, Series A, No. 132 (Judgment of April 29, 1988).

Hence, a statement denominated as an "understanding" might be treated as a reservation if it appears that it modifies the obligations assumed by a state. Under U.S. constitutional law, however, when the Senate conditions its consent to ratification on certain reservations, understandings or declarations, and the President ratifies the treaty subject to them, they are binding (and have been treated as such by U.S. courts as a matter of domestic law, provided they are within the Constitutional power of the treaty makers (i.e., the President and the Senate) to adopt. *See generally* RESTATEMENT (FOURTH) FOREIGN RELATIONS LAW § 305.

Certain categories of RUDs are now attached to all human rights treaties ratified by the United States. First, there are the reservations to any treaty provisions that might be deemed to conflict with the U.S. Constitution. This problem arises most often in the context of First Amendment rights. Typical is the following reservation the taken when the United States ratified the Racial Discrimination Convention:

> The Constitution and laws of the United States contain extensive protections of individual freedom of speech, expression and association. Accordingly, the United States does not accept any obligations under this Convention, in particular under Articles 4 and 7, to restrict those rights, through the adoption of legislation or any other measures, to the extent that they are protected by the Constitution and laws of the United States.

A similar reservation was taken in respect of Article 20 of the Covenant on Civil and Political Rights, which deals with war propaganda and advocacy of national, racial, and religious hatred.

That reservation provides "that Article 20 does not authorize or require legislation or any other action by the United States that would restrict the right of free speech and association protected by the Constitution and laws of the United States." Note that the reservation applies not only to the Constitution but also to U.S. laws according or protecting individual rights. The evident purpose was to reassure skeptics who were concerned that the Covenant provisions might restrict the broad freedoms of speech and expression currently protected under domestic law beyond the requirements of the First Amendment.

Second, as a rule, reservations (or understandings) will be attached to any provision of a human rights treaty to which the United States is unwilling to conform existing domestic law. Thus, the following reservation was taken with regard to the Torture Convention:

> The United States considers itself bound by the obligation under Article 16 to prevent "cruel, inhuman or degrading treatment or punishment," only insofar as the term "cruel, inhuman or degrading treatment or punishment" means the cruel, unusual, and inhuman treatment or punishment prohibited by the Fifth, Eighth and/or Fourteenth Amendments to the Constitution of the United States.

A similar reservation was attached to ratification of the ICCPR, relating to the undertaking concerning "degrading treatment."

A reservation was also taken relating to the application of the death penalty to persons under the age of 18. This type of reservation is designed to ensure that the treaty will not be deemed to have superseded existing domestic law in conflict with it and reflects a strong preference that changes to the law should be made through the ordinary legislative process.

Third, it has now become U.S. practice to attach an understanding containing a so-called "federalism" clause to any human rights treaty to be ratified by this country. Here, the principal concern has been to indicate that ratification is not intended to alter the existing allocation of authority and responsibility between the federal government, on the one hand, and the states and other constituent governmental entities, on the other, with regard to subjects that are dealt with in the treaty. The language of these understandings has been refined over the past few years.

One of the more recent, attached to the Racial Discrimination Convention, reads as follows:

> That the United States understands that this Convention shall be implemented by the Federal Government to the extent that it exercises jurisdiction over the matters covered therein, and otherwise by the state and local governments. To the extent that state and local governments exercise jurisdiction over such matters, the Federal Government shall, as necessary, take appropriate measures to ensure the fulfillment of this Convention.

Specifically, the purpose of this understanding is to emphasize, for legal as well as policy reasons, that U.S. ratification will not have the effect of federalizing those subjects regulated by the treaty over which the states and local governments have heretofore exercised jurisdiction.

In other words, this understanding seeks to prevent the application of the rule enunciated in Missouri v. Holland, *supra*, which would empower the federal government to legislate on the matters covered by the treaty that would otherwise be within the exclusive legislative power of the states. Unlike traditional federal-state clauses, however, this understanding is not designed to limit the international obligations of the United States. It is intended instead to make clear that the ratification of the treaty does not extend federal legislative power to all matters to which the treaty applies, while recognizing the international obligation of the United States to "take appropriate measures to ensure the fulfillment of this Convention."

Fourth, it has now also become the practice of the United States to ratify human rights treaties with a declaration to the effect that the United States considers their substantive provisions to be "non-self-executing." The doctrine of non-self-execution is shrouded in technical controversy and not-a-little confusion, and is discussed in greater detail below at § 6–12. For present purposes, it is sufficient to say that the evident purpose of this declaration has been to ensure that the particular treaty will not be deemed, in and of itself, to create rights directly enforceable in U.S. courts. *See, e.g.*, Medellín v. Texas, 552 U.S. 491, 527 (2008) ("A non-self-executing treaty, by definition, is one that was ratified with the understanding that it is not to [be domestically enforceable] of its own force."). Generally, *see* RESTATEMENT (FOURTH) FOREIGN RELATIONS LAW § 310. The stated concern of the Administration and the Senate was to avoid generating new "causes of action" for private litigants in U.S. courts based solely on the provisions of the treaties.

Finally, as indicated above in § 6–4, the Senate typically attaches a statement or "proviso" to its resolution giving advice and consent to the ratification of a human rights treaty, making clear that "[n]othing in this Convention requires or authorizes legislation, or other action, by the United States of America prohibited by the Constitution of the United States as interpreted by the United States." The proviso is not generally included in the U.S. instrument of ratification.

Thus, when the United States ratifies a human rights treaty today, it attempts to ensure that it has assumed no international obligations not effectively guaranteed by (or in conflict with) relevant U.S. law. To put it differently, the underlying policy is one of compliance with treaty commitments, either by making sure that the relevant law is in fact adequate to satisfy the obligations which will become binding when the treaty is ratified, or by enacting the necessary implementing legislation.

This practice does not imply categorical opposition to changing domestic law in order to comport with the treaty in question. It does, however, signal opposition to changing the law directly through the treaty power itself. In that sense, it reflects a long-standing view, particularly on the part of the U.S. Congress, that any amendments to existing U.S. law necessary to implement human rights treaty obligations should be made through the normal legislative process. That is the reason the United States defers ratification of non-self-executing treaties until any necessary implementing legislation has been enacted.

By making the treaty non-self-executing, the practice seeks to prevent individuals from instituting legal actions in U.S. courts based solely on provisions of the treaty (i.e., making clear the treaty does not by itself provide a federal "cause of action"). By including the federalism understanding, the Executive and the Congress together make clear their intent to avoid "federalizing" matters that would otherwise be within the exclusive legislative power of the states. It is ironic that this approach for all practical purposes accomplishes some of the goals that the proponents of the Bricker Amendment sought to achieve with respect to human rights treaties. *See* § 6–3, *supra*.

It is important to emphasize that none of these practices excuse the federal government from the obligation of complying with the treaties the United States has ratified. On the contrary, the position of the various Administrations has been that existing U.S. law amply recognizes and protects most of the rights guaranteed by the treaties, so that no new implementing legislation is necessary.

In fact, by Exec. Order No. 13107, 63 FR 68991 (Dec. 10, 1998), President Clinton proclaimed that "it shall be the policy and practice of the Government of the United States . . . fully to respect and implement its obligations under the international human rights treaties to which it is a party, including the ICCPR, the CAT, and the CERD." *Id.* at § 1(a). The order established an Interagency Working Group on Human Rights Treaties to provide guidance, oversight and coordination with respect to "questions concerning the adherence to and implementation of human rights obligations and related matters." *Id.* at § 4(b). The duties of that Working Group were later transferred to a Policy Coordination Committee of the National Security Council. *See* National Security Presidential Directive, Organization of the National Security Council System, available at *https://fas.org/irp/offdocs/nspd/nspd-1.htm* (Feb. 13, 2001), revised by Presidential Policy Directive 1; (Fb. 13, 2009), available at *https://www.hsdl.org/?abstract&did=34560*.

The debate over federal versus state implementation must be understood against the background of the continuing legal and political debate over the contours of the U.S. federal system. *See, e.g.*, Exec. Order No. 13132 on Federalism, 64 FR 43255 (August 4, 1999). Where existing U.S. law is inconsistent with, or falls short of the treaty's requirements, then new legislation should be adopted in the ordinary course prior to ratification (so that no RUDs would be needed). (It is of course possible that legislation could be adopted following ratification, permitting the withdrawal of any relevant reservations could be withdrawn. That situation might arise, for instance, in regard to such controversial issues as capital punishment, the juvenile death penalty or abortion).

Some implementing legislation has in fact been adopted. *See, e.g.*, the Genocide Convention Implementation Act, 18 U.S.C. §§ 1091–93 (2008), amended by the Genocide Accountability Act of 2007, Pub. L. 110–151, codified at § 1091(d) and the criminal statute implementing part of the Torture Convention, 18 U.S.C. § 2340A; *cf.* the Torture Convention Implementation Act, Pub. L. No. 102–256, 106 Stat. 73 (1992), codified at 28 U.S.C. § 1350 note (2008) (providing a civil remedy for actions of torture under color of foreign law).

It is clear, of course, that the United States cannot ratify a treaty the provisions of which, without an appropriate reservation, would violate the U.S. Constitution. It does have the constitutional power, however, to ratify a human rights treaty that conflicts with other domestic laws. Under the later-in-time rule, the treaty (or its implementing legislation, if any) would then supersede the incompatible domestic law. The decision of the Senate to insist on reservations so that the treaty itself will effect no changes whatsoever in the relevant domestic law is a policy decision not compelled by any constitutional mandate. The Constitution authorizes the President (with the consent of the Senate) to ratify treaties that become law and, if they are self-executing, that will supersede conflicting provisions of prior domestic law. The argument of the proponents of the Bricker Amendment and their contemporary disciples that this result should only be achieved by legislation passed by both Houses of Congress is in no way required by the Constitution when applied to human rights treaties. The same can be said about the need for the non-self-executing declaration and the federal-state clause. These are all policy decisions with which one may or may not agree, but they certainly are not compelled by the Constitution.

It should also be noted that a number of western European States, including The Netherlands, Germany, France, Italy, Belgium, and various Scandinavian countries, formally objected to some of the U.S. reservations to the Covenant on Civil and Political Rights as being incompatible with the object and purpose of the treaty and therefore invalid. These objections were addressed in particular to U.S. reservations relating to the death penalty and to cruel and usual treatment and punishment. The views of these States are echoed by a General Comment of the UN Human Rights Committee with regard to reservations in general. *See* General Comment No. 24 (52) on Issues Relating to Reservations, U.N. Doc. CCPR/C/21/Rev.1/Add.6 (1994). For the U.S. response to that General Comment, rejecting much of its legal analysis, *see* 16 Hum. Rts. L. J. 422 (1995).

III. HUMAN RIGHTS LEGISLATION

§ 6–6. INTRODUCTION

In the early 1970's, the U.S. Congress began a thorough assessment of international human rights issues and their foreign policy implications. The person principally responsible for initiating this process was Congressman Donald M. Fraser of Minnesota, who at that time chaired the Subcommittee on International Organizations and Movements of the House Committee on Foreign Affairs. In 1973, Congressman Fraser's subcommittee held extensive hearings on the subject. Subcommittee on International Organizations and Movements of the House Committee on Foreign Affairs, Hearings on International Protection of Human Rights, 93d Cong., 1st Sess., Aug. 1–Dec. 7, 1973.

A year later, the subcommittee presented a comprehensive set of recommendations calling for legislation and other action to ensure that human rights considerations would receive serious consideration in the formulation and execution of U.S. foreign policy. Subcommittee on International Organizations and Movements of the House Committee on Foreign Affairs, Human Rights in the World Community: A Call for Leadership, 93d Cong., 2d Sess., 1974.

The legislative and bureaucratic underpinnings of contemporary U.S. human rights foreign policy have their origin in the efforts of the Fraser committee and the policies of President Jimmy Carter, who was elected in 1976. The latter enthusiastically espoused many of Congressman Fraser's recommendations and made the promotion of human rights the cornerstone of his administration's foreign policy.

The legislation and other measures that the initial Fraser committee hearings produced have been significantly transformed and amplified since then. Today there exists a substantial, indeed expanding, body of law on the subject. The subsequent sections examine the major provisions of that law.

§ 6–7. TERMINATING MILITARY AND ECONOMIC AID: LAWS OF GENERAL APPLICABILITY

The cornerstone of U.S. human rights legislation consists of two laws of general applicability. The relevant laws are § 502B of the Foreign Assistance Act of 1961, as amended (22 U.S.C.A. § 2304), and § 116 of the same Act (22 U.S.C.A. § 2151n). These laws tie the grant of military and economic assistance to the human rights policies of the recipient governments. Their underlying policy is well articulated in § 502B(a)(1), which reads as follows:

> The United States shall, in accordance with its international obligations as set forth in the Charter of the United Nations and in keeping with the constitutional heritage and traditions of the United States, promote and encourage increased respect for human rights and fundamental freedoms throughout the world without distinction as to race, sex, language, or religion. Accordingly, a principal goal of the

> foreign policy of the United States shall be to promote the increased observance of internationally recognized human rights by all countries.

Although § 502B deals with military or security assistance and § 116 applies to economic aid and development assistance, both laws have the same purpose: to deny such assistance to countries the governments of which engage in activities that reveal "a consistent pattern of gross violations of internationally recognized human rights." The concept of "gross violation of internationally recognized human rights" is defined in § 502B(d)(1) as "including" violations such as:

> torture or cruel, inhuman, or degrading treatment or punishment, prolonged detention without charges and trial, causing the disappearance of persons by the abduction and clandestine detention of those persons, and other flagrant denial of the right to life, liberty, or the security of person.

22 U.S.C.A. § 2304(d)(1). Section 116(a) uses almost identical language. 22 U.S.C.A. § 2151n(a). The use of the word "including" indicates that Congress recognized that other human rights may also qualify as being "internationally recognized."

The phrase "consistent pattern of gross violations" mirrors the language of UN Economic and Social Council Resolution 1503 (1970). That resolution is at the heart of the UN Charter-based system for dealing with human rights complaints and reflects the view that a state guilty of such violations is in breach of its obligations under the Charter. *See* § 2–25, *supra*. Resort by the U.S. Congress to the UN language was no accident and indicates a desire to ensure that these laws not be considered as constituting illegal intervention in the domestic affairs of other countries.

The language also suggests that the Congress wished to reach only governments which systematically engaged in or tolerated massive violations of human rights. Isolated instances of even serious violations presumably would not be covered by the statute, particularly if they revealed that these acts were not the result of a governmental policy. For an analysis of the manner in which the U.S. State Department has applied this test, *see* Forsythe, "Congress and Human Rights in U.S. Foreign Policy: The Fate of General Legislation," 9 Hum. Rts. Q. 382 (1987). For a critical analysis of the application of these laws, *see* Lawyers Committee for Human Rights, *Human Rights and U.S. Foreign Policy* 6 (1992).

Over time, the Congress has adopted additional restrictions on assistance to other countries, using the "consistent pattern of gross violations" standard or very similar language. *See, e.g.*, § 403(j)(1) of the Agricultural Trade and Development Act of 1954, 7 U.S.C. § 1733(j)(1) (providing and financing of agricultural commodities); bilateral debt relief under the enhanced HIPC legislation, 22 U.S.C.A. § 262p–8(c)(4); § 104 (a) of the Africa Growth and Opportunity Act, 19 U.S.C. § 3703(a)(3); § 2(b)(6) and

(14) of the Export-Import Bank Act of 1945, as amended, 12 U.S.C. § 635(b)(6) and 635i–8(c) (certain functions of the Ex-Im Bank); § 498A of the Foreign Assistance Act of 1961 as amended, 22 U.S.C. § 2295a(b)(1) (assistance to the governments of the independent states of the former Soviet Union); and benefits under the Americas Initiative, 22 U.S.C. § 2430b(a)(4).

Section 116 also establishes an elaborate reporting requirement under which the Department of State must provide an annual human rights status report for all states receiving aid. This requirement has in the meantime been extended to all UN Member States. Similar obligations are imposed by § 502B. These annual "country conditions" reports have become a valuable source of information about world-wide human rights conditions and violations. In compiling the reports, the State Department relies on information provided by U.S. embassies as well as on findings of inter-governmental and non-governmental human rights organizations. The annual reports are available on-line at *https://www.state.gov/j/drl/rls/hrrpt*.

The legislation requires the Department of State, in determining whether a foreign State is a gross violator of human rights, to take into account, among other considerations, "the relevant findings of appropriate international organizations, including nongovernmental organizations, such as the International Committee of the Red Cross. . . ." Section 502B(b)(1). Similar language is found in § 116(c)(1). Both laws also attach considerable weight to the extent to which the particular country cooperates with and permits such organizations "an unimpeded investigation of alleged violations of internationally recognized human rights." *See* § 116(c)(1) and § 502B(b)(2). These requirements strengthen the effectiveness of public and private human rights institutions that investigate and judge violations. Hence, findings—for example, by the UN Human Rights Council or a regional human rights body such as the Inter-American Court or Commission on Human Rights—that a government has engaged in large-scale violations of human rights, should be taken into account by the State Department in preparing its reports and in deciding on the action to be taken in application of §§ 116 or 502B.

Each provision contains exceptions. Thus, economic aid does not have to be terminated if "such assistance will directly benefit the needy people in such country." § 116(a). Moreover, the President may continue security assistance to a gross violator if he or she certifies to the Congress "that extraordinary circumstances exist warranting provision of such assistance." § 502B(a)(2). These and other provisions give the Executive Branch considerable latitude in administering the law with more or less vigor.

Ultimately, of course, the question of whether a government is a human rights violator within the meaning of this legislation is a matter of judgment. For one thing, it is not always easy to determine whether conditions have improved in a country to justify resumption of aid. Much also depends upon the political will of the Executive Branch in implementing a strong or weak human rights policy. Generally, *see* Foreign Assistance Act of 1961: Authorizations and Corresponding Appropriations updated to January 18, 2023 (CRS 40089). Additional reporting requirements were imposed by the 1998 International Religious Freedom Act, recently amended by Pub. L. 114–281, 130 Stat 1426 (2016), codified at 22 U.S.C. § 6401 et seq. (2016). That Act mandated the establishment of an Office of International Religious Freedom within the Department of State, headed by an Ambassador-at-Large who acts as the principal advisor to the President and Secretary of State in matters concerning religious freedom abroad.

The law also created an independent, bipartisan United States Commission on International Religious Freedom. The Act made it U.S. policy "to seek to channel United States security and development assistance to governments other than those found to be engaged in gross violations of the right to freedom of religion, as set forth in the Foreign Assistance Act of 1961, in the International Financial Institutions Act of 1977, and in other formulations of United States human rights policy." 22 U.S.C. § 6401(b)(2). The President must annually designate every country "the government of which has engaged in or tolerated violations described in this subparagraph as a country of particular concern for religious freedom." 22 U.S.C. § 6442(b)(1)(A). A report covering every foreign country, coupled with an identification of severe violators, is submitted each year. The 2022 International Religious Freedom

Report may be found at *https://www.state.gov/reports/2022-report-on-international-religious-freedom/*.

§ 6–8. COUNTRY-SPECIFIC LEGISLATION

In addition to the legislation of general applicability described in the preceding section, the Congress has from time-to-time enacted so-called country-specific human rights laws. One purpose of such legislation is to force the Executive Branch to cut off aid to a particular country to which the laws of general applicability, in Congress's view, are not being applied as strictly as they should be.

Another purpose is to focus attention on especially serious human rights violations in a given country. Among the states thus singled out at one time or another have been Argentina, Burma, Cambodia, Chile, Cuba, Guatemala, Haiti, Iran, Iraq, Libya, Salvador, South Africa, Sudan and Yugoslavia. This legislation usually has a one year duration and may be renewed or extended depending upon the actions of the target government.

Country-specific legislation can be very useful in complementing the laws of general applicability by providing the Congress with a more powerful instrument to compel action by an uncooperative or timid Executive Branch. Sometimes the Congress will also simply refuse the Administration's request for security assistance to a country it considers to be a gross violator of human rights.

Another provision of country-specific application is the prohibition against the obligation or expenditure of funds to finance directly any assistance to any country whose duly elected head of state is deposed by decree or military coup. *See, e.g.,* § 7008 of the 2014 Consolidated and Further Continuing Appropriations Act, 2015, Pub. L.113–235 (Dec. 16, 2014), 128 Stat. 2130.

§ 6–9. INTERNATIONAL FINANCIAL INSTITUTIONS

The United States channels substantial amounts of economic aid to developing countries through international financial institutions, the so-called IFIs. These include the World Bank, the International Finance Corporation, the International Development Association, and various regional development banks. Although in most of these institutions the United States lacks the power to veto loans or grants to a specific country, it is a major contributor and as such has substantial influence on the decision-making process of the IFIs. This fact explains why, once Congress began to use economic and technical aid as a lever in seeking to reduce human rights violations, it also started to look at the role the U.S. Government could play in the IFIs in promoting that same policy. (Congressman, later Senator, Tom Harkin was the leading advocate of the policy that introduced human rights considerations into the decision-making process of the IFIs and the principal sponsor of the legislation on the subject.)

Section 701 of the International Financial Institutions Act of 1977 requires the U.S. Government and U.S. representatives to the IFIs to advance the cause of human rights by using their "voice and vote" to prevent development aid from going to countries whose governments engage in gross violations of human rights. *See* 22 U.S.C. § 262d(a) (2014). The test for determining what types of violations of human rights are covered by this law and how they are to be assessed mirrors the "pattern of gross violations of internationally recognized human rights" criteria contained in the legislation that has been described in § 6–7, *supra*. The same is true, as a general proposition, of the certification requirements and escape clauses.

For a report on how the Executive Branch complies with these provisions of the law, *see,* Oversight of State Department Country Reports on Human Rights Practices for 1992 and U.S. Human Rights Policy (Hearing before the Subcommittee on International Security, International Organizations, and Human Rights, 103rd Cong., 1st Sess., March 4, 1993), which also contains testimony by various human rights organizations criticizing the Executive Branch's performance in specific cases.

§ 6–10. THE BUREAU OF DEMOCRACY, HUMAN RIGHTS AND LABOR

The principal spokesperson and policy adviser on international human rights issues within the United States Government is found in the U.S. Department of State. The U.S. Department of State is divided into so-called functional and geographic bureaus through which it carries on its work. Each of these bureaus is headed by an assistant secretary of state (or the equivalent). Until the mid-1970's, human rights subjects were handled by relatively low-level State Department officials working in different bureaus. As a result, human rights policy questions were poorly coordinated and rarely received high-level attention within the Department.

In 1976, the Congress took the first steps to deal with this problem. It mandated the establishment of an office of Coordinator for Human Rights and Humanitarian Affairs. A year later, the Congress adopted legislation changing the Coordinator's rank to that of an Assistant Secretary of State, who would head the Bureau of Human Rights and Humanitarian Affairs. *See* Pub. L. 95–105, 91 Stat. 846 (1977). By taking this action, the Congress wished to demonstrate that human rights concerns should have a bureaucratic status within the Department of State comparable to that enjoyed by other major foreign policy subjects. In the Clinton Administration this office was renamed the Bureau for Democracy, Human Rights and Labor (DRL). Pub. L. 103–236, § 161, 108 Stat. 402 (April 30, 1994). The powers and functions of the Assistant Secretary of State for Democracy, Human Rights and Labor are set out at 22 U.S.C. § 2651a(c)(2) (2016).

This legislation requires the Assistant Secretary to report through the Under Secretary for Global Affairs to the Secretary of State on matters relating to the formulation and implementation of U.S.

human rights foreign policy. The Assistant Secretary is also responsible for the preparation of the human rights country reports, prescribed by § 116 and § 502B, as well as the reports mandated by other applicable legislation. The Bureau for Democracy, Human Rights and Labor has a sizeable specialized staff, which plays an important role in administering and coordinating U.S. laws and policies relating to the promotion of human rights, democracy and labor rights. Information about the Bureau's activities is available at *https://www.state.gov/policy-issues/human-rights-and-democracy/*.

The effectiveness of the Bureau depends on the Assistant Secretary's commitment to human rights, bureaucratic skill and clout and, above all, the political will of the President and Secretary of State to have a strong U.S. human rights foreign policy. The attitude of the Executive Branch towards international human rights in general also influences the manner in which U.S. legislation on that subject is applied as well as the foreign policy initiatives the United States is likely to take.

While DRL coordinates U.S. human rights policy at the international level, the Bureau does not perform any oversight functions with respect to domestic U.S. compliance with international human rights norms or otherwise function as a "national human rights institution." Within the federal government, the various departments and agencies (such as Education, Interior, and Health and Human Services) each have some responsibility for domestic implementation of human rights law and obligations within their respective domains, with overall guidance provided by the NSC's Policy Coordination Committee discussed in § 6–5 *supra*.

Many states, counties and cities within the United States have independent human rights commissions or councils. Some (such as the State of California and the City of Berkeley) have opted to prepare their own reports under certain human rights treaties. In 2016, the State of Hawaii called upon its departments and counties to affirm the principles of the Convention on the Elimination of All Forms of Discrimination Against Women and to work with the State Commission on the Status of Women to develop gender analysis guidelines, including the examination of race, disability, immigration status, sexual orientation, and other demographic characteristics linked to gender. *See* 2015 Hawaii Senate Resolution No. 97–16, Hawaii Twenty-Eighth Legislature (April 7, 2016).

IV. INTERNATIONAL HUMAN RIGHTS LAW IN U.S. COURTS

§ 6–11. INTRODUCTION

As a general proposition, treaties and customary international law are the principal sources of international human rights law. States incorporate these principles and provisions into their domestic law in different ways. To understand how American courts deal with international human rights law, it is necessary to review the place given to treaties and customary international law in U.S. law.

In general, U.S. constitutional law accords treaties the same normative rank as federal statutes, meaning that once ratified, they are part of the Supreme Law of the Land. Treaty provisions cannot contravene the Constitution or violate any constitutional rights. However, they supersede prior inconsistent federal law and (at least to the extent the relevant provision is directly applicable or "self-executing") to the extent of conflict or inconsistency. RESTATEMENT (FOURTH) FOREIGN RELATIONS LAW §§ 301, 302, 307, 311 (2018).

Customary international law is generally equated law to federal common law. *See* Banco Nacional de Cuba v. Sabbatino, 376 U.S. 398, 425 (1964); RESTATEMENT (THIRD) FOREIGN RELATIONS LAW § 131. *But cf.* Bradley & Goldsmith, "Customary International Law as Federal Common Law: A Critique of the Modern Position," 110 Harv. L. Rev. 815 (1997); Vázquez , "Customary International Law as U.S. Law: A Critique of the Revisionist and Intermediate Positions and a Defense of the Modern Position," 86 Notre Dame L. Rev. 1495 (2011).

A federal statute will take precedence over an earlier conflicting treaty provision and any customary international law rule in conflict with it. Whitney v. Robertson, 124 U.S. 190, 194 (1888); Cook v. United States, 288 U.S. 102 (1933). Wherever possible, however, U.S. courts will attempt to reconcile U.S. law with the country's international obligations to avoid unintended conflicts. RESTATEMENT (THIRD) FOREIGN RELATIONS LAW

§ 114 and 115; *cf.* Murray v. The Schooner Charming Betsy, 6 U.S. (2 Cranch) 64, 118 (1804).

In sum, when an international human rights norm has become binding on the United States either as a result of a treaty obligation or, according to the "modern position," as customary international law, it has the status of U.S. law. How that law will be applied by domestic courts and what legal effect it will be accorded depends, among other things, on whether it has been superseded (displaced) by a federal statute and whether, in the case of a treaty, it can be applied without implementing legislation—that is, whether it is "self-executing." The sections that follow will look at the manner in which U.S. courts have applied international human rights law.

§ 6–12. HUMAN RIGHTS TREATIES

The human rights provisions of the UN Charter have been invoked in U.S. courts on a number of occasions. The most important case on the subject is Sei Fujii v. California, 38 Cal.2d 718, 242 P.2d 617 (1952), discussed *supra* in § 6–3. Although the California Supreme Court struck down the law in question as being in violation of the Fourteenth Amendment of the U.S. Constitution, it declared that the human rights provisions of the UN Charter were non-self-executing and that, consequently, they lacked the necessary domestic legal force to invalidate the challenged California law.

Although that decision might also have been challenged on the ground that the treaty provision (even though "non-self-executing") reflected a "preemptive" federal policy on the subject, so that a state law in conflict with that policy must yield to it, *see* Zschernig v. Miller, 389 U.S. 429 (1968), U.S. courts have generally followed the Sei Fujii view, holding the human rights provisions of the Charter to be "non-self-executing."

The distinction between a "self-executing" and "non-self-executing" treaty concerns the domestic effect of the treaty in question. Doctrinally, a "self-executing" treaty has the force of federal law in the United States and is "directly enforceable" in U.S. courts without the need for implementing legislation, while a "non-self-executing" treaty is not domestically enforceable by U.S. courts in the absence of implementing legislation, even while it remains binding on the United States under international law. *See* RESTATEMENT (FOURTH) FOREIGN RELATIONS LAW § 301.

The exact meaning of the distinction has been controversial ever since the Supreme Court first spoke to the issue in Foster v. Neilson, 27 U.S. (2 Pet.) 253 (1829):

> A treaty is in its nature a contract between two nations, not a legislative act. It does not generally effect, of itself, the object to be accomplished, especially so far as its operation is infra-territorial; but is carried into execution by the sovereign power of the respective parties to the instrument.
>
> In the United States a different principle is established. Our constitution declares a treaty

> to be the law of the land. It is, consequently, to be regarded in courts of justice as equivalent to an act of the legislature, whenever it operates of itself without the aid of any legislative provision. But when the terms of the stipulation import a contract, when either of the parties engages to perform a particular act, the treaty addresses itself to the political, not the judicial department; and the legislature must execute the contract before it can become a rule for the Court.

Id. at 314.

The "self-executing" terminology was first used by the Court in Whitney v. Robertson, 124 U.S. 190, 194 (1888):

> When the stipulations [of a treaty] are not self-executing, they can only be enforced pursuant to legislation to carry them into effect. . . . If the treaty contains stipulations which are self-executing, that is, require no legislation to make them operative, to that extent they have the force and effect of a legislative enactment.

Over the years, this distinction has become an accepted doctrine. *See, e.g.,* RESTATEMENT (THIRD) FOREIGN RELATIONS LAW § 111(3) (1986) ("a non-self-executing agreement will not be given effect as [U.S.] law in the absence of implementing legislation.) and § 111(4) ("[a]n international agreement of the United States is 'non-self-executing' (a) if the agreement manifests an intention that it shall not become effective as domestic law without the enactment of implementing legislation, (b) if the Senate in giving consent to a treaty, or Congress by resolution, requires implementing legislation, or (c) if implementing legislation is constitutionally required.").

In 2008, the Supreme Court addressed the issues again Medellín v. Texas, 552 U.S. 491 (2008). The case arose from the failure of U.S. officials to advise José Ernesto Medellín, a Mexican national, of his right under Article 36 of the Vienna Convention on Consular Relations to report his detention to the Mexican consulate. Medellín had been found guilty of murder by the Texas courts and sentenced to death. His petitions for habeas corpus were deemed barred by the "procedural default" doctrine because he had not raised his claims under the Convention at trial or on appeal.

Before his appeals were exhausted, the International Court of Justice held that because the United States had violated its obligations under the Vienna Convention, Medellín and other Mexican nationals with similar claims were entitled under the treaty to review of their state court convictions. The ICJ did not specify a particular procedure for this review but held that the United States was obligated "to provide, by means of its own choosing, review and reconsideration of the convictions and sentences" to determine whether the failure to provide the notice required by the treaty prejudiced the petitioners. Avena and Other Mexican Nationals (Mex. v. U.S.), 2004 I.C.J. 12 at 72 (Mar. 31).

In response, President Bush issued a memorandum purporting to instruct the Texas courts to give effect to the ICJ's judgment. It said: "I have determined, pursuant to the authority vested in me as President by the Constitution and the laws of the United States of America, that the United States will discharge its international obligations under the decision of the International Court of Justice in [Avena], by having State courts give effect to the decision in accordance with general principles of comity in cases filed by the 51 Mexican nationals addressed in that decision." The Texas Court of Criminal Appeals rejected that instruction, however, on the ground that the President's memorandum was not "binding federal law" and thus could not displace the relevant state law.

Writing for a majority of the Court, Chief Justice Roberts concluded that neither the Avena decision nor the President's memorandum entitled Medellín to the review and reconsideration he sought. As to the first, the Chief Justice focused primarily on Article 94 of the UN Charter, under which the United States "under[took] to comply with the decision of the International Court of Justice in any case to which it is a party." Because Article 94 did not say that the States Parties 'shall' or 'must' comply, 552 U.S. 491, 508 (2008), and for a variety of other reasons, the Court concluded that the ICJ's judgment in Avena did not of its own force constitute binding federal law that pre-empts state restrictions on the filing of successive habeas petitions.

On the second issue, the Medellín majority noted that while treaties may comprise international commitments "they are not domestic law unless Congress has either enacted implementing statutes or the treaty itself conveys an intention that it be 'self-executing' and is ratified on these terms [citing to Igartua-De La Rosa v. United States, 417 F.3d 145, 150 (1st Cir. 2005)]." *Id.* at 505. In a footnote, it said that a "non-self-executing" treaty is one that "does not by itself give rise to domestically enforceable federal law." 552 U.S. at 505 n. 2. Because the treaty in question (i.e., the UN Charter) was not self-executing, the President therefore lacked constitutional authority bind the state courts to follow the Avena decision. The Court noted that "[t]he President may comply with the treaty's obligations by some other means, so long as they are consistent with the Constitution. But he may not rely upon a non-self-executing treaty to 'establish binding rules of decision that preempt contrary state law.' " *Id.* at 530.

Several aspects of this decision give rise to concern from the human rights perspective. Perhaps the most important is that the executive branch was found, in the circumstances of this case, to lack the constitutional ability to require one of the constituent states of the Union to comply with a national obligation under international law. For many, this result illustrates the difficulties posed by the federal system when it comes to human rights treaty obligations.

Second, some commentators have worried that some of the Court's language might be read to establish a presumption against self-execution. Commentators have also questioned the Court's suggestion that the domestic effect of the treaty turns on the intent of the political branches ("[o]ur cases simply require courts to decide whether a treaty's terms reflect a determination by the President who negotiated it and the Senate that confirmed it that the treaty has domestic effect.") *Id.* at 521.

Third, concern has been expressed about the Court's dictum that "[e]ven when treaties are self-executing in the sense that they create federal law, the background presumption is that '[i]nternational agreements, even those directly benefiting private persons, generally do not create private rights or provide for a private cause of action in domestic courts.'" *Id.* at 505 n.3. This statement seems to signal a restrictive approach to the status of even self-executing treaties in U.S. law.

Finally, some worry that the Court's statement that a non-self-executing treaty is not "domestically enforceable federal law" and lacks "any domestic effect of its own force" will effectively deprive such treaties of any normative influence whatsoever. Even if they do not provide the basis for bringing a lawsuit, for example, might they nonetheless be invoked by litigants or relied on by courts as providing evidence of customary international law or otherwise relevant standards? Do they still fall within the President's constitutional obligations to 'take care' to enforce the law? These and other questions continue to be vigorously debated in the wake of the Medellín decision.

More recently, the RESTATEMENT (FOURTH), FOREIGN RELATIONS LAW § 310(1) (2018) notes that a treaty provision "is directly enforceable in courts in the United States only if it is self-executing." It also states that U.S. courts "will evaluate whether the text and content of the provision . . . are consistent with an understanding by the U.S. treatymakers that the provision would be directly enforceable" and that courts will defer to a specification in the relevant Senate resolution of advice and consent on this question. Id. §§ 310(2) and (3).

§ 6–13. CUSTOMARY INTERNATIONAL LAW

The place of customary international law in the U.S. legal system has similarly been the subject of differing conclusions. At the Founding, it appears that the "law of nations" was considered part of the general common law and thus applicable in federal as well as state courts. In The Paquete Habana, 175 U.S. 677, 700 (1900), the U.S. Supreme Court appeared to endorse this view when it famously said that "[i]nternational law is part of our law, and must be ascertained and administered by the courts of appropriate jurisdiction as often as questions of right depending on it are duly presented for their determination." The Court continued:

> For this purpose, where there is no treaty and no controlling executive or legislative act or judicial decision, resort must be had to the customs and usages of civilized nations, and, as evidence of

> these, to the works of jurists and commentators who by years of labor, research, and experience have made themselves particularly well acquainted with the subjects of which they treat.

175 U.S. at 700.

However, the import of this statement can be debated. Not only did the Court ascribe a secondary or "gap-filling" role to customary international law, but the context of the case suggests to some a limited application. The case involved a claim that two Spanish-flagged coastal fishing vessels had been wrongly seized by the U.S. Navy during its blockade of Cuba, and thus arose under the Court's admiralty and maritime jurisdiction (which traditionally relied on customary international law and still does today).

Moreover, the concept of a general common law (as opposed to specific doctrines) applicable in federal courts is debatable. *See* Erie R. Co. v. Tompkins, 304 U.S. 64, 78 (1938) ("[t]here is no federal general common law"); *cf.* David M. Howard, "A Revised Revisionist Position in the Law of Nations Debate," 15 Duke J. Const. L. & Pub. Pol'y 532 (2020); Bradley, Goldsmith & Moore, "Sosa, Customary International Law, and the Continuing Relevance of Erie," 120 Harv. L. Rev. 869 (2007).

Still, the question remains whether, and to what extent, customary international law may play a role in domestic litigation in the absence of an applicable human rights treaty provision. A growing list of international human rights can be characterized as customary international law (*e.g.*, genocide, torture, and prolonged arbitrary detention). RESTATEMENT (THIRD) FOREIGN RELATIONS LAW § 702. Much of that law has evolved from rights and principles proclaimed in international human rights instruments that have their basis in the Charter of the UN and other treaties of a universal character. *See* Chapter 2, *supra*. In fact, U.S. courts have from time to time relied on this law to grant judicial relief.

The Alien Tort Statute. For a number of years, one important vehicle for bringing these issues into U.S. courts has been the Alien Tort Statute (ATS), codified at 28 U.S.C. § 1350 (2014) (sometimes wrongly referred to as the "Alien Tort Claims Act"). This unique (and antique) provision - initially adopted as part of the Judiciary Act of 1789 - gives federal district courts original jurisdiction over civil actions brought by aliens (non-U.S. citizens) "for a tort only, committed in violation of the law of nations or a treaty of the United States." Exactly why the first Congress enacted this law remains in dispute.

Three things are significant about the ATS. First, it expressly incorporates the "law of nations" (or customary international law) directly into U.S. domestic law. Second, it appears (and was initially interpreted by the judiciary) to permit U.S. courts to adjudicate claims of human rights abuses even when the alleged abuses took place in foreign countries and involved no U.S. persons or entities or other connections to the United States. In this sense, the statute uniquely provided a kind of "universal civil jurisdiction" allowing foreigners to sue foreigners in U.S. courts on the basis of non-codified customary international law for human rights abuses occurring outside the United States. Third, it has not been warmly embraced by the U.S. Supreme Court.

The first modern case to discuss these issues was Filártiga v. Peña-Irala, 630 F.2d 876 (2d Cir.1980), in which the Court of Appeals held that the right to be free from torture "has become part of customary international law, as evidenced and defined by the Universal Declaration of Human Rights." *Id.* at 882. That case was brought by a Paraguayan family against a former Paraguayan police official for the death of their son in Paraguay. The court was required to determine whether torture was a "tort . . . in violation of the law of nations." To substantiate its conclusion, the court traced the evolution of the prohibition against torture from the UN Charter, the Universal Declaration and other major international human rights instruments.

In the wake of the *Filártiga* decision, litigants brought hundreds of § 1350 cases concerning a broad range of human rights violations occurring in various parts of the world. In most of those cases, however, the respondents did not appear in court to defend themselves, and most of the proceedings resulted in default judgments. Moreover, the defendants seldom had assets in the United States, meaning plaintiffs were typically unable to recover on the resulting judgments: given the statute's unique jurisdictional reach, foreign courts were generally unable or unwilling to enforce them. Nonetheless, ATS litigation was frequently used by human rights advocates as a means of giving public voice to complaints about violations of international law occurring in foreign countries.

The U.S. Supreme Court first considered the question of the scope of the ATS in Sosa v. Alvarez-Machain, 542 U.S. 692 (2004). The central issue before the Court was whether an alien could bring a private claim under the ATS as a matter of federal common law or only pursuant to a supplementary congressional statute authorizing such claims. The Court, in an opinion by Justice Souter, held that by its terms the ATS is merely a jurisdictional grant and does not itself create a cause of action. However, it said, the First Congress could not have meant the statute to be "stillborn," an empty vessel to be filled by subsequent legislation (none was enacted) but must have been intended to allow the federal courts to adjudicate claims in violation of "the law of nations" under their common law power. Although "general" federal common law no longer exists today (given the effect of Erie Railroad v. Tompkins, 304 U.S. 64 (1938)), the Court said that the law of nations continues to be one of the "limited enclaves in which federal courts may derive some substantive law in a common law way." *Id.* at 729.

The Court considered the criteria to be applied in determining which of the "limited enclaves" provides a cause of action falling within the ATS. When the ATS was originally enacted in 1789, it observed, a tort remedy was available for violation of safe conducts, infringement of the rights of ambassadors, and piracy. "It was this narrow set of violations of the law of nations, admitting of a judicial remedy and at the same time threatening serious consequences in international affairs, that was probably on minds of the men who drafted the ATS with its reference to tort." 542 U.S. at 715. Accordingly, U.S. courts "should require any claim based on the present-day law of nations to rest on a norm of international character accepted by the civilized world and defined with a specificity comparable to the features of the 18th-century paradigms we have recognized." *Id.* at 725.

The Court took care to emphasize the limited scope of this authority. "The door to further independent judicial recognition of actionable international norms," the Court said, "is still ajar subject to vigilant doorkeeping, and thus open to a narrow class of international norms today." *Id.* at 729. Since the "decision to create a private right of action is one better left to legislative judgment," the Court stressed, "courts should not recognize private claims under federal common law for violations of any international law norm with less definite content and acceptance among civilized nations than the historical paradigms familiar when § 1350 was enacted." *Id.* at 727 and 732. Concerning Sosa's specific claim, the Court found that "a single illegal detention of less than a day, followed by the transfer of custody to lawful authorities and a prompt arraignment, violates no norm of customary international law so well defined as to support the creation of a federal remedy." *Id.* at 738.

In emphasizing the need in ATS cases for "great caution in adapting the law of nations to private rights," the Court noted concern over the possible "collateral consequences" of a given decision.

> [T]he potential implications for the foreign relations of the United States of recognizing such causes should make courts particularly wary of impinging on the discretion of the Legislative and Executive Branches in managing foreign affairs. It is one thing for American courts to enforce constitutional limits on our own State and Federal Governments' power, but quite another to consider suits under rules that would go so far as to claim a limit on the power of foreign governments over their own citizens, and to hold that a foreign government or its agent has transgressed those limits.

Id. at 728. Accordingly, "there is a strong argument that federal courts should give serious weight to the Executive Branch's view of the case's impact on foreign policy 'a policy of case-specific deference to the political branches'." *Id.* at 733, n.21. The Court also suggested that lower courts should look to international law to determine whether each particular norm extends the scope of liability to private actors such as corporations or individuals. *Id.* at 733 n.20.

The Sosa decision also appeared to indicate the Court's receptivity to an "exhaustion of domestic remedies" requirement in ATS cases. *See* 542 U.S. at 733, n.21. After initially rejecting such a condition, the Ninth Circuit said in Sarei v. Rio Tinto, PLC, 550 F.3d 822 at 824 (9th Cir. 2008) that "[w]here the 'nexus' to the United States is weak, courts should carefully consider the question of exhaustion, particularly—but not exclusively—with respect to claims that do not involve matters of 'universal concern.' "

In *Kiobel v. Royal Dutch Petroleum Co.*, 569 U.S. 108 (2013), however, the U.S. Supreme Court took a more restrictive view, holding that the presumption against extraterritoriality applies to the ATS and that the statute does not extend to cases in which "all the relevant conduct took place outside the United States." Id. at 124.

In that case, Nigerian nationals residing in the United States had sued Dutch, British, and Nigerian corporations claiming that through their joint subsidiary which was engaged in oil exploration and production in Ogoniland, they had aided and abetted the Nigerian Government in committing extrajudicial killings, crimes against humanity, torture and cruel treatment, arbitrary arrest and detention, and violations of the rights to life, liberty, security, and association among other violations of international law. The Second Circuit had dismissed the complaint, reasoning that the law of nations does not recognize corporate liability. After initially granting certiorari on that issue, the Court ordered supplemental briefing on the question whether U.S. courts can consider claims for violations of the law of nations occurring in another country.

In its judgment, the Court answered that question in the negative, relying on a canon of statutory interpretation known as "the presumption against extraterritorial application." Under that presumption, the Court said, "[w]hen a statute gives no clear indication of an extraterritorial application, it has none" (*id.* at 108, citing to Morrison v. National Australia Bank Ltd., 561 U.S. 247 (2010)). That rule in turn reflects the "presumption that United States law governs domestically but does not rule the world" (*id.*, at 105, citing to Microsoft Corp. v. AT&T Corp., 550 U.S. 437, 454 (2007)). The presumption "serves to protect against unintended clashes between our laws and those of other nations which could result in international discord" (*id.*, at 115, citing to EEOC v. Arabian American Oil Co., 499 U.S. 244 at 248).

The Court recalled its caution in Sosa that "the danger of unwarranted judicial interference in the conduct of foreign policy is magnified in the context of the ATS, because the question is not what Congress has done but instead what courts may do." *Id.* at 109. It noted that in Sosa it had "repeatedly stressed the need for judicial caution in considering which claims could be brought under the ATS, in light of foreign policy concerns." *Id.* at 116. Further, it said, "[t]hese concerns, which are implicated in any case arising under the ATS, are all the more pressing when the question is whether a cause of action under the ATS reaches conduct within the territory of another sovereign." *Id.* at 117.

Nothing in the text of the statute, the Court continued, suggested that Congress intended causes of action recognized under it to have extraterritorial reach. *Id.* at 118. Neither could "the historical background against which the ATS was enacted overcome the presumption against application to conduct in the territory of another sovereign." *Id.* at 119. Finally, the Court found "no indication that the ATS was passed to make the United States a uniquely hospitable forum for the enforcement of international norms." *Id.* at 123. In consequence, it concluded that "the presumption against extraterritoriality applies to claims under the ATS, and that nothing in the statute rebuts that presumption." *Id.* at 1669. Nevertheless, it phrased its ultimate holding in narrow terms:

> On these facts, all the relevant conduct took place outside the United States. And even where the claims touch and concern the territory of the United States, they must do so with sufficient force to displace the presumption against extraterritorial application. *See Morrison,* 561 U.S. 247, 130 S.Ct., at 2883–2888. Corporations are often present in many countries, and it would reach too far to say that mere corporate presence suffices. If Congress were to determine otherwise, a statute more specific than the ATS would be required.

Id. at 124–25.

Precisely how claims might "touch and concern the territory of the United States" sufficiently to overcome the presumption against extraterritoriality was not further explained. Justice Kennedy's concurrence noted that the majority was "careful to leave open a number of significant questions regarding the reach and interpretation of the Alien Tort Statute." *Id.* at 125. In his concurrence, Justice Breyer (joined by Justices Ginsburg, Sotomayor and

Kagan) said that jurisdiction under the ATS could be proper where "(1) the alleged tort occurs on American soil, (2) the defendant is an American national, or (3) the defendant's conduct substantially and adversely affects an important American national interest, and that includes a distinct interest in preventing the United States from becoming a safe harbor (free of civil as well as criminal liability) for a torturer or other common enemy of mankind." *Id.* at 127.

In *Jesner v. Arab Bank, PLC*, 584 U.S. 241 (2018), the Court further narrowed the reach of the ATS by holding that foreign corporations could not be sued under its provisions. That case had been brought by individuals (and representatives of individuals) allegedly killed or injured by terrorist acts committed outside the United States. They sought to recover damages from Arab Bank, PLC, a foreign corporation, because some of its officials had allegedly allowed the Bank to be used to transfer funds to terrorist groups in the Middle East, thus enabling or facilitating the terrorist acts that caused the deaths or injuries in question. Writing for a 5-4 majority, Justice Kennedy noted that the statute itself does not provide that foreign corporations can be defendants in ATS suits. Given the sensitivity of the issue, it was for the Congress, not the Judiciary, to decide whether to expand the scope of liability under the ATS to include foreign corporations and, if so, when and under what conditions. "[J]udicial deference requires that any imposition of corporate liability on foreign corporations for violations of international law must be determined in the first instance by the political branch" *Id*, 584 U.S. at 274.

Finally, in *Nestlé USA, Inc. v. Doe,* 593 U.S. 628 (2021), the plaintiffs were six individuals from Mali who claimed they had been trafficked into Côte d'Ivoire to work as child slaves on cocoa farms. The defendants were two U.S. corporations, Nestlé USA and Cargill; neither owned or operate cocoa farms in Côte d'Ivoire but were sued under the ATS for aiding and abetting child slavery. The defendants not only purchased cocoa from the farms where the plaintiffs were forced to work but were alleged to have "provided those farms with technical and financial resources—such as training, fertilizer, tools, and cash—in exchange for the exclusive right to purchase cocoa." To further support those claims, the plaintiffs contended that the defendants "knew or should have known" of the child slavery but continued to do business with the farms; in other words, that they had "economic leverage over the farms but failed to exercise it to eliminate child slavery." *Id.* at 631.

The Ninth Circuit had held that the plaintiffs had satisfied the domestic application of the ATS requirements of *Kiobel* because, even though the defendants' "resource distribution and [plaintiff's] injuries occurred outside the United States," the defendants' decision-making on financing and operations had occurred in the United States. The Supreme Court disagreed with that analysis, however, stating that "allegations of general corporate activity—like decisionmaking—cannot alone establish domestic application of the ATS."

To reach this conclusion, the Court applied the "two-step framework" from *RJR Nabisco, Inc. v.*

European Community to determine the extraterritoriality question. As applied, step one asks whether the statute clearly indicated it was meant to apply extraterritorially. The Court found that it did not and accordingly it moved to step two, which asks whether "the conduct relevant to the statute's focus occurred in the United States." Although the parties disagreed about what the focus of the ATS actually was, the Court characterized the defendants' domestic conduct (decision making on financing and operations) as "general corporate activity" and therefore insufficient to justify extraterritorial application of the ATS under either party's contentions.

In *Doe I v. Cisco Systems, Inc.*, 73 F.4th 7 (9th Cir. 2023), the Ninth Circuit upheld the assertion of aiding and abetting liability under the ATS against a U.S. corporation for knowingly providing assistance in the United States to the Chinese government's violations of international human rights norms within its own territory.

There continues to be a spirited debate over the role of customary international law in U.S. courts and the legitimacy and propriety of ATS suits. For a sampling, *see* Thomas Ellis, "The Rise, Fall, and Resurrection of the Alien Tort Statute," 57 UIC L. Rev. 863 (2024); Phillip Ayers, "Nestlé v. Doe: A Death Knell to Corporate Human Rights Accountability?", 46 Seattle U. L. Rev. 909 (2023); Hassan Ahmad, "Judicial Activism in Transnational Business and Human Rights Litigation," 41 Berkeley J. Int'l L. 145 (2023).

Congress has explicitly provided federal causes of action for torture and extrajudicial killing under the Torture Victims Protection Act, Pub. L. No. 102–256, 106 Stat. 73 (1992), codified at 22 U.S.C. § 1350 (note) (2008). Note that the somewhat related issue of universal criminal jurisdiction to prosecute and punish individuals for human rights violations that constitute international crimes has not yet been raised in U.S. courts.

Selected References and Further Reading

André Nollkaemper, Yuval Shany, Antonios Tzanakopoulos, The Engagement of Domestic Courts with International Law: Comparative Perspectives (Oxford 2024); D. Shelton, ed., International Law and Domestic Legal Systems: Incorporation, Transformation, and Persuasion (2011); Buergenthal, "International Human Rights: U.S. Policy and Priorities," 14 Va. J. Int'l L. 611, 614–17 (1974); L. Henkin, Foreign Affairs and the United States Constitution (2d ed. 1996).

Treaties in U.S. Law:

Alyssa Moinet, "CEDAW: United States Federal Ratification and the Case for a CEDAW Ordinance in Chicago,?" 72 DePaul L. Rev. 755 (2023); Benjamin A. Barsky, "Dual Federalism, Constitutional Openings, and the Convention on the Rights of Persons with Disabilities," 24 U. Pa. J. Const. L. 345 (2022); David Sloss, The Death of Treaty Supremacy: An Invisible Constitutional Change (2016); Glennon and Sloane, "The Sad, Quiet Death of Missouri v. Holland: How Bond Hobbled the Treaty Power," 41

Yale J. Int'l L. 51 (2016); Hollis, "An Inter-Subjective Treaty Power," 90 Notre Dame L. Rev. 1415 (2015); Ku and Yoo "Bond, The Treaty Power, and the Overlooked Value of Non-Self-Executing Treaties," 90 Notre Dame L. Rev. 1607 (2015); Ramsey, "A Textual Approach to Treaty Non-Self-Execution," 2015 B.Y.U. L. Rev. 1639 (2015); Ku and Yoo, "Bond, The Treaty Power, and the Overlooked Value of Non-Self-Executing Treaties," 90 Notre Dame L. Rev. 1607 (2015); Ramsey, "A Textual Approach to Treaty Non-Self-Execution," 2015 B.Y.U. L. Rev. 1639 (2015); Bradley, "Federalism, Treaty Implementation, and Political Process: Bond v. United States," 108 Am. J. Int'l L. 486 (2014); Bradley, "Intent, Presumption, and Non-Self-Executing Treaties," 102 Am. J. Int'l L. 540 (2008); Stewart, "Ratification of the Convention on the Rights of the Child," 5 Geo. J. Fighting Poverty 161 (1998); Stewart, "U.S. Ratification of the Covenant on Civil and Political Rights: The Significance of the Reservations, Understanding and Declarations," 14 Hum. Rts. L.J. 77, 79–81 (1993); Buergenthal, "Self-Executing and Non-Self-Executing Treaties in National and International Law," 235 Recueil des Cours 303 (1992 IV); Buergenthal, "Modern Constitutions and Human Rights Treaties," 36 Colum. J. Trans'l L. 211, 221–23 (1997).

Bricker Amendment / Federalism:

Richards, "The Bricker Amendment and Congress' Failure to Check the Inflation of the Executive's Foreign Affairs Powers, 1951–1954," 94 Cal. L. Rev. 175 (2006); Henkin, "U.S. Ratification of Human

Rights Treaties: The Ghost of Senator Bricker," 89 Am. J. Int'l L. 341 (1995); D. Tananbaum, *The Bricker Amendment Controversy: A Test of Eisenhower's Political Leadership* (1988); Kaufman & Whiteman, "Opposition to Human Rights in the United States Senate: The Legacy of the Bricker Amendment," 10 Hum. Rts. Q. 309 (1988).

The Alien Tort Statute:

Phillip Ayers, "Nestlé USA, Inc. v. Doe: A Death Knell To Corporate Human Rights Accountability?," 46 Seattle U. L. Rev. 909 (2023); Clara Petch, "What Remains of the Alien Tort Statute After Nestlé USA, Inc. v. Doe?," 42 Nw. J. Int'l L. & Bus. 397 (2022); Christopher Ewell, Oona A. Hathaway, Ellen Nohle, "Has The Alien Tort Statute Made A Difference?: A Historical, Empirical, and Normative Assessment," 107 Cornell L. Rev. 1205 (2022); Lindsey Roberson and Johanna Lee, "The Road to Recovery After Nestlé: Exploring the TVPA As A Promising Tool For Corporate Accountability," 6 Colum. Hum. Rts. L. Rev. Online 1 (2021); Lee, "The Three Lives of the Alien Tort Statute: The Evolving Role of the Judiciary in U.S. Foreign Relations," 89 Notre Dame L. Rev. 1645 (2014); Vázquez, "Things We Do With Presumptions: Reflections on Kiobel v. Royal Dutch Shell," 89 Notre Dame L. Rev. 1719 (2014); Stephens, "The Curious History of the Alien Tort Statute," 89 Notre Dame L. Rev. 1467 (2014).

Customary International Law/Law of Nations:

Garvey, "The Long Arm of the Law: Customary International Law in Domestic Courts," 91 Fordham

L. Rev. Online 123 (2023); David M. Howard, "A Revised Revisionist Position in the Law of Nations Debate," 15 Duke J. Const. L. & Pub. Pol'y 53 (2020); Ingrid Wuerth, "The Future of the Federal Common Law of Foreign Relations," 106 Geo. L.J. 1825 (2018); Gary Born, "Customary International Law in United States Courts," 92 Wash. L. Rev. 1641 (2017); Moon, "The Original Meaning of the Law of Nations," 56 Va. J. Int'l L. 51 (2016); Buergenthal, "Self-Executing and Non-Self-Executing Treaties in National and International Law," 235 Recueil des Cours 303 (1992 IV).

CHAPTER 7

NON-STATE ACTORS AND INTERNATIONAL HUMAN RIGHTS LAW

I. INTRODUCTION

At its origins, international human rights law mainly addressed the relationship between national governments and their own citizens. In consequence, it focused primarily on the domestic duties and responsibilities of States and their governmental agencies and entities. Indeed, that was the cause of much early criticism (echoes of which can still be heard today): that by addressing how a government deals with its own citizens within its own territory, international human rights improperly interferes in the domestic affairs of sovereign States.

Over time, however, the elaboration of international human rights norms, institutions, and procedures has been broadly accepted as a legitimate, even necessary, constraint on governmental actions in general, so that States are now understood to owe basic human rights protections to all people, including foreigners (non-citizens) within their territories and subject to their jurisdiction—and even those outside the State's national borders, at least in some circumstances.

In addition, the scope of human rights obligations is increasingly understood to extend beyond the government and its entities to impose duties on private entities as well as individuals. As a result, the field of international human rights law today encompasses an increasing variety of non-state actors.

This development has clear roots, of course, in the Universal Declaration of Human Rights, which recognizes that governments are not the only ones with human rights obligations and responsibilities. It describes human rights as

> a common standard of achievement for all peoples and nations, to the end that every individual and every organ of society, keeping this Declaration constantly in mind, shall strive by teaching and education to promote respect for these rights and freedoms and by progressive measures, national and international, to secure their universal and effective recognition and observance, both among the peoples of Member States themselves and among the peoples of territories under their jurisdiction.

UDHR, preambular para. 8. The notion that entities other than States and individuals may be rights-holders as well as bearers of responsibilities has gained increasing acceptance during the intervening decades.

This chapter describes the relevant roles and responsibilities of several categories of non-state actors. The term "non-state actor" can be wide-reaching, even encompassing entities such as non-governmental organizations (NGOs), some inter-governmental organizations (IGOs), and private bodies as diverse as multinational corporations ("enterprises" in UN usage), and voluntary associations. Although these entities may fall collectively under the "non-state actors" umbrella, they are quite different and play varying roles. To date, no specific treaty obligation or rule of customary international law explicitly holds *all* actors liable for committing human rights violations or provides a forum for redress for all interferences with human rights. However, parts of the international community have increasingly viewed some non-state (non-governmental) actors as being covered by some international human rights instruments.

Moreover, non-state actors can have the capacity to contribute positively to the protection and promotion of human rights around the world. Some NGOs have been established precisely for that purpose and they frequently play an important and dynamic role in advancing human rights, both domestically and globally. Increasingly, multinational enterprises and financial institutions (both domestic and international) are in a position to either be heroes or villains in upholding human rights, depending on their governing rules and practices. Intergovernmental organizations can also play an influential role in determining how each of those groups operates.

This chapter offers an overview of the evolving role of two groups of non-state actors, each raising different issues about the international human rights field: "non-governmental actors" and private business enterprises.

II. NON-GOVERNMENTAL ORGANIZATIONS

§ 7–1. TYPES AND ROLES

Some 1200 NGOs attended the San Francisco Conference during the drafting of the UN Charter and many played an important role. They lobbied for the inclusion of human rights provisions in the Charter and for a system that would give NGOs formal institutional affiliation with and standing before UN organs.

The result was Article 71 of the UN Charter, which provides that "the Economic and Social Council may make suitable arrangements for consultation with non-governmental organizations which are concerned with matters within its competence." Article 71 was implemented in due course by ECOSOC and over time it has come to be interpreted broadly to allow NGOs to involve themselves in UN human rights activities. The subject was first regulated by ECOSOC Resolution 1296 (XLIV) of May 23, 1968, which was revised and expanded in 1996 by ECOSOC Resolution 1996/31. It established a formal system that enables qualified NGOs to obtain one of three types of consultative status (general, special, and roster) with the Organization. *See https://ecosoc.un.org/en/ngo/consultative-status*.

The existence of this system has encouraged the creation of more NGOs and the adoption of similar consultative systems by other international and regional organizations, such as the Council of Europe, the Organization for the Security and

Cooperation for Europe, the African Union (including the African Commission for Human Rights), and the Organization of American States. As a result, a myriad of these groups exists today around the world, helping to promote human rights standards and compliance. While most are domestically oriented, many are internationally active. Generally, *see https://www.humanrightscareers.com/issues/types-of-ngos.*

The term "NGO" is generally understood to exclude entities established by governments (known as "government organized NGOs" (or "GONGOs") or through intergovernmental agreements as well as private for-profit enterprises. Nevertheless, human rights NGOs come in all sizes and varieties. They can be classified in several categories. On the one hand, generalist NGOs have broad mandates and agendas, covering all categories of human rights, e.g., Human Rights Watch or the International Federation for Human Rights (FIDH). By contrast, many NGOs have specific mandates, for example covering a specific right (the right to health or water or housing or a clean environment) or the rights of a specific category of persons (such as women, children, persons with disabilities, minorities, or indigenous peoples). Some concentrate only on local or national situations, while others have a regional focus and still others work on global issues.

The activities of human rights NGOs typically focus on the overall promotion and protection of human rights. Some aim at changing the domestic or international policies of their own (or foreign) governments, while others engage exclusively in education and training, building domestic constituencies, or carrying out international relief efforts. They may conduct inquiries, fact-finding missions, monitoring and investigations into human rights abuses, visit detention facilities to monitor detainees' rights and detention conditions, or assist asylum-seekers and refugees. Some exclusively litigate human rights issues in national courts, including by offering free legal assistance to alleged victims. Others mount grass-roots campaigns against specific types of violations (such as torture, police abuse, or racial or gender discrimination) while still others engage in standard-setting efforts (for example, aimed at improving corporate social responsibility).

NGOs may be active in the formulation or negotiation of international human rights instruments, in advocating for their ratification by States, or involved in drafting national reports to be submitted to international bodies. They may also assist States in implementing recommendations made by international bodies. Some governments consult with NGOs during the drafting of domestic legislation with human rights dimensions.

Many NGOs work closely with international bodies such as the United Nations and its specialized agencies (*see* § 7–3 *infra*) as well as regional bodies. Whether or not they have a formal affiliation with an intergovernmental organization, human rights NGOs have increasingly played an important role in the evolution of the international system for the protection of human rights and in efforts to make it work. Because governments that do not respect human rights are often disposed to undermine international human rights norms, institutions, and procedures, human rights NGOs frequently provide a needed and effective counterweight by highlighting the issues and bringing public pressure to bear (for example, by "naming and shaming" abusers). To a significant extent, NGOs deserve credit for the progress in international human rights compliance that has been made in recent decades.

The NGO field is diverse, constantly adapting and evolving. As the range of human rights concerns has expanded, NGOs have similarly diversified their work and enlarged their interests. With their increasing numbers and functions, networks of international and national NGOs have emerged. In recent years, this expanding web of transnational NGOs, other groups, and individuals has frequently been referred to as the "global civil society." and the nature and merits of its increasing role have been debated. Generally, *see https://www.un.org/en/get-involved/un-and-civil-society*.

Consider, for example, the disparate nature and activities of the following human rights organizations. The list is far from exhaustive and includes only a small fraction of the NGOs in the international human rights field. It is included here simply to illustrate the varied nature of NGOs involved in human rights work.

Amnesty International describes itself as a "global movement of people fighting injustice and promoting human rights" through "high-level legislative work, media outreach and grassroots mobilization to shape and promote legislation and policies to advance human rights, protect individuals and free prisoners of conscience." It is active in the areas of arms control, corporate accountability, freedom of expression, the rights of the indigenous people, and international justice, to name a few. *See https://www.amnesty.org/en/what-we-do*.

The International Federation for Human Rights (FIDH) includes some 188 national human rights organizations from 116 countries. It works at the national, regional, and international levels to defend "all civil, political, economic, social and cultural rights as set out in the Universal Declaration of Human Rights" and to "consolidate democratic processes." *See https://www.fidh.org/en*.

The European Roma Rights Centre works to combat anti-Romani racism and human rights abuse of Roma through strategic litigation, research and policy development, advocacy, and human rights education. *See http://www.errc.org/*.

The Association of Women's Rights in Development is an international feminist membership organization committed to achieving gender equality, sustainable development, and women's human rights, *inter alia* by providing comprehensive information and analysis on women's human rights and global issues. *See https://www.awid.org*.

The International Commission of Jurists aims to promote and protect human rights through the Rule of Law by using the legal expertise of its members to "develop and strengthen national and international justice systems" through the progressive development and effective implementation of international human rights and humanitarian law. It comprises up to sixty lawyers from around the world who are known for their experience, knowledge, and fundamental commitment to human rights. *See https://www.icj.org*.

Human Rights Watch is a nonprofit, nongovernmental organization dedicated to fact-finding, impartial reporting, effective use of media, and targeted advocacy for human rights. Each year, HRW publishes more than 100 reports and briefings on human rights conditions in some 90 countries, with governments, the United Nations, regional groups like the African Union and the European Union, financial institutions, and corporations. *See https://www.hrw.org*.

Médecins Sans Frontières, also known as "Doctors Without Borders," works in war-torn regions and developing countries to provide medical care and assistance through medical professionals, logistical experts, water and sanitation engineers and administrators, the majority of whom are volunteers. *See http://www.msf-me.org*.

Human Rights First is an "advocacy and action" organization that works "to promote respect for human rights and the rule of law," to encourage the U.S. government and private companies to respect the rule of law, and to "create the political environment and policy solutions necessary to ensure consistent respect for human rights." *See https://humanrightsfirst.org/about-us/.*

The Global Fund for Human Rights works to strengthen human rights around the world by finding and funding "the most effective human rights activists, offering "flexible funding with no strings attached because activists know best how to use their resources . . . [to] overturn unjust laws, push for progressive policies, and challenge entrenched systems of oppression." *See https://globalhumanrights.org.*

Minority Rights Group works to secure rights for ethnic, religious, and linguistic minorities and indigenous people around the world through advocacy publications, litigation, and training projects. *See http://minorityrights.org.*

The International Dalit Solidarity Network advocates for Dalit human rights, promotes national Dalit solidarity, and works internationally against caste-based discrimination. *See http://idsn.org/about-us/.*

Freedom House is "founded on the core conviction that freedom flourishes in democratic nations where governments are accountable to their people." It conducts research and advocacy "to defend human rights and promote democratic change, with a focus on political rights and civil liberties." *See https://freedomhouse.org.*

Article 19 focuses on the defense and promotion of "two interlocking freedoms: the Freedom to Speak, and the Freedom to Know" as articulated in Article

19 of the Universal Declaration of Human Rights, in the belief that these particular human rights are central to freedom and democracy. where all people everywhere can freely communicate. *See https://www.article19.org.*

The Public International Law & Policy Group provides free legal assistance to states and governments in such areas as peace negotiations, drafting post-conflict constitutions, prosecuting war criminals, and promoting democratic governance and transitional justice. *See http://www.publicinternationallawandpolicygroup.org.*

Habitat For Humanity is a nonprofit organization that "helps families build and improve places to call home." It works in more than 70 countries "so that more people are able to live in affordable and safe homes." Its advocacy focuses on "policy reform to remove systemic barriers preventing low-income and historically underserved families from accessing adequate, affordable shelter. *See http://www.habitat.org.*

International Coalition for the International Criminal Court is a partnership of over 2,500 member organizations in 150 countries that together fight for global justice by supporting the International Criminal Court established by the Rome Statute to prosecute genocide, crimes against humanity, war crimes, and aggression and through prosecutions in national courts. *See http://www.coalitionfortheicc.org.*

The International Service for Human Rights is dedicated to promoting and protecting human rights by supporting human rights defenders, promoting rights and accountability, and strengthening human rights laws and systems. *See http://www.ishr.ch.*

Most NGOs are formed, established, or registered as private non-profit organizations or associations under domestic (national) law. Only a very few, such as the International Committee of the Red Cross, are recognized as having international legal personality in their own right. Once formed or registered, NGOs often work closely with local populations to engage in advocacy and policy work within a state. Some NGOs work through local implementing partners to further human rights norms in foreign countries; others comprise networks or federations of affiliated organizations in different countries.

Both international and domestic NGOs engage in advocacy with state actors to further the implementation of human rights norms through recommendations for changes in policy as well as legislation. Some focus on foreign governments, while others aim to change the approach and practices of their own governments. Governmental policies are of course made on the national level, and national political considerations necessarily affect decisions about whether to ratify human rights treaties or which methods should be employed to promote respect for human rights abroad. Many NGOs actively engage in lobbying governments in an effort to influence the formulation and execution of relevant policies. Some human rights NGOs also cooperate (or work directly) with UN field activities.

§ 7–2. NGO ENGAGEMENT WITH INTERNATIONAL BODIES

In order to engage with the UN and its various commissions, committees, and specialized agencies, NGOs working in the international human rights field must have some form of consultative status (with the exception of the UN human rights treaty bodies, which do not require such status). This status permits their representatives (subject to certain conditions and restrictions) to attend meetings of these organizations, to present reports, to be heard by their committees and commissions, and, in certain cases, to influence the agendas of these bodies. According to ECOSOC's NGO Branch, as of April 2023, nearly 6500 NGOs held consultative status with the United Nations. *See generally* UN Doc. E/2022/INF/5 (April 4, 2023), accessible at *https://esango.un.org/civilsociety/displayConsultativeStatusSearch.do?method=search*.

Within Europe, NGOs participate in standard-setting at the Council of Europe through the International Non-Governmental Organizations (INGO) Conference. They can provide comments on state reports under the European Social Charter and have standing to file complaints under the 1995 Additional Protocol to the European Social Charter providing a System of Collective Complaints. NGOs also participate as *amici curiae* in cases before the European Court of Human Rights. Similar arrangements can be made with other international organizations working in the human rights field, such as the Organization of American States (OAS) through its program for the participation of civil society, the Organization for Security and Cooperation in Europe, and the African Commission on Human and Peoples' Rights.

At the UN level, human rights NGOs mostly engage with the UN Human Rights Council and its subsidiary bodies and procedures (including the Universal Periodic Review) as well as with the various human rights treaty bodies. All of the UN human rights treaty bodies have developed procedures for interaction with NGOs in the various phases of their work. For example, in the context of a State Party's report to a treaty body, NGOs may provide an "alternative" or "shadow" report on that state's progress in implementing its treaty obligations. They may brief Committee members on country conditions, either formally during a meeting before the review or informally over a coffee. They may also approach Committee members individually to lobby for the consideration of pressing concerns to raise during the dialogue with the delegation during the review.

Often, the NGO reports provide first-hand information to balance or supplement the information states include in their reports. In addition, they may contribute to the elaboration of General Comments or Recommendations by providing analyses, views, and position papers. NGOs have the ability to represent individuals who submit "communications" to treaty bodies and may act as amicus curiae. Lastly, they can provide input to the preparation of *in situ* visits by the UN Sub-Committee on the Prevention of Torture. *See generally* S. Farrior, "International Reporting Procedures," *in* Hannum (ed.), *Guide to International Human Rights Practice* 189 (4th ed. 2004); Buergenthal, "The U.N. Human Rights Committee," 5 Max Planck YB U.N. Law 341, 352–53 (2001).

The more recent treaties have expressly provided a role for NGOs in the work of the relevant treaty body, recognizing that NGOs can sometimes be in a better position than individuals to gather reliable information and prepare the necessary legal documentation. For example, the Committee on the Rights of the Child (CRC) has received reports, documentation, and other information from NGOs since its first session in 1991 based on the Committee's explicit authority to invite expert advice on the implementation of the Convention from "competent bodies" to assist in "the effective implementation of the Convention and to encourage international co-operation in the field covered by the Convention." *See* Article 45(a) of the CRC. The term "competent bodies" has been interpreted to include NGOs.

All of the treaty bodies that consider periodic country reports invite NGOs to provide reports containing country-specific information on States Parties under review or consideration. The more recent treaties expressly provide for the submission of such information. *See, e.g.,* art. 74(4) of the

Convention on the Protection of the Rights of All Migrant Workers and Members of Their Families, and Article 38(a) of the Convention on the Rights of Persons with Disabilities. All treaty bodies that examine State Party reports also set aside time (ordinarily a half-day each week) for a briefing by NGOs in public session regarding the countries being examined in that week. Some also set aside time for their pre-sessional working groups to hear statements from NGOs and others. Some also allow NGOs to appear and brief committee members orally in private. Many contemporary human rights instruments can be traced to proposals and/or drafts prepared by NGOs, including the Convention against Torture and the Convention on the Rights of the Child, as well as the regional African and Arab Charters.

Regarding the UN Human Rights Council, NGOs have made contributions to consideration of major human rights violations in the political bodies of the UN, as they did for its predecessor, the UN Commission on Human Rights. In concrete terms, NGOs can intervene at the Human Rights Council's sessions, which provides them with a unique opportunity to draw attention to the human rights violations that occur in some countries and to speak on behalf of the victims. Under the Council's complaint mechanism (formerly called the 1503 procedure), NGOs draw the Council's attention to human rights violations in specific states. By putting forth written and oral interventions and by lobbying key representatives and delegations, they have on many occasions helped to focus attention on specific human rights violations which might otherwise not have received attention. NGOs also participate in the Universal Periodic Review and in the work of the Advisory Committee and the working groups created by the Council.

§ 7–3. UNIVERSAL PERIODIC REVIEW

A main mechanism for engagement with non-governmental organizations in the UN human rights system is the Universal Periodic Review (UPR). The UPR, which operates under the auspices of the Human Rights Council, was created by UN General Assembly Resolution 60/251 on March 15, 2006. This unique mechanism involves reviewing the human rights records of every UN member state every four and a half years in light of the human rights obligations and commitments expressed in the various human rights instruments to which the state under review is a party. *See* § 2–23, *supra*.

The UPR consists primarily of three stages. First, a working group in the UN Human Rights Council in Geneva undertakes a review of the human rights situation in the state under consideration. That review is based on reports submitted by that state, the Office of the High Commissioner for Human Rights, and NGOs and human rights institutions. The state's representatives present their report and respond to questions and recommendations. Next, a three-member panel "troika of rapporteurs" and members of the OHCHR Secretariat prepare a response with recommendations, which is debated and ultimately adopted by the Council. The state under review accepts, in whole or in part, or notes recommendations, and it makes a policy commitment to take action accordingly. In the four and a half years between the two reviews, states are expected to take the necessary action to implement the voluntary pledges they have made, and they report on their progress at their next appearance before the Council.

NGOs are permitted to engage in the UPR process in several ways. They may participate in national consultations held by the state under review (for example, in the United States, through the Department of State's "UPR Town Hall and Civil Society Consultation" process). NGOs may also submit information directly to the Human Rights Council and may make statements at the regular sessions of the Human Rights Council during which the outcomes of the state reviews are considered. NGOs may monitor the UPR working group sessions, lobby members of the UPR working group, and monitor and participate in the States' implementation of UPR recommendations. However, they are not authorized to make statements during the review itself.

Generally, *see https://www.ohchr.org/en/hr-bodies/upr/upr-home.*

§ 7–4. ENGAGEMENT IN JUDICIAL AND QUASI-JUDICIAL PROCESSES

In addition to participating in the individual petition or communications processes before the UN Human Rights Council and the various treaty bodies, NGOs can file complaints with the Inter-American

Commission on Human Rights, both under the American Convention and under the OAS Charter-based petition system (*see* Chapter 4 *supra*). Thus, for example, a decision by the Inter-American Commission deciding that the United States had violated the right to life by permitting the execution of minors originated from a complaint filed by the American Civil Liberties Union and the International Human Rights Law Group. Case No. 9647 (United States), Resolution No. 3/87, Annual Report of the Inter-American Commission on Human Rights 1986–1987, OEA/Ser.L/V/II.71, doc.9, rev.1, at 147 (1987).

NGOs can also participate in the various matters that reach the Inter-American Court of Human Rights either in the form of requests for advisory opinions or as contentious cases. The Court has permitted NGOs to file *amicus curiae* briefs in advisory proceedings, and a number of them have done so regularly. *See, e.g.*, Advisory Opinion on Restrictions to the Death Penalty, OC–3/83 of Sept. 8, 1983, Inter-American Court of Human Rights, Series A: Judgments and Opinions, No. 3, para. 5 (1983). Rules of Court now provide that the victim's representatives have separate standing to participate in cases submitted to the Court; as such they no longer appear as part of the Commission's legal team. *See* Rules of Procedure of the Inter-American Court of Human Rights, art. 25 (2009).

In the first three contentious cases referred to the Inter-American Court by the Inter-American Commission in 1986, the latter invited the lawyers of the NGOs that had originally filed the cases to join its legal team before the Court. Annual Report of the Inter-American Commission on Human Rights 1986–1987, OAS/Ser.L/V/II.71, doc.9, rev.1, at 25–26 (1987). *See* Grossman, "Disappearances in Honduras: The Need for Direct Victim Representation in Human Rights Litigation," 15 Hastings Int'l & Comp. L. Rev. 363, 378–82 (1992). The Commission now routinely resorts to this practice.

Human rights NGOs have also pioneered the practice of using distinguished foreign lawyers or judges as observers at trials of individuals who have been charged with or appear to be tried for political offenses. Amnesty International and the International Commission of Jurists try to make frequent use of trial observers to ensure due process of law for the accused. *See, e.g.*, the annual reports of Amnesty International. The mere presence at such trials of foreign lawyers acting as trial observers has tended to prevent some abuses; at times it has even produced acquittals.

A related practice, utilized with considerable success—particularly by the International Committee of the Red Cross—consists of inspections of prisons and detention centers. The ICRC attempts to ensure that those in detention are treated humanely and that they are provided with medical services and other basic necessities. Other NGOs have carried out important *in loco* investigations of human rights violations for use by intergovernmental human rights organizations and international tribunals. *See, e.g.*, International

Human Rights Law Group, *No Justice, No Peace: Accountability for Rape and Gender-Based Violence in the Former Yugoslavia* (1993).

These illustrations demonstrate how national and international NGOs can work together towards a common goal in and through the various international human rights bodies.

§ 7–5. NGOs AND NATIONAL POLICIES AND LEGISLATION

A national government's human rights laws, policies, and practices are increasingly likely to be influenced by domestic or international non-governmental organizations. National political considerations obviously affect governmental decisions on whether to ratify human rights treaties or what methods, national or international, should be employed to promote respect for human rights abroad. The same is true of the policies that determine the degree to which a nation is willing to confer authority on international organizations like the UN to deal with such violations. All of these and related issues must be addressed by a country's human rights foreign policy. Decisions affecting the formulation and execution of these policies are as much subject to various forms of lobbying as are other foreign policy decisions.

NGOs act in many regions, particularly where countries are in transition from repressive rule or armed conflicts, in order to foster democracy and build institutions. One question that has yet to be broadly explored is whether, as participants in the international human rights field, NGOs are themselves bound by relevant human rights principles and if so, which ones and where (how) might allegations of violations be addressed and resolved.

Selected References and Further Reading

For more information, *see* the list of Intergovernmental and Governmental Organizations at *http://www.humanrights.com/voices-for-human-rights/human-rights-organizations/governmental.html*; the UN Human Rights Treaty Information *Portal, at http://www.humanrightsinfo.com/links-ngo.html*; the Council of Europe's "Compass: Manual for Human Rights Education with Young People," at *http://www.coe.int/en/web/compass/human-rights-activism-and-the-role-of-ngos*; and UN High Commissioner for Human Rights, "National human rights institutions: history, principles roles and responsibilities" (UN Doc. HR/P/PT/4/Rev.1, 2010), available at *http://www.ohchr.org/Documents/Publications/PTS-4Rev1-NHRI_en.pdf.*

See also Alfred de Zayas, The Human Rights Industry (Clarity 2023); Clark and Danyi, *The Protection Roles of Human Rights NGO's* (Brill 2023); Crowley and Ryan, *Navigating Change for International NGOs: A Practical Handbook* (Kumarian 2016); Boulding, *NGOs, Political Protest, and Civil Society* (Cambridge 2016); Cotton-Betteridge, "An Emerging International Norm for Non-Governmental Organizations, 11 B.Y.U. Int'l L. & Mgmt. Rev. 1 (2015); Shelton, "The Participation of Nongovernmental Organizations in International

Judicial Proceedings," 88 Am. J. Int'l L. 611 (1994); Edwards, "Assessing the Effectiveness of Human Rights Non-Governmental Organizations (NGOs) from the Birth of the United Nations to the 21st Century: Ten Attributes of Highly Successful Human Rights NGOs," 18 Michigan State J. Int'l L. 165 (2010); Charnovitz, Non-Governmental Organizations and International Law, 100 Am. J. Int'l L. 348 (2006); Shelton, "The Participation of Nongovernmental Organizations in International Judicial Proceedings," 88 Am. J. Int'l L. 611 (1994).

III. BUSINESS AND HUMAN RIGHTS

§ 7–6. THE ROLE AND RESPONSIBILITY OF CORPORATIONS

By some estimates, over half of the 100 largest economies (economic units) of the world today are multinational enterprises (corporations), not States. According to one, when measured by revenue, over two-thirds of the top 100 economic entities are private businesses, not governments. *See https://www.accountancydaily.co/corporations-dominate-worlds-top-100-economic-entities; also see* also *https://inequality.org/research/richest-entities-corporations-governments/*. There can be little doubt that such corporations now enjoy unprecedented power and influence over local communities as well as the global economy in general.

Until relatively recently, however, corporate law and international human rights law rarely intersected. In theory, the obligors of human rights were understood to be governments, and the beneficiaries were people. In the few instances in which corporate failure to uphold high standards of conduct was addressed, the focus was primarily on domestic violations concerning corrupt practices, unfair business dealings, or labor laws. The rapid pace of "globalization" has meant, however, that large private corporations increasingly operate in multiple countries and thus have greater potential to contribute to human rights progress—and to "sustainable development—at the international level. In consequence, greater attention has been given to the broader implications of their activities—beyond narrow economic and business goals. Put otherwise, there has been an increasing realization that cross-border corporate activity is a legitimate and important area of international human rights consideration.

Whether, as a matter of law, private entities such as corporations are proper "subjects" of international human rights law (and therefore directly bound by its obligations) remains debated (It was, in part, for this reason that allegations of human rights violations by corporations were frequently pursued in U.S. courts under the Alien Tort Statute, discussed previously in Chapter 6). Yet many corporate entities have today accepted that acting as "good global citizens," with appropriate attention to human rights norms along with broader social goals such as ethical labor practices, concern for the environment, and the well-being of employees, the community and civil society in general, is in their economic interests. Sometimes, the incentive comes from corporate leadership; at other times, it comes from the corporation's investors or customers; it can also be generated by government regulators or "civil society" including NGO advocacy groups. Whatever the source, the fact is that today businesses, including those ranging from large corporations to smaller enterprises, can and do play a significant role today in shaping the human rights landscape.

That landscape is broad. Workers' rights, of course, are fundamental human rights and ensuring their protection by fostering fair and dignified working conditions is essential. Labor rights violations can encompass exploitative labor practices (e.g., forced labor, child labor, discrimination, unsafe working conditions, etc.), as well as occupational health and safety, fair wages and benefits, freedom of association and collective bargaining, and the protection of workers, specifically migrant workers. A truly compelling example was the April 2013 collapse at Rana Plaza in Dhaka, Bangladesh, that resulted in the deaths of over 1,100 garment workers (more than 2500 others were injured), including some from the United States, the United Kingdom, Spain, Germany, Italy, and Denmark), as a result of poor working conditions and the absence lack of safety measures.

In an increasingly globalized economy, businesses are not infrequently implicated in a broader range of human rights violations. In the extractive industries, for example, it is not uncommon to encounter claims that corporate activities have caused or contributed to environmental degradation, deforestation, pollution, and climate change affecting the health of those living in affected communities (often of indigenous peoples). Additionally, the right of individuals and communities to a clean and healthy environment is increasingly understood to encompass access to clean air, water, natural resources, and essential services as well as protection from environmental degradation, land rights violations, and interference with privacy and data rights. These issues are often discussed under the concept of "sustainable development."

One response has been described as a call for "corporate social responsibility" or taking a "business and human rights" approach. Broadly considered, the term is often used to refer to business practices by which corporations commit themselves to conducting their business in a socially responsible manner. Among other steps, for instance, this might mean prioritizing environmentally conscious investments, reducing carbon footprints, participating in fair trade, improving labor policies and conditions, pursing "sustainable marketing," and promoting "equality, diversity, and inclusion" among its employees.

Another method of energizing private entities to take human rights considerations into account has been to call upon them to disclose their relevant activities. Some companies have been publicly shamed by civil society into changing their practices. Activist groups frequently bring workers from corporations with human rights violations to speak in the United States and other countries. Their discussions are often covered by the media, inspiring consumers and organizations across the United States, Europe, and Asia to put pressure on the companies.

The mining and raw material extractive industries have attracted particular attention in recent years. The extraction sites are often in politically or socially unstable countries facing armed conflicts, so the multinational companies hire local military forces to protect their assets. Not infrequently, these forces are ill-trained and poorly led and therefore prone to committing grave human rights violations. The violators may go unpunished by the host nation either because the government is incapable of taking appropriate steps or because it benefits from (or perhaps even supports) the atrocities in question. Here, CSR efforts directed at the parent company or headquarters may have a positive effect.

As transnational businesses have expanded their reach and influence, there has been increasing recognition that voluntary compliance by private entities with international human norms and principles may not be sufficient.

§ 7–7. U.S. HUMAN RIGHTS LITIGATION AGAINST CORPORATIONS

For a number of years in the United States, the venerable Alien Tort Statute [§ 6.13 *supra*] provided one of the main legal pathways for challenging corporate activities abroad on human rights grounds. Many suits were brought in an effort to subject international corporations (including those established under foreign law) to liability for alleged human rights violations committed in other countries through their own actions or their alleged collusion with or complicity in abuses committed by foreign governments and officials. Because the statute does not specify who or what can be a defendant, the question arose whether it could support litigation against corporate entities. A number of decisions answered that question in the affirmative.

In Kiobel v. Royal Dutch Petroleum Co., 621 F.3d 111 (2d Cir. 2010) ("Kiobel I"), however, the Second Circuit held that the ATS does not provide subject-matter jurisdiction over ATS cases against corporate defendants. Liability under the statute, it said, rests on customary international law, but corporate liability for violations of international law is not an established rule of customary international law. "[T]he principle of individual liability for violations of international law has been limited to natural persons" and international law "has steadfastly rejected the notion of corporate liability for international crimes, and no international tribunal has ever held a corporation liable for a violation of the law of nations." *Id.* at 119, 120. The U.S. Supreme Court granted certiorari on that issue but subsequently revised its grant to focus on the issue of extraterritoriality, and its 2013 decision addressed only the latter issue, leaving open the issue of corporate liability. *See* Kiobel v. Royal Dutch Petroleum Co., 569 U.S.108 (2013) ("Kiobel II").

However, in Jesner v. Arab Bank, PLC, 584 U.S. 241 (2018), the U.S. Supreme Court concluded that, absent further action from Congress, it would be inappropriate for the judiciary to extend ATS liability to foreign corporations. Noting that the "various considerations that must shape and instruct the formulation of principles of international and domestic law are matters that the political branches are in the better position to define and articulate," the Court concluded that "judicial deference requires that any imposition of corporate liability on foreign corporations for violations of international law must be determined in the first instance by the political branches of the Government." *Id.* at 274.

The Court further restricted the reach of the ATS in Nestlé USA, Inc. v. Doe, 593 U.S. 628 (2021), holding that to show jurisdiction under the ATS, a plaintiff must establish that "the conduct relevant to the statute's focus occurred in the United States" and that "allegations of general corporate activity" are insufficient to create statutory standing. *Id.* at 634. In that case, for example, the plaintiffs alleged that the company had purchased cocoa from farms in the Ivory Coast and provided "technical and financial resources—such as training, fertilizer, tools, and cash," to those farms, which "aided and abetted child slavery." *Id.* at 631. To establish a domestic connection, they alleged that "all major operational decisions" by Nestlé occurred in the United States, including originating financial agreements. Yet the Court held that those allegations were insufficient to show that "the conduct relevant to the statute's focus occurred in the United States" because they did "not draw a sufficient connection between the cause of action" *Id.* at 634.

The Court's opinion repeated its view that under the ATS, federal courts should not recognize new causes of action "beyond the three historical violations of international law" in Sosa v. Alvarez-Machain, 542 U.S. 692 (2004), namely: "violation of safe conducts, infringement of the rights of ambassadors, and piracy." *Id.* It went further, noting that its decisions since *Sosa* "have clarified that courts must refrain from creating a cause of action whenever there is even a single sound reason to defer to Congress." *Id.* at 635.

While to date no other country has enacted a statute identical to the ATS, it is nonetheless possible to pursue litigation against corporate human rights violators in foreign courts on other jurisdictional and substantive bases, such as ordinary tort suits. Some countries have enacted legislation aimed at curbing corporate involvement in or liability for human rights abuses, especially within their own territories.

§ 7–8. INTERNATIONAL STANDARDS AND CODES OF CONDUCT FOR BUSINESS

While most of the international human rights instruments adopted within the UN address the obligations and commitments of States (and their government entities), many of the principles they articulate can also be applied to the activities of private business entities. One can, in fact, identify a trend, in the UN and other international organizations, towards increased regulation and accountability, specifically regarding legislation on supply chain due diligence.

1. UN Measures

UN Global Compact. Among the first efforts to focus particular attention on this aspect was the UN Global Compact, a voluntary initiative intended to encourage the international business community to adopt sustainable and socially responsible policies and to report on their implementation. Since its initiation in 2000 on the basis of a UN General Assembly resolution, the Global Compact has become the world's largest corporate sustainability and corporate social responsibility initiative, with more than 20,000 corporate participants and other stakeholders in over 167 countries. The organization consists of a global agency and local "networks" or agencies for each participating country. It works to promotes responsible business practices and UN values among the global business community and the UN System. *See https://unglobalcompact.org/about/faq*.

At the heart of the UN Global Compact are ten principles in the areas of human rights, labor, the environment, and anti-corruption, which participants and stakeholders agree to embrace and pursue in their business activities around the world. Participants agree to "mainstream" these principles and to work in support of broader UN goals such as the Millennium Development Goals (MDGs) and the Sustainable Development Goals (SDGs). The organization solicits commitments to specific sustainability and social responsibility goals from CEOs and highest-level executives and in turn, offers training, peer networks, and a functional framework for responsibility, taking a "learning model" for corporate change rather than a regulatory one. *See https://unglobalcompact.org/what-is-gc/mission/principles.*

In the same vein, the Ten Principles adopted by the United Nations Global Compact call upon businesses to support and respect internationally proclaimed human rights and to "make sure" that they are not complicit in human rights abuses. (Principles 1 and 2). The Principles are derived from the Universal Declaration on Human Rights, the International Labour Organization's Declaration on Fundamental Principles and Rights at Work, the Rio Declaration on Environment and Development, and the United Nations Convention Against Corruption. If a corporation fails to abide by these ideals and fails to address the violations, it may be removed from the public list of business participants associated with the compact. *See https://www.unglobalcompact.org.*

UN Guiding Principles on Business and Human Rights. Another early initiative resulted in the adoption of the Guiding Principles on Business and Human Rights: Implementing the United Nations "Protect, Respect and Remedy" ("UNGPs"), developed by John Ruggie, the Special Representative of the UN Secretary- General on the issue of human rights and transnational corporations and endorsed by the UN Human Rights Council in 2011 (U.N. Doc. A/HRC/17/31). *See https://www.ohchr.org/sites/default/files/documents/publications/guiding principlesbusinesshr_en.pdf.*

The first formal set of guidelines endorsed by the UN, the Principles speak broadly to the role human rights should play in business. They address the obligations of business entities as well as obligations of States, providing (in Principle 11) that "[b]usiness enterprises should respect human rights. This means that they should avoid infringing on the human rights of others and should address adverse human rights impacts with which they are involved." They also encourage the establishment of various dispute-resolution mechanisms. Although nonbinding, the Guiding Principles have contributed to the progress of corporate social responsibility.

The UNGPs are grounded in three pillars: (i) the State's duty to protect human rights, (ii) the corporate responsibility to respect human rights, and (iii) the need for access to remedy human rights abuses linked to business activities. While the UNGPs represented a significant step towards advancing the business and human rights agenda, the implementation of the principles has faced many challenges, including a lack of awareness and understanding among businesses, weak enforcement mechanisms, and the sheer complexity of addressing these human rights violations across supply chains that span many States and jurisdictions.

At the same time, the UN Human Rights Council established a five-member "working group on the issue of human rights and transnational corporations and other business enterprises," commonly referred to as the "Working Group on Business and Human Rights," with a mandate to promote, disseminate and support the implementation of the UNGPs. The Working Group also guides and chairs the annual UN Forum on Business and Human Rights, which is the world's largest annual gathering on business and human rights with more than 2,000 participants from government, business, community groups and civil society, law firms, investor organizations, UN bodies, national human rights institutions, trade unions, academia, and the media. *See https://www.ohchr.org/en/hrc-subsidiary-bodies/united-nations-forum-business-and-human-rights; see also https://www.ohchr.org/en/business-and-human-rights.*

In some cases, investors have also become involved in trying to motivate corporations to uphold human rights. For example, Dreyfus' Third Century Fund and Merrill Lynch's Ecological Trust are ethical-investment mutual funds available for consumers interested in only supporting companies with strong human rights records. Moreover, a growing number of ethical consulting firms have been established to counsel companies on how to avoid infringing on human rights. In some instances, institutional investors have pulled out of countries or companies they felt were non-compliant with human rights principles.

2. Regional Initiatives

EU Directives. Within the European Union, for example, several recent measures impose requirements on businesses *inter alia* with respect to human rights. The Corporate Sustainability Reporting Directive (CSRD), in force since January

2023, sets out a number of environmental, social, and governance (ESG) reporting requirements for companies.

In March 2024, the European Council adopted a Corporate Sustainability Due Diligence Directive (CSDDD) requiring companies to identify, prevent, and, where necessary, mitigate and cease the adverse impacts of business activities on human rights and the environment. The Directive is intended to foster sustainable and responsible corporate behavior by anchoring human rights and environmental considerations in companies' operations and corporate governance. It focuses on shaping companies' management of environmental, social, and governance (ESG) matters and creates legal liability for companies relating to environmental and human rights violations within their supply chains.

Even when not legally binding, such principles, standards, and codes of conduct can be an effective means for encouraging companies to incorporate human rights principles into their business operations. In many instances, the instruments are formulated by (or in close collaboration with) the corporations themselves. Voluntary adherence can help guide a company's activities and provide strong reputational benefits even when no compulsory external monitoring and enforcement mechanisms are established.

Voluntary Principles on Security and Human Rights. These principles are the product of an initiative begun in 2000 by NGOs, corporations, and governments to address the problems that often arise when companies in the extractive sector employ security forces to protect their assets. They are designed to guide companies in maintaining the safety and security of their operations within an operating framework that encourages respect for human rights. Unlike some other multi-stakeholder approaches, they set forth concrete guidelines instead of generalized recommendations, although they lack a reliable enforcement mechanism. *See http://www.voluntaryprinciples.org* and *https://globalnetworkinitiative.org/*.

OECD Guidelines. Among the international organizations that have long promoted corporate accountability for actions that violate their human rights responsibilities is the Organization for Economic Co-operation and Development (OECD), which first adopted Guidelines for Multinational Enterprises on Responsible Business Conduct (including human rights due diligence, stakeholder engagement, and proper disclosure) in 1976. These Guidelines reflect social, environmental, and technological priorities facing societies and businesses as well as expectations from governments about what constitutes "responsible business conduct." *See https://www.oecd.org/industry/inv/responsible-business-conduct-and-human-rights.htm*.

The Guidelines call on each OECD Member State to appoint a National Contact Point to hear grievances from any interested party, including individuals and NGOs. Amended in 2011 to incorporate the UN Guiding Principles' "protect, respect, and remedy" framework, they specifically call upon enterprises to "contribute to economic, environmental and social progress with a view to achieving sustainable development" and "respect the internationally recognized human rights of those affected by their activities." While non-binding, they do provide for non-judicial review of businesses that have failed to abide by the guidelines.

The 2023 edition provides updated recommendations in such areas as climate change, biodiversity, technology, business integrity, and supply chain due diligence, as well as updated implementation procedures. *See https://mneguidelines.oecd.org/*.

APEC Principles. The Asia-Pacific Economic Cooperation (APEC) has also played a role in initiatives to combat corruption, including the recent APEC Principles on the Prevention of Bribery and Enforcement of Anti-Bribery Laws, *see www.apec.org/docs/default-source/Groups/ATCWG/APEC-ACT-Principles-on-Enforcement.docx. See also* the APEC General Elements of Effective Voluntary Corporate Compliance Programs adopted by APEC Leaders in 2014, available at *https://mddb.apec.org/Documents/2014/SOM/CSOM/14_csom_041.pdf*.

3. Other Actions

U.S. National Action Plan. In 2016 the U.S. Government adopted a "National Action Plan on Responsible Business Conduct" with the goals *inter alia* of enhancing coordination within the government, pushing for higher global standards, strengthening public-private coordination, and promoting high standards globally, in accordance with the OECD Guidelines and UN Guiding Principles. *See https://www.state.gov/responsible-business-conduct-national-action-plan/*.

That Plan was updated in 2024 *inter alia* to establish a Federal Advisory Committee on Responsible Business Conduct, with the purpose of strengthening coordination with the private sector, affected communities, labor unions, civil society (including human rights defenders), academia, and other relevant stakeholders on RBC policies, programming, and initiatives. In addition, it provided that the U.S. Department of Defense will evaluate whether to encourage or require its private security vendors to participate in the International Code of Conduct Association for Private Security Providers' Association, a multistakeholder initiative that provides oversight and certification of private security providers in line with international human rights and humanitarian law standards.

The text of the National Action Plan can be found at *https://www.state.gov/u-s-governments-national-action-plan-on-responsible-business-conduct/*. *See* also *https://www.csis.org/analysis/updates-release-us-national-action-plan-responsible-business-conduct*.

As awareness of business of human rights issues continues to grow, the trend towards increased voluntary regulation and accountability will also gain momentum. The most significant development, however, may come in the form of a legally binding convention.

§ 7–9. THE DRAFT UN TREATY ON BUSINESS AND HUMAN RIGHTS

In June 2014, the UN Human Rights Council undertook to draft a new legally binding instrument to regulate the activities of "transnational corporations and other business enterprises with respect to human rights." The effort had its origins in the growing appreciation of the role that private businesses play in the international human rights arena and a sense that it was necessary to clarify and ensure their responsibilities and obligations to "respect and fulfill" the human rights obligations set forth in the UN Guiding Principles on Business and Human Rights, in particular (1) providing for prevention of abuses and protection for victims, (2) ensuring that victims have access to a remedy, (3) creating a "treaty body," and (4) enabling relevant international cooperation between States party.

Negotiations have taken place under the Council's auspices in an open-ended intergovernmental working group on transnational corporations and other business enterprises with respect to human rights beginning in 2018. The Working Group produced a revised draft in 2019, a third draft in 2021, and an "updated draft" in July 2023. *See https://www.ohchr.org/sites/default/files/documents/hrbodies/hrcouncil/igwg-transcorp/session9/igwg-9th-updated-lbi-with-proposals.pdf.* The next session was scheduled for October 2024. *See https://www.business-humanrights.org/en/big-issues/binding-treaty* and *https://www.ohchr.org/en/business-and-human-rights/bhr-treaty-process.*

As stated in Art. 2 of the "updated draft," the purposes of the treaty are:

(a) To clarify and facilitate effective implementation of the obligation of States to respect, protect, fulfill and promote human rights in the context of business activities, particularly those of transnational character;

(b) To clarify and ensure respect and fulfillment of the human rights responsibilities of business enterprises;

(c) To prevent the occurrence of human rights abuses in the context of business activities by effective mechanisms for monitoring, enforceability and accountability;

(d) To ensure access to gender-responsive, child-sensitive and victim-centred justice and effective, adequate and timely remedy for victims of human rights abuses in the context of business activities;

(e) To facilitate and strengthen mutual legal assistance and international cooperation to prevent and mitigate human rights abuses in the context of business activities, particularly those of transnational character, and provide access to justice and effective, adequate, and timely remedy for victims.

As currently formulated, the draft treaty would require State parties to ensure that their domestic legislation provides for the legal liability for human rights abuses arising from the business activities of natural and legal persons and for reparations to the victims of human rights violations in accordance with international standards. It would apply to "all business activities, including business activities of an international character" and would "cover all internationally recognized human rights and fundamental freedoms binding on the States Parties" to the agreement. Art. 3(a). However, the specific responsibilities imposed on business enterprises could vary depending on the size, nature, sector, location, operational context, and risks associated with the business activities.

To guarantee that victims have access to an effective remedy for damages. it would require States Party to provide jurisdiction (i) where the human rights abuse or omission contributing to the human rights abuse occurred and/or produced effects, (ii) where legal or natural persons alleged to have committed a relevant act are domiciled, or (iii) where the victim is domiciled or is a national. Courts of a State Party would also have jurisdiction to adjudicate cases over claims against legal or natural persons not domiciled in the territory of the forum State, in the event that no other effective forum guaranteeing a fair judicial process is available, and if there is a connection to the presence of the victim, assets of the business enterprise, or substantial activity of the business enterprise in the territory of the forum chosen.

To ease victims' right to access remedy, States parties would be obligated to enact or amend their domestic laws to allow judges to reverse the burden of proof in appropriate cases and circumstances. It would also require adoption of legislative or other measures necessary to ensure that statutory and other limitations do not apply in relation to international human rights violations, particularly in cases where the abuses occurred in another state or when the harm may be identifiable only after a long period of time.

It would preclude application of the doctrine of *forum non-conveniens* in relevant cases. Additionally, States party would be required to ensure that court fees and legal cost rules do not place an unreasonable burden on victims, including by waiving such fees in appropriate cases. An International Fund for Victims would be established to provide legal and financial aid to victims, with special consideration for vulnerable and marginalized groups.

States party would also be required to ensure that business enterprises subject to their jurisdiction undertake human rights due diligence, proportionate to their size, risk of human rights abuse, or the nature and context of their business activities and relationships, including appropriate measures to prevent and mitigate potential human rights abuses which the business entity causes or contributes to through its business activity; (ii) to monitor the effectiveness of their measures to prevent human rights abuses; (iii) to communicate regularly and in an accessible manner to affected or potentially affected people.

Further, business entities subject to a Sate's jurisdiction would have to publish regular human rights, labor rights, environment, and climate impact assessments, conduct consultations with individuals or communities whose human rights can potentially be affected by business activities, and integrate human rights due diligence requirements in their contracts.

To oversee the operation of the Draft Treaty, a committee of experts would be established (initially consisting of 12 experts and expanding to 18 after an additional sixty ratifications. State parties would be required to submit reports to this committee on the measures they have taken to give effect to their undertakings under the Draft Treaty; the Committee would be authorized to provide concluding observations and recommendations on these reports submitted by State Parties. It would also have the power to make normative recommendations on the implementation of the treaty, provide recommendations on reports by state parties, and provide support to state parties for the compilation of such reports. This committee would also be required to provide support to the State Parties in the.

Disputes between States Party to the treaty (about their compliance with its provisions) would be resolved by the International Court of Justice or arbitration in accordance with the procedures and organization mutually agreed by those States.

Selected References and Further Reading

Generally, *see https://www.business-humanrights.org/en/big-issues/binding-treaty/*; *https://www.ohchr.org/en/business-and-human-rights/reports*; *https://www.ohchr.org/en/business-and-human-rights/bhr-treaty-process*.

See also Blog of the Center for Transnational Business and the Law, Georgetown University Law Center, 3.9.2023, at *https://www.law.georgetown.edu/ctbl/blog/an-overview-of-the-proposed-legally-binding-instrument-to-regulate-in-international-human-rights-law-the-activities-of-transnational-corporations-and-other-business-enterprises/*.

Robert McCorquodale, Business and Human Rights (Oxford Elements of International Law 2024); Peterson and Ulferts, "An Interdisciplinary Approach to the Study of Business Ethics, CSR, Sustainability and Human Rights," 30 J.L. Bus. & Eth. 49 (2024); Correa, "Business and Human Rights: A Rocky Road Towards a Binding Treaty," 51 Ga. J. Int'l & Comp. L. 907 (2023); Butler, "The Corporate Keepers of International Law," 114 Am. J. Int'l L. 189 (2020); King, "The UN Global Compact: Responsibility for Human Rights, Labor Relations and the Environment in Developing Nations," 34 Cornell Int'l L.J. 481 (2001). *See also* Umpula & Dummett, The Blood Cobalt Narrative: Addressing Human Rights Concerns or Scaremongering?, published online in *Business and Human Rights Journal, First View* (April 2024), available at *https://www.cambridge.org/core/journals/business-and-human-rights-journal*.

IV. FINANCIAL INSTITUTIONS

Attention has also focused on the responsibilities of financial institutions for respecting and advancing international human rights. For example, in 2007, the UN Environment Program Finance Initiative released the Human Rights Guidance Tool for the Financial Sector (available at *https://www.unepfi.org/humanrightstoolkit/*). Last updated in 2014, the Guidance Tool focuses on "human rights issues relevant to the assessment of business relationships and transactions" and aims at helping finance sector professionals to identify potential human rights risks in lending operations, assess the materiality of the human rights risk, and identify possible risk-mitigating factors. It is based on the proposition that human rights are important in relation to all financial sector activity. *See also* the Initiative's publication on Banks and Human Rights, A Legal Analysis (2015), at *https://www.unepfi.org/industries/banking/banks-and-human-rights-a-legal-analysis-2/*.

In 2012, the International Finance Corporation (IFC), a member of the World Bank Group, updated its Environmental and Social Performance Standards, which provide guidance primarily intended for the institution's project financing, bridge loans, and advisory services. These standards are enforceable when they are incorporated into a loan agreement, thereby giving leverage over an offending party to improve its human rights impact or risk violating the legal agreement. They highlight the responsibility of businesses to protect individuals' human rights and the IFC's interest in engaging in sustainable business. For additional information, *see https://www.ifc.org/en/insights-reports/2012/ifc-performance-standards.*

The so-called Equator Principles provide a risk management framework, adopted by financial institutions, for determining, assessing, and managing environmental and social risk in projects. They were drafted by a group of banks to apply to project finance, project finance advisory services, project-related corporate loans, and bridge loans. Using the IFC Performance Standards as the minimum benchmark, these Principles require banks and their clients to perform sufficient human rights due diligence, especially when the project involves high-risk circumstances. Some 82 large financial institutions in over 35 countries (conducting around 70% of the international project finance in emerging markets) have adopted the Principles. For the 2020 version of the Equator Principles, *see https://equator-principles.com/about-the-equator-principles/.*

Banks and other financial institutions may also be subject to human rights scrutiny on other bases. For example, anti-money laundering laws prohibit financial institutions from processing funds that have ties to criminal activity, including those from rogue governments or armed insurgencies. By depriving the perpetrators of their ability to take advantage of the banking system, these laws serve to reduce the ability of human rights abusers to store and grow their illicit financial assets.

Sanctions (whether imposed under international or domestic authority) may provide additional tools for curbing human rights abuses. Different types of sanctions exist. The most restrictive forbid all transactions with an offending country; others may be selectively targeted at individuals or entities. Sanctions may forbid banks from accepting money or engaging in any sort of business transaction with States, companies, or individuals, engaged in human rights violations. As the use of sanctions increases, financial institutions are likely to be held accountable for violations in a variety of contexts. Consider, for instance, the challenge brought against Riggs Bank in Spain for having allegedly transferred over $8,000,000 of former Chilean President Augusto Pinochet's frozen assets, thereby contributing to his reign of terror. The Bank eventually entered into a settlement agreement with the plaintiffs for its role in facilitating Pinochet's abusive regime.

The UN's Guiding Principles on Business and Human Rights (§ 7–8 *supra*), also apply to financial institutions. Because of the financial sector's role in projects, many of the human rights violations with which they are associated are not a direct result of their actions but are instead caused by the actions of their business partners. The banks typically do not have control over the offending company and thus may be unable to resolve the issue themselves. However, depending on the amount of leverage the bank has in the business relationship, it might be able to persuade the company to change its practices. A lack of leverage or a business partner's refusal to abide by human rights norms does not, however, obviate any of the financial institution's responsibility to identify, prevent, or mitigate any human rights violations.

In 2013, seven European banks comprising the Thun Group of Banks released a paper discussing the impact of the UN Guiding Principles on large banks. The paper emphasized the importance of upholding human rights norms, noting that this responsibility should lie within the banks at all levels and across all disciplines. In order to accomplish that goal, it recommended that banks develop broader risk management models that allow the banks to identify and address their potential human rights issues. *See* "The UN Guiding Principles on Business and Human Rights: Discussion Paper for Banks" (2015), at *https://www.credit-suisse.com/media/assets/corporate/docs/about-us/responsibility/banking/thun-group-discussion-paper.pdf.*

Generally, *see https://www.bsr.org/en/primers/10-human-rights-priorities-for-the-financial-sector* and *https://www.ohchr.org/en/special-procedures/wg-business/financial-sector-and-human-rights.*

§ 7–10. FUTURE DEVELOPMENTS

Advancements in technology will continue to transform the business landscape and raise new and complex questions about the human rights implications of private (non-governmental) activity in the areas, *inter alia*, of digital rights, data privacy, surveillance and monitoring, ethical uses of artificial intelligence (AI), algorithmic biases, and the impact that automation will have on labor, job displacement, and reskilling. Moreover, the phenomenon generally called "globalization" means that more and more private commercial activities will have a greater international impact and will likely have human rights impact.

These developments raise some fundamental questions about the future direction of international human rights law. In its origins, human rights concerns focused on the actions of States (governments) with respect to individuals who were their citizens or over whom they exercised jurisdiction, initially in their own country but then anywhere in the world under certain conditions. Today, that focus has expanded to include the actions of commercial businesses, particularly but not exclusively in the transnational realm, whether publicly or privately owned, and with regard to the consequences of their activities for individuals with whom they may not have a business or contractual relationship. What might be the implications of this expansion in the focus (scope) of international human rights law? Should other large (non-governmental) institutions also be subject to human rights constraints? Consider, for example, manufacturers (for consequences beyond the limits of product liability), commercial banks, investment houses and brokerages, perhaps consulting firms, or even universities.

Selected References and Further Reading

Guiding Principles on Business and Human Rights: Implementing the United Nations "Protect, Respect, and Remedy" Framework, UNHCR HR/

PUB/11/04 (2011) at *http://www.ohchr.org/Documents/Publications/GuidingPrinciplesBusinessHR_EN.pdf*; The Corporate Responsibility to Respect Human Rights: An Interpretive Guide, Office of the United Nations High Commissioner for Human Rights (2012), *at http://www.ohchr.org/Documents/Publications/HR.PUB.12.2_En.pdf.*

Robert McCorquodale, Business and Human Rights (Oxford 2024); Angelica Bonfanti, ed., The Corporate Keepers of International Law, Business and Human Rights in Europe (2019); Umpula & Dummett, "The Blood Cobalt Narrative: Addressing Human Rights Concerns or Scaremongering?" 9 Business and Human Rights Journal 308 (2024); Kishanthi Parella, International Law in the Boardroom, 108 Cornell L. Rev. 839 (2023); Gloria María Corre, Business and Human Rights: A Rocky Road Towards a Binding Treaty, 51 Ga. J. Int'l & Comp. L. 907 (2023); Backer, Moving Forward: the UN Guiding Principles for Business and Human Rights: Between Enterprise Social Norm, State Domestic Legal Orders, and the Treaty Law that Might Bind Them All," 38 Fordham Int'l L.J. 457 (2015); Laine, "Integrated Reporting: Fostering Human Rights Accountability for Multinational Corporations," 47 Geo. Wash. Int'l L. Rev. 639 (2015). Weissbrodt, "Human Rights Standards Concerning Transnational Corporations and Other Business Entities," 23 Minn. J. Int'l L. 135 (2014). Lucy Amis, A Guide for Business: How to Develop a Human Rights Policy (2011), at *http://www.ohchr.org/Documents/Publications/DevelopHumanRightsPolicy_en.pdf.*

For additional information about the UPR, *see* *http://www.ohchr.org/EN/HRBodies/UPR/Pages/BasicFacts.aspx* and *https://www.state.gov/universal-periodic-review*. *See also* Storey, Improving Recommendations from the UN's Universal Periodic Review: A Case Study on Domestic Abuse in the UK, 35 Pace Int'l L. Rev. 193 (2023); Storey, Challenges and Opportunities for the United Nations' Universal Periodic Review: A Case Study on Capital Punishment in the United States, 90 UMKC L. Rev. 129 (2021); Levin, "The Reporting Cycle to the United Nations Human Rights Treaty Bodies: Creating a Dialogue between the State and Civil Society—The Israeli Case Study," 48 Geo. Wash. Int'l L. Rev. 315 (2016).

INDEX

References are to Pages

ADVISORY OPINIONS
See Inter-American Court of Human Rights, this index

AFRICA
Generally, 269 et seq.
African Charter
Generally, 269 et seq.
Individual complaints, 292
Interstate complaints, 289
Measures of implementation, 281 et seq.
Peoples' rights, 277
Rights and duties, 272 et seq.
State obligations, 281 et seq.
African Commission on Human and Peoples' Rights, 283
African Court of Human Rights, 306
Court of Justice of the Economic Community of West African States, 315
Individual complaints, 292
Interstate complaints, 289
Organization of African Union, 269, 294

AGENCY FOR FUNDAMENTAL RIGHTS (FRA), 179

AGRICULTURE
See Migrant Workers Convention, this index

ALIEN PROTECTIONS
Alien Tort Statute (ATS)
Generally, 391
Convention on Human Rights, 128
Historical background, 2, 14
Stateless persons, 15

AMERICAN CONVENTION ON HUMAN RIGHTS
Generally, 216 et seq.
Civil-law/common-law distinctions, 217
Death penalty
Generally, 219
Protocol to abolish, 218
Derogation provisions, 221
Federal state clause, 222
Guarantees of the Convention, 218
Historical background, 216
IACHR as organ of the Convention, 222
Inter-American Court of Human Rights as organ of, 222
Organs of the Convention, 222
Progressive measures undertaking, 220
Ratifications, 216
San Salvador Protocol, 218

AMERICAN DECLARATION OF THE RIGHTS AND DUTIES OF MAN, 201, 211

ARAB CHARTER ON HUMAN RIGHTS, 318 et seq.

ASSOCIATION OF SOUTH-EAST ASIAN NATIONS, 325 et seq.

BUSINESS ENTITIES
See Multinational Corporations, this index

CAMBODIA
UN creation of *ad hoc* international tribunal, 6

CAPITAL PUNISHMENT
See Death Penalty, this index

CAT
See Convention Against Torture, this index

CEDAW
See Elimination of Discrimination Against Women, this index

CERD
See International Convention on the Elimination of Racial Discrimination, this index

CHARTER FOR REGIONAL OR MINORITY LANGUAGES, 123, 166

CHARTER OF FUNDAMENTAL RIGHTS, 177

CHILDREN
Committee on the Rights of the Child, this index
Recruitment in military service, 93
Trafficking, this index

CLONING
European Union protocol, 123

COLD WAR ERA, 5, 24, 338

COMMISSION AGAINST RACISM AND INTOLERANCE (ECRI), 124

COMMISSION FOR DEMOCRACY THROUGH LAW, 124

COMMISSION ON THE STATUS OF WOMEN
Generally, 106
Historical background, 107

COMMISSIONER FOR HUMAN RIGHTS
See European Union, this index

COMMITTEE ON THE RIGHTS OF THE CHILD (CRC)
Generally, 91 et seq.
Complaints, 94
Military service recruitment, 93
Optional protocols, 93
Pornography and prostitution prohibitions, 93
Reporting procedures, 92
Scope of protections, 92

COMPLAINT PROCEDURES
See also Petition Processes, this index
Collective complaints, European Social Charter, 160, 163
Convention on the Rights of Persons with Disabilities, 96
CRC, 94
European Social Charter, collective complaints, 160, 163
European Union, this index
Human Rights Committee, 56, 64

Human Rights Council, 105
ICCPR
First Optional Protocol, 65
Second Optional Protocol, 68
ICESCR
Generally, 74
Individual complaints proposals, 75
International Labor Organization, 114
Migrant Workers Convention, 95
UNESCO, 115

CONFERENCES ON HUMAN RIGHTS, 110

CONVENTION AGAINST TORTURE (CAT)
Generally, 89
Committee Against Torture, 90
Confidential meetings, 91
Definitions, 89
European Union, 165
Investigations, 90, 91
Jurisdiction, 89
Optional protocol, 90
Private party acts prohibited, 89

CONVENTION FOR THE PREVENTION OF TORTURE AND INHUMAN OR DEGRADING TREATMENT OR PUNISHMENT, 123

CONVENTION FOR THE PROTECTION OF HUMAN RIGHTS AND BIOMEDICINE, 123, 169

CONVENTION ON ACTION AGAINST TRAFFICKING IN HUMAN BEINGS, 123, 171

CONVENTION ON HUMAN RIGHTS (EUROPE)
Generally, 125 et seq.
See also European Union, this index
Absorbing the convention in the EU, 174
Alien protections, 128
Enactment, 126
Enforcement mechanism, 128, 135 et seq.
Historical background, 126, 130

Implementing legislation to enforce, 135
Institutions in support of, 128
Parliamentary Assembly responsibilities, 129
Ratifying states, 176
Remedies, 127
Scope of protections, 126

CONVENTION ON THE RIGHTS OF PERSONS WITH DISABILITIES
Generally, 96
Complaints, 96
Monitoring mechanisms, 97
Reporting procedures, 97
Scope of protections, 97

CORPORATIONS
See Multinational Corporations, this index

COUNCIL OF EUROPE
See European Union, this index

COURT OF HUMAN RIGHTS (EUROPE)
Generally, 129 et seq.
See also European Union, this index
Abolition of Commission of Human Rights, 130
Abuse the right of petition, 143
Admissibility of petitions, 143
Case management, 132
Composition, 129
Constitutional court operation as, 157
Due process jurisprudence, 157
Enforcement mechanism of the Convention on Human Rights, 135 et seq.
Enforcement of judgments, 155
Evidentiary rules, 153
Execution of judgments, 154
Exhaustion of domestic remedies, 145
Freedom of expression rights, 158
Hearings, 153
Historical background, 130
Incompatible or ill-founded petitions, 143

Indirect victims of violations, 140
Individual petitions, 140
Inter-state complaints, 136
Judgments, 154
Jurisdiction
Generally, 131
Individual complaints, 136
Inter-state complaints, 136
Limitations periods, 131
Proceedings on the merits, 153
Significant disadvantage doctrine, 149
Six-months rule, 145

COURT OF JUSTICE (ECJ)
Generally, 174
Religious freedom, 175

CRC
See Committee on the Rights of the Child, this index

CUSTOMARY INTERNATIONAL LAW, 389 et seq.

DEATH PENALTY
American Convention on Human Rights
Generally, 219
Protocol to abolish, 218
ICCPR, Second Optional Protocol, 67

DISABILITIES
See Convention on the Rights of Persons with Disabilities, this index

DISAPPEARANCES
Committee on Enforced Disappearances, 79
International Convention for the Protection of All Persons from Enforced Disappearance, 79, 97

DISCRIMINATION
Commission against Racism and Intolerance, European Union, 124
Commission on the Status of Women, this index
European Social Charter cases, 164
ICESCR provisions, 73

International Convention on the Elimination of Racial Discrimination, this index
Migrant Workers Convention, national treatment provision, 95

DUE PROCESS JURISPRUDENCE
Court of Human Rights (Europe), 157

ECRI
Commission against Racism and Intolerance, 124

ELIMINATION OF DISCRIMINATION AGAINST WOMEN (CEDAW)
Generally, 85 et seq.
Definitions, 85
Powers, 88
Reporting procedures, 87
Reservations of ratifying states, 87

ENFORCEMENT
See Jurisdiction and Power, this index

EQUATOR PRINCIPLES, 452

ESC
See European Union, this index

EUROPEAN UNION
Generally, 121 et seq.
Abolition of Commission of Human Rights, 130
Agency for Fundamental Rights (FRA), 179
Alien protections, Convention on Human Rights, 128
Catalog of rights
OSCE, 188
Social Charter, 160
Charter for Regional or Minority Languages, 123, 166
Charter of Fundamental Rights, 177
Collective complaints, Social Charter, 160, 163
Commission against Racism and Intolerance, 124
Commission for Democracy through Law, 124
Commissioner for Human Rights, 123
Commission of Human Rights, abolition, 130
Committee of Ministers
Enforcement of judgments of Court of Human Rights, 155

Monitoring, 156
Committee of Social Rights (ECSR), 163
Complaint procedures, Social Charter, 164
Constitutional court, Court of Human Rights as, 157
Convention Against Torture, 165
Convention for the Prevention of Torture and Inhuman or Degrading Treatment or Punishment, 123
Convention for the Protection of Human Rights and Biomedicine, 123, 169
Convention on Action against Trafficking in Human Beings, 123, 171
Convention on Human Rights (Europe), this index
Conventions
Domestic treatment, 135
Interpretations of rights guaranteed, 157
Remedies, below
Council of Europe
EU distinguished, 174, 176
Responsibilities, 121
Court of Human Rights (Europe), this index
Court of Justice (ECJ)
EU distinguished, 174
Religious freedom, 175
Discrimination cases, Social Charter, 164
Domestic remedies, exhaustion, 145
Domestic treatment of Convention on Human Rights
Domestic treatment of Convention, 135
Individual petitions, 143
Due process jurisprudence, Court of Human Rights, 157
Enforcement mechanism of Convention on Human Rights
Generally, 128, 135 et seq.
Domestic treatment of Convention, 135
Implementing legislation, 135
Enforcement of remedies, 156
ESC. Social Charter, below
Evidentiary rules, Court of Human Rights, 153
Execution of judgments of Court of Human Rights, 154
Exhaustion of domestic remedies, 145
Freedom of expression rights, 158
Helsinki Document, 188

Helsinki Final Act, 183
High Commissioner on National Minorities (HCNM), 191
Historical background
Generally, 121
Convention on Human Rights, 130
Court of Human Rights, 130
Court of Justice, 174
OSCE, 182
Social Charter, 159
Human dimension mechanism, OSCE, 189
Implementing legislation to enforce Convention on Human Rights, 135
Indirect as well as direct victims if violations, 140
Institutions in support of Convention on Human Rights, 128
Interpretation of rights guaranteed, 157
Inter-state complaints, Court of Human Rights, 136
Judgments, Court of Human Rights, 154
Jurisdiction. See Court of Human Rights (Europe), this index
Limitations periods
Court of Human Rights, 131
Six-months rule, 145
Maastricht Treaty, 176
Member states, 121
Monitoring, Committee of Ministers, 156
Moscow Concluding Document, 188
NGO activities, 419
Non-judicial EU human rights bodies, 179
Ombudsman creation, 181
Organization for Security and Cooperation in Europe, this index
Parliamentary Assembly responsibilities, Convention on Human Rights, 129
Press and media freedoms, OSCE, 193
Process, OSCE, 186
Protocol on the Prohibition of Cloning Human Beings, 123
Religious freedom, Court of Justice, 175
Remedies
Enforcement, 156
Exhaustion of domestic remedies, 145
Reporting procedures, OSCE, 190
Safety and health regulations, Social Charter, 162

Settlement mechanisms, Court of Human Rights, 153
Significant disadvantage doctrine, Court of Human Rights, 149
Six-months rule, Court of Human Rights, 145
Social Charter (ESC)
Generally, 159
Catalog of rights, 160
Collective complaints, 160, 163
Committee of Social Rights (ECSR), 163
Complaint procedure, 164
Discrimination cases, 164
Historical background, 159
International measures for enforcement of charter rights, 163
Legal obligations assumed by contracting parties, 162
Revised Charter, 160 et seq.
Safety and health regulations, 162
Working conditions, 162
Trafficking issues, OSCE, 191
Treaty of European Union, 175
Treaty of Lisbon, 177
Venice Commission, 124
Working conditions, Social Charter, 162

FARM WORKERS
See Migrant Workers Convention, this index

FINANCIAL INSTITUTIONS
Generally, 451
Equator Principles, 452
UN's Guiding Principles on Business and Human Rights, 453
United States foreign aid channels, 376

FORCE EXERCISES
Humanitarian intervention doctrine, 4

FOREIGN NATIONALS
See Alien Protections, this index

FRA
Agency for Fundamental Rights, 179

FRIENDSHIP, COMMERCE AND NAVIGATION (FCN) TREATIES, 17

GENOCIDE CONVENTION
Generally, 80
International Court of Justice referrals, 82
Jurisdictional provisions, 82
Rwanda tribunal, 82
United States ratification, 366
Universal jurisdiction, 83
Yugoslavia tribunal definitions, 82

GLOBALIZATION
Multinational corporations' human rights activities, 429
Workers' rights impacts, 114

GROSS VIOLATIONS OF HUMAN RIGHTS, 108

HANDICAPPED PERSONS
See Convention on the Rights of Persons with Disabilities, this index

HIGH COMMISSIONER ON NATIONAL MINORITIES (HCNM), 191

HISTORICAL BACKGROUND
Generally, 2 et seq.
American Convention on Human Rights, 216
Business entities' responsibilities, 19
Cold War era, 5, 24, 338
Commission on the Status of Women, 107
Criminal organization violations, 18
Early human rights treaties, 7
European Union, this index
Friendship, commerce and navigation (FCN treaties), 17
Gross violations of human rights, 108
Group protections, 22
Holocaust, 35
Humanitarian intervention doctrine, 2, 4
Humanitarian law, 2, 20
Individual vs state protections, 3, 23
Individuals responsibilities, 18

Inter-American Commission on Human Rights, 203
International Criminal Court, this index
International humanitarian law, 2
League of Nations, this index
Natural law theory, 4
Non-governmental organizations, 408
Non-state actors' responsibilities, 19
Organization of American States, 200
Paramilitary group violations, 18
Private entity responsibilities, 18
Restatement of the Foreign Relations Law of the United States, 16
Revolution in human rights protections, 24
Slave trade treaties, 7
State responsibility for injuries to aliens, 2, 14
Stateless persons protections, 15
States vs individual approach to human rights, 3
Terrorist violations, 18
UN creation, 35
United States, 338 et seq.
War crimes laws, 21

HOLOCAUST
Generally, 35, 80
See also Genocide Convention, this index

HUMAN RIGHTS COMMITTEE
Generally, 56 et seq.
Complaints, 56, 64
General comments by the Committee, 62
Inter-state communications, 64
Investigations, 58
Jurisdiction, 58
Petition process, 56
Reporting procedure, 57
Shadow reports, 59
Special Rapporteur on New Communications, 66

HUMAN RIGHTS COUNCIL
Generally, 104
Functions, 105

Mandates procedures
    Generally, 109
  Historical background, 106
NGO contributions, 422
Procedures, 109 et seq.
Special Procedures, 109
Working groups, 109

HUMAN RIGHTS LAW, HUMANITARIAN LAW DISTINCTIONS
  Generally, 22
ICJ rulings, 103

HUMANITARIAN INTERVENTION DOCTRINE
Force exercises, 4
Historical background, 2, 4

HUMANITARIAN LAW
Children, recruitment in military service, 93
Definition, 20
Historical background, 2, 20
Human rights law distinctions
    Generally, 22
  ICJ rulings, 103
Nuremberg and Tokyo Tribunals, 18
War crimes laws, 21

IA CT HR
See Inter-American Court of Human Rights, this index

IACHR
See Inter-American Commission on Human Rights, this index

ICCPR
See International Covenant on Civil and Political Rights, this index

ICESCR
See International Covenant on Economic, Social and Cultural Rights, this index

ICJ
See International Court of Justice, this index

ILO
See International Labor Organization, this index

IMMIGRANTS
See Alien Protections, this index

INDIVIDUAL VS STATE PROTECTIONS, 3, 23

INTER-AMERICAN COMMISSION ON HUMAN RIGHTS (IACHR)
Generally, 203 et seq., 223 et seq.
American Convention on Human Rights implementation, 222
Charter organ, Commission as, 203
Charter organ treatment, 208
Convention organ, commission as, 223
Court, referrals to, 228
Exhaustion of domestic remedies, 225
Historical background, 203
Individual petitions, 205
Inter-state communications, 230
Non OAS member states, 208
Opinions, 229
Petitions
Examination, 224
Exhaustion of domestic remedies, 225
Individual petitions, 205
Repetitive, 226
State parties petition system, 224
Powers, 204
Precautionary measures, 214
Recommendations
Generally, 229
Inter-state communications, 230
Repetitive petitions, 226
Reporting procedures, 205
Reports, 228
Role of Commission before the court, 231
Settlements, 228
State parties petition system, 224

INTER-AMERICAN COURT OF HUMAN RIGHTS (IA CT HR)
Generally, 203, 232 et seq.
Advisory jurisdiction, 243
Advisory opinions
Generally, 232
Legal effects, 246
American Convention on Human Rights implementation, 222
Commission referrals, 228
Jurisdiction, 232 et seq.
Petitions, 228
Provisional measures, 242
Role of Commission before the court, 231

INTER-AMERICAN HUMAN RIGHTS SYSTEM
Generally, 197 et seq.
American Convention on Human Rights, this index
Conventions, 259
Democracy and human rights, 260
Organization of American States, this index

INTER-GOVERNMENTAL ORGANIZATIONS (IGO), 408

INTERNATIONAL BILL OF HUMAN RIGHTS, 42, 77

INTERNATIONAL CONVENTION FOR THE PROTECTION OF ALL PERSONS FROM ENFORCED DISAPPEARANCE, 79, 97

INTERNATIONAL CONVENTION ON THE ELIMINATION OF RACIAL DISCRIMINATION (CERD)
Generally, 83 et seq.
Jurisdiction, 85
Monitoring committee, 84
Petition system, 85
State parties, 85
State vs state disputes, 85
Urgent action procedures, 99

INTERNATIONAL COURT OF JUSTICE (ICJ)
Generally, 102
Genocide Convention matters referred to, 82

Human rights rulings, 103
Judicial appointments, 102
Jurisdiction, 102
Parties to proceedings, 102

INTERNATIONAL COVENANT ON CIVIL AND POLITICAL RIGHTS (ICCPR)
Generally, 52 et seq.
Complaints
First Optional Protocol, 65
Second Optional Protocol, 68
Death penalty, Second Optional Protocol, 67
First Optional Protocol, 65
Human Rights Committee, this index
ICESCR approaches compared, 69
Non-derogable rights, 53
Second Optional Protocol, 67
UN creation, 51

INTERNATIONAL COVENANT ON ECONOMIC, SOCIAL AND CULTURAL RIGHTS (ICESCR)
Generally, 68 et seq.
Committee
Generally, 74
Closed session proceedings, 76
Complaints
Generally, 74
Individual complaints mechanism proposals, 75
Discrimination provisions, 73
Enforcement, 74
ICCPR approaches compared, 69
Measurements of compliance, 72
Reporting procedures, 74
UN creation, 51
Undertakings of parties, 69
Universal Declaration compared, 68

INTERNATIONAL CRIMINAL COURT
Establishment, 19
Jurisdiction, 82
Supporting states, 417

INTERNATIONAL LABOR ORGANIZATION (ILO)
Generally, 112
Complaint procedures, 114
Core standards, 114
Creation, 10
Globalization impacts on workers' rights, 114
Investigations, 110
Migrant Workers Convention relationship, 94
Reports of member states, 113
US ratification, 343

INVESTIGATIONS
See also Monitoring Mechanisms, this index
Committee Against Torture, 90, 91
Human Rights Committee, 58
ILO, 110
NGO activities, 426
Organization of American States, 208

JURISDICTION AND POWER
Aliens, state responsibilities, 14
CEDAW, 88
Committee Against Torture, 89
Court of Human Rights (Europe), 131
Court of Human Rights (Europe), this index
Domestic jurisdiction
Treaties creating, 7
UN human rights system, jurisdictional implications, 40
Enforcement
European Convention on Human Rights, 128
Genocide Convention
Generally, 82
Universal jurisdiction, 83
Human Rights Committee, 58
ICESCR enforcement, 74
Inter-American Commission on Human Rights, 204
See also Inter-American Court of Human Rights, this index
International Convention on the Elimination of Racial Discrimination, 85
International Court of Justice, 102
International Criminal Court, 82

Treaties creating domestic jurisdiction, 7
UN committees, authority of, 79
UN human rights system, jurisdictional implications, 40
United States, this index
Universal jurisdiction, Genocide Convention, 83

LABOR PROTECTIONS
International Labor Organization, this index
League of Nations, 10
Migrant Workers Convention, this index
Working conditions, European Social Charter, 162

LAW OF WAR
See Humanitarian Law, this index

LEAGUE OF NATIONS
Historical background, 8
Labor protections, 10
Mandates System, 2, 8
Minorities System, 2, 10
Polish Treaty, 11

LIMITATIONS PERIODS
Court of Human Rights (Europe), 131

MANDATE PROCEDURES
Human Rights Council mandates procedures
Generally, 109
Historical background, 106
League of Nations, Mandates System, 2, 8

MIGRANT WORKERS CONVENTION
Generally, 94
Committee membership, 95
ILO relationship, 94
National treatment provision, 95
Rights of all migrant workers, 95

MILITARY SERVICE
See Humanitarian Law, this index

MINORITIES SYSTEM
League of Nations, 2, 10

MONITORING MECHANISMS
See also Investigations, this index
CAT compliance, 90
CERD monitoring committee, 84
Convention on the Rights of Persons with Disabilities, 97
CRC compliance, 94
European Union Committee of Ministers, 156
ILO compliance, 10
Inter-American Court of Human Rights, 259
OSCE compliance, 190
UN covenants, 51, 77

MULTINATIONAL CORPORATIONS
Generally, 429 et seq.
Boycott powers, 433
Globalization impacts, 429
Historical background, 19
Human rights litigation against, 433
International standards and codes of conduct, 436
Obligations of, 430
OECD Guidelines for Multinational Enterprises, 442
Security forces employed by, 441
Shareholders' roles, 440
Social responsibility principle, 432
UN's Guiding Principles on Business and Human Rights, 439
United Nations Global Compact, 437

NON-CITIZENS
See Alien Protections, this index

NON-GOVERNMENTAL ORGANIZATIONS (NGO)
Generally, 410 et seq.
Alternative or shadow reports on treaty compliance, 420
Consultative status, 410
European Union activities, 419
Historical background, 408
International Conference (INGO), 420
Investigative activities, 426
Judicial and quasi-judicial processes, engagement in, 424
Major NGOs, 413
Naming and shaming activities, 413

National policies and legislation influences, 427
UN Human Rights Council contributions, 422
UN, cooperative associations with, 413, 419
Universal Periodic Review (UPR), 423

NON-STATE ACTORS' RESPONSIBILITIES
Generally, 407
Historical background, 19

OECD
See Organization for Economic Co-operation and Development, this index

OFFICE OF THE HIGH COMMISSIONER FOR HUMAN RIGHTS (OHCHR)
Generally, 101

OMBUDSMAN
European Union creation, 181

ORGANIZATION FOR ECONOMIC CO-OPERATION AND DEVELOPMENT (OECD)
Grievance procedures, 442
Guidelines for Multinational Enterprises, 442

ORGANIZATION FOR SECURITY AND COOPERATION IN EUROPE (OSCE)
Generally, 182 et seq.
Catalog of rights, 188
Copenhagen Concluding Document, 13, 188
Helsinki Document, 188
High Commissioner on National Minorities (HCNM), 191
Historical background, 182
Human dimension mechanism, 189
Impact in human rights areas, 186
Moscow Concluding Document, 188
Non-binding character of commitments, 187
Press and media freedoms, 193
Process, 186
Reporting procedures, 190
Trafficking issues, 191
Vienna Concluding Document, 189

ORGANIZATION OF AMERICAN STATES (OAS)
Generally, 197 et seq.
American Convention on Human Rights, this index
American Declaration of the Rights and Duties of Man, 201
Charter as legal source, 198
Charter organ, IACHR as
Generally, 208 et seq.
Inter-American Commission on Human Rights, this index
Charter-based system
Generally, 199 et seq.
American Declaration of the Rights and Duties of Man, 201
Constitution, Charter as, 200
Human rights norms, 199
Inter-American Court of Human Rights, 203
U.S. Government influences, 200
Constitution, Charter as, 200
Country studies and on-site investigations, 208
Democracy and human rights, 260
General Assembly, 198
Historical background, 200
Human rights norms, 199
Individual petitions, 212
Investigations, 208
Member states, 197
Organization, 198
Permanent Council, 198
Petitions, individual, 212
Treaties as legal sources, 198

OSCE
See Organization for Security and Cooperation in Europe, this index

PETITION PROCESSES
See also Complaint Procedures, this index
European Union, this index
Gross violations of human rights, 108
Human Rights Committee, 56
Individual petitions
Inter-American Commission on Human Rights, 205
Inter-American Court of Human Rights, 228

Organization of American States, 212
Inter-American Commission on Human Rights, this index
OECD grievance procedures, 442
UNESCO, 115

POWER
See Jurisdiction and Power, this index

PRIVACY RIGHTS
American Declaration of the Rights and Duties of Man, 201
UDHR, 43

REMEDIES
See also Mandates Procedures, this index
Convention on Human Rights, 127
European Union, this index
Exhaustion of domestic remedies
Court of Human Rights, 145
Inter-American Commission on Human Rights, 225

REPORTING PROCEDURES
Committee on the Rights of the Child (CRC), 92
Convention on the Rights of Persons with Disabilities, 97
Elimination of Discrimination Against Women (CEDAW), 87
Human Rights Committee, 57
ICESCR, 74
ILO member states, 113
Inter-American Commission on Human Rights, 205, 228
NGO alternative or shadow reports on treaty compliance, 420
OSCE, 190
Universal Periodic Review (UPR), 423

RESERVATIONS OF RATIFYING STATES
CEDAW, 87
United States, this index

RESTATEMENT OF THE FOREIGN RELATIONS LAW OF THE UNITED STATES, 16

RWANDA TRIBUNAL
Genocide Convention definitions, 82
UN creation of *ad hoc* international tribunal, 6, 19

SELF-EXECUTING TREATIES
Generally, 135
United States, 344, 382

SETTLEMENT MECHANISMS
European Union, this index
Inter-American Commission on Human Rights, 228

SIGNIFICANT DISADVANTAGE DOCTRINE
See European Union, this index

SOCIAL CHARTER (ESC)
See European Union, this index

SOUTH AMERICA
Inter-American Human Rights System, this index
Organization of American States, this index

STATE ACTION
CERD, 85
Non-state actors' responsibilities, 19

STATE VS INDIVIDUAL PROTECTIONS, 3, 23

STATELESS PERSONS PROTECTIONS, 15

TORTURE
Convention Against Torture, this index
European Convention for the Prevention of Torture and Inhuman or Degrading Treatment or Punishment, 123, 165

TRAFFICKING
Convention on Action against Trafficking in Human Beings, 123, 171
OSCE, 191

UDHR
See Universal Declaration of Human Rights, this index

UNESCO
See United Nations, this index

UNITED NATIONS
Ad hoc international tribunals, 6
Authorities of UN committees, 79

Charter-based institutions, 99
Conferences on human rights, 110
Core human rights treaties, 77 et seq.
Educational, Scientific and Cultural Organization (UNESCO)
Generally, 114
Complaints procedures, 115
Petitions, 115
General Assembly, 99
Global Compact for multinationals, 442
Gross violations of human rights, 108
Guiding Principles on Business and Human Rights, 439, 453
Human Rights Council, 104
Human rights system
Generally, 35
Article 55, 38
Article 56, 38
Charter protections, 35, 37
International Bill of Human Rights, 42
Jurisdiction, 40
Universal Declaration of Human Rights, 43
Multinationals, Global Compact for, 442
NGOs, cooperative associations with, 413, 419
Office of the High Commissioner for Human Rights, 101
Reports of committees, 77
Security Council, 100
Specialized agencies, 112
United States support, 338
Universal Periodic Review (UPR), 423

UNITED STATES
Generally, 335 et seq.
Alien Tort Statute, 391
Bricker Amendment impact on treaty enforcement, 347, 364
Cold War Era, 338
Constitutional treaties provisions, 344
Country-specific legislation, 375
Customary international law, 389 et seq.
Department of State responsibilities, 377
Domestic vs international protection tensions, 335
Federal law, treaty conflicts with, 381

Federalism and treaty enforcement, 365
Financial institutions channels for foreign aid, 376
Fraser Committee, 368
Historical background, 338 et seq.
ILO ratification, 343
International human rights law in US courts
Generally, 380
Alien Tort Statute, 391
Customary international law, 389 et seq.
Law of nations doctrine, 389
Self-executing treat issues, 382
International vs domestic protection tensions, 335
Law of nations doctrine, 389
Legal and policy considerations affecting treaty ratifications, 351
Legislation, enactment and enforcement, 368 et seq.
Military and economic aid as enforcement levers, 369
Reservations
Ratifications with, 357 et seq.
Understandings and declarations affecting treaty ratifications, 358
Restatement of the Foreign Relations Law of the United States, 16
Self-executing treaties, 344, 382
Senate treatment of treaties, 345
Treaty conflicts with federal law, 381
Treaty ratifications enforcement, 342 et seq.
United Nations support, 338

UNIVERSAL DECLARATION OF HUMAN RIGHTS (UDHR)
Generally, 43
ICESCR, 68

UNIVERSAL JURISDICTION
Genocide Convention, 83

UNIVERSAL PERIODIC REVIEW (UPR)
Generally, 423

VENICE COMMISSION, 124

WAR CRIMES
See Humanitarian Law, this index

WOMEN'S RIGHTS
Commission on the Status of Women, this index
Elimination of Discrimination Against Women, this index
Trafficking, this index

WORLD HEALTH ORGANIZATION
Human rights work, 116

YUGOSLAVIA
UN creation of *ad hoc* international tribunal, 6, 19